FOREIGN DIRECT INVESTMENT AND THE MULTINATIONAL ENTERPRISE: A BIBLIOGRAPHY

Foreign Direct Investment and the Multinational Enterprise: A Bibliography

edited by

Cynthia Day Wallace

1988

MARTINUS NIJHOFF PUBLISHERS
A MEMBER OF THE KLUWER ACADEMIC PUBLISHERS GROUP
DORDRECHT / BOSTON / LANCASTER

Distributors

for the United States and Canada: Kluwer Academic Publishers, 101 Philip Drive, Norwell, MA 02061, USA
for the UK and Ireland: Kluwer Academic Publishers, MTP Press Limited, Falcon House, Queen Square, Lancaster LA1 1RN, UK
for all other countries: Kluwer Academic Publishers Group, Distribution Center, P.O. Box 322, 3300 AH Dordrecht, The Netherlands

Library of Congress Cataloging in Publication Data

Wallace, Cynthia Day.
Foreign direct investment and the multinational enterprise : a bibliography / Cynthia Day Wallace, editor.
p. cm.
ISBN 9024736579
1. International business enterprises--Law and legislation--Bibliography. 2. Investments, Foreign--Law and legislation--Bibliography. 3. International business enterprises--Bibliography. 4. Investments, Foreign--Bibliography. I. Title.
K1322.A12W35 1988
016.34673'07--dc19
[016.3473067] 87-34828
CIP

ISBN 90-247-3657-9

Copyright

PRINTED IN THE NETHERLANDS

TABLE OF CONTENTS

INTRODUCTION

The volume of literature on the subject of foreign direct investment (FDI) and the multinational enterprise (MNE), still sparse through the 1960's, began to proliferate in the mid-1970's and has become a veritable flood in the 1980's. My own serious involvement with the subject matter began in the mid-1970's when control considerations regarding multinationals were perhaps at their peak.

While concerns over control have largely subsided, MNEs are still as active as ever, and the importance of FDI is rivaling more traditional trade considerations for prominence on the international economic agenda. Meanwhile, the American share is diminishing proportionate to the increasing number of multinationals from the industrialized as well as the newly industrializing and even developing nations.

A recognized authority on international economics, writing recently in the _Wall Street Journal_, expressed the view that FDI is already overshadowing trade _per se_ as the viable international commercial priority of the near future. The same economist, in another _Journal_ article which appeared yesterday as I write, speaks of a "world-wide boom in transnational direct investments" which are "becoming imperative for any business that aims at a leadership position any place in the developed world."[1]

You, the reader, are already sufficiently interested in foreign direct investment to have opened these pages in a search for more literature on the subject, so I need not belabour the importance and timeliness of the issues.

This Bibliography stems initially from researching my book, _Legal Control of the Multinational Enterprise_ (Nijhoff, 1983), and was inspired by preiiminary research done in preparation for a new edition of that work. The selections therefore focus on the legal, operational and policy aspects of MNE activities, though much related literature is included to encompass a broader area for those whose particular interests extend beyond the scope of my own work.

---

1 See Peter F. Drucker, "From World Trade to World Investment," _Wall Street Journal_ 26 May 1987; _idem_, "The Transnational Economy," _Wall Street Journal_ 25 August 1987.

It is impossible, while attempting to be comprehensive, to compile an exhaustive Bibliography on the subject at hand. Some significant works will regrettably have been omitted, and I would be happy to hear from any author whose work has been overlooked or who has been mis-cited in any way. I invite correction also from other readers who discover an error of citation in the following pages. Comments as to how future editions might be made more useful will also be welcomed.

The cutoff date for this compilation is January 1, 1987.

HINTS FOR THE USER

The Bibliography is broken down into subject matter and geographical categories. The various categories are listed alphabetically, with page references, in the Table of Contents (p. v). Within each category, individual works are listed alphabetically according to authors' names (or titles where no author is attributed). The alphabetized categories thus serve as a broad subject index, while the alphabetical listings by author's name within each category serve as an author index.

The user will find some categories rather lengthy, notably: "Antitrust," " Europe," and "United States." He/she should not be put off by this. Selections are entered under each and every relevant category. It is therefore suggested that the user look under the category that most narrowly defines his/her interest. For example, if the particular concern is joint ventures in the United States, the user should look under "Joint Ventures" rather than under "United States," even though the entry can be found in both categories. If, on the other hand, the aim is to check into every issue concerning FDI in the United States, it is more useful to peruse the entire category "United States," for all aspects of FDI as it relates to U.S. multinationals abroad or to foreign MNEs operating in the United States.

The objective is for this Bibliography to be "user-friendly" and as efficient as possible while responding to the broadest range of needs. Any suggestions by users as to how this objective can be improved upon for future editions will be most welcome.

ACKNOWLEDGMENTS

I would like to thank CSIS interns Jed Schaeffer and Raoul Jain for the help they lent to the effort of deciphering my cryptic abbreviations and tracking down incomplete citations. Intern Troy Tanner also interrupted his other tasks to provide one important additional proofread when my own eyes lost some of their earlier acuity on the manuscript; Troy was also diligent to track down remaining bibliographical lacunae.

A superb job of transposing entries in several languages into a methodical and unified format was accomplished by my secretary, Mary Marik, whose degree of accuracy made one phase of my editing infinitely less arduous.

Special recognition goes to CSIS intern Ann Galloway for innumerable hours of all of the above activities, in addition to countless days, weeks and months of faithful implementation of each stage of my preparations, categorizations and edits, with all the intricacies and frustrations of word processor technology.

I trust that the process of any future updates or supplements to this Bibliography will be hugely facilitated by the elimination of "bugs" in the present process and further advancements in computer technology which, in this instance, left much to be desired and left much to the ad hoc ingenuity of my computer quasi-literate self with ultra-perfectionist tendencies.

Every bit of help by the above-named individuals contributed to a highly arduous and lengthy undertaking. It is hoped that the results will substantially justify the efforts.

1. ANTI-TRUST/COMPETITION

Abrams, Lee N., et al. "Antitrust and U.S. Trade Law." (Various articles) Proceedings of the Twenty-Ninth Annual Spring Meeting of the Section of Antitrust Law of the American Bar Association, Washington, D.C., 1981. Antitrust Law Journal Vol. 50, 1981, pp. 751-799.

Abrams, Lee N., et al. "Critical Issues in International Antitrust and Unfair Competition Law." (Various articles) Proceedings of the Twenty-Ninth Annual Spring Meeting of the Section of Antitrust Law of the American Bar Association, Washington, D.C., 1981. Antitrust Law Journal Vol. 50, 1981, pp. 447-452.

Abrams, Lee N., et al. "Litigating in an International Context." (Various articles) Proceedings of the Twenty-Ninth Annual Spring Meeting of the Section of Antitrust Law of the American Bar Association, Washington, D.C., 1981. Antitrust Law Journal Vol. 50, 1981, pp. 555-616.

"Act of State Doctrine - Anti-Trust Law." Denver Journal of International Law and Politics Vol. 3, 1973, pp. 133-140.

Adams, G.B. "European and American Antitrust Regulation of Pricing by Monopolists." Vanderbilt Journal of Transnational Law Vol. 18, 1985, pp. 1-70.

Adisert, R.J. "Federal Courts and Extraterritorial Antitrust Law: Enlightened Self-Interest or Yankee Imperialism?" Journal of Law and Commerce Vol. 5, 1985, pp. 415-432.

Adler, Howard Jr. and Murray J. Belman. "Antimerger Enforcement in Europe - Trends and Prospects." Journal of International Law and Economics Vol. 8, 1973, pp. 31-51.

Albulescu, P.R. "Prospective Exemptions Under EEC Competition Law: A Proposal." Law and Policy in International Business Vol. 16, 1984, pp. 1137-1180.

"Anhaltender Konzentrationstrend in Deutschland: Jahresbericht des Bundeskartellamtes." Neue Zuercher Zeitung 6 June 1979, p. 16.

"Antitrust and International Business Transactions," Part I. Antitrust Law Journal Vol. 43, 1974, pp. 517-643.

Antitrust Cases: Cartels. London: European Law Centre Ltd., 1979.

Antitrust Cases: Monopolies and Mergers, 2 vols. London: European Law Centre Ltd., 1979.

Antitrust Cases: Restrictive Agreements. London: European Law Centre Ltd., 1976.

"Antitrust - Foreign Import Cartels are Liable under the Sherman Act Although Domestic Export Competitors are Shielded within Webb-Pomerance Exemption; Daishowa International v. No. Coast Export Co. 1982-Z Tr.Cas. No. 64,774." Vanderbilt Journal of Transnational Law Vol. 16, 1983, pp. 645-665.

"Antitrust Implications of Trade Law: Japan, the European Communities, and the United States: A Panel." American Society of International Law Proceedings Vol. 76, 1982, pp. 120-130.

"Antitrust Law: Commission of the European Communities Suspends Proceedings Against International Business Machines Corporation - 3 Common Market Law Review 147 (1984)." Harvard International Law Journal Vol. 26, 1985, pp. 189-201.

"Antitrust - Noerr-Pennington [Eastern R.R. Presidents Conf. v. Noerr Motor Freight, Inc., 81 S.Ct. 523] Extends Immunity from Sherman Act to Foreign Litigation and Foreign Acts that Result in Alleged Antitrust Violations. Coastal States Marketing, Inc. v. Hunt, 694 F.2d 1358." Vanderbilt Journal of Transnational Law Vol. 16, 1983, pp. 623-644.

Applebaum, Harvey M. "Are U.S. International Trade and Commerce Conduct Laws in Harmony With Traditional Antitrust Law and Policy?" Antitrust Law Journal Vol. 49, 1980, pp. 1207-1216.

"Arbitration: Public Policy Exception to Arbitration of Antitrust Issues - Mitsubishi Motors Corp. v. Soler Chrysler-Plymouth, Inc., 723 F.2d 155." Harvard International Law Journal Vol. 25, 1984, pp. 427-433.

Ariga, Michiko and Luvern V. Rieke. "The Antimonopoly Law of Japan and its Enforcement." Washington Law Review Vol. 39, 1964, pp. 437-478.

Ariga, Michiko. "International Trade of Japan and the Antimonopoly Act." Journal of International Law and Economics Vol. 8, 1973, pp. 185-202.

Arthur, T.C. "Farewell to the Sea of Doubt: Jettisoning the Constitutional Sherman Act." California Law Review Vol. 74, 1986, pp. 263-376.

Articles 85 and 86 of the EEC Treaty and the Relevant Regulations: A Manual for Firms. London, Washington, DC: Information Service of the European Communities, n.d.

Askari, H. "International Trade Implications of the Oil Cartel." Texas International Law Journal Vol. 12, 1977, pp. 47-55.

Athos, E. "Antitrust Law: United Nations Guidelines." Harvard International Law Journal Vol. 22, 1981, pp. 405-411.

Atkins, P.A. "Defense Against Creeping Acquisitions." Institute on Security Regulations Vol. 13, 1982, pp. 57-84.

Atwood, James R. and Kingman Brewster. Anti-Trust and American Business Abroad, 2d edition. New York: McGraw Hill, 1981.

Atwood, James R. "International Ventures and the U.S. Anti-Trust Laws." Akron Law Review Vol. 10, 1976-1977, pp. 609-621.

Augustyn, F.M. "An Antitrust Analysis of Joint Research and Development Agreements in the European Economic Community and the United States." Georgia Journal of International and Comparative Law Vol. 16, 1986, pp. 45-71.

Autenruth, K. "Britischen Protection of Trade Interests Acts im System des Internationalen Kartellrechts." Recht der internationalen Wirtschaft Vol. 29, 1983, pp. 15-18.

Baker, Donald I. "Antitrust and World Trade: Tempest in an International Teapot?" Cornell International Law Journal Vol. 8, 1974, pp. 16-44. (Followed by J.A. Rahl, "Rejoinder.")

Baker, Donald I. "Antitrust Conflicts Between Friends: Canada and the United States in the Mid-1970s." Cornell International Law Journal Vol. 11, 1978, pp. 165-194.

Bechtold, R. "Die Entwicklung des deutschen Kartellrechts im Jahre 1979." Neue Juristische Wochenschrift Vol. 33, 1980, pp. 1265-1269.

Bechtold, R. "Die Entwicklung des deutschen Kartellrechts von 1981 bis 1983." Neue Juristische Wochenschrift Vol. 37, 1984, pp. 145-152.

Becker, J.D. "Antitrust and International Arbitration - the New American Synthesis." International Business Lawyer Vol. 13, 1985, pp. 445-447.

Behrens, Peter. "Durchgriff ueber die Grenze." Rabels Zeitschrift fuer auslaendisches und internationales Privatrecht Vol. 46, 1982, pp. 308-356.

Beier, F.-K. "The Law of Unfair Competition in the European Community - Its Development and Present Status." European Intellectual Property Review Vol. 7, 1985, pp. 284-291.

Bellamy, Christopher and Graham D. Child. Common Market Law of Competition. London: Sweet & Maxwell, 1973.

Berger, Daniel and R. Bernstein. "An Analytical Framework for Anti-Trust Standing." *Yale Law Journal* Vol. 86, 1976-1977, pp. 809-883.

Bilder, R.B. "Comments on the Legality of the Arab Oil Boycott." *Texas International Law Journal* Vol. 12, 1977, pp. 41-46.

Binkowski, E.S. "*Timberlane*: Three Steps Forward, One Step Backwards." *International Lawyer* Vol. 15, 1981, pp. 419-431.

Blake, Harlan Morse and Robert Pitofsky. *Antitrust Law*. Mineola, New York: The Foundations Press, Inc., 1967, supplement: 1969.

Blechman, Michael D. "Antitrust Jurisdiction, Discovery and Enforcement in the International Sphere: An Appraisal of American Developments and Foreign Reactions." *Antitrust Law Journal* Vol. 49, 1980, pp. 1197-1206.

Blechman, Michael D. "Neue Entwicklungen in der amerikanischen Wettbewerbspolitik." *Wirtschaft und Wettbewerb* Vol. 32, March 1982, pp. 173-188.

Blythe, M.A. "Extraterritorial Impact of the Anti-Trust Laws: Protecting British Trading Interests." *American Journal of Comparative Law* Vol. 31, 1983, pp. 99-129.

"Boersenaufsichtsbehoerde: Mitspracherecht bei Fusionen." *Frankfurter Allgemeine Zeitung* 12 December 1979, p. 12.

Bollack, G. "Verhindert die deutsche Fusionskontrolle die Wettbewerbsfahigkeit der deutschen Wirtschaft auf den Weltmarkt?" *Gewerblicher Rechtsschutz und Urheberrecht* Vol. 85, 1983, pp. 229-234.

Bondurant, Ward S. "Extraterritorial Jurisdiction - Antitrust - The Impact of the British Protection of Trading Interests Act on the United States Antitrust Suit Brought by Laker Airways against British Airways and British Caledonian." (Recent Developments) *Georgia Journal of International and Comparative Law* Vol. 14, 1984, pp. 181-200.

Bowen, S. "Defenses Against Takeovers - Selected Tax Problems." *Taxes* Vol. 64, 1986, pp. 835-845.

Boyer, A. "Form as Substance: A Comparison of Antitrust Regulation by Consent Decrees in the U.S.A., Reports of the Monopolies and Mergers Commission in the U.K., and Grants of Clearance by the European Commission" *International and Comparative Law Quarterly* Vol. 32, 1983, pp. 904-930.

Brewer, T.L. "International Regulation of Restrictive Business Practices." *Journal of World Trade Law* Vol. 16, 1982, pp. 108-118.

Brill, J.-P. "Renforcement de la lutte contre les abus de position dominante." *Recueil Dalloz Sirey* June 1981, pp. 165-174.

"The British Telecommunications (250 J. Eur. Comm. [No. L360] 36) Decision: Toward a New Telecommunications Policy in the Common Market." *Harvard International Law Journal* Vol. 95, 1984, pp. 299-328.

g Brusick, P. "UN Control of Restrictive Business Practices." *Journal of World Trade Law* Vol. 17, 1983, pp. 337-351.

Bushman, K. "British Protection of Trading Interests Act of 1980: An Analysis." *Journal of International Law and Economics* Vol. 14, 1980, pp. 253-280.

Cairns, J.P. "Economics in Court: the Consumers Glass [R.V. Consumers Glass Co. Ltd., 124 D.L.R. 3d. 274] Case." *Canadian Business Law Journal* Vol. 11, 1986, pp. 212-220.

Campbell, Alan Robertson. *Restrictive Trading Agreements in the Common Market: Texts, Commentaries*. London: Stevens & Sons, 1964.

Campbell, Barry R. "Canadian Combines Law: A Perspective on the Current Combines Investigation Act and Recent Case Law." *North Carolina Journal of International Law and Commercial Regulation* Vol. 5, 1980, pp. 57-90.

Campbell, Dennis and C. Rohwer, eds. Legal Aspects of International Business Transactions - I. (The Edinburgh Institute on International Transactions 1983) New York: Elsevier, 1984.

Campbell, T.J. "The Antitrust Record of the First Reagan Administration." Texas Law Review Vol. 64, 1985, pp. 353-369.

"The Canada-United States Memorandum of Understanding Regarding Application of National Antitrust Law: New Guidelines for Resolution of Multinational Antitrust Enforcement Disputes." New England Journal of International Law and Business Vol. 6, 1984/1985, pp. 1065-1095.

"Canadian Merger Policy and Its International Implications." Michigan Yearbook of International Legal Studies Vol. 2, 1981, pp. 172-200.

"Capacity of a Foreign Government to Bring an Action for Treble Damages under the Federal Anti-Trust Laws." George Washington Law Review Vol. 44, 1976, pp. 287-298.

Carnulutti, A. and F. Delon. "États face aux éffets extraterritoriaux du droit de la concurrence des États-Unis d'Amérique: l'exemple de la France." Revue Française de Droit Aérien Vol. 36, 1982, pp. 15-41.

Carrera, V.M. and J.L. Wood. "International Uranium Cartel: International Economic Contingencies and Contractual Excuse under Section 2-615 of the Uniform Commercial Code." Texas International Law Journal Vol. 14, 1979, pp. 277-288.

Cartel and Monopoly in Modern Law. Report of conference on Restraints of Competition, Frankfurt am Main, 1960. Karlsruhe: Mueller, 1961.

Champaud, C. "Contrôle des concentrations en France depuis 1977." Revue Trimestrielle de Droit Commercial et de Droit Économique Vol. 33, 1980, pp. 421-439.

"The Changing Complexion of Intra-Enterprise Conspiracy under the Sherman Antitrust Act (Copperweld Corp. v. Independence Tube Corp., 104 S.Ct. 2731, 1984)." Georgia Law Review Vol. 19, 1984, pp. 189-220.

Cira, Jr., Carl A. "The Challenge of Foreign Laws to Block American Antitrust Actions." Stanford Journal of International Law Vol. 18, 1982, pp. 247-278.

"City Code on Take-Overs and Mergers: Amendments (1985)." Business Law Review Vol. 6, 1985, pp. 77-80.

Clanton, D.A. "Horizontal Agreements, the Rule of Reason, and the General Motors-Toyota Joint Venture." Wayne Law Review Vol. 30, 1984, pp. 1239-1266.

Clanton, D.A. "Major Merger and Joint Venture Decisions of the Past Year." Antitrust Law Journal Vol. 53, 1984, pp. 321-357.

Cohen, N.B. and C.A. Sullivan. "The Herfindahl-Hirschman Index and the New Antitrust Merger Guidelines: Concentrating on Concentration." Texas Law Review Vol. 62, 1983, pp. 453-508.

Collins, C.J. "Antitrust: EEC Treaty: Joint-Venture Agreement." Vanderbilt Journal of Transnational Law Vol. 12, 1979, pp. 775-785.

"A Comparative Analysis of the Efficacy of Bilateral Agreements in Resolving Disputes Between Sovereigns Arising from Extra-territorial Application of Antitrust Law: The Australian Agreement." Georgia Journal of International and Comparative Law Vol. 13, 1983, pp. 49-82.

"Comparative Aspects of Anti-Trust Law in the U.S., the U.K., and the EEC: Report of a Conference, 14-16 June 1963." International and Comparative Law Quarterly: Supplementary Publication, No. 6. (1963).

"Constriction of the Intra-Enterprise Conspiracy Doctrine (Copperweld Corp. v. Independence Tube Corp., 104 S.Ct. 2731, 1984)." Detroit College of Law Review Vol. 1985, 1985, pp. 189-200.

"The Costs of the Consensual Myth: Antitrust Enforcement and Institutional Barriers to Litigation in Japan." Yale Law Journal Vol. 94, 1985, pp. 604-645.

Czako, J.M. "Set of Multilaterally Agreed Equitable Principles and Rules for Restrictive Business Practices." Law and Policy in International Business Vol. 13, 1981, pp. 313-337.

Danaher, M.J. "Antitrust Law: The Clawback and Other Features of the U.K. Protection of Trading Interests Act, 1980." Law and Policy in International Business Vol. 12, 1980, pp. 947-972.

Daverat, G. "Approche administrative et judiciaire actuelle de la distribution sélective dans le secteur de l'automobile." Revue Trimestrielle de Droit Commercial et de Droit Économique Vol. 38, 1985, pp. 645-724.

Davidow, Joel. "Antitrust, International Policy, and Merger Control." Journal of International Law and Economics Vol. 15, 1981, pp. 519-532.

Davidow, Joel. "Recent Developments in International Antitrust." Akron Law Review Vol. 10, 1977, pp. 603-608.

Davidow, Joel. "UNCTAD Restrictive Business Practices Code." International Lawyer Vol. 13, 1979, pp. 587-617.

Davidow, Joel. "U.S. Antitrust and Doing Business Abroad: Recent Trends and Developments." North Carolina Journal of International Law and Commercial Regulation Vol. 5, 1980, pp. 23-36.

Davidow, Joel. "U.S. Antitrust and Doing Business Abroad: Recent Trends and Developments." North Carolina Journal of International Law and Commercial Regulation Vol 5, 1980, pp. 23-36.

Davis, R.W. "Antitrust Analysis of Mergers, Acquisitions, and Joint Ventures in the 1980's: A Pragmatic Guide to Evaluation of Legal Risks." Delaware Journal of Corporate Law Vol. 11, 1986, pp. 25-133.

Davis, R.W. "Antitrust, the Trade Deficit, and U.S. International Competitiveness: A Time for Rethinking." New York University Journal of International Law and Politics Vol. 18, 1986, pp. 1235-1279.

De Angelis, L. "Il nuovo 'city code on take-overs and mergers.'" Rivista della Societá Vol. 30, 1985, pp. 1170-1188.

deKieffer, Donald E. "Antitrust and the Japanese Auto Quotas." Antitrust Law Journal Vol. 50, 1981, pp. 779-790.

Deringer, Arved. "Current Trends of EEC Competition Policy." Journal of International Law and Economics Vol. 8, 1973, pp. 203-222.

de Smith, B. "The Laker Name Lives On: Litigation, Deregulation and the Airline Industry." Public Law Vol. 1985, 1985, pp. 22-32.

"Determining the Arbitrability of International Antitrust Disputes." Journal of Comparative Business and Capital Market Law Vol. 8, 1986, pp. 197-218.

"Developments in Corporate Takeover Techniques: Creeping Tender Offers, Lockup Arrangements, and Standstill Agreements." Washington and Lee Law Review Vol. 39, 1982, pp. 1095-1122.

"Developments in International Commercial Arbitration (including ICSID and anti-trust in international commerce)." Harvard International Law Journal Vol. 17, 1976, pp. 89-154.

Dinkins, C.E. "Merger Guidelines: A Return to Reason." South Texas Law Journal Vol. 27, 1986, pp 507-518.

Dreher, M. and C. Stewart. "Merger Guidelines des U.S. Department of Justice." Recht der internationalen Wirtschaft Vol. 29, 1983, pp. 906-915.

Dunfee, T.W. and A.S. Friedman. "The Extraterritorial Application of United States Antitrust Laws: A Proposal for an Interim Solution." Ohio State Law Journal Vol. 45, 1984, pp. 883-932.

Dunlop, B. "Bora Laskin and Competition." University of Toronto Law Journal Vol. 35, 1985, pp. 425-437.

"EEC Plans Antitrust Crackdown on State-Controlled Companies." International Herald Tribune 25 October 1979, p. 1.

"EEC Regulation of Exclusive Dealing Arrangements." International Tax and Business Lawyer Vol. 3, 1985, pp. 81-101.

Ebel, H.-R. "Marktbeherrschungsvermutungen im Gesetz gegen Wettbewerbsbeschraenkungen." Neue Juristische Wochenschrift Vol. 34, August 1981, pp. 1763-1767.

"The Economic Unity Doctrine in the EEC: A Limited Exemption to Article 85 of the Treaty of Rome." Fordham International Law Journal Vol. 9, 1985/1986, pp. 373-399.

Ehrenhaft, Peter D. Review of James A. Rahl, "Common Market and American Antitrust - Overlap and Conflict." Law and Policy in International Business Vol. 3, 1971, pp. 649-658.

Eser, G. "Fusionskontrollrechtliche Problematik internationaler joint venture im Kartellrecht der Bundesrepublik Deutschland." Recht der internationalen Wirtschaft Vol. 28, March 1982, pp. 161-167.

"The Expanding Extraterritorial Jurisdiction of the Sherman Antitrust Act: Intent and Effects in the Balance?" Loyola of Los Angeles International and Comparative Law Journal Vol. 6, 1983, pp. 463-482.

"Extraterritorial Application of the Sherman Act to Foreign Corporations." Delaware Journal of Corporate Law Vol. 11, 1986, pp. 513-534.

"The Extraterritorial Enforcement of U.S. Antitrust Laws and Retaliatory Legislation in the United Kingdom and Australia. Denver Journal of International Law and Policy Vol. 13, 1984, pp. 377-386.

Feuring, W. "Anwendbarkeit des Sec. 23 I Satz 8 GWB auf die Zusammenschlusstatbestaende des Sec. 23 II Nr. 3, 4 und 5 GWB." Wirtschaft und Wettbewerb Vol. 32, 1982, pp. 517-522.

Fisher, B.M. "Product Distribution in Canada." International Lawyer Vol. 20, 1986, pp. 45-79.

1974 Fordham Corporate Law Institute - International Antitrust. New York: Matthew Bender and Co., 1975.

"Foreign Sovereign Compulsion and the Arab Boycott: A State Action Analogy." Georgetown Law Journal Vol. 65, 1976-1977, pp. 1001-1023.

"Foreign Statutory Response to Extraterritorial Application of United States Antitrust Law." Dickinson International Law Annual Vol. 1, 1982, pp. 125-155.

"Forum Non Conveniens and the Extraterritorial Application of United States Antitrust Law." Yale Law Journal Vol. 94, 1985, pp. 1693-1714.

Fox, D.W. "The EEC Treaty: 'Abusive Exploitation' and Provision of Discount." Solicitor's Journal Vol. 130, 18 April 1986, pp. 294-296.

Fox, E.M. "Updating the Antitrust Guide on International Operations: A Greener Light for Export and Investment Abroad." Vanderbilt Journal of Transnational Law Vol. 15, 1982, pp. 709-750.

Friedman, A.S. "Laker Airways [Laker Airways, Ltd. v. Sabena, 731 F.2d. 909]: the Dilemma of Concurrent Jurisdiction and Conflicting National Policies." Brooklyn Journal of International Law Vol. 11, 1985, pp. 181-236.

Fugate, Wilbur L. "Antitrust Aspects of the Revised Restatement of Foreign Relations Law." Virginia Journal of International Law Vol. 25, 1984, pp. 49-71.

Fugate, Wilbur L. "Antitrust Aspects of U.S.-Japanese Trade." Case Western Reserve Journal of International Law Vol. 15, 1983, pp. 505-525.

Fugate, Wilbur L. "Export Trade Exceptions to the Antitrust Laws: The Old Webb-Pomerane Act and the New Export Trading Company Act." Vanderbilt Journal of Transnational Law Vol. 15, 1982, pp. 673-707.

Fugate, Wilbur L. "An Overview of Anti-Trust Enforcement and the Multinational Corporation." The Journal of International Law and Economics Vol. 8, 1973, pp. 1-9.

"Fusionsstatistik sagt nicht alles." Frankfurter Allgemeine Zeitung 19 February 1980, p. 12.

Garner, S.S. "Hoffman-LaRoche and Dominant Position in the EEC." Journal of International Law and Economics Vol. 14, 1980, pp. 485-508.

Garvey, G.E. "Foreign Trade Antitrust Improvements Act of 1981." Law and Policy in International Business Vol. 14, 1982, pp. 1-46.

Garvey, G.E. "Transnational Joint Ventures and Antitrust Analysis." Stanford Journal of International Law Vol. 21, 1985, pp. 331-372.

Gellhorn, E. "Government Merger Policy and Practice - 1983." Antitrust Law Journal Vol. 52, 1983, pp. 419-434.

"The G.M.-Toyota Joint Venture and Its Implications under the National Labor Relations Act." Detroit College Law Review Vol. 1984, 1984, pp. 647-685.

"The G.M.-Toyota Joint Venture: Legal Cooperation or Illegal Combination in the World Automobile Industry?" Texas International Law Journal Vol. 19, 1984, pp. 699-728.

Gerber, D.J. "The Extraterritorial Application of the German Antitrust Laws." American Journal of International Law Vol. 77, 1983, pp. 756-783.

Gerster, Richard. "Zur Diskussion um den Entwurf fuer ein neues Kartellgesetz: Aktive Kartellpolitik als Entwicklungsforderung." Neue Zuercher Zeitung, 17 August 1979, p. 11.

Gill, David. "The UNCTAD Restrictive Business Practices Code: A Code for Competition?" International Lawyer Vol. 13, 1979, pp. 607-617.

Goebel, R.J. "The Uneasy Fate of Franchising Under EEC Antitrust Laws." European Law Review Vol. 10, April 1985, pp. 87-118.

Goldman, B. "Fusion des sociétés et le projet de convention sur la fusion internationale des sociétés anonymnes." Cahiers de Droit Européen Vol. 17, 1981, pp. 4-14, 57-69.

Goldsweig, David N., et al. "Survey of Foreign Antitrust Laws." (Various articles) Proceedings of the Twenty-Ninth Annual Spring Meeting of the Section of Antitrust Law of the American Bar Association, Washington, D.C., 1981. Antitrust Law Journal Vol. 50, 1981, pp. 645-750.

Grabar, N.H. "Antitrust: Effect of Foreign Disclosure Limitation on Discovery in United States Courts." Harvard International Law Journal Vol. 22, 1981, pp. 177-186.

Grendell, Timothy J. "The Antitrust Legislation of the United States, the European Community, Germany and Japan." International and Comparative Law Quarterly Vol. 29, 1980, pp. 64-86.

Gribbin, J.D. "U.K. Regulation of Transnational Corporate Concentration." Michigan Year Book of International Legal Studies Vol. 2, 1981, pp. 93-127.

Griffin, Joseph P. "Antitrust Constraints on Acquisitions by Aliens in the United States." International Lawyer Vol. 13, 1979, pp. 427-448.

Griffin, S. "UN Set of Multilaterally Agreed Equitable Principles and Rules for the Control of Restrictive Business Practices." Georgia Journal of International and Comparative Law Vol. 11, 1981, pp. 709-721.

Grippando, J.M. "Declining to Exercise Extraterritorial Antitrust Jurisdiction on Grounds of International Comity: An Illigitimate Extension of the Judicial Abstention Doctrine." Virginia Journal of International Law Vol. 23, 1983, pp. 395-428.

Gumpel, P.E. "International Implications of Conglomerate Merger Legislation." Virginia Journal of International Law Vol. 22, 1982, pp. 715-774.

Gurley, Franklin L. "Zur Diskussion um den Entwurf fuer ein neues Kartellgesetz: Das amerikanische Wettbewerbsrecht." Neue Zuercher Zeitung 7 September 1979, p. 14.

Guyénot, Jean. "La décision 'Continental Can' de la Commission CEE et la naissance du droit antitrust européen." Rivista della Societá Vol. 17, 1972, pp. 722-741.

Guzzardi, Jr., Walter. "A Search for Sanity in Antitrust." Fortune 30 January 1978, pp. 72-83.

Gyselen, L. and N. Kyriazis. "Artice 86 EEC: the Monopoly Power Measurement Issue Revisited." European Law Review Vol. 11, April 1986, pp. 134-148.

Haley, J.O. "Oil Cartel Cases: The End of an Era." Law in Japan: An Annual Vol. 15, 1982, pp. 1-11.

Halverson, J.T. "60 Minutes With Douglas H. Ginsburg, Assistant Attorney General, Antitrust Division." Introductory remarks. (Interview with Douglas H. Ginsburg: a panel) Antitrust Law Journal Vol. 55, 1986, pp. 253-273.

Halverson, J.T. "U.S. Industrial Competitiveness and Section 7 of the Clayton Act: Are they Compatible?" Introductory remarks. Other articles: "Some Form of Secton 7 Relief Must Be Granted to United State Industries." R.B. Peabody; "Necessary Flexibility Is Already Present Under the 1982 and 1984 Merger Guidelines." J.P. McGrath; "Antitrust and Problems of Adjustment in Distressed Industries." R. Pitofsky; "The Administration's Legislative Proposal and Its Ramifications." M. Baldridge; Panel discussion. Antitrust Law Journal Vol. 55, 1986, pp. 3-49.

Hammesfahr, R.W. and R.L. Blatt. "Extraterritorial Application of American Antitrust Laws: An Overview." Chicago Bar Record Vol. 65, 1983, pp. 106-112.

Haubert, William H., III. "Continental Can - New Strength for Common Market Anti-Trust." (Comment) San Diego Law Review Vol. 11, 1973, pp. 227-244.

Hawk, Barry E., et al. "Antitrust and International Trade - Special Rules." (Various articles) Proceedings of the Twenty-Eighth Annual Spring Meeting of the Section of Antitrust Law of the American Bar Association, Washington, D.C., 1980. Antitrust Law Journal Vol. 49, 1980, pp. 1185-1223.

Hawk, Barry E. "Antitrust in the EEC - The First Decade." Fordham Law Review Vol. 41, 1972, pp. 229-292.

Hawk, Barry E., ed. International Antitrust: Annual Proceedings of the Fordham Corporate Law Institute (1978). New York: Law and Business, 1979.

Hawk, Barry E. International Anti-Trust Manual: U.S., Common Market, and International Antitrust: A Comparative Guide. New York: Law and Business, 1979.

Hawk, Barry E. "International Antitrust Policy and the 1982 Acts: The Continuing Need for Reassessment." Fordham Law Review Vol. 51, 1982, pp. 201-254.

Henry, D.H.W., Q.C. "Anti-Monopoly Legislation in Canada," in Hahlo, Economic and Managerial Aspects. Dobbs Ferry, New York: Oceana, 1973.

Heywood, J.S. "Horizontal Mergers and International Competition." Detroit College Law Review Vol. 1984, 1984, pp. 871-875.

Hoelzer, Heinrich. "Neuere Initiativen zum U.S. Antitrust - Ein Ueberblick -." Wirtschaft und Wettbewerb Vol. 30, 1980, pp. 728-740.

Hopt, Klaus J., ed. Legal and Economic Analyses on Multinational Enterprises. New York: Walter de Gruyter, 1982. (2 Vols.) Vol. 1: European Merger Control; Vol. 2: Groups of Companies in European Laws.

Hunter, Lawson. "Survey of Canadian Antitrust Laws." Antitrust Law Journal Vol. 50, 1981, pp. 699-708.

Huntley, A. K. "Protection of Trading Interests Act, 1980: Some General Aspects of Enforcement of Antitrust Laws." International and Comparative Law Quarterly Vol. 30 1981, pp. 213-233.

Hurwitz, James D. "The Impact of the Continental Can Case on Combinations and Concentrations Within the Common Market." Hastings Law Journal Vol. 25, 1973-1974, pp. 469-517.

Hutcheson, N.L. and P.M. Kliger. "Current Antitrust Enforcement Policies Affecting Mergers and Joint Ventures." Michigan Bar Journal Vol. 64, 1985, pp. 55-58.

Imurenga, U. "Schwerpunkte der Vierten Novelle zum Gesetz gegen Wettbewerbsbeschraenkungen." Neue Juristische Wochenschrift Vol. 33, 1980, pp. 1417-1423.

International Bar Association, Committee C - Antitrust Law and Monopolies. Enforcing Antitrust Against Foreign Enterprises: Procedural Problems in the Extraterritorial Application of Antitrust Laws. Boston: Kluwer, 1981.

"International Implications of the 1982 Merger Guidelines." Georgia Journal of International and Comparative Law Vol. 13, 1983, pp. 797-824.

"International Joint Ventures and Antitrust Policy: FTC Puts GM and Toyota in the Driver's Seat." Wisconsin International Law Journal Vol. 4, 1985, pp. 64-85.

"International Joint Ventures and Section (1) of the Sherman Act: per se as the Meaningful Standard." American University Law Review Vol. 23, 1974, pp. 689-729.

"International Joint Ventures in the United States: The GM-Toyota Deal." Columbia Journal of Transnational Law Vol. 22, 1984, pp. 505-540.

"International Law - Act of State Doctrine: An Emerging Corruption Exception in Antitrust Cases?" Notre Dame Law Review Vol. 59, 1984, pp. 455-470.

"Intra-Enterprise Conspiracy Under Section 1 of the Sherman Act: A Suggested Standard." Michigan Law Review Vol. 75, 1976-1977, pp. 717-744.

Jackson, Bruce H. "Application of U.S. Antitrust Law to International Investment: Joint Ventures, Mergers and Aquisitions." North Carolina Journal of International Law and Commercial Regulation Vol. 5, 1980, pp. 141-164.

Jennings, R.Y. "Extraterritorial Jurisdiction and the United States Anti-Trust Laws." British Yearbook of International Law Vol. 33, 1957, pp. 146-175.

Joelson, Mark R. "Challenges to United States Foreign Trade and Investment: Antitrust Law Perspectives." International Lawyer Vol. 14, 1980, pp. 103-114.

Joelson, Mark R. "International Antitrust: Problems and Defenses." Law and Policy in International Business Vol. 15, 1983, pp. 1121-1134.

Joelson, Mark R. "International Technology Transfers and U.S. Anti-Trust Laws." Journal of International Law and Economics Vol. 8, 1973, p. 85-112.

Joelson, Mark R. and Joseph P. Griffin. "Legal Status of Nation-State Cartels under United States Anti-Trust and Public International Law." International Lawyer Vol. 9, 1975, pp. 617-645.

Joelson, Mark R. and Joseph P. Griffin. "Multinational Joint Ventures and the U.S. Anti-Trust Laws." Virginia Journal of International Law Vol. 15, 1975, pp. 487-538.

Joelson, Mark R. "Proposed International Codes of Conduct as Related to Restrictive Business Practices." Law and Policy in International Business Vol. 8, 1976, pp. 837-874.

Johnson, J.C. and K.C. Schneider. "Fifty Years (1936-1986) of the Robinson-Patman Act Mystique." Transportation Practitioners Journal Vol. 53, 1986, pp. 400-412.

Joliet, René. Monopolization and Abuse of Dominant Position: Study of the American and European Approaches to the Control of Economic Power. (Lièges Faculté de droit: Collection scientifique de la faculté de droit de l'Université de lièges 31) The Hague: Nijhoff, 1970.

Joliet, René. The Rule of Reason in Anti-Trust Law: American, German and Common Market Laws in Comparative Perspective. The Hague: Nijhoff, 1967.

Jones, J.C.H. and P.J. Coxon. "Positive Economics and Public Policy: Some Canadian Evidence on Policy Change and Antitrust." Antitrust Bulletin Vol. 30, 1985, pp. 365-399.

Jones, Robert T. "Extraterritoriality in U.S. Antitrust: An International 'Hot Potato'." International Lawyer Vol. 11, 1977, pp. 415-435.

Kaiser, Joseph H. "Fusionskontrolle oder Fusionsverbot?: Die Vermutungstatbestaende des Entwurfs der IV. GWB-Novelle." Wirtschaft und Wettbewerb Vol. 28, 1978, pp. 344-363.

"Kartell-Hearing: ASU: Fusionskontrolle noch immer lueckenhaft." Handelsblatt 3 March 1979, p. 3.

"Kartellnovelle 'kein grosser Wurf': Einstimmige Verabschiedung im Wirtschaftsausschuss." Frankfurter Allgemeine Zeitung 25 January 1970, p.11.

Kennish, J.T. "Competition Law and Enforcement in Canada." International Lawyer Vol. 20, 1986, pp. 81-123.

Kestenbaum, L. "Antitrust's 'Extraterritorial' Jurisdiction: A Progress Report on the Balancing of Interests Test." Stanford Journal of International Law Vol. 18, 1982, pp. 311-346.

King, H.T., Jr. "International Operations: Current Antitrust Environment." Case Western Reserve Journal of International Law Vol. 8, 1976, pp. 452-467.

Kintner, Joelson and Vaghi. "Groping for a Truly International Antitrust Law." Virginia Journal of International Law Vol. 14, 1973, pp. 85-100.

Kitch, E.W. "The Antitrust Economics of Joint Ventures." Antitrust Law Journal Vol. 54, 1985, pp. 957-966.

Klawitter, C. "Nochmals: die Aufloesung von Unternehmenszusammenschlussen im Fusionskontrollverfahren." Wirtschaft und Wettbewerb Vol. 31, 1981, pp. 245-251.

Knoepfle, R. "Wettbewerbsbeschraenkung durch Anwendung des Gesetzes gegen Wettbewerbsbeschraenkungen bei Zusammenschlussen." Juristenzeitung Vol. 37, 1982, pp. 521-530.

Koppensteiner, Hans-Georg. "International Enterprises under the Antitrust Law of the European Economic Community." Journal of World Trade Law Vol. 9, 1975, pp. 287-317.

Korah, Valentine. "The Control of Mergers under Article 86 of the Rome Treaty: Continental Can." Current Legal Problems Vol. 26, 1973, pp. 82-113.

Korah, Valentine. "Group Exemptions for Exclusive Distribution and Purchasing in the EEC." Common Market Law Review Vol. 21, 1984, pp. 53-80.

Krause, Harry D. "The Multi-Corporate International Business under Section 1 of the Sherman Act - Intra-Enterprise Conspiracy Revisited." Business Lawyer Vol. 17, 1962, pp. 912-938.

"Laker Airways v. Sabena [731 F.2d. 909]: Comity and Conflict." Law and Policy in International Business Vol. 17, 1985, pp. 157-176.

"The Laker [British Airway Bd. v. Laker Airways, Ltd. (1984) 3 All E.R. 39] Jurisdictional Affair: the Judiciary Temporarily Avoids a Political Showdown." Wakeforest Law Review Vol. 20, 1984, pp. 951-974.

"The Laker [Laker Airways, Ltd. v. Sabena, Belgian World Airlines, 731 F.2d. 909] Antitrust Litigation: the Jurisdictional 'Rule of Reason' Applied to Transnational Injunctive Relief." Cornell Law Review Vol. 71, 1986, pp. 645-667.

Lang, J.T. "Community Antitrust Law - Compliance and Enforcement." Common Market Law Review Vol. 18, 1981, pp. 335-362.

Lang, J.T. "Selective Distribution." Fordham International Law Journal Vol. 8, 1984/1985, pp. 323-361.

Lawson, R.G. "The Competition Act: A Review." New Law Journal Vol. 133, 1983, pp. 908-910.

"The Long-Awaited Death Knell of the Intra-Enterprise Doctrine." Villanova Law Review Vol. 30, 1985, pp. 521-569.

Lopez-Balboa, V.M. and J. Myers. "Jurisdictional Standards Under EEC Competition Law: The Evolution of the Economic Entity Test." Journal of Comparative Business and Capital Market Law Vol. 6, 1984, pp. 383-407.

Maitland-Walker, J., ed. International Anti-Trust Law Oxford: ESC Publishing, 1984. (2 Vols.) Vol. 1: A review of national laws; Vol. 2: Recent developments in EEC and U.S. Anti-Trust Laws.

Mannick, C.V. "Antitrust: British Restrictions on Enforcement of Foreign Judgments." Harvard International Law Journal Vol. 21, 1980, pp. 727-735.

Marinelli, Jr., A.J. "Competition Policy in Britain." Southern Illinois University Law Journal Vol. 1985, 1985, pp. 153-164.

Markert, Kurt E. "Anti-Monopoly Legislation in Europe," in H.R. Hahlo, ed., Nationalism and the Multinational Enterprise: Legal, Economic and Managerial Aspects. Dobbs Ferry, NY: Oceana, 1973.

Markert, Kurt E. "Recent Developments in German Antitrust Law." Fordham Law Review Vol. 43, 1975, pp. 697-718.

Markert, Kurt E. "Recent Developments in International Antitrust Cooperation." Antitrust Bulletin Vol. 13, 1968, pp. 355-372.

Matsushita, M. "Problems and Analysis of the Oil Cartel Case Decisions." Law in Japan: An Annual Vol. 15, 1982, pp. 79-94.

McClaren, Richard. "International Investment and the U.S. Antitrust Laws." Address delivered in London, 1 December 1969.

McDermid, John F. "Merger Directions: The United States and EEC: An Ominous Picture for United States Multinationals." George Mason University Law Review Vol. 3, 1980, pp. 1-62.

McFetridge, D.G. and S. Wong. "Predatory Pricing in Canada: The Law and the Economics." Canadian Business Review Vol. 63, 1985, pp. 685-733.

Meal, D.H. "Governmental Compulsion as a Defense under United States and European Community Antitrust Law." Columbia Journal of Transnational Law Vol. 20, 1981, pp. 51-131.

Meesen, K.M. "Antitrust Jurisdiction under Customary International Law." American Journal of International Law Vol. 78, 1984, pp. 783-810.

Meng, Werner. "Neuere Entwicklungen im Streit um die Jurisdiktionshoheit der Staaten im Bereich der Wettbewerbsbeschraenkungen." Zeitschrift fuer auslaendisches oeffentliches Recht und Voelkerrecht Vol. 41, 1981, pp. 469-513.

"Merger Policy and Enforcement." J. Sims, introductory remarks. Other articles: "Merger Policy and Enforcement at the Antitrust Division: The Lawyer's View." R.B. Andewelt; "Merger Policy and Enforcement at the Federal Trade Commission: The Lawyer's View." J.E. McCarty; "Merger Policy and Enforcement at the Antitrust Division: The Economist's View." F.R. Warren-Boulton; "Merger Policy and Enforcement at the Federal Trade Commisssion: The Economist's View." D.T. Scheffman; Panel discussion. Antitrust Law Journal Vol. 54, 1985, pp. 93-128.

Merkin, R. "The Legality of Effective Competition in EEC Law: AEG Telefunken [AEG Telefunken v. Commission of European Communities, Case 107/82] in the European Court of Justice." Liverpool Law Review Vol. 6, 1984, pp. 139-165.

Mestmaecker, E.-J. and R. Richter, eds. "Competition Policy: German and American Experiences - A Symposium." Zeitschrift fuer die gesamte Staatswissenschaft No. 3, 1980, pp. 385-592.

Metzger, Stanley D. "Cartels, Combines, Commodity Agreements and International Law." Texas International Law Journal Vol. 11, 1976, pp. 527-539.

Millstein, Ira M., et al. "Extraterritorial Application of U.S. Antitrust Law (Economic Imperialism or Protecting Competition Against Foreign Invasion?)." (Debate) Proceedings of the Twenty-Ninth Annual Spring Meeting of the Section of Antitrust Law of the American Bar Association, Washington, D.C., 1981. Antitrust Law Journal Vol. 50, 1981, pp. 617-644.

Moeschel, W. "Konglomerate Zusammenschlusse im Antitrustrecht der Vereinigten Staaten von Amerika." Rabels Zeitschrift fuer auslaendisches und internationales Privatrecht Vol. 44, 1980, pp. 203-256.

Mongoven, J.F. "Theory of Actual and Potential Competition: British Oxygen Co. v. Federal Trade Commission." Columbia Journal of Transnational Law Vol. 18, 1979, pp. 289-307.

"Monopolkomission will unabhaengig bleiben: Gegen Beschwerderecht/ Professoren: Fusionsverbote fuer 'Grosse'." Frankfurter Allgemeine Zeitung 13 March 1979, p. 11.

"More Speech, Less Litigation: Extending the Noerr-Pennington Doctrine to the Law of Defamation." The John Marshall Law Review Vol. 18, 1985, pp. 683-702.

Morris, V. "Interim Measures in EEC Competition Cases." International Tax and Business Law Vol. 3, 1985, pp. 102-118.

Mueller, Rudolf and Hannes Schneider. Gesetz gegen Wettbewerbsbeschraenkungen: Deutsch-Englische Textausgabe. Frankfurt am Main: Fritz Knapp Verlag, 1973.

"The Multinational's Dilemma: The IBM [IBM Corp. v. Commission of European Communities (1981) Common Market Law Reports Vol. 32 p. 93] Proceeding in Europe." Dickinson Journal of International Law Vol. 3, 1985, pp. 255-280.

Murphy, D.T. "Moderating Antitrust Subject Matter Jurisdiction: the Foreign Trade Antitrust Improvements Act and the Restatement of Foreign Relations Law (Revised)." University of Cincinnati Law Review Vol. 54, 1986, pp. 779-827.

Myers, James D. "EEC Antitrust Law: Its Development and Philosophy with Special Attention to Intellectual Property Rights." North Carolina Journal of International Law and Commercial Regulation Vol. 5, 1980, pp. 37-56.

Neale, A.D. The Antitrust Laws of the United States of America: A Study of Competition Enforced by Law, 2d ed. Cambridge: Cambridge University Press, 1970.

Niessen, H. "Proposition de septième directive concernant les comptes du groupe." Cahiers de Droit Européen Vol. 17, 1981, pp. 26-37, 57-69.

Norton, Joseph J. "The European Court of Justice Judgment in United Brands: Extraterritorial Jurisdiction and Abuse of a Dominant Position." Denver Journal of International Law and Policy Vol. 8, 1979, pp. 379-414.

Oakley, L. "Laker Probe: Who Will Gain?" Sunday Times (London) 3 July 1983, p. 20.

Oesterle, D.A. "United Nations Conference on Restrictive Business Practices." Cornell International Law Journal Vol. 14, 1981, pp. 1-55.

Ongman, John Will. "Be No Longer a Chaos: Constructing a Normative Theory of the Sherman Act's Extraterritorial Jurisdictional Scope." Northwestern University Law Review Vol. 6, 1977, pp. 733-766.

Organisation for Economic Co-operation and Development. Competition Policy in OECD Countries 1983-1984. Paris: OECD Publications, 1986.

Organisation for Economic Co-operation and Development. Glossary of Terms Relating to the Restrictive Business Practices Committee. Paris: OECD Publications, 1965.

Organisation for Economic Co-operation and Development. Merger and Competition Policy, Report of the Committee of Experts on Restrictive Business Practices. Paris: OECD Publications, 1975.

Organisation for Economic Co-operation and Development. Mergers and Competition Policy, Report of the Committee of Experts on Restrictive Business Practices. Paris: OECD Publications, 1974.

Organisation for Economic Co-operation and Development. Merger Policies and R cent Trends in Mergers. Paris: OECD Publications, 1984.

Organisation for Economic Co-operation and Development. Restrictive Business Practices of Multinational Enterprises, Report of the Committee of Experts on Restrictive Business Practices. Paris: OECD Publications, 1977.

Painter, Therese Eve and Dianne Zomper. "A Bibliography of Current Issues in International Business Transactions: Investment Regulation, Antitrust, Acquisitions and Mergers, Transfer of Technology, Joint Ventures, Taxation, Dispute Resolution, Transnational Tort Claims, and Export Controls." Texas International Law Journal Vol. 21, 1985, pp. 165-197.

Park, J.G. "Extraterritorial Impact of United States Antitrust Laws and Commercial Bribery Considerations." Dickinson International Law Annual Vol. 1, 1982, pp. 105-124.

Paugh, Jon. "The Application of U.S. Economic Regulations to International Commerce: A Comparison of the Sherman Act and U.S. International Trade Regulation Laws." Law and Policy in International Business Vol. 13, 1981, pp. 961-995.

Payne, Kenneth E. and Richard L. Stroup. "U.S. Antitrust Aspects of the International Transfer of Technology." North Carolina Journal of International Law and Commercial Regulation Vol. 5, 1980, pp. 91-120.

Pengilley, W. "Competition Policy and Law Enforcement: Ramblings on Rhetoric and Reality." Australian Journal of Law and Society Vol. 2, 1984, pp. 1-29.

Pikua, R.J., Jr. "Uranium Cartel Saga." Case Western Reserve Journal of International Law Vol. 12, 1980, pp. 591-639.

"Potential Havens from American Jurisdiction and Discovery Laws in International Antitrust Enforcement." University of Florida Law Review Vol. 33, 1981, pp. 240-271.

Preston, Leslie J. "The Defense of Coercive Foreign Legislation in Competition Proceedings before the Commission of the European Economic Community." Unpublished manuscript.

"Private International Couriers: A Challenge to the West German Postal Monopoly and EEC Law." Cornell International Law Journal Vol. 19, 1986, pp. 35-63.

Rahl, James A. Common Market and American Antitrust - Overlap and Conflict. New York: McGraw-Hill, 1970.

Ramsey, S.D. "The United States-Australia Antitrust Cooperation Agreement: A Step in the Right Direction." Virginia Journal of International Law Vol. 24, 1983, pp. 127-169.

Ramseyer, J.M. "Japanese Antitrust Enforcement after the Oil Embargo." American Journal of Comparative Law Vol. 31, 1983, pp. 395-430.

Ramseyer, J.M. "Oil Cartel Criminal Cases: Translations and Postscript." Law in Japan: An Annual Vol. 15, 1982, pp. 57-78.

Rauschenbach, G. "Die Entwicklung des deutschen Kartellrechts 1977." Neue Juristische Wochenschrift 1 February 1978, p. 190.

Rauschenbach, G. "Die Entwicklung des deutschen Kartellrechts im Jahre 1978." Neue Juristische Wochenschrift 11 April 1979, p. 737.

Rauschenbach, G. "Die Entwicklung des deutschen Kartellrechts in den Jahren 1975/1976." Neue Juristische Wochenschrift 1 December 1976, pp. 2185-2191.

Reicin, C.V. "Act of State Doctrine: Applicability of United States Antitrust Laws." Harvard International Law Journal Vol. 23, 1982, pp. 117-123.

"Ressourcenwuerdigung bei konglomeratem Zusammenschluss." Wirtschaft und Wettbewerb/Entscheidungsammlung [des Oberlandesgerichts] zum Kartellrecht Vol. 4, 1977, p. 1745.

Reynolds, M.J. "Merger Control in the EEC." Journal of World Trade Law Vol. 17, 1983, pp. 407-426.

Riechmann, V. "Funf Jahre 4. Kartellgesetz-Novelle - Eine Bestandsaufnahme zur Rechtsprechungs- und Verwaltungspraxis." Wettbewerb in Recht und Praxis Vol. 31, 1985, pp. 323-330.

Riedweg, A.J. "The Extra-Territorial Application of Restrictive Trade Legislation - Jurisdiction and International Law," in International Law Association, Report on the Fifty-First Conference, 1965.

Rinck, Gerd. "Information Agreements in Comparative Competition Law." Current Legal Problems Vol. 29, 1976, pp. 150-167.

Roberts, R.J. and C.A. Hewat. "Pre-Merger Notification in Canada." Canadian Business Law Journal Vol. 11, 1986, pp. 135-146.

Robinson, Stanley D. "Recent Antitrust Developments - 1979. Record of the Association of the Bar of the City of New York Vol. 34, 1979, pp. 671-728.

"The Robinson-Patman Act Revisited in Its 50th Year." Introduction by R.D. Paul; Other articles: "The Robinson-Patman Act: The Great Issues and Personalities." P.H. LaRue; "The Robinson-Patman Act: A Critical Appraisal." H.L. Shniderman; Panel discussion. Antitrust Law Journal Vol. 55, 1986, pp. 133-170.

Rogers, C.P. "Still Running Against the Wind: A Comment on Antitrust Jurisdiction and Laker Airways, Ltd. v. Sabena, Belgian World Airlines [731 F.2d. 909]. Journal of Air Law and Commerce Vol. 50, 1985, pp. 931-967.

Rosen, J.P. "Protection of Trading Interests Act." International Lawyer Vol. 15, 1981, pp. 213-232.

Rosenthal, Douglas E. "Relationship of U.S. Antitrust Laws to Formulation of Foreign Economic Policy, Particularly Export and Overseas Investment Policy." Antitrust Law Journal Vol. 49, 1980, pp. 1189-1196.

Roth, H. "Fusionkontrolle internationaler Unternehmens-zusammenschlusse." Rabels Zeitschrift fuer auslaendisches und internationales Privatrecht Vol. 45, 1981, pp. 501-544.

Rowe, Frederick M. "Antitrust Aspects of European Acquisitions or Joint Ventures in the United States." Paper presented at a conference on "The U.S. Antitrust Laws/Die U.S. Antitrust Gesetze: the legal implications for those entering or operating in the U.S. market." Practising Law Institute (New York)/ German-American Lawyers Association (Bonn), Cologne, June 1979.

Rule, C.F. "The Administration's Views on Joint Ventures." *Antitrust Law Journal* Vol. 54, 1985, pp. 1121-1136.

Sandrock, O. "Das Kollisionsrecht des unlauteren Wettbewerbs zwischen dem internationalen Immaterialgutterrecht und dem internationalen Kartellrecht." *Gewerblicher Rechtsschutz und Urheberrecht, Internationaler Teil* 1985, pp. 507-522.

Sayler, R.H. and A. Heck. "Neue Rechtlinien zur Fusionskontrolle in den USA und ihre praktischen Auswirkungen." *Recht der internationalen Wirtschaft* Vol. 29, 1983, pp. 77-81.

Schachter, Oscar, and Robert Hellawell, eds. *Competition in International Business: Law and Policy on Restrictive Practices.* New York: Columbia University Press, 1981.

Schlieder, Willy C. "European Competition Policy." *Antitrust Law Journal* Vol. 50, 1981, pp. 647-698.

Schlieder, Willy C. "Wettbewerbsregeln fur den Technologietransfer." *Gewerblicher Rechtschutz und Uhrheberrecht* Vol. 82, 1980, pp. 451-456.

Schmidt, H.R. "The Extraterritorial Application of the United States Antitrust Laws." *Journal of Law and Commerce* Vol. 5, 1985, pp. 321-345.

Schmidt, I. "Different Approaches and Problems in Dealing with Control of Market Power: A Comparison of German, European, and U.S. Policy Towards Market-Dominating Enterprises." *Antitrust Bulletin* Vol. 28, 1983, pp. 417-460.

Schmidt, K. "Vertraegliche Wettbewerbsverbote im deutschen Kartellrecht." Zeitschrift fur das gesamte Handelsrecht und Wirtschaftsrecht Vol. 149, 1985, pp. 1-27.

Schnor, Thomas. "Trust-Busting with a German Accent: The Control of Corporate Merger and Acquisition Activities under Increasingly Aggressive West German Law." Virginia Journal of International Law Vol. 19, 1979, pp. 595-631.

Schroter, H.R.B. "The Application of Article 85 of the EEC Treaty to Exclusive Distribution Agreements." Fordham International Law Journal Vol. 8, 1984-1985, pp. 1-38.

Schultz, K.-P. "Ausgestaltung der fusionsrechtlinien in der Praxis." Wirtschaft und Wettbewerb Vol. 32, 1982, pp. 429-444.

Schwartz, Louis B. Free Enterprise and Economic Organization, 3d edition. Vol. 1: Concentration and Restrictive Practices; Vol. 2: Regulation of Entry, Rules and Discrimination (University Casebook Series). Mineola, New York: Foundation Press, 1966.

"Selective Distribution of Personal Computers in the EEC: Is Article 85 IBM Compatible?" Journal of Law and Commerce Vol. 5, 1985, pp. 505-534.

Sennett, M. and A.I. Gavil. "Antitrust Jurisdiction, Extraterritorial Conduct and Interest-Balancing." International Lawyer Vol. 19, 1985, pp. 1185-1214.

"The Sham Exception to the Noerr-Pennington Doctrine: A Commercial Speech Interpretation." Brooklyn Law Review Vol. 49, 1983, pp. 573-603.

Shenefeld, J.H. "Extraterritoriality in Antitrust." Law and Policy in International Business Vol. 15, 1983, pp. 1109-1120.

Shenefeld, J.H. "Thoughts on Extraterritorial Application of the United States Antitrust Laws." Fordham Law Review Vol. 52, 1983, pp. 350-373.

Sherliker, C. "Merger Regulation in the EEC." New Law Journal Vol. 134, 1984, pp. 809-812.

"Shortening the Long Arm of American Antitrust Jurisdiction: Extraterritoriality and the Foreign Blocking Statutes." Loyola Law Review Vol. 28, 1982, pp. 213-280.

Silcox, C.R. "Unfair Methods of Competition: The Courts Revive Proof of Injury to Competition in Antitrust Cases under Section 5 of the Act." Antitrust Bulletin Vol. 29, 1984, pp. 423-474.

Silverstein, D. "Antitrust Guide for International Operations - Another Point of View." International Lawyer Vol. 13, 1979, pp. 693-701.

Simson, G.J. "Return of American Banana: A Contemporary Perspective on American Anti-Trust Abroad." Journal of International Law and Economics Vol. 9, 1974, pp. 233-265.

Sinau, I.M. "Tied-House Agreements and the EEC Competition Rules: A Brief History." New Law Journal Vol. 135, 1985, pp. 1063-1065.

Smith, Robert E. "Cartels and the Shield of Ignorance." The Journal of International Law and Economics Vol. 8, 1973, pp. 53-83.

Snyder, J.L. "International Competition: Toward a Normative Theory of United States Antitrust Law and Policy." Boston University International Law Journal Vol. 3, 1984, pp. 257-324.

Sornarajah, M. "Extraterritorial Enforcement of U.S. Antitrust Laws: Conflict and Compromise." International and Comparative Law Quarterly Vol. 31, 1982, pp. 127-149.

Stanbury, W.T. "Half a Loaf: Bill C-29, Proposed Amendments to the Combines Investigation Act." Canadian Business Law Journal Vol. 10, February 1985, pp. 1-34.

Stanbury, W.T. "The New Competition Act and Competition Tribunal Act: 'Not With a Bang, but a Whimper.'" Canadian Business Law Journal Vol. 12, October 1986, pp. 2-42.

Stanford, J.S. "The Application of the Sherman Act to Conduct Outside the United States: A View from Abroad." Cornell International Law Journal Vol. 11, 1978, pp. 195-214.

Steindorff, E. "Kartellrecht und Schiedsgerichtbarkeit." Wirtschaft und Wettbewerb Vol. 34, 1984, pp. 189-200.

Stephanou, C.A. "Code des Nations Unies sur les Pratiques Commerciales Restrictives." Revue Hellenique de Droit International Vol. 34, 1981, pp. 21-47.

"A Survey of the Patent-Anti-Trust Controversy in International Trade." Notre Dame Lawyer Vol. 52, 1977, pp. 957-994.

Sutherland, P.D. "The Competition Policy of the European Community." St. Louis University Law Journal Vol. 30, October 1985, pp. 149-170.

Swan, George S. "EEC United Brands Decision: Can Chiquita Banana Find Happiness in Europe?" California Western International Law Journal Vol. 7, 1977, pp. 385-417.

Thieffry, J. "La distribution des produits a l'étranger." Revue Trimestrielle de Droit Commercial et de Droit Économique Vol. 38, 1985, pp. 725-736.

Thiesing, Jochen. "Antitrust and International Law as Viewed from the United States and the European Common Market." Record of the Association of the Bar of the City of New York Vol. 25, 1970, pp. 206-224.

Thomas, B.S. "Internationalization of the Securities Markets: An Empirical Analysis." George Washington Law Review Vol. 50, 1982, pp. 155-190.

Thompson, D. "UNCTAD: Model Law on Restrictive Business Practices." Journal of World Trade Law Vol. 14, 1980, pp. 444-449.

Thompson, M.J. "Antitrust and the Multinational Corporation: Competition or Cartels." International Lawyer Vol. 8, 1974, pp. 618-625.

Tillotson, John. "The GKN - Sachs Affair: A Case Study in Economic Law." Journal of World Trade Law Vol. 14, 1980, pp. 39-67.

Timberg, Sigmund. "An International Antitrust Convention: A Proposal to Harmonize Conflicting National Policies Towards the Multinational Corporation." Journal of International Law and Economics Vol. 8, 1973, pp. 157-184.

Timberg, Sigmund. "International Combines and National Sovereigns." University of Pennsylvania Law Review Vol. 95, 1947, pp. 575-620.

Tindall, Robert E. Multinational Enterprises: Legal and Management Structures and Interrelationship with Ownership, Control, Antitrust, Labor, Taxation and Disclosure. Dobbs Ferry, New York: Oceana, 1975.

Toepke, U. "EEC Law of Competition: Distribution Agreements and Their Notification." International Lawyer Vol. 19, 1985, pp. 117-158.

Toms, B.C., III. "French Response to the Extraterritorial Application of U.S. Antitrust Laws." International Lawyer Vol. 15, 1981, pp. 585-614.

Toyama, K., N. Tateishi and J. Palenberg. "Trade Friction, Administrative Guidance and Antimonopoly Law in Japan." Case Western Reserve Journal of International Law Vol. 15, 1983, pp. 601-610.

Tsoris, S.A. "Section C of Great Britain's Protection of Trading Interests Act: The Claw and the Lever." Cornell International Law Journal Vol. 14, 1981, pp. 457-479.

Tuomi, K. "Mergers and Acquisitions in Canada: The Interrelationship Between Foreign Ownership and Competition Policy." Canadian Business Law Journal Vol. 11, 1986, pp. 316-330.

Uesugi, Akinori. "Japan's Cartel System and Its Impact on International Trade." *Harvard International Law Journal* Vol. 27, 1986, pp. 389-424.

Uesugi, Akinori. "Japanese Antimonopoly Policy - Its Past and Future." *Antitrust Law Journal* Vol. 50, 1981, pp. 709-720.

Ulmer, P. "Gemeinschaftsunternehmen in EG-Kartellrecht." *Wirtschaft und Wettbewerb* Vol. 29, 1979, pp. 433-447.

"Um die Fusionskontrolle wird weiter gepokert." *Frankfurter Allgemeine Zeitung* 3 December 1979, p. 13.

"U.N. Set of Multilaterally Agreed Equitable Principles and Rules for the Control of Restrictive Business Practices. General Assembly Resolution 35/63 (1980)." *Georgia Journal of International and Comparative Law* Vol. 11, 1981, pp. 709-721.

United Kingdom. "A Review of Monopolies and Mergers Policy: A Consultative Document." Cmnd. 7198, HMSO, London, May 1978.

United Nations Conference on Trade and Development. "A Set of Multilaterally Agreed Equitable Principles and Rules for the Control of Restrictive Business Practices." UNCTAD Document No. TD/RBP/CONF/10. 2 May 1980. Also No. A/C.2/35/6. 23 October 1980.

United States. Federal Trade Commission, Bureau of Competition, Premerger Notification Office. *Premerger Notification Compliance Guide: An explanation of the application and operation of the premerger notification rules implementing the Hart-Scott-Rodino Anti-Trust Improvements Act of 1976*. 18 September 1978.

United States. National Commission for the Review of Antitrust Laws and Procedures. *Report to the President and the Attorney General* Washington, DC, 22 January 1979.

United States Department of Justice, Antitrust Division. *Antitrust Guide for International Operations.* Washington, D.C.: Department of Justice, 1977.

"United States Antitrust Law and Industrial Policy: International Joint Ventures and Global Competition After GM-Toyota [103 F.T.C. 374]." Fordham International Law Journal Vol. 9, 1985/1986, pp. 257-294.

"U.S. Challenges BASF's Purchase." International Herald Tribune 19 April 1979, p. 7.

Van Cise, Jerrold G. Understanding the Antitrust Laws. New York: Practising Law Institute, 1955.

van Roy, Y. "Commerce Amendment Act 1983 - Necessary Procedural Change for Mergers and Takeovers." Victoria University Wellington Law Review Vol. 14, May 1984, pp. 203-219.

Veltius, M.A. "Neueste Entwicklungen der extraterritorialen Anwendung des U.S. Antitrust-Rechts." Recht der internationalen Wirtschaft Vol. 28, 1982, pp. 157-161.

Velvel, Lawrence R. "Antitrust Suits by Foreign Nations." Catholic University Law Review Vol. 25, 1975, pp. 1-41.

Venit, J.S. "EEC Patent Licensing Revisited: The Commisssion's Patent License Regulation." Antitrust Bulletin Vol. 30, 1985, pp. 457-526.

Venit, J.S. "Exclusive Distribution Agreements and Their Automatic Exemption from the Prohibition on Restrictive Agreements in the European Economic Community." Tidskrift, utgiven ar Juridiska Foereningen 1985, pp. 173-210.

Victor, A. Paul, et al. "International Acquisitions, Joint Ventures, and Other Agreements - the Applicable Substantive and Procedural Law." (Various articles) Proceedings of the Twenty-Ninth Annual Spring Meeting of the Section of Antitrust Law of the American Bar Association, Washington, D.C., 1981. Antitrust Law Journal Vol. 50, 1981, pp. 453-496.

Victor, A. Paul. "Multinational Corporations: Anti-Trust Extraterritoriality and the Prospect of Immunity." Journal of International Law and Economics Vol. 8, 1973, pp. 11-29.

Vogelenzang, P. "Abuse of a Dominant Position in Article 86; The Problem of Causality and Some Applications." Common Market Law Review Vol. 13, 1976, pp. 61-78.

von Gamm, O.-F. "Wein- und Bezeichnungsvorschriften des Gemeinschaftsrechts und Nationales Recht gegen den enlauteren Wettbewerb." Gewerblicher Rechtsschutz und Urheberrecht Vol. 86, 1984, pp. 165-169.

"Wall Street's Rush to Beat the New Merger Rules." The Economist 17 March 1979, pp. 113-114.

Waller, S.W. "Redefining the Foreign Compulsion Defense in U.S. Antitrust Law: The Japanese Auto Restraints and Beyond." Law and Policy in International Business Vol. 14, 1982, pp. 747-817.

"West Germany: Monopolies Commission." Journal of World Trade Law Vol. 13, 1979, pp. 448-462.

"West Germany Probes Alleged Japanese Cartel." International Herald Tribune 7-8 March 1981, p. 11.

Withrow, James R. and Richard P. Larm. "The 'Big' Anti-Trust Case: Twenty-Five Years of Sisyphean Labor." Cornell Law Review Vol. 61, 1976, pp. 1-49.

Wittman, Joseph I. "International Mergers Under Section 7 of the Clayton Act and Article 86 of the Common Market Treaty of Rome: A Comparative Perspective." Washburn Law Journal Vol. 18, 1979, pp. 512-534.

Wolf, D. "Fortentwicklung der Fusionskontrolle." Wirtschaft und Wettbewerb Vol. 30, 1980, pp. 462-474.

Wood, Jeffrey and Victor M. Carrera. "The International Uranium Cartel: Litigation and Legal Implications." Texas International Law Journal Vol. 14, 1979, pp. 59-114.

Yoshikawa, Seichi. "Fair Trade Commission vs. MITI: History of the Conflicts Between the Antimonopoly Policy in the Post War Period of Japan." Case Western Reserve Journal of International Law Vol. 15, 1983, pp. 489-504.

Zanon, DiValgiurata L. "Price Discrimination and Hoffman-LaRoche." Journal of World Trade Law Vol. 15, 1981, pp. 305-322.

Zanon, DiValgiurata L. "Price Discrimination under Article 86 of the EEC Treaty: The United Brands Case." International and Comparative Law Quarterly Vol. 31, 1982, pp. 36-58.

"Zum Verhaeltnis der Monopol- und der Oligopol-vermutung in Nr. 22 Abs. 3 GWB: Kritische Anmerkungen zur Entscheidung des Kammergerichts in der Sache 'Blei-' und Silber-huette Braubach' vom 16.1.1980." Betriebs-Berater Vol. 36, 1981, pp. 149-153.

Zwarensteyn, Hendrik. Some Aspects of the Extraterritorial Reach of the American Antitrust Laws. Deventer: Kluwer, 1970.

2. ARBITRATION/DISPUTE SETTLEMENT

Amerasinghe, C.F. "Model Clauses for Settlement of Foreign Investment Disputes." Arbitration Journal Vol. 28, December 1973, pp. 232-257.

Amerasinghe, C.F. "Submissions and the Jurisdiction of the International Center for the Settlement of Investment Disputes." Journal of Maritime Law Vol. 5, 1974, pp. 211-250.

"Arbitration and Securities Regulation - Conflict between the Federal Arbitration Act and the Securities Exchange Act in an International Transaction." Missouri Law Review Vol. 40, 1975, pp. 527-535.

"Arbitration Clauses in International Contracts and the Extraterritorial Reach of the Securities Exchange Act of 1934 in Light of Scherk v. Alberto-Culver Co. (94 S.Ct. 2449)." Syracuse Law Review Vol. 26, 1975, pp. 995-1015.

"Arbitration: Public Policy Exception to Arbitration of Antitrust Issues - Mitsubishi Motors Corp. v. Soler Chrysler-Plymouth, Inc., 723 F.2d 155." Harvard International Law Journal Vol. 25, 1984, pp. 427-433.

Becker, J.D. "Antitrust and International Arbitration - the New American Synthesis." International Business Lawyer Vol. 13, 1985, pp. 445-447.

Bishop, R.D. and S. Burnette. "United States Practice Concerning the Recognition of Foreign Judgments." International Lawyer Vol. 16, 1982, pp. 425-442.

"The Canada-United States Memorandum of Understanding Regarding Application of National Antitrust Law: New Guidelines for Resolution of Multinational Antitrust Enforcement Disputes." New England Journal of International Law and Business Vol. 6, 1984/1985, pp. 1065-1095.

Cherian, J. Investment Contracts and Arbitration. The World Bank Convention on the Settlement of Investment Disputes. Leyden: Sijthoff, 1975.

"Commercial Dispute Settlement in China-United States Trade: Conciliation in Perspective." Fordham International Law Journal Vol. 6, 1982-1983, pp. 172-201.

Cremades, B.M. "The Impact of International Arbitration on the Development of Business Law." American Journal of Comparative Law Vol. 31, 1983, pp. 526-534.

Delaume, G.R. "ICSID Arbitration and the Courts." American Journal of International Law Vol. 77, 1983, pp. 784-803.

"Determining the Arbitrability of International Antitrust Disputes." Journal of Comparative Business and Capital Market Law Vol. 8, 1986, pp. 197-218.

"Developments in International Commercial Arbitration (including ICSID and anti-trust in international commerce)." Harvard International Law Journal Vol. 17, 1976, pp. 89-154.

Dore, I.I. "Peaceful Settlement of International Trade Disputes: Analysis of the Scope of Application of the UNCITRAL Conciliation Rules." Columbia Journal of Transnational Law Vol. 21, 1983, pp. 339-352.

Ebenroth, C.T. and L.E. Teitz. "Winning (or Losing) by Default: The Act of State Doctrine, Sovereign Immunity and Comity in International Business Transactions." International Lawyer Vol. 19, 1985, pp. 225-258.

"Establishment of Mechanisms for the Settlement of Economic Disputes." Georgia Journal of International and Comparative Law Vol. 5, 1975, pp. 145-171.

Evans, C.L. and R.W. Ellis. "International Commercial Arbitration: A Comparison of Legal Regimes." Texas International Law Journal Vol. 8, 1973, pp. 17-55.

Fawcett, J.E.S. International Economic Conflicts: Prevention and Resolution. London: Europa for the David Davies Memorial Institute of International Studies, 1977. (Includes text of relevant legislation.)

Fleischhauer, C.A. "UNCITRAL and International Commercial Dispute Settlement." Arbitration Journal Vol. 38, 1983, pp. 9-13.

"Foreign Investment in the People's Republic of China: Compensation Trade, Joint-Ventures, Industrial Property Protection and Dispute Settlement." Georgia Journal of International and Comparative Law Vol. 10, 1980, pp. 233-270.

"Foreign Investment: International Chamber of Commerce Court of Arbitration - Southern Pacific Properties (Middle East) Ltd. v. Arab Republic of Egypt, reprinted in 22 International Legal Materials 752 (1983)." Harvard International Law Journal Vol. 25, 1984, pp. 463-470.

Gopal, G. "International Center for the Settlement of Investment Disputes" Case Western Reserve Journal of International Law Vol. 14, 1982, pp. 591-611.

Grzybowski, K. "Arbitral Tribunals for Foreign Trade in Socialist Countries." Law and Contemporary Problems Vol. 37, 1972, pp. 592-610.

Holtzmann, H.M. "Arbitration: An Indispensable Aid to Multinational Enterprise." Journal of International Law and Economics Vol. 10, 1975, pp. 337-345.

Houzhi, T. "UNCITRAL's Work on a Model Law on International Commercial Disputes." Pace Law Review Vol. 4, 1983-84, pp. 519-627.

International Bank for Reconstruction and Development. "Convention on the Settlement of Investment Disputes between States and Nationals of Other States." Washington, D.C.: IBRD, 18 March 1965.

International Bank for Reconstruction and Development. "Regional consultative meetings of legal experts on settlement of investment disputes; Chairman's report on issues raised and suggestions made with respect to the preliminary draft of a convention on the settlement of investment disputes between states and nationals of other states." Washington, D.C.: IBRD Legal Department Report No. z-11, 1964.

"The International Center for the Settlement of Investment Disputes: Selected Case Studies." International Trade Law and Practice Vol. 7, 1982-1983, pp. 306-326.

Jenks, C. Wilfred. "The Prospects of International Adjudication". London: Stevens & Sons, 1964.

Jhong, Chun Ryo. "The Settlement of Disputes Arising from International Trade and Investment." Lawasia Vol. 1, December 1969, pp. 21-32.

Klitgaard, T.J. "People's Republic of China Joint Venture Dispute Resolution Procedures." UCLA Pacific Basin Law Journal Vol. 1, 1982, pp. 1-40.

Layton, R. "Arbitration in International Commercial Agreements: The Noose Draws Tighter." International Lawyer Vol. 9, 1975, pp. 741-750.

Lillich, R.B. "International Claims: Their Settlement by Lump Sum Agreements," in P. Sanders, ed., International Arbitration: Liber Amicorum for Martin Domke. The Hague: Nijhoff, 1967.

Lindencrona, G. and N. Mattson. "Arbritration in Taxation." [Summaries in English, French, and German] Intertax 1982, pp. 76-82.

Lizares, E.P. "New International Economic Order and the International Center for the Settlement of Investment Disputes." Philippine Law Journal Vol. 55, 1980, pp. 298-326.

Painter, Therese Eve and Dianne Zomper. "A Bibliography of Current Issues in International Business Transactions: Investment Regulation, Antitrust, Acquisitions and Mergers, Transfer of Technology, Joint Ventures, Taxation, Dispute Resolution, Transnational Tort Claims, and Export Controls." Texas International Law Journal Vol. 21, 1985, pp. 165-197.

Peter, Wolfgang. Arbitration and Renegotiation of International Investment Agreements. The Hague: Nijhoff, 1986.

Ramos, F. "First Application by the Spanish Supreme Court of the New York Convention of June 10, 1958 to the Exequatur of Foreign Arbitral Awards." [Summary in French] Droit et Pratique du Commerce International Vol. 10, 1984, pp. 95-116.

Ryans, John K., Jr. and James C. Baker. "The International Center for the Settlement of Investment Disputes." Journal of World Trade Law Vol. 10, 1976, pp. 65-79.

Sanders, P., ed. International Arbitration: Liber Amicorum for Martin Domke. The Hague: Nijhoff, 1967.

Schmidt, John T. "Arbitration under the Auspices of the International Center for the Settlement of Investment Disputes." (Case Note) Harvard International Law Journal Vol. 17, 1976, pp. 90-109.

Scholsen, J.-U. "EC: The Proposal for a Council Directive on the Elimination of Double Taxation (Arbitration Procedure)." [Summaries in English, French, and German] Intertax 1982, pp. 424-435.

"Settlement of Disputes in Overseas Investment Guaranty Contracts: The Problem of Investor Behaviour in the Host Country." Columbia Journal of Transnational Law Vol. 12, 1973, pp. 557-580.

Snijder, E. "Foreign Investment Protection: The Dispute-Solving Aspect." The California Journal of Transnational Law Vol. 3, 1965, pp. 127-151.

Stein, S.J. and D.R. Wotman. "International Commercial Arbitration in the 1980s: A Comparison of the Major Arbitral Systems and Rules." Business Lawyer Vol. 38, 1983, pp. 1685-1728.

"U.S.-Soviet Commercial Arbitration under the 1972 Trade Agreement." Case Western Reserve Journal of International Law Vol. 7, 1974, pp. 121-139.

Vafai, John. "Conflict Resolution in the International Petroleum Industry." Journal of World Trade Law Vol. 5, 1971, pp. 427-460.

Waller, S.W. and A.M. Simon. "Analyzing Claims of Sovereignty in International Economic Disputes." Northwestern Journal of International Law and Business Vol. 7, 1985, pp. 1-11.

Wilner, Gabriel M. "Applicable Law and Dispute Settlement in the Transfer of Technology Code." Journal of World Trade Law Vol. 17, 1983, pp. 389-396.

3. CANADA

Abrutyn, M. and N. Boidman. "The New Canada-United States Tax Convention." International Lawyer Vol. 20, 1986, pp. 125-152.

Arnett, E. James. "Canadian Regulation of Foreign Investment: The Legal Parameters." Canadian Bar Review Vol. 50, 1972, pp. 213-247.

Arnett, E. James. "From FIRA to Investment Canada." Petroleum Law Supplement, Alberta Law Review Vol. 24, 1985, pp. 1-33.

Arnold, B.J. and C.F.L. Young. "International Taxation and Federalism: the Canadian Perspective." [In English and French] Revue de Droit des Affaires Internationales 1985, pp. 541-558.

Baker, Donald I. "Antitrust Conflicts Between Friends: Canada and the United States in the Mid-1970s." Cornell International Law Journal Vol. 11, 1978, pp. 165-194.

Beck, D. "Law and Policy in the Operations of Canada's Foreign Investment Review Agency." Saskatchewan Law Review Vol. 45, 1980-1981, pp. 183-201.

Boidman, N. "Canada: New Legislation Respecting Treaty Interpretation." [Summaries in English, French, and German] Intertax 1983, pp. 383-389.

Boidman, N. "Canada: Supreme Court Interprets Canada-Germany Tax Treaty." [Summaries in English, French, and German] Intertax 1983, pp. 17-21.

Boidman, N. "Interpretation of Tax Treaties in Canada." Bulletin for International Fiscal Documentation Vol. 34, 1980, pp. 388-401.

Bonney, William H. "Foreign Investment Review Act." Alberta Law Review Vol. 13, 1975, pp. 83-89.

Brean, Donald J.S. International Issues on Taxation: The Canadian Perspective Toronto: Canadian Tax Foundation, 1984.

Brown, R.D. "Tax Aspects of Technology Transfers Between the United States and Canada: A Canadian Viewpoint." Canada-United States Law Journal Vol. 11, 1986, pp. 227-246.

Caflisch, Lucius C. "The Protection of Corporate Investments Abroad in the Light of the Barcelona Traction Case." Zeitschrift fuer auslaendisches oeffentliches Recht und Voelkerrecht Vol. 31, 1971, p. 162.

Cairns, J.P. "Economics in Court: the Consumers Glass [R. v. Consumer Glass Co. Ltd. 124 D.L.R. 3d 274] Case." Canadian Business Law Journal Vol. 11, 1986, pp. 212-220.

Campbell, Barry R. "Canadian Combines Law: A Perspective on the Current Combines Investigation Act and Recent Case Law." North Carolina Journal of International Law and Commercial Regulation Vol. 5, 1980, pp. 57-90.

Canada. Eleventh Report of the Standing Committee on External Affairs and National Defence Respecting Canada-U.S. Relations 28th Parliament, Second Session; Ottawa, 1970.

Canada. Foreign Direct Investment in Canada ("Gray Report"). Ottawa: Information Canada, 1972.

Canada. Privy Council. Foreign Ownership and the Structure of Canadian Industry. Report of the Task Force on the Structure of Canadian Industry. ("Watkins Report") Ottawa, 1968.

"The Canada-United States Memorandum of Understanding Regarding Application of National Antitrust Law: New Guidelines for Resolution of Multinational Antitrust Enforcement Disputes." New England Journal of International Law and Business Vol. 6, 1984/1985, pp. 1065-1095.

"Canada-United States Transnational Business Activities: Current Tax and Other Developments." (Various articles) Canada-United States Law Journal Vol. 4, 1981, pp. 90-173.

Carasco, E.F. "The Foreign Investment Review Agency and the General Agreement on Tariffs and Trade: Incompatible?" Georgia Journal of International and Comparative Law Vol. 13, 1983, pp. 441-463.

Corcoran, J.I.W. "The Trading with the Enemy Act: The Impact of the Amended Foreign Assets Control Regulations On Canadian Corporations Owned by Americans." McGill Law Journal Vol. 16, 1970, pp. 460-487.

Derrak, B. "Canada and the Challenge of Foreign Investment: The First Decade of Foreign Investment Review." Dalhousie Law Journal Vol. 7, 1983, pp. 194-234.

"The Development of Canadian Law on Transborder Data Flows." Georgia Journal of International and Comparative Law Vol. 13, 1983, pp. 825-855.

Dewhirst, G. and M. Rudiak. "From Investment Screening to Investment Development: The Impact of Canada's Foreign Investment Review Agency (FIRA) and Investment Canada in Canada's Technological Development." Canada-United States Law Journal Vol. 11, 1986, pp. 149-160.

Donaghue, H.P. "Transborder Flows: Its Implications in Canada-U.S. Relations." Canada-United States Law Journal Vol. 11, 1986, pp. 289-294.

Donaldson, R.A. and J.D.A. Jackson. "Foreign Investment Review Act - An Analysis of the Legislation." Canadian Bar Review Vol. 53, 1975, pp. 171-236.

"Dow Jones and Co., Inc. v. Attorney General of Canada: The Canadian Foreign Investment Review Act." Law and Policy in International Business Vol. 14, 1982, pp. 505-519.

Espinosa, W.H. "Canadian Foreign Investment Review Act: Red, White and Gray." Law and Policy in International Business Vol. 5, 1973, pp. 1018-1041.

Feltham, Ivan R. and William R. Rauenbusch. "Canada and the Multinational Enterprise," in H.R. Hahlo, ed., Nationalism and the Multinational Enterprise: Legal, Economic and Managerial Aspects. Dobbs Ferry, New York: Oceana, 1973.

Feltham, Ivan R. and William R. Rauenbusch. "Economic Nationalism," in R. St. J. Macdonald, et al., eds., Canadian Perspectives on International Law and Organization. Toronto: University of Toronto Press, 1974.

Fisher, B.M. "Canada's Foreign Investment Review Act as a Model for Foreign Investment Regulation in the United States." Canada-United States Law Journal Vol. 7, 1984, pp. 61-91.

Fisher, B.M. "Product Distribution in Canada." International Lawyer Vol. 20, 1986, pp. 45-79.

Flowers, Edward B. "Oligopolistic Reaction in European and Canadian Direct Investment in the United States." Journal of International Business Studies Vol. 7, Fall/Winter 1976, pp. 43-56.

Franck, T.M. and K.I. Gudgeon. "Canada's Foreign Investment Control Experiment: The Law, the Context and the Practice." New York University Law Review Vol. 50, 1975, pp. 76-146.

Glover, G.C., Jr. "Canada's Foreign Investment Review Act." Business Lawyer Vol. 29, 1974, pp. 805-822.

Glover, G.C., Jr., D.C. New, and M.M. Lacourcière. "The Investment Canada Act: A New Approach to Regulation of Foreign Investment in Canada." Business Lawyer Vol. 41, 1985, pp. 83-98.

Goodrich, G.G. "U.S. Tax Aspects of Technology Transfers Between the United States and Canada." Canada-United States Law Journal Vol. 11, 1986, pp. 213-226.

Gotlieb, A.E. "Canadian-U.S. Relations: Legislation, Regulation and the Management of Conflict." Canadian Business Law Journal Vol. 9, 1984, pp. 485-496.

Gotlieb, A.E. "Extraterritoriality: A Canadian Perspective." Northwestern Journal of International Law and Business Vol. 5, 1983, pp. 449-461.

Gotlieb, A.E. "The Legal Aspects of International Investment: The Canadian-U.S. Experience." American Society of International Law Proceedings Vol. 76, 1982, pp. 47-55.

Graham, W.C. "The Foreign Extraterritorial Measures Act." The Canadian Business Law Journal Vol. 11, 1986, pp. 410-444.

Grover, W. "The Investment Canada Act." Canadian Business Lawyer Vol. 10, 1985, pp. 475-482.

Hayden, P.R. and J.H. Burns. "Canadian Foreign Investment Review Act." Practical Lawyer Vol. 21, 1975.

Henderson, G.F. and E.S. Binavince. "Doing Business in Canada and the Judicial Review of Wrongful Government Statutory and Regulatory Action." Canada-United States Law Journal Vol. 7, 1984, pp. 1-60.

Henry, D.H.W., Q.C. "Anti-Monopoly Legislation in Canada," in H.R. Hahlo, ed., Nationalism and the Multinational Enterprise: Legal, Economic and Managerial Aspects. Dobbs Ferry, New York: Oceana, 1973.

Hogg, R.D. "Intercompany Pricing: A Canadian Tax Overview." [Summaries in English, French, and German] Intertax 1983, pp. 224-238.

Hughes, Graeme C. Foreign Investment Law in Canada Toronto: Carswell, 1983.

Hunter, Lawson. "Survey of Canadian Antitrust Laws." Antitrust Law Journal Vol. 50, 1981, pp. 699-708.

bHyde, A. "Rights for Canadian Members of International Unions Under the (U.S.) Labor-Management Reporting and Disclosure Act." Washington Law Review Vol. 61, 1986, pp. 1007-1039.

Jones, J.C.H. and P.J. Coxon. "Positive Economics and Public Policy: Some Canadian Evidence on Policy Change and Antitrust." Antitrust Bulletin Vol. 30, 1985, pp. 365-399.

Kennish, J.T. "Competition Law and Enforcement in Canada." International Lawyer Vol. 20, 1986, pp. 81-123.

Kindred, H.M. and W. Biggs. "Trade and Investment Issues: Pattern of Canadian-American Economic Problems." Canada-United States Law Journal Vol. 1, 1978, pp. 114-131.

King, H.T., Jr. "The Changing Context for the Foreign Investor in Canada. Introductory Remarks," in Private Investors Abroad - 1982. New York: Matthew Bender, 1982.

Lalonde, M. "Foreign Banks in Canada: Their Impact on the Canadian Banking System and Investment." Detroit College of Law Review Vol. 1985, 1985, pp. 1151-1160.

Lillich, R.B. "Two Perspectives on the Barcelona Traction Case: The Rigidity of Barcelona." (Editorial Comment) American Journal of International Law Vol. 65, 1971, pp. 522-532.

Litvak, I. and C.J. Maule. "Canadian Small Business Investment in the U.S. - Corporate Forms and Characteristics." Business Quarterly Winter 1978, pp. 69-77.

Macdonald, D.S. "The Pacific Basin: The View from Canada." Private Investors Abroad - 1985. New York: Matthew Bender, 1985.

McFetridge, D.G. and S. Wong. "Predatory Pricing in Canada: The Law and the Economics." Canadian Business Review Vol. 63, 1985, pp. 685-733.

a Menck, T. "Qualifitsationsconflikt im neuen deutsch-kanadischen Doppelbesteuerungsabkommen." [Summary in English] Intertax 1982, pp. 417-423.

Mendes, E.P. "Canadian National Energy Program: An Example of Assertion of Economic Sovereignty or Creeping Expropriation in International Law." Vanderbilt Journal of Transnational Law Vol. 14, 1981, pp. 475-507.

Metzger, Stanley D. "Two Perspectives on the Barcelona Traction Case: Nationality of Corporate Investment under Investment Guaranty Schemes - The Relevance of Barcelona Traction." (Editorial Comment) American Journal of International Law Vol. 65, 1971, pp. 532-541.

Nixon, J.B. and J.H. Burns. "An Examination of the Legality of the Use of the Foreign Investment Review Act by the Government of Canada to Control Intra- and Extraterritorial Commercial Activity by Aliens." International and Comparative Law Quarterly Vol. 33, 1984, pp. 57-80.

Olmstead, Cecil J., E.J. Krauland and D.F. Orentlicher. "Expropriation in the Energy Industry: Canada's Crown Share Provision as a Violation of International Law." McGill Law Journal Vol. 29, 1984, pp. 439-467.

Osgood, R.K. "Interpreting Tax Treaties in Canada, the United States, and the United Kingdom." Cornell International Law Journal Vol. 17, 1984, pp. 255-297.

Paterson, R.K. "The Economic Cooperation Agreement Between Canada and ASSAN: Charting a Foreign Investment Course in South East Asia." University of British Columbia Law Review Vol. 19, 1985, pp. 389-404.

Paterson, R.K. "The GATT and Restrictions on Foreign Investment: the U.S. Challenge to Canada's Foreign Investment Law." UCLA Pacific Basin Law Journal Vol. 1, 1985, pp. 224-246.

Pauwels, J.R. "FIRA: Instrument of Regulation or Vote-Maximization?" Osgoode Hall Law Journal Vol. 23, 1985, pp. 131-170.

Roberts, R.J. and C.A. Hewat. "Pre-Merger Notification in Canada." Canadian Business Law Journal Vol. 11, 1986, pp. 135-146.

Rose, W.B. "Foreign Investment in Canada: The New Investment Canada Act." International Lawyer Vol. 20, 1986, pp. 19-44.

Ross, J.L. and D.A. Rubin. "Investment Canada Act: A New Regime for Foreign Investment in Canada." Commercial Law Journal Vol. 91, 1986, pp. 141-152.

Rugman, Alan M. The Multinationals in Canada: Theory, Performance and Economic Impact. Boston: Nijhoff, 1980.

Rugman, Alan M. "The Results of Foreign Investment in Canada." Journal of World Trade Law Vol. 11, 1977.

"Should Investment Capital Stay Home? A Canadian-U.S. Dialogue." Proceedings of the 68th Annual Meeting (1974). Washington, D.C.: American Society of International Law, 1975.

Smith, S. "Should There Be More Canadian Government Intervention in Technology Transfer Arrangements Between Canadian and Foreign Firms?" Canada-United States Law Journal Vol. 11, 1986, pp. 321-329.

"Some Guiding Principles of Good Corporate Behaviour for Subsidiaries in Canada of Foreign Companies." Trade and Commerce, 1967.

Spence, J.M. "Current Approaches to Foreign Investment Review in Canada." McGill Law Journal Vol. 31, 1986, pp. 508-526.

Stanbury, W.T. "Half a Loaf: Bill C-29, Proposed Amendments to the Combines Investigation Act." Canadian Business Law Journal Vol. 10, February 1985, pp. 1-34.

Stanbury, W.T. "The New Competition Act and Competition Tribunal Act: 'Not With a Bang, but a Whimper.'" Canadian Business Law Journal Vol. 12, October 1986, pp. 2-42.

Tuomi, K. "Mergers and Acquisitions in Canada: The Interrelationship Between Foreign Ownership and Competition Policy." Canadian Business Law Journal Vol. 11, 1986, pp. 316-330.

Turner, J. "Canadian Regulation of Foreign Direct Investment." Harvard International Law Journal Vol. 23, 1983, pp. 333-356.

United States Department of Commerce, International Trade Administration. _Investment Climate in Foreign Countries_. (Vol.1: OECD and Other European Countries [includes Canada and Japan]; Vol. 2: Africa; Vol. 3: Asia [excluding Japan]; Vol. 4: Western Hemisphere [excluding Canada]) August, 1985.

United States Department of Commerce, Office of Foreign Investment in the United States. _Canadian Direct Investment in the United States_ July 1980.

United States General Accounting Office. _Should Canada's Screening Practices Be Used by the United States?_ 6 September 1979.

Wigdor, M. "Canada and the New International Economic Order: Some Legal Implications." _Canadian Yearbook of International Law_ Vol. 20, 1982, pp. 161-192.

4. CAPITAL MOVEMENTS

Adler, J.H., ed. Capital Movements and Economic Development. New York: St. Martins Press, 1967.

Borts, G.H. "The International Firm, the Tariff, and Long-Run Capital Movements." Paper presented at a Conference on the Multinational Firm and Economic Analysis, Bellagio, Italy, July 1972.

Bruck, N. and F. Lees. Foreign Investments, Capital Controls, and the Balance of Payments. New York University Graduate School of Business Administration, 1968.

"China ebnet den Weg zu 'Joint Ventures': Gesetz gestattet Kapitalbeteiligungen und Transfer von Gewinnen." Sueddeutsche Zeitung 9 July 1979, p. 15.

"The Economic Analysis of Capital Flight in Hong Kong." New York University Journal of International Law and Policy Vol. 17, 1985, pp. 683-716.

"Ende britischer Kapitalverkehrskontrollen." Neue Zuercher Zeitung 25 October 1979, p. 11.

"England jetzt ohne Devisenkontrollen." Frankfurter Allgemeine Zeitung 24 October 1979, p. 13.

Fedders, J.M. "Policing Internationalized U.S. Capital Markets: Methods to Obtain Evidence Abroad." International Lawyer Vol. 18, 1984, pp. 89-108.

Fedders, J.M., F.B. Wade, and M.D. Mann. "Waiver by Conduct? - A Possible Response to the Internationalization of the Securities Markets." Journal of Comparative Business and Capital Market Law Vol. 6, March 1984, pp. 1-54.

"Foreign Investment - Capital Controls, Termination of the Interest Equalization Tax, the Foreign Direct Investment Regulations and the Voluntary Foreign Credit Restraint Guidelines." Law and Policy in International Business Vol. 6, 1974, pp. 1263-1270.

"Freedom for Capital Movement." International Chamber of Commerce Information Vol. 40, 1974.

Gold, Joseph. "International Capital Movements Under the Law of the International Monetary Fund." International Monetary Fund Pamphlet Series No. 21 Washington, D.C., International Monetary Fund, 1977.

Gomez-Palacio, I. "Mexico's Foreign Exchange Controls. Two Administrations: Two Solutions. Thorough and Benign." Legal Issues of European Integration Vol. 16, 1984, pp. 267-299.

Jouanjean, H. "Mouvements des capitaux dans le cadre de l'adhésion de la Grèce à la Communauté européen." Revue du Marché Commun Vol. 24, 1981, pp. 14-20.

"La Grande-Bretagne abolit tous les contrôles." Le Monde 25 October 1979, p. 42.

Leech, N. "International Banking: Effects of Nationalization and Exchange Controls." Journal of Comparative Business and Capital Market Law Vol. 8, 1986, pp. 123-147.

Louis, J.-V. "Free Movement of Capital in the Community: The Casati Judgment." Common Market Law Review Vol. 19, 1982, pp. 443-452.

Machlup, F., W. Salant and L. Tarshis, eds. International Mobility and Movement of Capital. New York: Columbia University Press, 1972.

MacNaughton, B. "Japan's Trade and Currency Regulations: Do the Changes Put Japan in the Mainstream of World Commerce or Are They Merely an Illusion?" Texas International Law Journal Vol. 16, 1981, pp. 245-259.

Maskall, M.E. "United Kingdom: Tax Consequences of the Abolition of Exchange Controls." [Summaries in English, French, and German] Intertax 1981, pp. 32-38.

Onitsuka, Y. "International Capital Movements and the Patterns of Economic Growth." The American Economic Review Vol. 64, 1974, pp. 24-36.

Petersen, M. "Capital Movements and the Payments under the EEC Treaty after Casati." European Law Review Vol. 7, 1982, pp. 167-182.

Spitaller, E. "A Survey of Recent Quantitative Studies of Long-Term Capital Movements." IMF Staff Papers March 1971.

Steindorff, E. "Kapitalverkehrsfreiheit in EG nach Casati." Werner Collection pp. 877-891.

Strohmeier, R.W. "Europaisches Wahnungsystem (EWS) u. seine Auswirkung auf die Autonomie der Deutschen Bundesbank." [Summary in English] German Yearbook of International Law Vol. 25, 1982, pp. 352-375.

Thomas, B.S. "Internationalization of the Securities Markets: An Empirical Analysis." George Washington Law Review Vol. 50, 1982, pp. 155-190.

"U.K. Removes Foreign Exchange Curbs." International Herald Tribune 24 October 1979, p. 1.

"Verstaerkte Kapitalausfuhr aus Japan: Direktinvestitionen im Ausland auf Rekordhoehe." Neue Zuercher Zeitung 6 September 1979, p. 17.

Willey, H. David. "Direct Investment Controls and the Balance of Payments," in Charles P. Kindleberger, ed., The International Corporation: A Symposium. Cambridge, Massacusetts: MIT Press, 1970.

Williams, Harold R. "Exchange Rate Systems, the Marginal Efficiency of Investments and Foreign Direct Capital Movements." Kyklos Vol. 26, 1973, pp. 58-74.

5. CORRUPT PRACTICES/ILLICIT PAYMENTS

"The Act of State Doctrine: A Shield for Bribery and Corruption. Clayco Petroleum Corp. v. Occidental Petroleum Corp., 712 F.2d 404." University of Miami Inter-American Law Review Vol. 16, 1984, pp. 167-176.

"Amending the Foreign Corrupt Practices Act of 1977: A Step Toward Clarification and Consolidation." Journal of Criminal Law and Criminology Vol. 73, 1982, pp. 1740-1773.

"The Antibribery Provisions of the Foreign Corrupt Practices Act of 1977: Are They Really As Valuable As We Think They Are?" Delaware Journal of Corporate Law Vol. 10, 1985, pp. 71-95.

Atchinson, B.K. "Foreign Corrupt Practices Act: A Practical Look." New York State Bar Journal Vol. 53, 1981, pp. 342-347.

Bagby, J.W. "Enforcement of Accounting Standards in the Foreign Corrupt Practices Act." American Business Law Journal Vol. 21, 1983, pp. 213-235.

Brennan, B.A. "Amending the Foreign Corrupt Practices Act of 1977: 'Clarifying' or 'Gutting' a Law?" Journal of Legislation Vol. 11, 1984, pp. 56-89.

Brock, W.E. "Progress Report on Efforts to Amend the Foreign Corrupt Practices Act." Detroit College of Law Review Vol. 1983, 1983, pp. 1083-1093.

"Comparison of the F.C.P.A. and the Draft International Agreement on Illegal Payments." Vanderbilt Journal of Transnational Law Vol. 13, 1980, pp. 795-823.

Dunn, R.R. "Taxation: Foreign Corrupt Practices Act." Texas International Law Journal Vol. 18, 1983, pp. 407-412.

"FCPA: Curse or Cure?" American Business Law Journal Vol. 19, 1981, pp. 73-86.

"Foreign Corrupt Practices Act: Domestic and International Implications: A Symposium." App. I: "FCP Act of 1977"; App. II: "Senate Bill 708"; App. III: "ITT Code of Corporate Conduct." Syracuse Journal of International Law and Commerce Vol. 9, 1982, pp. 235-378.

Hibey, R.A. "Practical Necessity for Amendment of the Foreign Corrupt Practices Act: S708 - the Current Legislative Initiative." Hofstra Law Review Vol. 10, 1982, pp. 1121-1136.

"International Law - Act of State Doctrine: An Emerging Corruption Exception in Antitrust Cases?" Notre Dame Law Review Vol. 59, 1984, pp. 455-470.

"Is the SEC the Appropriate Federal Agency for Policing Bribery of Foreign Nationals by Multinational Public Corporations?" Case Western Reserve Journal of International Law Vol. 13, 1981, pp. 517-540.

Johnson, J. "Business Judgment Rule: A Review of its Application to the Problem of Illegal Foreign Payments." Journal of Corporation Law Vol. 6, 1981, pp. 481-510.

"Modifying the Foreign Corrupt Practices Act: The Search for a Practical Standard." Northwestern Journal of International Law and Business Vol. 4, 1982, pp. 203-233.

Porrata-Doria, Jr., R.A. "Amending the Foreign Corrupt Practices Act of 1977: Repeating the Mistakes of the Past?" Rutgers Law Review Vol. 38, Fall 1985, pp. 29-67.

Slade, D.R. "Foreign Corrupt Payments: Enforcing a Multilateral Agreement." Harvard International Law Journal Vol. 22, 1981, pp. 117-155.

"Taxation - Congress Amends Internal Revenue Code to Comport with the Foreign Corrupt Practices Act, Tax Equity and Fiscal Responsibility Act of 1982. Public Law No. 97-248, 96 Stat. 324 [codified as amended in scattered sections of 26 U.S.C." Texas International Law Journal Vol. 18, 1983, pp. 407-412.

United Nations. "Report of the *Ad Hoc* Intergovernmental Working Group on the Problem of Corrupt Practices on Its First, Second, Third and Resumed Third Sessions." UN Document E/6006. 5 July 1977.

United Nations. "Report of the Committee on an International Agreement on Illicit Payments on its First and Second Sessions (29 January-9 February and 7-18 May 1979)." UN Document E/1979/104. 25 May 1979.

United States Congress. Senate Committee on Banking, Housing and Urban Affairs. *Report to the Securities and Exchange Commission on Questionable and Illegal Corporate Payments and Practices*. 94th Cong. 2d sess. 3-5, 1976.

Witherspoon, R.A. "Multinational Corporations - Governmental Regulation of Business Ethics under the Foreign Corrupt Practices Act of 1977: An Analysis." *Dickinson Law Review* Vol. 87, 1983, pp. 531-593.

6. DISCLOSURE/DISCOVERY

Abrams, Lee N., et al. "Litigating in an International Context." (Various articles) Proceedings of the Twenty-Ninth Annual Spring Meeting of the Section of Antitrust Law of the American Bar Association, Washington, D.C., 1981. Antitrust Law Journal Vol. 50, 1981, pp. 555-616.

Bartlett, J.W., III. "In re: Oil Spill by Amoco Cadiz [1984 A.M.C. 2123] - Choice of Law and A Pierced Corporate Veil Defeat the 1969 Civil Liability Convention." Maritime Law Vol. 10, 1985, pp. 1-23.

Batista, P.A. "Confronting Foreign 'Blocking' Legislation: A Guide to Securing Disclosure for Non-Resident Parties to American Litigation." International Lawyer Vol. 17, 1983, pp. 61-85.

Blechman, Michael D. "Antitrust Jurisdiction, Discovery and Enforcement in the International Sphere: An Appraisal of American Developments and Foreign Reactions." Antitrust Law Journal Vol. 49, 1980, pp. 1197-1206.

Bobrow, D.B. and R.T. Kudrle. "Multinational Enterprise Disclosure Alternatives and Their Consequences." Journal of World Trade Law Vol. 18, 1984, pp. 437-454.

Brent, A.S. "Illegally Obtained Evidence: An Historical and Comparative Analysis." Saskatchewan Law Review Vol. 48, 1983-1984, pp. 1-27.

Carroll, Terence M. "Securities and Exchange Commission," in the chapter "Administrative Survey: October 1975 to September 1976: IV Investment Regulation," in Law and Policy in International Business Vol. 9, 1977, pp. 231-236.

Cole, P.E. "New Challenges to the U.S. Multinational Corporation in the European Economic Community: Data Protection Laws." New York University Journal of International Law and Politics Vol. 17, 1985, pp. 893-947.

"Compelling Production of Documents in Violation of Foreign Law: An Examination and Reevaluation of the American Position." Fordham Law Review Vol. 50, 1982, pp. 877-908.

"Conflict of Laws: Discovery Abroad Under Provisions of the Hague Convention - Laker Airways Ltd. v. Pan American World Airways," et. al., Nos. 82-3362, 83-0416, 83-2791 (D.D.C. June 26, 1984) reported in 23 International Legal Materials 748 (1984)." Harvard International Law Journal Vol. 26, 1985, pp. 201-208.

Convention on Service Abroad of Judicial and Extrajudicial Documents in Civil or Commercial Affairs. Opened for signature February 10, 1969, 20 U.S.T. 361, T.I.A.S. No. 6638.

Convention on Taking of Evidence Abroad in Civil or Commercial Matters. Opened for signature March 18, 1970, 23 U.S.T. 2555, T.I.A.S. No. 2555.

"Discovery in Great Britain: The Evidence (Proceedings in Other Jurisdictions) Act." Cornell International Law Journal Vol. 11, 1978, pp. 323-342.

Dockray, M. "Discovery: Recent Developments." New Law Journal Vol. 136, 1986, pp. 219-221.

"Extraterritorial Discovery: An Analysis Based on Good Faith." Columbia Law Review Vol. 83, 1983, pp. 1320-1350.

"Extraterritorial Discovery - Hague Evidence Convention - The Hague Convention Procedures Are Not Exclusive, and Courts May Issue Discovery Orders Using Alternative Means." Virginia Journal of International Law Vol. 25, Fall 1984, pp. 249-280.

"Extraterritorial Discovery Under the Hague Evidence Convention." Villanova Law Review Vol. 31, 1986, pp. 253-290.

"Extraterritoriality: Australian Limitations on Foreign Judgement and Discovery - Foreign Proceedings (Excess of Jurisdiction) Act 1984, No. 3 Australian Acts (1984)." Harvard International Law Journal Vol. 26, 1985, pp. 578-584.

Fedders, J.M. "Policing Internationalized U.S. Capital Markets: Methods to Obtain Evidence Abroad." International Lawyer Vol. 18, 1984, pp. 89-108.

Fedders, J.M., F.B. Wade, and M.D. Mann. "Waiver by Conduct? - A Possible Response to the Internationalization of the Securities Markets." Journal of Comparative Business and Capital Market Law Vol. 6, March 1984, pp. 1-54.

Feingold, F. and P.A. Glicklich. "Onerous FIRPTA Reporting Requirements Replaced by New Broad Withholding Rules." Journal of Taxation Vol. 61, 1984, pp. 298-305.

Fishman, R.G. "Reporting Requirements Imposed on Foreign-Controlled Corporations." Taxes Vol. 63, 1985, pp. 773-779.

"Foreign Investment: Investment Disclosure Requirements - Amended Regulations to Implement the International Investment Survey Act of 1976, 46 Fed. Reg. 23,225 (1981) (to be codified in 15 C.F.R. Part 806)." Harvard International Law Journal Vol. 22, 1981, pp. 694-697.

Garfinkel, E.I. "Disclosure of Confidential Documents under the Trade Agreements Act of 1979: A Corporate Nightmare?" Law and Policy in International Business Vol. 13, 1981, pp. 465-493.

Grabar, N.H. "Antitrust: Effect of Foreign Disclosure Limitation on Discovery in United States Courts." Harvard International Law Journal Vol. 22, 1981, pp. 177-186.

Griffin, Joseph P. "The Power of Host Countries over the Multinational: Lifting the Veil in the European Economic Community and the United States." Law and Policy in International Business Vol. 6, 1974, pp. 375-435.

"Hague Evidence Convention: A Practical Guide to the Convention, United States Case Law, Convention-Sponsored Review Commissions (1978 and 1985), and Responses of Other Signatory Nations; with digest of cases and bibliography." Georgia Journal of International and Comparative Law Vol. 16, 1986, pp. 73-107.

Harter, P.R. "Taxation Summons to Secure Business Records of a Foreign Subsidiary." Harvard International Law Journal Vol. 22, 1981, pp. 704-710.

Heck, A. "U.S. Misinterpretation of the Hague Evidence Convention." Columbia Journal of Transnational Law Vol. 24, 1986, pp. 231-278.

Herzog, B.E. "Nineteen-Eighty French Law on Documents and Information." American Journal of International Law Vol. 75, 1981, pp. 382-386.

"Information Disclosure and Competent Authority: A Proposal." Case Western Reserve Journal of International Law Vol. 17, 1985, pp. 485-513.

"Institutional Investor Disclosure Act: An Analysis of the Consumer Benefits." Yale Law Journal Vol. 83, 1974, pp. 1271-1290.

"International Trade: Court of International Trade Disclosure of Confidential Information - American Spring Wire Corp. v. U.S." Harvard International Law Journal Vol. 24, 1983, pp. 219-225.

Kennelly, J.J. "Effective Discovery Vis-a-Vis Abuse Discovery - Which Is Which?" Trial Lawyer Guide Vol. 29, 1985, pp. 261-297.

Kripke, Homer. The SEC and Corporate Disclosure: Regulation in Search of a Purpose New York: Harcourt, Brace, Jovanovich, 1979.

Larose, L.A. "Conflicts, Contacts, and Cooperation: Extraterritorial Application of the United States Securities Laws." Securities Regulation Law Journal Vol. 12, Summer 1984, pp. 99-137.

Lichtenstein, Cynthia Crawford. "Current Proposals for Marshalling Data on and Disclosure by Multinationals." International Lawyer Vol. 11, 1977, pp. 61-68.

Light, John R. "Discovery Abroad and the Consequences When Discovery is not Possible." Antitrust Law Journal Vol. 50, 1981, pp. 577-598.

McNamara, D.E. "Foreign Direct Investment in the United States: Disclosure Regulations." Georgia Journal of International and Comparative Law Vol. 12, 1982, pp. 193-207.

Olmstead, Cecil J., ed. Extraterritorial Application of Laws and Responses Thereto. (Various articles: "General Theory of State Jurisdiction and Limitations Under General International Law and Under International Agreements." Cecil J. Olmstead, Chairman; "Specific Extra-territorial Applications of Jurisdiction Resulting in Conflicts." Gunther Jaenicke, Chairman; "Securities Regulation: Extra-territorial Aspects." Maarten Bos, Chairman; "Corporate Governance: Responsibilities of Directors and Officers for Acts of Foreign Subsidiaries and Affiliates." A.E. von Overbeck, Chairman; "Discovery of Documentary and Other Evidence in a Foreign Country." Richard Bentham, Chairman; "Responses to Extra-territorial Exercises of Jurisdiction." Sir Francis Vallat, Q.C., Chairman) Oxford: ESC Publishing, 1984.

Onkelinx, Ivo T. "Conflict of International Jurisdiction: Ordering the Production of Documents in Violation of the Law of the Situs." Northwestern University Law Review Vol. 64, 1969-1970, pp. 487-533.

O'Reilly, James T. Federal Information Disclosure: Procedures, Forms, and the Law. (Two looseleaf volumes) Colorado Springs, Colorado: Shepard's/McGraw-Hill, 1977.

Oxman, B.H. "The Choice Between Direct Discovery and Other Means of Obtaining Evidence Abroad: The Impact of the Hague Evidence Convention." University of Miami Law Review Vol. 37, 1983, pp. 733-795.

"Potential Havens from American Jurisdiction and Discovery Laws in International Antitrust Enforcement." Univerisity of Florida Law Review Vol. 33, 1981, pp. 240-271.

"Reaching for Documents in a Foreign Country: Marc Rich & Company vs. United States." [707 F.2d. 663]. Houston Journal of International Law Vol. 8, 1985, pp. 119-130.

"Responses to Fedders ["Waiver by Conduct"]." Journal of Comparative Business and Capital Market Law Vol. 6, 1984, pp. 307-318.

Robinson, D.R. "Compelling Discovery and Evidence in International Litigation." International Lawyer Vol. 18, 1984, pp. 533-540.

Sadoff, M.J. "The Hague Evidence Convention: Problems at Home of Obtaining Foreign Evidence." The International Lawyer Vol. 20, 1986, pp. 659-676.

Scarborough, K. "The Foreign Investor in the United States: Disclosure, Taxation and Visa Laws." International Lawyer Vol. 19, 1985, pp. 85-115.

"The Securities Acts and International Discovery: the Hague Evidence Convention After Anschuetz [754 F.2d. 602] and Messerschmitt Bolkow Blohm [757 F.2d. 729]." Syracuse Journal of International Law and Commerce Vol. 12, 1986, pp. 600-612.

"Securities Regulation - Exterritorial Application - Continental Grain (Australia) Pty. Ltd. v. Pacific Oilseeds, Inc. [592 F.2d 409]." New York Law School Journal of International and Comparative Law Vol. 4, 1982, pp. 187-204.

Shemanski, Donald R. "Obtaining Evidence in the Federal Republic of Germany: The Impact of the Hague Convention on German-American Judicial Cooperation." International Lawyer Vol. 17, 1983, pp. 465-487.

Stephens, Richard A. "Reevaluation of Disclosure Requirements for Foreign Issuers: Securities Exchange Act of 1934." George Washington Law Review Vol. 45, 1977, pp. 135-178.

Stevenson, Russell B., Jr. "The SEC and the New Disclosure." Cornell Law Review Vol. 62, 1976, pp. 50-93.

Strawn, D. U. "Discovering Computerized Records." American Bar Association Journal Vol. 71, April 1984, pp. 72-74.

"Strict Enforcement of Extraterritorial Discovery." Stanford Law Review Vol. 38, 1986, pp. 841-890.

Stuermer, U. "Neuere Entwicklung der extraterritorialen Anwendung amerikanischen Securities Regulations." Recht der internationalen Wirtschaft Vol. 29, 1983, pp. 641-646.

"Subject Matter Jurisdiction in Transnational Securities Frauds." Ohio Northern University Law Review Vol. 3, 1976, pp. 1305-1331.

"Taxation: Summons to Secure Business Records of a Foreign Subsidiary." Harvard International Law Journal Vol. 22, 1981, pp. 704-710.

Teschner, P.A. "Foreign Discovery of Head Office Tax Records: By Invitation Only." Taxes Vol. 64, 1986, pp. 326-334.

Thomas, B.S. "Extraterritoriality in an Era of Internationalization of the Securities Markets: The Need to Revisit Domestic Policies." Rutgers Law Review Vol. 35, 1983, pp. 453-471.

Tindall, Robert E. Multinational Enterprises: Legal and Management Structures and Interrelationship with Ownership, Control, Antitrust, Labor, Taxation and Disclosure. Dobbs Ferry, New York: Oceana, 1975.

Toms, B.C., III. "French Response to the Extraterritorial Application of U.S. Antitrust Laws." International Lawyer Vol. 15, 1981, pp. 585-614.

"Transnational Discovery: The Balancing Act of American Trial Courts and the Northern District of Illinois' New Approach to the Hague Convention." Washington and Lee Law Review Vol. 42, 1985, pp. 1285-1310.

United Kingdom, Department of Trade. Disclosure of Interests in Shares: A Consultative Document. London, 11 August 1980.

"Waiver of Rights Under the Hague Convention on the Taking of Evidence Abroad in Civil or Commercial Matters." Loyola of Los Angeles International and Comparative Law Journal Vol. 7, 1984, pp. 409-438.

Wallace, Cynthia Day. "Control through Disclosure Legislation: Industrialized States Clamp Down on Foreign Multinational Enterprises." International and Comparative Law Quarterly Vol. 32, 1983, pp. 141-174.

Weems, P.R. "Reporting Requirements for U.S. Corporations: The International Investment and Trade in Services Survey Act." International Lawyer Vol. 19, 1985, pp. 1293-1302.

Zeitler, Arthur W. "Foreign Investment in the United States - Reporting Requirements." Houston Journal of International Law Vol. 3, 1981, pp. 221-240.

7. DOMESTIC LEGISLATION

Allen, D.G.M. "Regulating Foreign Investments in the United States." Solicitors' Journal Vol. 125, 1981, pp. 838-840.

"Amending the Foreign Corrupt Practices Act of 1977: A Step Toward Clarification and Consolidation." Journal of Criminal Law and Criminology Vol. 73, 1982, pp. 1740-1773.

American Law Institute. Restatement of the Law: Conflict of Laws. St. Paul, Minnesota: American Law Institute Publishers, 1934.

American Law Institute. Restatement of the Law (Second): Conflict of Laws. St. Paul, Minnesota: American Law Institute Publishers, 1971.

American Law Institute. Restatement of the Law (Second): Foreign Relations Law of the United States. St. Paul, Minnesota: American Law Institute Publishers, 1965.

Andrews, Gregory E. "An Evaluation of the Need for Further Statutory Controls on Foreign Direct Investment in the United States." Vanderbilt Journal of Transnational Law Vol. 8, 1974, pp. 147-188.

"The Antibribery Provisions of the Foreign Corrupt Practices Act of 1977: Are They Really As Valuable As We Think They Are?" Delaware Journal of Corporate Law Vol. 10, 1985, pp. 71-95.

Arnett, E. James. "Canadian Regulation of Foreign Investment: The Legal Parameters." Canadian Bar Review Vol. 50, 1972. pp. 213-247.

Arnett, E. James. "From FIRA to Investment Canada." Petroleum Law Supplement, Alberta Law Review Vol. 24, 1985, pp. 1-33.

Atchinson, B.K. "Foreign Corrupt Practices Act: A Practical Look." New York State Bar Journal Vol. 53, 1981, pp. 342-347.

Bagby, J.W. "Enforcement of Accounting Standards in the Foreign Corrupt Practices Act." American Business Law Journal Vol. 21, 1983, pp. 213-235.

Batista, P.A. "Confronting Foreign 'Blocking' Legislation: A Guide to Securing Disclosure for Non-Resident Parties to American Litigation." International Lawyer Vol. 17, 1983, pp. 61-85.

Bierman, J.N. "The 1983 Export Administration Act Legislation: The Extraterritoriality Issue." Law and Policy in International Business Vol. 15, 1983, pp. 1181-1185.

Boidman, N. "Canada: New Legislation Respecting Treaty Interpretation." [Summaries in English, French, and German] Intertax 1983, pp. 383-389.

Bonney, William H. "Foreign Investment Review Act." Alberta Law Review Vol. 13, 1975, pp. 83-89.

Brennan, B.A. "Amending the Foreign Corrupt Practices Act of 1977: 'Clarifying' or 'Gutting' a Law?" Journal of Legislation Vol. 11, 1984, pp. 56-89.

Bringezu, Volker. "Parent-Subsidiary Relations under German Law." International Lawyer Vol. 7, 1973, pp. 138-157.

Brock, W.E. "Progress Report on Efforts to Amend the Foreign Corrupt Practices Act." Detroit College of Law Review Vol. 1983, 1983 pp. 1083-1093.

Brown, J.T. "International Joint Venture Contracts in English Law." [Summary in French] Droit et Pratique du Commerce International Vol. 5, June 1979, pp. 193-243.

Bruyneel, A. "Restrictions on Foreign Investment: Developments in U.S. Law." Journal of Comparative Corporate Law and Securities Regulation Vol. 3, 1981, pp. 330-338.

Bushman, K. "British Protection of Trading Interests Act of 1980: An Analysis." Journal of International Law and Economics Vol. 14, 1980, pp. 253-280.

Butler, E.B. "The Extraterritorial Reach of the U.S. Export Administration Act: Reflections on the Yamal Pipeline Controversy." Journal of Business Law Vol. 1983, 1983, pp. 275-283.

Cherol, R.L. and S. Zalduendo. "Legal Framework for Foreign Investment in the Caribbean and Central America." International Lawyer Vol. 57, 1984, pp. 957-982.

Chrysostomides, K. "The Legal Aspects of Foreign Investments in Cyprus." Annuaire de l'Association des Auditeurs et Anciens Auditeurs de l'Academie de Droit International de la Haye Vol. 47-48, 1977-1978, pp. 63-86.

Clagett, Brice M. "Protection of Foreign Investment under the Revised Restatement." Virginia Journal of International Law Vol. 25, 1984, pp. 73-98.

Cohen, B.E. "In Personam Jurisdiction in Federal Courts Over Foreign Corporations: The Need for a Federal Long-Arm Statute." Denver Journal of International Law and Policy Vol. 14, 1985, pp. 59-73.

Cole, P.E. "New Challenges to the U.S. Multinational Corporation in the European Economic Community: Data Protection Laws." New York University Journal of International Law and Politics Vol. 17, 1985, pp. 893-947.

"Comparison of the F.C.P.A. and the Draft International Agreement on Illegal Payments." Vanderbilt Journal of Transnational Law Vol. 13, 1980, pp. 795-823.

Craig, William L. "Application of the Trading with the Enemy Act to Foreign Corporations Owned by Americans: Reflections on Fruehauf v. Massardy." Harvard Law Review Vol. 83, 1970, pp. 579-601.

Cremades, B.M. "The Impact of International Arbitration on the Development of Business Law." American Journal of Comparative Law Vol. 31, 1983, pp. 526-534.

Danaher, M.J. "Antitrust Law: The Clawback and Other Features of the U.K. Anti-Protection of Trading Interests Act, 1980." Law and Policy in International Business Vol. 12, 1980, pp. 947-972.

"The Development of Canadian Law on Transborder Data Flows." Georgia Journal of International and Comparative Law Vol. 13, 1983, pp. 825-855.

Dickey, W.L. "Aspects of the Legal, Political and Policy Issues That Will Confront the U.S.-Japan Trading Community During the Remainder of the 1980's." Case Western Reserve Journal of International Law Vol. 15, 1983, pp. 445-468.

"Draft Restatement Revised." American Society of International Law Proceedings Vol. 76, 1982, pp. 184-205.

Dunn, R.R. "Taxation: Foreign Corrupt Practices Act." Texas International Law Journal Vol. 18, 1983, pp. 407-412.

Ebenroth, C.T. and A. Sura. "Transnationale Unternehmen und deutsches Mitbestimmungs-Gesetz." Zeitschrift fuer das gesamte Handelsrecht und Wirtschaftsrecht Vol. 144, 1980, pp. 610-627.

Ellicott, J. "Trends in Export Control Regulation." Business Lawyer Vol. 38, 1983, pp. 533-553.

Fletcher, William M. Cyclopedia of the Law of Private Corporations. Chicago: Callaghan and Co., 1931-1933.

"Foreign Corrupt Practices Act: Domestic and International Implications: A Symposium." App. I: "FCP Act of 1977"; App. II: "Senate Bill 708"; App. III: "ITT Code of Corporate Conduct." Syracuse Journal of International Law and Commerce Vol. 9, 1982, pp. 235-378.

"Foreign Investment: Foreign Economic Contract Law - the Foreign Economic Contract Law of the People's Republic of China, reprinted in 24 ILM 799 (1985) (unofficial transcript); and The Regulation of the People's Republic of China Governing Contracts for the Imports of Technology, reprinted in 24 ILM 801 (1985) (unofficial transcript)." Harvard International Law Journal Vol. 27, 1986, pp. 275-283.

"Foreign Investment: Investment Dislosure Requirements - Amended Regulations to Implement the International Investment Survey Act of 1976, 46 Fed. Reg. 23,225 (1981) (to be codified in 15 C.F.R. Part 806)." _Harvard International Law Journal_ Vol. 22, 1981, pp. 694-697.

Fugate, Wilbur L. "Export Trade Exceptions to the Antitrust Laws: The Old Webb-Pomerane Act and the New Export Trading Company Act." _Vanderbilt Journal of Transnational Law_ Vol. 15, 1982, pp. 673-707.

Fulda, Carl H. and Warren F. Schwartz. _Regulation of International Trade and Investment_. (University Casebook Series) Mineola, New York: Foundation Press, 1970.

Garfinkel, E.I. "Disclosure of Confidential Documents under the Trade Agreements Act of 1979: A Corporate Nightmare?" _Law and Policy in International Business_ Vol. 13, 1981, pp. 465-493.

"The G.M.-Toyota Joint Venture and Its Implications under the National Labor Relations Act." _Detroit College Law Review_ Vol. 1984, 1984, pp. 647-685.

Gerster, Richard. "Zur Diskussion um den Entwurf fuer ein neues Kartellgesetz: Aktive Kartellpolitik als Entwicklungsforderung." _Neue Zuercher Zeitung_ 17 August 1979, p. 11.

"Gesetzenwuerfe in chinesischen Volkskongress." _Frankfurter Allgemeine Zeitung_ 28 June 1979, p. 3.

Glover, G.C., Jr., D.C. New, and M.M. Lacourciere. "The Investment Canada Act: A New Approach to Regulation of Foreign Investment in Canada." _Business Lawyer_ Vol. 41, 1985, pp. 83-98.

Gordon, William C. "Tests for Determining the Status of a Treaty Provision as Domestic Law." (Comment) _Michigan Law Review_ Vol. 48, 1950, pp. 852-860.

Graham, W.C. "The Foreign Extraterritorial Measures Act." _The Canadian Business Law Journal_ Vol. 11, 1986, pp. 410-44.

Grover, W. "The Investment Canada Act." Canadian Business Lawyer Vol. 10, 1985, pp. 475-482.

Hadden, Tom. Company Law and Capitalism. London: Weidenfeld and Nicolson, 1972.

Han, A.M. "People's Republic of China's Foreign Enterprises Income Tax Law and Regulations." Hasting's International and Comparative Law Review Vol. 6, 1983, pp. 689-717.

Hayden, P.R. and J.H. Burns. "Canadian Foreign Investment Review Act." Practical Lawyer Vol. 21, 1975.

Hibey, R.A. "Practical Necessity for Amendment of the Foreign Corrupt Practices Act: S708 - the Current Legislative Initiative." Hofstra Law Review Vol. 10, 1982, pp. 1121-1136.

Hodges, J.W. "The Trading with the Enemy Act of 1917 and Foreign-Based Subsidiaries of American Multinational Corporations: A Time to Abstain from Restraining." (Comment) San Diego Law Review Vol. 11, 1973, pp. 206-226.

Hofbauer, M.A. "Die Einbeziehung von Fremdkapitalzinsen in die Herstellungskosten nach geltenden und kuenftigem Bilanzrecht." Wallis Collection pp. 383-395.

Honigsberg, C.C. "Uniform Foreign Money-Judgments Recognition Act: A Survey of the Case Law." Vanderbilt Journal of Transnational Law Vol. 14, 1981, pp. 171-196.

Houck, J.B. "The New American Law Institute Restatement of the Foreign Relations Law of the United States - Problems for Practitioners." Private Investors Abroad Vol. 1983, 1983, pp. 37-61.

Houzhi, T. "UNCITRAL's Work on a Model Law on International Commercial Disputes." Pace Law Review Vol. 4, 1983-1984, pp. 519-627.

Huntley, A. K. "Protection of Trading Interests Act, 1980: Some General Aspects of Enforcement of Antitrust Laws." International and Comparative Law Quarterly Vol. 30 1981, pp. 213-233.

"International Transactions: Jurisdictional Developments; Applicability of American Employment Discrimination Legislation to Domestically Based Foreign Companies; and Governmental Restrictions on International Economic Transactions." 1985 Annual Survey of American Law Vol. 1985, 1986, pp. 409-438.

International Legal Center. Law and Public Enterprise in Asia. London: Praeger, 1976.

Jackson, John Howard. Legal Problems of International Economic Relations: Cases, Materials, and Text on the National and International Regulation of Transnational Economic Relations. St. Paul, Minnesota: West Publishing Company, 1977.

Johnson, J. "Business Judgment Rule: A Review of its Application to the Problem of Illegal Foreign Payments." Journal of Corporation Law Vol. 6, 1981, pp. 481-510.

Langley, M. "International Investment Survey Act: The High Cost of Knowledge." Law and Policy in International Business Vol. 14, 1982, pp. 481-504.

Legislation - The Overseas Private Investment Corporation Amendment of 1974. OPIC's functions are to be gradually phased out and its programs are to be transferred to the private insurance industry. 22 U.S.C.A. Sec. 2191-2200a, as amended (- U.S.C.A Sec. -)." (Note) Texas International Law Journal Vol. 10, 1975, pp. 402-410.

Leigh, M. "Restating the Restatement: The Foreign Relations Law of the United States," in Private Investors Abroad. New York: Matthew Bender, 1985.

Lipstein, Kurt. The Law of the European Economic Community. London: Butterworth, 1974.

Lowe, A.V. "Blocking Extraterritorial Jurisdiction: The British Protection of Trading Interests Act, 1980." American Journal of International Law Vol. 75, 1981, pp. 257-282.

McClure, C.E. "Federal Law and State Corporate Income Taxes." Vanderbilt Journal of Transnational Law Vol. 18, 1985, pp. 275-310.

McFadden, D.L. "A Selected Bibliography on Hazardous Activity, Technology and the Law: Bhopal and Beyond." International Lawyer Vol. 19, 1985, pp. 1459-1475.

McNamara, D.E. "Foreign Direct Investment in the United States: Disclosure Regulations." Georgia Journal of International and Comparative Law Vol. 12, 1982, pp. 193-207.

Mierzwa, A.M. and A.K.P. Drab. "New Legislation on Foreign Private Firms in Poland." Review of Socialist Law Vol. 10, 1984, pp. 119-128.

"Modifying the Foreign Corrupt Practices Act: The Search for a Practical Standard." Northwestern Journal of International Law and Business Vol. 4, 1982, pp. 203-233.

Murphy, D.T. "Moderating Antitrust Subject Matter Jurisdiction: The Foreign Trade Antitrust Improvements Act and the Restatement of Foreign Relations Law (Revised)." University of Cincinnati Law Review Vol. 54, 1986, pp. 779-827.

Olmstead, Cecil J. Extraterritorial Application of Laws and Responses Thereto. (Various articles: "General Theory of State Jurisdiction and Limitations Under General International Law and Under International Agreements." Cecil J. Olmstead, Chairman; "Specific Extra-territorial Applications of Jurisdiction Resulting in Conflicts." Gunther Jaenicke Chairman; "Securities Regulation: Extra-territorial Aspects." Maarten Bos, Chairman; "Corporate Governance: Responsibilities of Directors and Officers for Acts of Foreign Subsidiaries and Affiliates." A.E. von Overbeck, Chairman; "Discovery of Documentary and Other Evidence in a Foreign Country." Richard Bentham, Chairman; "Responses to Extraterritorial Exercises of Jurisdiction." Sir Francis Vallat Q.C., Chairman) Oxford: ESC Publishing Limited, 1984.

Ott, K.T. "Economic Recovery Tax Act of 1981, Section 223: The Suspension of IRC Regulations Regarding the Allocation of R&D Expenses to Foreign and Domestic Source Income." Law and Policy in International Business Vol. 14, 1982, pp. 885-904.

Parker, Paul S. "Foreign Relations Law." (Recent Decisions) Vanderbilt Journal of Transnational Law Vol. 8, 1974, pp. 223-230.

Paterson, R.K. "The GATT and Restrictions on Foreign Investment: the U.S. Challenge to Canada's Foreign Investment Law." UCLA Pacific Basin Law Journal Vol. 1, 1985, pp. 224-246.

Porrata-Doria, Jr., R.A. "Amending the Foreign Corrupt Practices Act of 1977: Repeating the Mistakes of the Past?" Rutgers Law Review Vol. 38, 1985, pp. 29-67.

"The Protection of Trading Interests Bill." Law Society's Gazette Vol. 76, 1979, p. 1230.

Robinson, D.R. "Conflicts of Jurisdiction and the Draft Restatement." Law and Policy in International Business Vol. 15, 1983, pp. 1147-1155.

Rose, W.B. "Foreign Investment in Canada: The New Investment Canada Act." International Lawyer Vol. 20, 1986, pp. 19-44.

Rosen, J.P. "Protection of Trading Interests Act." International Lawyer Vol. 15, 1981, pp. 213-232.

Ross, J.L. and D.A. Rubin. "Investment Canada Act: A New Regime for Foreign Investment in Canada." Commercial Law Journal Vol. 91, Spring 1986, pp. 141-152.

Ruiz, J.J. "Participation étrangère dans des activités économiques en Espagne: regime juridique des investissements étrangers." Thesaurus Acroasium Vol. 12, 1982, pp. 651-670.

Schachter, Oscar, and Robert Hellawell, eds. Competition in International Business: Law and Policy on Restrictive Practices. New York: Columbia University Press, 1981.

Schweitzer, Thomas A. "The United Nations as a Source of Domestic Law: Can Security Council Resolutions Be Enforced in American Courts?" Yale Studies in World Public Order Vol. 4, 1978, pp. 162-273.

Singer, Stuart R. Regulation of Foreign Investments in the United States. New York: Practicing Law Institute, 1976.

Skol, A.G. and C.H. Peterson. "Export Control Laws and Multinational Enterprises." International Lawyer Vol. 11, 1977, pp. 29-44.

Steefel, Ernest C. and Bernhard von Falkenhausen. "The New German Stock Corporation Law." Cornell Law Quarterly Vol. 52, 1967, pp. 518-550.

"A Summary of the Forthcoming Restatement of the Foreign Relations Law of the United States (Revised)." The Columbia Journal of Transnational Law Vol. 24, 1986, pp. 677-685.

"Tax Reform Act of 1984 - Netherlands Antilles - Effect of the Repeal of the Withholding Tax on Portfolio Interest Payments to Foreign Investors." Georgia Journal of International and Comparative Law Vol. 15, 1985, pp. 111-123.

"Taxation - Congress Amends Internal Revenue Code to Comport with the Foreign Corrupt Practices Act, Tax Equity and Fiscal Responsibility Act of 1982. Public Law No. 97-248, 96 Stat. 324 [codified as amended in scattered sections of 26 N.S.C.]" Texas International Law Journal Vol. 18, 1983, pp. 407-412.

Thompson, D. "UNCTAD: Model Law on Restrictive Business Practices." Journal of World Trade Law Vol. 14, 1980, pp. 444-449.

"Title VII of the Civil Rights Act of 1964 and the Multinational Enterprise." Georgia Law Journal Vol. 73, 1985, pp. 1465-1498.

Tobi, N. "Legal Aspects of Foreign Investment in Nigeria." Annuaire de l'Association des Auditeurs et Anciens Auditeurs de l'Academie de Droit International de la Haye Vol. 47-48, 1977-1978, pp. 31-56.

Trotier, B. "Le controle juridique des entreprises multinationales." Cahiers de Droit Vol. 27, 1986, pp. 419-435.

Tunc, Andre. "Multinational Companies in French Law," in Fritz Fabricus, ed., Law and International Trade, Festschrift fuer Clive M. Schmitthoff. Frankfurt: Athenaum Verlag, 1973.

Vagts, Detlev F. "Law and Accounting in Business Associations," in Vol. XIII "Business and Private Organizations," International Encyclopedia of Comparative Law. Dobbs Ferry, New York: Oceana, 1972.

Vila, A.M. "Legal Aspects of Foreign Direct Investment in the United States." International Lawyer Vol. 16, 1982, pp. 1-49.

Weems, P.R. "Reporting Requirements for U.S. Corporations: The International Investment and Trade in Services Survey Act." International Lawyer Vol. 19, 1985, pp. 1293-1302.

Weis, H. "Verstaatlichungen aus gemeinschaftsrechlicher Sicht." Neue Juristische Wochenschrift Vol. 35, 1982, pp. 1910-1914.

Willens, R. "The Corporate Provisions of the Tax Reform Act of 1986." The Advisor Vol. 17, 1986, pp. 624-661.

Wilner, Gabriel M. "Applicable Law and Dispute Settlement in the Transfer of Technology Code." Journal of World Trade Law Vol. 17, 1983, pp. 389-396.

Witherspoon, R.A. "Multinational Corporations - Governmental Regulation of Business Ethics under the Foreign Corrupt Practices Act of 1977: An Analysis." Dickinson Law Review Vol. 87, 1983, pp. 531-593.

Wootton, R.R. "Section 382 After the Tax Reform Act of 1986." _Taxes_ Vol. 64, 1986, pp. 874-889.

Zimbler, B.L. "Constitutional Law: French Nationalizations." _Harvard Journal of International Law_ Vol. 23, 1983, pp. 381-388.

8. EUROPE

Adler, Howard Jr. and Murray J. Belman. "Antimerger Enforcement in Europe - Trends and Prospects." *Journal of International Law and Economics* Vol. 8, June 1973, pp. 31-51.

Albulescu, P.R. "Prospective Exemptions Under EEC Competition Law: A Proposal." *Law and Policy in International Business* Vol. 16, 1984, pp. 1137-1180.

Allen, D.G.M. "Controlled Foreign Corporations in France and Domicile." *Solicitor's Journal* Vol. 130, 1986, pp. 707-708.

American Subsidiaries of German Firms. New York: German American Chamber of Commerce, 1971.

"Anhaltender Konzentrationstrend in Deutschland: Jahresbericht des Bundeskartellamtes." *Neue Zuercher Zeitung* 6 June 1979, p. 16.

"Antitrust Implications of Trade Law: Japan, the European Communities, and the United States: A Panel." *American Society of International Law Proceedings* Vol. 76, 1982, pp. 120-130.

"Antitrust Law: Commission of the European Communities Suspends Proceedings Against International Business Machines Corporation - 3 Common Market Law Review 147 (1984)." *Harvard International Law Journal* Vol. 26, 1985, pp. 189-201.

Aronson, S. and S. Nyman. "Doing Business in Sweden." *Brooklyn Journal of International Law* Vol. 12, 1986, pp. 73-94.

Arpan, Jeffrey S. *International Intracorporate Pricing: Non-American Systems and Views*. New York: Praeger, 1972.

Articles 85 and 86 of the EEC Treaty and the Relevant Regulations: A Manual for Firms. London, Washington, DC: Information Service of the European Communities, n.d.

"Auf dem Weg zu einem Verhaltenskodex fuer Multis: Tagung der UNO-Kommission fuer transnationale Gesellschaften." Neue Zuercher Zeitung 30 May 1979, p. 10.

Augustyn, F.M. "An Antitrust Analysis of Joint Research and Development Agreements in the European Economic Community and the United States." Georgia Journal of International and Comparative Law Vol. 16, 1986, pp. 45-71.

Augustyn, F.M. "A Primer for Incorporating Under the Income Tax Laws of France, Germany, or the United Kingdom." New England Journal of International Law and Business Vol. 7, 1985, pp. 267-317.

Autenruth, K. "Britischen Protection of Trade Interests Acts im System des Internationalen Kartellrechts." Recht der internationalen Wirtschaft Vol. 29, 1983, pp. 15-18.

Bathurst, M.E., et al., eds. Legal Problems of an Enlarged European Community. (British Institute Studies in International and Comparative Law No. 6) London: Stevens and Sons, 1972.

Baxter, I.F.G. "The United Kingdom and Tax Havens: A Comparative Comment." American Journal of Comparative Law Vol. 33, 1985, pp. 707-719.

Bechtold, R. "Die Entwicklung des deutschen Kartellrechts im Jahre 1979." Neue Juristische Wochenschrift Vol. 33, 1980, pp. 1265-1269.

Bechtold, R. "Die Entwicklung des deutschen Kartellrechts von 1981 bis 1983." Neue Juristische Wochenschrift Vol. 37, 1984, pp. 145-152.

Behrens, Peter. "Garantien fuer auslaendisches Investoren." [Summaries in English and French] Deutsche Zivil-, Kollisions-, und Wirtschafts- rechtliche Beitraege Vol. 1978, 1978, pp. 111-149.

Behrens, Peter. "Kontrolle auslaendischer Direktinvestitionen." [Summary in English] *Rabels Zeitschrift fuer auslaendisches und internationales Privatrecht* Vol. 40, 1976, pp. 233-271.

Beier, F.-K. "The Law of Unfair Competition in the European Community - Its Development and Present Status." *European Intellectual Property Review* Vol. 7, 1985, pp. 284-291.

Bellamy, Christopher and Graham D. Child. *Common Market Law of Competition*. London: Sweet & Maxwell, 1973.

Berberian, D. and Menck, T. "Comparison of U.S. and German Intercompany Pricing Regulations." [Summaries in English, French and German] *Intertax* 1981, pp. 410-420.

xBernstein, H. and H. Koch. "Internationaler Konzern und deutsche Mitbestimmung." *Zeitschrift fuer das gesamte Handelsrecht und Wirtschaftsrecht* Vol. 143, 1979, pp. 522-538.

Blockmann, Albert. *Grundgesetz und Voelkerrecht*. Berlin: Duncker & Humbolt, 1975.

Blythe, M.A. "Extraterritorial Impact of the Anti-Trust Laws: Protecting British Trading Interests." *American Journal of Comparative Law* Vol. 31, 1983, pp. 99-129.

Boddewyn, J. "Western European Public Policies toward American Investors." Project working paper, New York University Graduate School of Business Administration, October 1972.

Boehme, R. "Current Issues in U.S.-German Financial and Economic Relations." [Summaries in English, French, and German] *Intertax* 1982, pp. 129-135.

"Boersenaufsichtsbehoerde: Mitspracherecht bei Fusionen." *Frankfurter Allgemeine Zeitung* 12 December 1979, p. 12.

Boidman, N. "Canada: Supreme Court Interprets Canada-Germany Tax Treaty." [Summaries in English, French and German] *Intertax* 1983, pp. 17-21.

Bondurant, Ward S. "Extraterritorial Jurisdiction - Antitrust - The Impact of the British Protection of Trading Interests Act on the United States Antitrust Suit Brought by Laker Airways against British Airways and British Caledonian." (Recent Developments) Georgia Journal of International and Comparative Law Vol. 14, 1984, pp. 181-200.

Born, G.B. "Recent British Responses to the Extraterritorial Application of United States Law: The Midland Bank [Midland Bank v. Laker Airways, Slip Op. (C.A. July 30, 1985)] Decision and Retaliating Legislation Involving Unitary Taxation." Virginia Journal of International Law Vol. 26, 1985, pp. 91-108.

Boyer, A. "Form as Substance: A Comparison of Antitrust Regulation by Consent Decrees in the U.S.A., Reports of the Monopolies and Mergers Commission in the U.K., and Grants of Clearance by the European Commission" International and Comparative Law Quarterly Vol. 32, 1983, pp. 904-930.

Brenscheidt, Michael H. "Petroleum Legislation in the North Sea Countries." Texas International Law Journal Vol. 11, 1976, pp. 281-304.

Briggs, Herbert W. "Barcelona Traction: The Jus Standi of Belgium." American Journal of International Law Vol. 65, 1971, pp. 327-345.

Brill, J.-P. "Renforcement de la lutte contre les abus de position dominante." Recueil Dalloz Sirey June 1981, pp. 165-174.

Bringezu, Volker. "Parent-Subsidiary Relations under German Law." International Lawyer Vol. 7, 1973, pp. 138-157.

"The British Telecommunications (250 J. Eur. Comm. [No. L360] 36) Decision: Toward a New Telecommunications Policy in the Common Market." Harvard International Law Journal Vol. 95, 1984, pp. 299-328.

Brooke, Michael Z. and H. Lee Remmers, eds. The Multinational Company in Europe: Some Key Problems. London: Longman, 1972.

Brown, J.T. "International Joint Venture Contracts in English Law." [Summary in French] Droit et Pratique du Commerce International Vol. 5, June 1979, pp. 193-243.

Bruyneel, A. "Restrictions on Foreign Investment: Developments in European Law." Journal of Comparative Corporate Law and Securities Regulation Vol. 3, 1981, pp. 339-356.

Buckley, P.J. "Entry Strategy of Recent European Direct Investors in the United States of America." Journal of Comparative Corporate Law and Securities Regulations Vol. 3, 1981, pp. 169-191.

xBurdeau, G. "La contribution des nationalisations françaises de 1982 au droit international des nationalisations." Revue Générale de Droit International Public Vol. 89, 1985, pp. 5-28.

Burkard, P.H. "Attorney-Client Privilege in the EEC: The Perspective of Multinational Corporate Counsel." International Lawyer Vol. 20, 1986, pp. 677-688.

Burton, F.N. "Direct Investment by Sogo-Shasha in Europe." Journal of World Trade Law Vol. 17, 1983, pp. 249-258.

Bushman, K. "British Protection of Trading Interests Act of 1980: An Analysis." Journal of International Law and Economics Vol. 14, 1980, pp. 253-280.

Campbell, Alan Robertson. Restrictive Trading Agreements in the Common Market: Texts, Commentaries. London: Stevens & Sons, 1964.

Campbell, Dennis, ed. Legal Aspects of Doing Business in Western Europe. (International Business Series) St.Paul, Minnesota: West Publishing Co., 1983.

Campbell, Dennis and C. Rohwer, eds. Legal Aspects of International Business Transactions - I. (The Edinburgh Institute on International Transactions 1983) New York: Elsevier, 1984.

Capelli, F. "Nationalisierungen im Gemeinsamen Markt." Recht der internationalen Wirtschaft Vol. 29, 1983, pp. 313-322.

Carnulutti, A. and F. Delon. "États face aux éffets extraterritoriaux du droit de la concurrence des États-Unis d'Amérique: l'exemple de la France." Revue Française de Droit Aérien Vol. 36, 1982, pp. 15-41.

Champaud, C. "Contrôle des concentrations en France depuis 1977." Revue Trimestrielle de Droit Commercial et de Droit Économique Vol. 33, 1980, pp. 421-439.

Chown, J.F. and W. Hopper. "Company Tax Harmonization in the European Economic Community." [Summaries in English, French, and German] Intertax 1982, pp. 275-284.

Chown, J.F. "European Tax Treatment of Foreign Investment." Boston University International Law Journal Vol. 4, 1986, pp. 55-65.

"City Code on Take-Overs and Mergers: Amendments (1985)." Business Law Review Vol. 6, 1985, pp. 77-80.

Cohen, B.C. and G. Schachter. "Recent Trends in European Investment in the U.S." Bankers Magazine Vol. 153, Spring 1970, pp. 82-86.

Coing, H.C. "Germany and the Multinational Enterprise," in H.R. Hahlo, ed., Nationalism and the Multinational Enterprise: Legal, Economic and Managerial Aspects. Dobbs Ferry, NY: Oceana, 1973

Cole, P.E. "New Challenges to the U.S. Multinational Corporaton in the European Economic Community: Data Protection Laws." New York University Journal of International Law and Politics Vol. 17, 1985, pp. 893-947.

Collins, C.J. "Antitrust: EEC Treaty: Joint-Venture Agreement." Vanderbilt Journal of Transnational Law Vol. 12, 1979, pp. 775-785.

Commission of European Communities, Principles and General Datelines of an Industrial Policy for the Community. Brussels: Commission of European Communities Secretariat, 1970.

Common Market Reporter: Doing Business in Europe. New York: Commerce Clearing House Publishers, 1976 (with supplements).

"Continental Can [Europemballage Corp. and Continental Can Inc. v. EEC Commission]." Common Market Law Reports Vol. 12, 1973, p. 199-229.

"The Continental Challenge." The Economist 4 February 1978, p. 78.

Crowley, C. and P. McGowan. "Irish Tax Law and the Foreign Investor." Vanderbilt Journal of Transnational Law Vol. 17, 1984, pp. 631-664.

Damm, W. "The Economic Aspects of European Direct Investment in the U.S.," in S.E. Rolfe and W. Damm, eds., The Multinational Corporation in the World Economy. New York: Praeger, 1970.

Danaher, M.J. "Antitrust Law: The Clawback and Other Features of the U.K. Protection of Trading Interests Act, 1980." Law and Policy in International Business Vol. 12, 1980, pp. 947-972.

Davies, David R. "United Kingdom: Inland Revenue Guidance Notes on Transfer Pricing and Multinational Enterprises." [Summaries in English, French, and German] Intertax 1982, pp. 12-18.

Davies, David R. "United Kingdom: Recent Tax Cases Concerning Parent Company and Subsidiary Branch Operations." [Summaries in English, French, and German] Intertax 1983, pp. 301-306.

De Angelis, L. "Il nuovo 'city code on take-overs and mergers.'" Rivista della Societá Vol. 30, 1985, pp. 1170-1188.

Deppe, F. "Wissenschaftlich-technischer Fortschritt, internationale Konzerne und Supranationalitaet," in Manfred Krueper, ed., Investitionskontrolle gegen die Konzerne? Reinbek bei Hamburg: Rowholt, 1974.

Deringer, Arved. "Current Trends of EEC Competition Policy." Journal of International Law and Economics Vol. 8, 1973, pp. 203-222.

"Deutsche Auslandsinvestitionen bzw. auslaendische Investitionen in der Bundesrepublik Deutschland." Archiv der Gegenwart 9 August 1980.

de Vries, E. "Intercompany Pricing Provisions in the United Kingdom." [Summaries in English, French, and German] Intertax 1980, pp. 294-300.

"Discovery in Great Britain: The Evidence (Proceedings in Other Jurisdictions) Act." Cornell International Law Journal Vol. 11, 1978, pp. 323-341.

Done, Kevin. "Beecham Expanding in North America." Financial Times: Finance and Company News, 9 March 1978.

Dunning, John H. American Investment in British Manufacturing Industry. London: Allen & Unwin, 1958.

Dunning, John H. "British Investment in the United States, 1860-1913," in J.H. Dunning, Studies in International Investment. London: Allen & Unwin, 1970.

Dunning, John H. The Location of International Firms in an Enlarged EEC: An Explanatory Paper. Manchester: Manchester Statistical Society, 1972.

Ebel, H.-R. "Marktbeherrschungsvermutungen im Gesetz gegen Wettbewerbsbeschraenkungen." Neue Juristische Wochenschrift Vol. 34, August 1981, pp. 1763-1767.

xEbenroth, C.T. and A. Sura. "Transnationale Unternehmen und deutsches Mitbestimmungs-gesetz." Zeitschrift fuer das gesamte Handelsrecht und Wirtschaftsrecht Vol. 144, 1980, pp. 610-627.

"The Economic Unity Doctrine in the EEC: A Limited Exemption to Article 85 of the Treaty of Rome." Fordham International Law Journal Vol. 9, 1985/1986, pp. 373-399.

"EEC Plans Antitrust Crackdown on State-Controlled Companies." International Herald Tribune 25 October 1979, p. 1.

"EEC Regulation of Exclusive Dealing Arrangements." International Tax and Business Law Vol. 3, Summer 1985, pp. 81-101.

Ehrenhaft, Peter D. Review of James A. Rahl, "Common Market and American Antitrust - Overlap and Conflict." Law and Policy in International Business, Vol. 3, 1971, pp. 649-658.

Ekblom, H.E. "European Direct Investment in the U.S." Harvard Business Review Vol. 51, July/August 1973, pp. 16-27.

Ellis, J.J.A. "Legal Aspects of European Direct Investment in the U.S.A.," in S.E. Rolfe and Walter Damm, eds., The Multinational Corporation in the World Economy. New York: Praeger, 1970.

"Ende britischer Kapitalverkehrskontrollen." Neue Zuercher Zeitung 25 October 1979, p. 11.

"England jetzt ohne Devisenkontrollen." Frankfurter Allgemeine Zeitung 24 October 1979, p. 13.

Eser, G. "Fusionskontrollrechtliche Problematik internationaler joint venture im Kartellrecht der Bundesrepublic Deutschland." Recht der internationalen Wirtschaft Vol. 28, March 1982, pp. 161-167.

"Exchange of Information under the OECD and U.S. Model Tax Treaties." Loyola of Los Angeles International and Comparative Law Journal Vol. 5, 1982, pp. 129-142.

"The Extraterritorial Enforcement of U.S. Antitrust Laws and Retaliatory Legislation in the United Kingdom and Australia. Denver Journal of International Law and Policy Vol. 13, 1984, pp. 377-386.

Faith, Nicholas. The Infiltrators: The European Business Invasion of America. New York: E.P. Dutton & Co., 1972.

Fallon, Ivan. "Look Out - the British Are Coming." Sunday Telegraph 27 February 1977, p. 25.

Fera, R.D. "The European Economic Community and the Vredeling Proposal: The Debate to Temper Ideology with Realism." California Western International Law Journal Vol. 16, 1986, pp. 250-281.

Feuring, W. "Anwendbarkeit des Sec. 23 I Satz 8 GWB auf die Zusammenschlusstatbestaende des Sec. 23 II Nr. 3, 4 und 5 GWB." Wirtschaft und Wettbewerb Vol. 32, 1982, pp. 517-522.

Fisher, W. Halder. Technology Transfer as a Motivation for United States Direct Investments by European Firms. Battelle Memorial Institute, Columbus Laboratories, 1977.

Flowers, Edward B. "Oligopolistic Reaction in European and Canadian Direct Investment in the United States." Journal of International Business Studies Vol. 7, Fall/Winter 1976, pp. 43-56.

Focke, Katharina. "From Lomé 1 Towards Lomé 2." Texts of the Report and Resolution Adopted on 26 September 1980 by the APC-EEC Consultative Assembly. Luxembourg: Office for Official Publications of the European Communities, 1980.

"Foreign Direct Investment in Germany DM 66.8b End 1978." Europe Agence internationale d'informations pour la presse Luxembourg, 4 February 1981.

Foreign Direct Investment in the Southeast: West Germany, the United Kingdom and Japan. Atlanta, Georgia: Southern Center for International Studies, August 1979.

Fox, D.W. "The EEC Treaty: 'Abusive Exploitation' and Provision of Discount." Solicitor's Journal Vol. 130, 18 April 1986, pp. 294-296.

Franko, Lawrence G. European Business Strategies in the United States. Geneva: Business International, 1971.

Franko, Lawrence G. The European Multinationals: A Renewed Challenge to American and British Big Business. London: Harper and Row, 1976.

Garner, S.S. "Hoffman-LaRoche and Dominant Position in the EEC." Journal of International Law and Economics Vol. 14, 1980, pp. 485-508.

Gerber, D.J. "The Extraterritorial Application of the German Antitrust Laws." American Journal of International Law Vol. 77, 1983, pp. 756-783.

German American Chamber of Commerce. American Subsidiaries of German Firms. New York: German American Chamber of Commerce, 1971.

"German Firms in the American Southeast: Problems and Prospects." Atlanta, Georgia: Georgia World Congress Institute, 1980.

"German-U.S. Tax Treaty: German Memorandum on the Questions of Dividend Taxation." [Summaries in English, French, and German] Intertax 1980, pp. 246-262.

Gerster, Richard. "Zur Diskussion um den Entwurf fuer ein neues Kartellgesetz: Aktive Kartellpolitik als Entwicklungsforderung." Neue Zuercher Zeitung 17 August 1979, p. 11.

Goebel, R.J. "The Uneasy Fate of Franchising Under EEC Antitrust Laws." European Law Review Vol. 10, April 1985, pp. 87-118.

xGoldman, B. "Décisions du conseil constitutionnel relative aux nationalisations et le droit international." Journal du Droit International Vol. 109, 1982, pp. 275-345.

Gordon, Edward. "Extraterritorial Application of United States Economic Law: Britain Draws the Line." International Lawyer Vol. 14, 1980, pp. 151-166.

Graham, E.M. "A Defensive Theory of Foreign Direct Investment and European Direct Investment in the United States." Massachusetts Institute of Technology: Sloan School of Management, 1976.

Graham, E.M. "Oligopolistic Imitation and European Direct Investment in the United States." Ph.D. dissertation, Massachusetts Institute of Technology, 1974.

Gramlich, L. "Zur Zulaessigkeit von Vergesellschaftungen (Nationalisierungen) nach dem Grundgesetz der Bundesrepublic Deutschland." Zeitschrift fuer vergleichende Rechtswissenschaft einschliesslich der ethnologischen Rechtsvorschung Vol. 82, May 1983, pp. 165-189.

"La Grande-Bretagne abolit tous les contrôles." Le Monde, 25 October 1979, p. 42.

Grendell, Timothy J. "The Antitrust Legislation of the United States, the European Community, Germany and Japan." International and Comparative Law Quarterly Vol. 29, 1980, pp. 64-86.

Gribbin, J.D. "U.K. Regulation of Transnational Corporate Concentration." Michigan Year Book of International Legal Studies Vol. 2, 1981, pp. 93-127.

Griffin, Joseph P. "The Power of Host Countries over the Multinational: Lifting the Veil in the European Economic Community and the United States." Law and Policy in International Business Vol. 6, 1974, pp. 375-435.

Guinezanes, N. "Loi no. 82-973 du 29 octobre, 1981 sur les conditions d'entrée et de séjour des étrangers en France." Recueil Dalloz Sirey July 1982, pp. 173-184.

Gurley, Franklin L. "Zur Diskussion um den Entwurf fuer ein neues Kartellgesetz: Das amerikanische Wettbewerbsrecht." Neue Zuercher Zeitung 7 September 1979, p. 14.

Guyénot, Jean. "La décision 'Continental Can' de la Commission C.E.E. et la naissance du droit antitrust européen." Rivista della Societá Vol. 17, 1972, pp. 722-741.

Gyselen, L. and N. Kyriazis. "Artice 86 EEC: The Monopoly Power Measurement Issue Revisited." European Law Review Vol. 11, April 1986, pp. 134-148.

Hamon, L. "Nationalisation devant le conseil constitutionnel." Recueil Dalloz Sirey Vol. 79, March 1983, pp. 79-84.

Harding, C.D.P. "Jurisdiction in EEC Competition Law: Some Recent Developments." Journal of World Trade Law Vol. 2, 1977, pp. 422-440.

Haubert, William H., III. "Continental Can - New Strength for Common Market Anti-Trust." (Comment) San Diego Law Review Vol. 11, 1973, pp. 227-244.

Hawk, Barry E. "Antitrust in the EEC - The First Decade." Fordham Law Review Vol. 41, 1972, pp. 229-292.

Hawk, Barry E. International Anti-Trust Manual: U.S., Common Market, and International Antitrust: A Comparative Guide. New York: Law and Business, 1979.

Heller, R. and N. Willatt. The European Revenge: How the American Challenge Was Rebuffed. London: Barrie & Jenkins, 1975.

Herzog, B.E. "Nineteen-Eighty French Law on Documents and Information." American Journal of International Law Vol. 75, 1981, pp. 382-386.

Hilinski, C.C. "U.S. Tax Aspects of European Direct Investment in the U.S." Commerce in Belgium September 1975.

Hoeppner, H.-D. "German Regulations on Transfer Pricing: A Tax Administrator's Point of View." [Summaries in English, French and German] Intertax 1983, pp. 208-223.

Hood, Neil and Stephen Young. Multinationals in Retreat: The Scottish Experience. Edinburgh: Edinburgh University Press, 1982.

Hopt, Klaus J., ed. Legal and Economic Analyses on Multinational Enterprises. New York: Walter de Gruyter, 1982. (2 Vols.) Vol. 1: European Merger Control; Vol. 2: Groups of Companies in European Laws.

Horn, Norbert. "Vertragsbindung unter veraenderten Umstaenden." Neue Juristische Wochenschrift Vol. 38, 1985, pp. 1118-1125.

Hornsby, S.B. "Public and Private Resale Price Maintenance Systems in the Publishing Sector: The Need for Equal Treatment in European Law." European Law Review Vol. 10, 1985, pp. 381-397.

Houin, R. "Sociétés multinationales et la Communauté Économique Européenne." Revue Juridique et Politique, Indépendence et Coopération Vol. 37, January-March 1983, pp. 464-469.

Huntley, A. K. "Protection of Trading Interests Act, 1980: Some General Aspects of Enforcement of Antitrust Laws." International and Comparative Law Quarterly Vol. 30 1981, pp. 213-233.

Hurwitz, James D. "The Impact of the Continental Can Case on Combinations and Concentrations within the Common Market." Hastings Law Journal Vol. 25, 1973-1974, pp. 469-517.

Imbert, Bernard. "French Investments in the American Southeast." Atlanta: Georgia World Congress Institute, August 1979.

Imurenga, U. "Schwerpunkte der Vierten Novelle zum Gesetz gegen Wettbewerbsbeschraenkungen." Neue Juristische Wochenschrift Vol. 33, 1980, pp. 1417-1423.

International Monetary Fund. "German Direct Investments in the United States." International Financial News Survey 15 May 1970.

"Der Investor sollte sich willkommen fuehlen." Frankfurter Allgemeine Zeitung 22 November 1979, p. 13.

Joliet, René. Monopolization and Abuse of Dominant Position: Study of the American and European Approaches to the Control of Economic Power. (Lièges Faculté de droit: Collection scientifique de la faculté de droit de l'Université de Lièges 31) The Hague: Nijhoff, 1970.

Joliet, René. The Rule of Reason in Anti-Trust Law: American, German and Common Market Laws in Comparative Perspective. The Hague: Nijhoff, 1967.

Jouanjean, H. "Mouvements des capitaux dans le cadre de l'adhésion de la Grèce a la Communauté européen." Revue du Marché Commun Vol. 24, 1981, pp. 14-20.

Juillard, P. "La succursale et le droit français des relations financières avec l'étranger." Droit et Pratique du Commerce Vol. 11, 1985, pp. 401-423.

Kaiser, Joseph H. "Fusionskontrolle oder Fusionsverbot?: Die Vermutungstatbestaende des Entwurfs der IV. GWB-Novelle." Wirtschaft und Wettbewerb Vol. 28, 1978, pp. 344-363.

"Kartell-Hearing: ASU: Fusionskontrolle noch immer lueckenhaft." Handelsblatt 3 March 1979, p. 3.

"Kartellnovelle 'kein grosser Wurf': Einstimmige Verabschiedung im Wirtschaftsausschuss." Frankfurter Allgemeine Zeitung 25 January 1970, p. 11.

Klawitter, C. "Nochmals: die Aufloesung von Unternehmens-zusammenschlussen im Fusionskontrollverfahren." Wirtschaft und Wettbewerb Vol. 31, 1981, pp. 245-251.

Knoepfle, R. "Wettbewerbsbeschraenkung durch Anwendung des Gesetzes gegen Wettbewerbsbeschraenkungen bei Zusammenschlussen." Juristenzeitung Vol. 37, 1982, pp. 521-530.

Knoepfler. "Les Nationalisations françaises face à l'ordre juridique Suisse." Schweizerisches Jahrbuch fuer Internationales Recht Vol. 39, 1983, pp. 149-173.

Kohler, Rainer M. "The New Corporate Laws in Germany (1966) and France (1967) and the Trend Towards a Uniform Corporation Law for the Common Market." Tulane Law Review Vol. 43, 1968, pp. 58-71.

Koppensteiner, Hans-Georg. "International Enterprises under the Antitrust Law of the European Economic Community." Journal of World Trade Law Vol. 9, 1975, pp. 287-317.

Korah, Valentine. "The Control of Mergers under Article 86 of the Rome Treaty: Continental Can." Current Legal Problems Vol. 26, 1973, pp. 82-113.

Korah, Valentine. "Group Exemptions for Exclusive Distribution and Purchasing in the EEC." Common Market Law Review Vol. 21, 1984, pp. 53-80.

Kozyris, P. John. "Equal Joint-Venture Corporations in France: Problems of Control and Resolution of Deadlocks." American Journal of Comparative Law Vol. 17, 1969, pp. 503-528.

Krueper, Manfred, ed. Investitionskontrolle gegen die Konzerne? Reinbek bei Hamburg: Rowholt, 1974.

Kubin, Konrad. "German Direct Investments in the U.S. and American Investments in the Federal Republic of Germany." Indiana University: Institute of German Studies, 1978.

Kuyper, P.J. "European Community Law and Extraterritoriality: Some Trends and New Developments." International and Comparative Law Quarterly Vol. 33, 1984, pp. 1013-1021.

bLandwehr, Martha L., ed. Private Investors Abroad - Problems and Solutions in International Business in 1982. Parts I, II, III, IV: "Privacy, Telecommunications and Transborder Data Flows - U.S. Multinational Response to European Expectations." (Articles: G.W. Coombe, Jr., R.E.L. Walker, H.P. Donaghue, and L.A. Hummer) New York: Matthew Bender, 1982.

Lang, J.T. "Community Antitrust Law - Compliance and Enforcement." Common Market Law Review Vol. 18, 1981, pp. 335-362.

Kohler, Rainer M. "The New Corporate Laws in Germany (1966) and France (1967) and the Trend Towards a Uniform Corporation Law for the Common Market." Tulane Law Review Vol. 43, 1968, pp. 58-71.

Koppensteiner, Hans-Georg. "International Enterprises under the Antitrust Law of the European Economic Community." Journal of World Trade Law Vol. 9, 1975, pp. 287-317.

Korah, Valentine. "The Control of Mergers under Article 86 of the Rome Treaty: Continental Can." Current Legal Problems Vol. 26, 1973, pp. 82-113.

Korah, Valentine. "Group Exemptions for Exclusive Distribution and Purchasing in the EEC." Common Market Law Review Vol. 21, 1984, pp. 53-80.

Kozyris, P. John. "Equal Joint-Venture Corporations in France: Problems of Control and Resolution of Deadlocks." American Journal of Comparative Law Vol. 17, 1969, pp. 503-528.

Krueper, Manfred, ed. Investitionskontrolle gegen die Konzerne? Reinbek bei Hamburg: Rowholt, 1974.

Kubin, Konrad. "German Direct Investments in the U.S. and American Investments in the Federal Republic of Germany." Indiana University: Institute of German Studies, 1978.

Kuyper, P.J. "European Community Law and Extraterritoriality: Some Trends and New Developments." International and Comparative Law Quarterly Vol. 33, 1984, pp. 1013-1021.

Landwehr, Martha L., ed. Private Investors Abroad - Problems and Solutions in International Business in 1982. Parts I, II, III, IV: "Privacy, Telecommunications and Transborder Data Flows - U.S. Multinational Response to European Expectations." (Articles: G.W. Coombe, Jr., R.E.L. Walker, H.P. Donaghue, and L.A. Hummer) New York: Matthew Bender, 1982.

Lang, J.T. "Community Antitrust Law - Compliance and Enforcement." Common Market Law Review Vol. 18, 1981, pp. 335-362.

Langer, S.H. "Israel-EEC Free Trade Agreement: An Analysis of the Agreement and Its Effect on Investments." _Syracuse Journal of International Law and Commerce_ Vol. 9, Spring 1982, pp. 63-113.

Lawrie, R.F.C. "Corporate Freezeouts: A Comparison of Controls in the United States and England." _New York University Journal of International Law and Politics_ Vol. 14, 1982, pp. 595-641.

Lawson, R.G. "The Competition Act: A Review." _New Law Journal_ Vol. 133, 1983, pp. 908-910.

Lazarski, H. "System of 'Territoriality': The Present Situation Possible Uses, Anti-Avoidance Measures." _European Taxation_ Vol. 22, 1982, pp. 175-182.

Lebedoff, G. and C. Raievski. "A French Perspective on the United States Ban on the Soviet Gas Pipeline Equipment." _Texas International Law Journal_ Vol. 18, 1983, pp. 483-507.

LeGall, J.-P. "Règle de l'arm's length serait-elle incompatible avec le traité de Rome?" [Text in French and English] _Droit et Pratique du Commerce International_ Vol. 8, July 1982, pp. 65-85.

Leleux, Paul. "Corporation Law in the U.S. and in the EEC." _Common Market Law Review_ Vol. 133, 1967-1968, pp. 133-176.

Leleux, Paul. "France, Belgium, European Economic Community and the Multinational Enterprise," in H.R. Hahlo, ed., _Nationalism and the Multinational Enterprise: Legal, Economic and Managerial Aspects_. Dobbs Ferry, New York: Oceana, 1973.

Leontiades, James. "The European Challenge: A Response." _Columbia Journal of World Business_ Vol 5, July-August 1970, pp. 9-16.

Lipstein, Kurt. _The Law of the European Economic Community_. London: Butterworth, 1974.

List, H. "Recent Cases of the German Supreme Tax Court on International Tax Law." Bulletin for International Fiscal Documentation Vol. 35, 1981, pp. 348-355.

Lopez-Balboa, V.M. and J. Myers. "Jurisdictional Standards Under EEC Competition Law: The Evolution of the Economic Entity Test." Journal of Comparative Business and Capital Market Law Vol. 6, 1984, pp. 383-407.

Louis, J.-V. "Free Movement of Capital in the Community: The Casati Judgment." Common Market Law Review Vol. 19, 1982, pp. 443-452.

Lowe, A.V. "Blocking Extraterritorial Jurisdiction: The British Protection of Trading Interests Act, 1980." American Journal of International Law Vol. 75, 1981, pp. 257-282.

Loyrette, J. and L. Gaillot. "French Nationalizations: The Decisions of the French Constitutional Council and Their Aftermath." George Washington Journal of International Law and Economics Vol. 17, 1982, pp. 17-62.

Maitland-Walker, J., ed. International Anti-Trust Law Oxford: ESC Publishing, 1984. (2 Vols.) Vol. 1: A review of national laws; Vol. 2: Recent developments in EEC and U.S. Anti-Trust Laws.

Mann, F.A. "The Dyestuffs Case in the Court of Justice of the European Communities." International and Comparative Law Quarterly Vol. 22, 1973, pp. 35-50.

Mannick, C.V. "Antitrust: British Restrictions on Enforcement of Foreign Judgments." Harvard International Law Journal Vol. 21, 1980, pp. 727-735.

Marinelli, Jr., A.J. "Competition Policy in Britain." Southern Illinois University Law Journal Vol. 1985, 1985 pp. 153-164.

Markert, Kurt E. "Anti-Monopoly Legislation in Europe," in H.R. Hahlo, ed., Nationalism and the Multinational Enterprise: Legal, Economic and Managerial Aspects. Dobbs Ferry, New York: Oceana, 1973.

Markert, Kurt E. "Recent Developments in German Antitrust Law." Fordham Law Review Vol. 43, 1975, pp. 697-718.

Maskall, M.E. "United Kingdom: Tax Consequences of the Abolition of Exchange Controls." [Summaries in English, French, and German] Intertax 1981, pp. 32-38.

McDermid, John F. "Merger Directions: The United States and EEC: An Ominous Picture for United States Multinationals." George Mason University Law Review Vol. 3, 1980, pp. 1-62.

Meal, D.H. "Governmental Compulsion as a Defense under United States and European Community Antitrust Law." Columbia Journal of Transnational Law Vol. 20, 1981, pp. 51-131.

Meessen, M. "Das Mitbestimmungsurteil des Bundesverfassungsgerichts." Neue Juristische Wochenschrift 25 April 1979, p. 833.

Menck, T. "Qualifitsationsconflikt im neuen deutsch-kanadischen Doppelbesteuerungsabkommen." [Summaries in English, French and German] Intertax 1982, pp. 417-423.

Merkin, R. "The Legality of Effective Competition in EEC Law: AEG Telefunken [AEG Telefunken v. Commission of European Communities, Case 107/82] in the European Court of Justice." Liverpool Law Review Vol. 6, 1984, pp. 139-165.

Merritt, Giles. "The EEC creeps up on the Multinationals." Financial Times 5 October 1979, p. 12.

Mestmaecker, E.-J. and R. Richter, eds. "Competition Policy: German and American Experiences - A Symposium." Zeitschrift fuer die gesamte Staatswissenschaft No. 3, 1980, pp. 385-592.

Meyers, J. "Coordination Centers in Belgium." Droit et Pratique du Commerce Vol. 11, 1985, pp. 459-477.

Miles, A. "Germany: Intercompany Prices and Charges." [Summaries in English, French, and German] Intertax 1985, pp. 335-340.

"Monopolkomission will unabhaengig bleiben: Gegen Beschwerderecht/ Professoren: Fusionsverbote fuer 'Grosse'," Frankfurter Allgemeine Zeitung 13 March 1979, p. 11.

Morris, V. "Interim Measures in EEC Competition Cases." International Tax and Business Law Vol. 3, Summer 1985, pp. 102-118.

Mueller, Rudolf and Hannes Schneider. Gesetz gegen Wettbewerbsbeschraenkungen: Deutsch-Englische Textausgabe. Frankfurt am Main: Fritz Knapp Verlag, 1973.

"The Multinational's Dilemma: The IBM [IBM Corp. v. Commission of European Communities (1981) Common Market Law Reports Vol. 32 p. 93] Proceeding in Europe." Dickinson Journal of International Law Vol. 3, 1985, pp. 255-280.

Multinationals in the 1980s - Trends in European Regulation and International Control. Brussels: Agence Européen d'information, 1980.

Myers, James D. "EEC Antitrust Law: Its Development and Philosophy with Special Attention to Intellectual Property Rights." North Carolina Journal of International Law and Commercial Regulation Vol. 5, 1980, pp. 37-56.

Negandhi, Anant R. and Martin Welge. Global Rationalization Strategies of American, German and Japanese Multinational Companies. Greenwich, Connecticut: JAI Press Inc., 1984.

Niessen, H. "Proposition de septième directive concernant les comptes du groupe." Cahiers de Droit Européen Vol. 17, 1981, pp. 26-37, 57-69.

"North Sea Oil: It's British." The Economist 6 March 1976.

"North Sea Oil: Survey." The Economist 26 July 1975.

"North Sea Participation: Hollow Agreement?" The Economist 8 January 1977.

"North Sea: Statesmen and Oilmen." The Economist 20 November 1976.

Norton, Joseph J. "The European Court of Justice Judgment in United Brands: Extraterritorial Jurisdiction and Abuse of a Dominant Position." Denver Journal of International Law and Policy Vol. 8, 1979, pp. 379-414.

Novicoff, M.L. "Blocking and Clawing Back in the Name of Public Policy: The United Kingdom's Protection of Private Economic Interests Against Adverse Foreign Adjudications." New England Journal of International Law and Business Vol. 7, 1985, pp. 12-36.

Osborn, J.E. "Renegotiation of the United States-British Virgin Islands Tax Convention: Prelude to the End of Treaty Shopping?" Virginia Journal of International Law Vol. 22, 1982, pp. 381-412.

Osgood, R.K. "Interpreting Tax Treaties in Canada, the United States, and the United Kingdom." Cornell International Law Journal Vol. 17, 1984, pp. 255-297.

Petersen, M. "Capital Movements and the Payments under the EEC Treaty after Casati." European Law Review Vol. 7, 1982, pp. 167-182.

Preston, Leslie J. "The Defense of Coercive Foreign Legislation in Competition Proceedings before the Commission of the European Economic Community." Unpublished manuscript.

"Private International Couriers: A Challenge to the West German Postal Monopoly and EEC Law." Cornell International Law Journal Vol. 19, 1986, pp. 35-63.

"The Protection of Trading Interests Bill." Law Society's Gazette Vol. 76, 1979, p. 1230.

"Pull up for a gallon of BNOC." The Economist 26 July 1975.

Rahl, James A. Common Market and American Antitrust - Overlap and Conflict. New York: McGraw-Hill, 1970.

Ramos, F. "First Application by the Spanish Supreme Court of the New York Convention of June 10, 1958 to the Exequatur of Foreign Arbitral Awards." [Summary in French] Droit et Pratique du Commerce International Vol. 10, 1984, pp. 95-116.

Raupach, A. "Die Verdeckte Nutzungseinlage in Kapitalgesellschaften, ein unbewaltigtes Problem bei der Besteuerung nationaler und unternationaler Konzerne?" Wallis Collection pp. 309-326.

Rauschenbach, G. "Die Entwicklung des deutschen Kartellrechts 1977." Neue Juristische Wochenschrift 1 February 1978, p. 190.

Rauschenbach, G. "Die Entwicklung des deutschen Kartellrechts im Jahre 1978." Neue Juristische Wochenschrift 11 April 1979, p. 737.

Rauschenbach, G. "Die Entwicklung des deutschen Kartellrechts in den Jahren 1975/1976." Neue Juristische Wochenschrift 1 December 1976, pp. 2185-2191.

"Ressourcenwuerdigung bei konglomeratem Zusammenschluss." Wirtschaft und Wettbewerb/Entscheidungsammlung [des Oberlandesgerichts] zum Kartellrecht Vol. 4, 1977, p. 1745.

Reynolds, M.J. "Merger Control in the EEC." Journal of World Trade Law Vol. 17, 1983, pp. 407-426.

Riechmann, V. "Fuenf Jahre 4. Kartellgesetz-Novelle-Eine Bestandsaufnahme zur Rechtsprechungs-und Verwaltungspraxis." Wettbewerb in Recht und Praxis Vol. 31, 1985, pp. 323-330.

Rocour, Jean-Luc. "Management of European Subsidiaries in the United States." Management International Review Vol. 1, 1966, pp. 13-28.

Rogers, Paolo N. "Multinational Corporations: A European View," in D.H. Blake, ed., "The Multinational Corporation." The Annals of the American Academy of Political and Social Science Vol. 403, 1972.

Rosen, J.P. "Protection of Trading Interests Act." International Lawyer Vol. 15, 1981, pp. 213-232.

Rowe, Frederick M. "Antitrust Aspects of European Acquisitions or Joint Ventures in the United States." Paper presented at a conference on "The U.S. Antitrust Laws/Die U.S. Antitrust Gesetze: The legal implications for those entering or operating in the U.S. market." Practising Law Institute (New York)/German-American Lawyers Association (Bonn), Cologne, June 1979.

Ruiz, J.J. "Participation etrangère dans des activités économiques en Espagne: regime juridique des investissements étrangers." Thesaurus Acroasium Vol. 12, 1982, pp. 651-670.

Schaffner, Hans. Die Multinationalen - Ausbeuter oder Triebkraft der Weltwirtschaft? Zurich: Edition Interfrom, 1974.

Schlieder, Willy C. "European Competition Policy." Antitrust Law Journal Vol. 50, 1981, pp. 647-698.

Schmidt, I. "Different Approaches and Problems in Dealing with Control of Market Power: A Comparison of German, European, and U.S. Policy Towards Market-Dominating Enterprises." Antitrust Bulletin Vol. 28, 1983, pp. 417-460.

Schmidt, K. "Vertragliche Wettbewerbsverbote im deutschen Kartellrecht." Zeitschrift fuer das gesamte Handelsrecht und Wirtschaftsrecht Vol. 149, 1985, pp. 1-27.

Schmitthoff, Clive M., ed., European Company Law Texts. London: Stevens & Sons, 1974.

Schmitthoff, Clive M. "The Multinational Enterprise in the United Kingdom," in H.R. Hahlo, ed., Nationalism and the Multinational Enterprise: Legal, Economic and Managerial Aspects. Dobbs Ferry, New York: Oceana, 1973.

Schmitthoff, Clive M. "The Role of the Multinational Enterprise in an Enlarged European Community," in M.E. Bathurst, et al., eds., Legal Problems of an Enlarged European Community (British Institute Studies in International and Comparative Law No. 6). London: Stevens & Sons, 1972.

Schnor, Thomas. "Trust-Busting with a German Accent: The Control of Corporate Merger and Acquisition Activities under Increasingly Aggressive West German Law." Virginia Journal of International Law Vol. 19, 1979, pp. 595-631.

Scholsen, J.-U. "EC: The Proposal for a Council Directive on the Elimination of Double Taxation (Arbitration Procedure)." [Summaries in English, French and German] Intertax 1982, pp. 424-435.

Schroeter, H.R.B. "The Application of Art. 85 of the EEC Treaty to Exclusive Distribution Agreements." Fordham International Law Journal Vol. 8, 1984-1985, pp. 1-38.

Schwabe, J. "Enteignung in der neueren Rechtssprechung des Bundesverfassungsgerichts." Juristenzeitung Vol. 38, April 1983, pp. 273-279.

Seidel, G. "Das Verhaeltnis von Voelkerrecht und innerstaatlichem Recht im Lichte der Rechtspraxis der Bundesrepublik Deutschland." Neue Justiz Vol. 38, 1984, pp. 17-20.

Seidl-Hohenveldern, Ignaz. "Chilean Copper Nationalization Cases before German Courts." American Journal of International Law Vol. 69, 1975, pp. 110-119.

"Selective Distribution of Personal Computers in the EEC: Is Article 85 IBM Compatible?" Journal of Law and Commerce Vol. 5, 1985, pp. 505-534.

Shemanski, Donald R. "Obtaining Evidence in the Federal Republic of Germany: The Impact of the Hague Convention on German-American Judicial Cooperation." International Lawyer Vol. 17, 1983, pp. 465-487.

Sherliker, C. "Merger Regulation in the EEC." New Law Journal Vol. 134, 1984, pp. 809-812.

Simma, Bruno. Das Reziprozitaetselement in der Entstehung des Voelkergewohnheitsrechts. Munich/Salzburg: Wilhelm Fink Verlag, 1970.

Sinau, I.M. "Tied-House Agreements and the EEC Competition Rules: A Brief History." New Law Journal Vol. 135, 1985, pp. 1063-1065.

Southern Center for International Studies. Foreign Direct Investment in the Southeast: West Germany, the United Kingdom and Japan. Atlanta, Georgia, August 1979.

Squartini, P. "The EEC and the Multinational Enterprise." paper read at the International Conference on Legal Problems of Multinational Enterprises, London, British Institute of International and Comparative Law, September 1976.

Stanford, J.S. "The Application of the Sherman Act to Conduct Outside the United States: A View from Abroad." Cornell International Law Journal Vol. 11, 1978, pp. 195-214.

Steefel, Ernest C. and Bernhard von Falkenhausen. The New German Stock Corporation Law." Cornell Law Quarterly Vol. 52, 1967, pp. 518-550.

Stein, Eric and Peter Hay. Cases and Materials on the Law and Institutions of the Atlantic Area. Ann Arbor: Overbeck, 1963.

Stein, Eric and Thomas L. Nicholson, eds. Enterprise (American) in the European Common Market: A Legal Profile. (2 Vols.) Ann Arbor: University of Michigan Law School, 1960.

Stein, Eric. Harmonization of European Company Laws: National Reform and Transnational Coordination. Indianapolis: Bobbs-Merrill, 1971.

Steindorff, E. "Kapitalverkehrsfreiheit in EG nach Casati." Werner Collection pp. 877-891.

Steindorff, E. "Kartellrecht und Schiedsgerichtbarkeit." Wirtschaft und Wettbewerb Vol. 34, 1984, pp. 189-200.

Steuer, M.D., et al. The Impact of Foreign Direct Investment of the United Kingdom. (Steuer Report) HMSO, London, 1973.

Stopford, J.M. "Changing Perspectives on Investment by British Manufacturing Multinationals." Journal of International Business Studies Vol. 7, Fall-Winter 1976, pp. 15-27.

Stopford, J.M. "The Evolution of U.K.-Based Multinational Enterprises." Unpublished paper prepared at the Harvard Business School, December 1972.

Strobl, J. "German Tax Audits of Foreign Subsidiaries in Germany: Practice and Experience." European Taxation Vol. 20, 1980, pp. 273-292.

Strohmeier, R.W. "Europaisches Wahnungsystem (EWS) u. seine Auswirkung auf die Autonomie der Deutschen Bundesbank." [Summary in English] German Yearbook of International Law, Vol. 25, 1982, pp. 352-375.

Sutherland, P.D. "The Competition Policy of the European Community." St. Louis University Law Journal Vol. 30, October 1985, pp. 149-170.

Swan, George S. "EEC United Brands Decision: Can Chiquita Banana Find Happiness in Europe?" California Western International Law Journal Vol. 7, 1977, pp. 385-417.

"Taxation of French Direct Investment Abroad." [Summaries in English, French, and German] Intertax [I] August 1980, pp. 301-308; [II] September 1980, pp. 350-355; [III] October 1980, pp. 395-400; [IV] November-December 1980, pp. 430-438.

"Taxation - Renegotiation of the United States-Netherlands Antilles Tax Treaty. Convention with Respect to Taxes on Income and Certain Other Taxes. April 29, 1948, United States-Netherlands, 62 Stat. 1757, T.I.A.S. No. 1855." Texas International Law Journal Vol. 18, 1983, pp. 400-407.

Thieffry, P. "L'internationalité des contrats conclus par la succursale française d'une société étrangère." Droit et Pratique du Commerce Vol. 11, 1985, pp. 371-384.

Theising, Jochen. "Antitrust and International Law as Viewed from United States and the European Common Market." Record of the Association of the Bar of the City of New York Vol. 25, 1970, pp. 206-224.

Third General Report on the Activities of the Community. European Communities Commission, 1960.

Tillotson, John. "The GKN-Sachs Affair: A Case Study in Economic Law." Journal of World Trade Law Vol. 14, 1980, pp. 39-67.

Tittman, H.H. "Extraterritorial Application of U.S. Export Control Laws on Foreign Subsidiaries of U.S. Corporations: An American Lawyer's View from Europe." International Lawyer Vol. 16, 1982, pp. 730-737.

Toepke, U. "EEC Law of Competition: Distribution Agreements and Their Notification." International Lawyer Vol. 19, 1985, pp. 117-158.

Toms, B.C., III. "French Response to the Extraterritorial Application of U.S. Antitrust Laws." International Lawyer Vol. 15, 1981, pp. 585-614.

Torem, Charles and William Laurence Craig. "Developments in the Control of Foreign Investment in France." Michigan Law Review Vol. 70, 1971, pp. 285-337.

Tsoris, S.A. "Section C of Great Britain's Protection of Trading Interests Act: The Claw and the Lever." Cornell International Law Journal Vol. 14, 1981, pp. 457-479.

Tunc, André. "Multinational Companies in French Law," in Fritz Fabricus, ed., Law and International Trade, Festschrift fuer Clive M. Schmitthoff. Frankfurt: Athenaum Verlag, 1973.

Ulmer, P. "Gemeinschaftsunternehmen in EG-Kartellrecht." _Wirtschaft und Wettbewerb_ Vol. 29, 1979, pp. 433-447.

"Um die Fusionskontrolle wird weiter gepokert." _Frankfurter Allgemeine Zeitung_, 3 December 1979, p. 13.

"U.K. Removes Foreign Exchange Curbs." _International Herald Tribune_, 24 October 1979, p. 1.

United Kingdom. "A Review of Monopolies and Mergers Policy: A Consultative Document." Cmnd. 7198, HMSO, London, May 1978.

United Kingdom, Department of Trade. _Disclosure of Interests in Shares: A Consultative Document_. London, 11 August 1980.

"United Kingdom: International Tax Avoidance." [Summaries in English, French, and German] _Intertax_ 1982, pp. 83-89.

"United Kingdom: Taxation of International Business." [Summaries in English, French, and German] _Intertax_ 1983, pp. 186-200.

"United Kingdom: The Transfer Pricing of Multinational Enterprises." [Summaries in English, French, and German] _Intertax_ 1981, pp. 301-306.

"United Kingdom versus Unitary Taxation." _Bulletin for International Fiscal Documentation_ Vol. 38, 1984, pp. 157-161, also pp. 51-59, 153-156.

United States Department of Commerce, International Trade Administration. _Investment Climate in Foreign Countries_. (Vol.1: OECD and Other European Countries [includes Canada and Japan]; Vol. 2: Africa; Vol. 3: Asia [excluding Japan]; Vol. 4: Western Hemisphere [excluding Canada]) August, 1985.

"U.S. Challenges BASF's Purchase." _International Herald Tribune_ 19 April 1979, p. 7.

Venit, J.S. "EEC Patent Licensing Revisited: The Commisssion's Patent License Regulation." Antitrust Bulletin Vol. 30, 1985, pp. 457-526.

Venit, J.S. "Exclusive Distribution Agreements and Their Automatic Exemption from the Prohibition on Restrictive Agreements in the European Economic Community." Tidskrift, utgiven av Juridiska Foreningen 1985, pp. 173-210.

Venit, J.S. "The Research and Development Block Exemption Regulaton." European Law Review Vol. 10, 1985, pp. 151-172.

Vernon, Raymond, ed. Big Business and the State: Changing Relations in Western Europe. Cambridge: Harvard University Press, 1974.

Vogelenzang, P. "Abuse of a Dominant Position in Article 86: The Problem of Causality and Some Applications." Common Market Law Review Vol. 13, 1976, pp. 61-78.

von Gamm, O.-F. "Wein- und Bezeichnungsvorschriften des Gemeinschaftsrect und nationales Recht gegen den enlauteren Wettbewerb." Gewerblicher Rechtsschutz und Urheberrecht Vol. 86, 1984, pp. 165-169.

Ward, James J. The European Approach to U.S. Markets: Product and Promotion Adaptation by European Multinational Corporations. New York: Praeger, 1973.

Ward, James J. "Product and Promotion Adaptation by European Firms in the U.S." Journal of International Business Studies Vol. 4, Spring 1973, pp. 79-85.

Wehle, Louis B. "Government-Controlled Business Corporations in America and Europe." Address delivered 8 May 1935 in Washington, D.C. Washington, D.C.: American Bar Association, 1935.

Weis, H. "Verstaatlichungen aus gemeinschaftsrechlicher Sicht." Neue Juristische Wochenschrift Vol. 35, 1982, pp. 1910-1914.

Wengler, Wilhelm. Die Mitbestimmung und das Voelkerrecht: Ein Gutachten ueber die Vereinbarkeit der Mitbestimmungsgesetzgebung in der Bundesrepublik mit dem deutsch-amerikanischen Handelsvertrag. Baden-Baden: Nomos Verlaggesellschaft, 1975.

Wengler, Wilhelm. "Parity Codetermination in West German Companies and International Law." Vanderbilt Journal of International Law Vol. 9, 1976, pp. 1-56.

"West Germany: Monopolies Commission." Journal of World Trade Law Vol. 13, 1979, pp. 448-462.

"West Germany Probes Alleged Japanese Cartel." International Herald Tribune 7-8 March 1981, p. 11.

Wittman, Joseph I. "International Mergers under Section 7 of the Clayton Act and Article 86 of the Common Market Treaty of Rome: A Comparative Perspective." Washburn Law Journal Vol. 18, 1979, pp. 512-534.

Woelker, U. "Nationalisierungen in Frankreich 1981-2." [Summary in English and French] Zeitschrift fuer auslaendisches oeffentliches Recht und Voelkerrecht Vol. 43, 1983, pp. 213-311.

Wolf, D. "Fortentwicklung der Fusionskontrolle." Wirtschaft und Wettbewerb Vol. 30, 1980, pp. 462-474.

Zanon, DiValgiurata L. "Price Discrimination under Article 86 of the EEC Treaty: The United Brands Case." International and Comparative Law Quarterly Vol. 31, 1982, pp. 36-58.

Zimbler, B.L. "Constitutional Law: French Nationalizations." Harvard Journal of International Law Vol. 23, 1983, pp. 381-388.

Zinn, K.G. "Moeglichkeiten der Machtkontrolle von Superkonzernen durch internationale Organisationen und nationale Regierungen," in M. Krueper, ed., Investitionskontrolle gegen die Konzerne? Reinbek bei Hamburg: Rowholt, 1974.

"Zum Verhaeltnis der Monopol- und der Oligopol-vermutung in Nr. 22 Abs. 3 GWB: Kritische Anmerkungen zur Entscheidung des Kammergerichts in der Sache 'Blei- und Silber-huette Braubach' vom 16.1.1980." Betriebs-Berater Vol. 36, 1981, pp. 149-153.

9. EXPROPRIATION/NATIONALIZATION

American Society of International Law. "International Protection of Acquired Rights: Selections from the Harvard Draft Convention on International Responsibility of State for Injuries to Aliens." (Panel Discussion) Proceedings of the Fifty-Fourth Annual Meeting, 28-30 April 1960, Washington, DC, 1960, pp. 102-120.

Bernstein, H. and H. Koch. "Internationaler Konzern und deutsche Mitbestimmung." Zeitschrift fuer das gesamte Handelsrecht und Wirtschaftsrecht Vol. 143, 1979, pp. 522-538.

Brand, C.M. and D.W. Williams. "Challenging Compulsory Purchase - Comyn Ching Style." New Law Journal Vol. 133, 1983, pp. 1075-1077.

Bryan, Greyson. "Overseas Investment: Liability of U.S. Government under Expropriation Insurance Contracts - ITT Corporation, S.A. v. Overseas Private Investment Corp., 13 ILM 1307 (American Arbitration Association, 1974)." Harvard International Law Journal Vol. 16, 1975, pp. 721-739.

Burdeau, G. "La contribution des nationalisations francaises de 1982 au droit international des nationalisations." Revue Generale de Droit International Public Vol. 89, 1985, pp. 5-28.

Burton, F.N. and H. Inoue. "Expropriations of Foreign-Owned Firms in Developing Countries." Journal of World Trade Law Vol. 18, 1984, pp. 396-414.

Buxbaum, R.M. "Extension of Parent Company Shareholders' Rights to Participate in the Governance of Subsidiaries." American Journal of Comparative Law Vol. 31, 1983, pp. 511-519.

Capelli, F. "Nationalisierungen im Gemeinsamen Markt." Recht der internationalen Wirtschaft Vol. 29, 1983, pp. 313-322.

Christie, G.C. "What Constitutes a Taking of Property under International Law?" British Yearbook of International Law: 1962. London: Oxford University Press, 1964.

Clagett, Brice M. "Protection of Foreign Investment under the Revised Restatement." Virginia Journal of International Law Vol. 25, 1984, pp. 73-98.

Cooper, R.M. "Act of State Doctrine: Ethiopian Spice v. Kalamazoo Spice." Denver Journal of International Law and Politics Vol. 12, 1983, pp. 285-295.

Dawson, Frank G. and Burns H. Weston. "'Prompt, Adequate and Effective': A Universal Standard of Compensation?" Fordham Law Review Vol. 30, 1962, pp. 727-758.

Dolzer, Rudolph. "Nationale Investitionsversicherung und voelkerrechtliches Enteignungsrecht." Zeitschrift fuer auslaendisches oeffentliches Recht und Voelkerrecht Vol. 42, 1982, pp. 480-507.

Dolzer, Rudolph. "New Foundations of Law of Expropriation of Alien Property." American Journal of International Law Vol. 75, 1981, pp. 553-589.

Domke, Martin. "Foreign Nationalizations: Some Aspects of Contemporary International Law." American Journal of International Law Vol. 55, 1961, pp. 585-616.

Ebenroth, C.T. and A. Sura. "Transnationale Unternehmen und deutsches Mitbestimmungs-gesetz." Zeitschrift fuer das gesamte Handelsrecht und Wirtschaftsrecht Vol. 144, 1980, pp. 610-627.

Evans, Alona E. "Expropriation - Cuba - Extraterritorial Effect - Act of State - Trademark Infringement - Bretton Woods Agreement - Hickenlooper Amendment." American Journal of International Law Vol. 68, 1974, pp. 325-330.

"An Examination of Compensation Terms in the U.S.-Egypt Bilateral Investment Treaty." Case Western Reserve Journal of International Law Vol. 16, 1984, pp. 287-302.

"Expropriated Property, Frozen Assets, and Sovereign Immunity: Legal Obstacles to United States-China Trade Regulations." Columbia Journal of Transnational Law Vol. 15, 1976, pp. 254-276.

Folsom, Victor C. "The Taking by a State of the Property, Acquired Right, or Other Interest of a Foreign National, When No Contract is Involved," in Rights and Duties of Private Investors Abroad. New York: Matthew Bender, 1965.

Goldman, B. "Decisions du conseil constitutionnel relative aux nationalisations et le droit international." Journal du Droit International Vol. 109, 1982, pp. 275-345.

Gramlich, L. "Zur Zulaessigkeit von Vergesellschaftungen (Nationalisierungen) nach dem Grundgesetz der Bundesrepublic Deutschland." Zeitschrift fuer vergleichende Rechtswissenschaft einschliesslich der ethnologischen Rechtsvorschung Vol. 82, May 1983, pp. 165-189.

Hamon, L. "Nationalisation devant le conseil constitutionnel." Recueil Dalloz Sirey Vol. 79, March 1983, pp. 79-84.

"The Harvest of Sabbatino (Banco Nacional de Cuba v. Chase Manhattan Bank [660 F.2d 854])." North Carolina Journal of International Law and Commercial Regulation Vol. 8, 1982, pp. 87-101.

"The International Law of Compensation for Expropriation and International Debt: A Dangerous Uncertainty." Hastings International and Comparative Law Review Vol. 8, Winter 1985, pp. 223-247.

"The International Law of Expropriation of Foreign-Owned Property: The Compensation Requirement and the Role of the Taking State." Loyola of Los Angeles International and Comparative Law Journal Vol. 6, 1983, pp. 355-425.

Ipsen, J. "Enteignung, enteignungsgleicher Eingriff und Staatshaftung." Deutsches Verwaltungsblatt Vol. 98, 1983, pp. 1029-1038.

"Iran-United States Claims Tribunal: Case Concerning Starett Housing Corp., et al. and the Government of the Islamic Republic of Iran." International Legal Materials Vol. 23, 1984, pp. 1090-1142.

"Jurisdiction to Expropriate and the Shell Game of Intangible Assets." _California Western International Law Journal_ Vol. 16, 1986, pp. 373-392.

Kahale, G., III. "Characterizing Nationalizations for Purposes of the Foreign Sovereign Immunities Act and the Act of State Doctrine." _Fordham International Law Journal_ Vol. 6, 1982-1983, pp. 391-420.

Kahn, P. "Contrats d'état et nationalisation." _Journal du Droit International_ Vol. 109, 1982, pp. 844-909.

Knoepfler. "Les Nationalisations françaises face à l'ordre juridique Suisse." _Schweizerisches Jahrbuch fuer Internationales Recht_ Vol. 39, 1983, pp. 149-173.

Koticha, K.C. "Comparative Analysis of Nationalization Laws: Objectives and Techniques." _Comparative and International Law Journal of South Africa_ Vol. 8, 1975, pp. 87-99.

Leech, N. "International Banking: Effects of Nationalization and Exchange Controls." _Journal of Comparative Business and Capital Market Law_ Vol. 8, 1986, pp. 123-147.

Loyrette, J. and L. Gaillot. "French Nationalizations: The Decisions of the French Constitutional Council and Their Aftermath." _George Washington Journal of International Law and Economics_ Vol. 17, 1982, pp. 17-62.

Mann, F.A. "Outlines of a History of Expropriation." _Law Quarterly Review_ Vol. 75, 1959, pp. 188-219.

McNair, Lord. "The Seizure of Property and Enterprises in Indonesia." _Nederlands Tijdschrift voor International Recht_ Vol. 6, 1959, pp. 217-256.

Meessen, M. "Das Mitbestimmungsurteil des Bundesverfassungsgerichts." _Neue Juristische Wochenschrift_ 25 April 1979, p. 833.

Mendes, E.P. "Canadian National Energy Program: An Example of Assertion of Economic Sovereignty or Creeping Expropriation in International Law." Vanderbilt Journal of Transnational Law Vol. 14, 1981, pp. 475-507.

"Nationalization: Appropriate Standard of Compensation" - [U.S./Iran]. Harvard International Law Journal Vol. 25, 1984, pp. 491-500.

"Nationalization: The Dichotomy between Western and Third World Perspectives in International Law." Howard Law Journal Vol. 26, 1983, pp. 1547-1577.

"Nationalizations - Standard of Compensation - Nationalizing State Must Compensate Shareholders Based on Going Concern Value, Taking into Account Social and Economic Conditions." Virginia Journal of International Law Vol. 24, 1984, pp. 993-1012.

Olmstead, Cecil J., E.J. Krauland and D.F. Orentlicher. "Expropriation in the Energy Industry: Canada's Crown Share Provision as a Violation of International Law." McGill Law Journal Vol. 29, 1984, pp. 439-467.

Organisation for Economic Co-operation and Development. Draft Convention on the Protection of Foreign Property and Resolution of the Council on the Draft Convention. Paris: OECD Publication No. 23081, November 1967.

Ossenbuehl, F. "Abschied vom Enteignungsgleichen Eingriff?" Neue Juristische Wochenschrift Vol. 36, January 1983, pp. 1-6.

Ray, Dennis M. "The Causes of Expropriation of American Property Abroad." Stanford Journal of International Studies Vol. 11, 1976, pp. 122-152.

Schachter, Oscar. "Compensation for Expropriation." American Journal of International Law Vol. 78, 1984, pp. 121-130.

Schwabe, J. "Enteignung in der neueren Rechtssprechung des Bundesverfassungsgerichts." Juristenzeitung Vol. 38, April 1983, pp. 273-279.

Seidl-Hohenveldern, Ignaz. "Austrian Practice on Lump-Sum Compensation by Treaty." American Journal of International Law Vol. 70, 1976, pp. 763-777.

Seidl-Hohenveldern, Ignaz. "Chilean Copper Nationalization Cases before German Courts." American Journal of International Law Vol. 69, 1975, pp. 110-119.

Sohn, L.B. and R.R. Baxter. "Responsibility of States for Injuries to the Economic Interests of Aliens." American Journal of International Law Vol. 55, 1961, pp. 545-584.

Steindorff, E. "Gemeinschaftsunternehmen mit zwei paritaetisch beteiligten Gesellschaftern." Neue Juristische Wochenschrift Vol. 33, 1980, pp. 1921-1924.

"A Treaty Exception to the Act of State Doctrine: A Framework for Judicial Application." Boston University International Law Journal Vol. 4, 1986, pp. 201-230.

Weis, H. "Verstaatlichungen aus gemeinschaftsrechlicher Sicht." Neue Juristische Wochenschrift Vol. 35, 1982, pp. 1910-1914.

Wengler, Wilhelm. Die Mitbestimmung und das Voelkerrecht: Ein Gutachten ueber die Vereinbarkeit der Mitbestimmungsgesetzgebung in der Bundesrepublik mit dem deutsch-amerikanischen Handelsvertrag. Baden-Baden: Nomos Verlaggesellschaft, 1975.

Wengler, Wilhelm. "Parity Codetermination in West German Companies and International Law." Vanderbilt Journal of International Law Vol. 9, 1976, pp. 1-56.

Weston, Burns H. "Charter of Economic Rights and Duties of States and the Deprivation of Foreign-Owned Wealth." American Journal of International Law Vol. 75, 1981, pp. 437-475.

Weston, Burns H. "'Constructive Takings' under International Law: A Modest Foray into the Problem of 'Creeping Expropriation'." Virginia Journal of International Law Vol. 16, Fall 1975, pp. 103-176.

Weston, Burns H. "International Law and the Deprivation of Foreign Wealth: A Framework for Future Inquiry," in R.A. Falk and C.E. Black, eds., The Future of the International Legal Order, Vol. II. Princeton, New Jersey: Princeton University Press, 1970.

White, Gillian. Nationalisation of Foreign Property. New York: Praeger, 1962.

Wilkinson, H.W. "Compulsory Acquisition: Compensation for Disturbance." New Law Journal Vol. 133, 26 August 1983, pp. 755-757.

Woelker, U. "Nationalisierungen in Frankreich 1981-2." [Summary in English and French] Zeitschrift fuer auslaendisches oeffentliches Recht und Voelkerrecht Vol. 43, 1983, pp. 213-311.

Wortley, B.A. Expropriation in Public International Law. Cambridge: Cambridge University Press, 1959.

Zimbler, B.L. "Constitutional Law: French Nationalizations." Harvard Journal of International Law Vol. 23, 1983, pp. 381-388.

10. FOREIGN DIRECT INVESTMENT - GENERAL

Abraham, Neville. Big Business and Government: The New Disorder. London: Macmillan, 1974.

Adler, M. and Guy Stevens. "Direct Investment and Trade: An Analysis of the Export Displacement Effect." Allied Social Sciences Meetings, New York, December 1973.

"Advising Foreign Investors: A Symposium." Chicago Bar Record Vol. 61, 1980, pp. 255-258.

Aharoni, Y. The Foreign Investment Decision Process. Boston: Graduate School of Business Administration, Harvard University, 1966.

Aho, C.M. "Foreign Direct Investment: Theories and Empirical Evidence." Council on International Economic Policy, 28 April 1974.

Aliber, R.Z. "A Theory of Direct Foreign Investment," in C.P. Kindleberger, ed., The International Corporation. Cambridge, Massachusetts: M.I.T. Press, 1970.

American Society of International Law. "East-West Investment." International Lawyer Vol. 10, January 1976, pp. 3-134.

"Arnold Toynbee: Are Businessmen Creating a New Pax Romana?" Forbes 15 April 1974, p. 70.

Baade, Hans W. "Individual Responsibility," in C.E. Black and R.A. Falk, eds., The Future of the International Legal Order, Vol. 4 of The Structure of the International Environment. Princeton, New Jersey: Princeton University Press, 1970, 1972 (Vol. 4).

Bade, R. "Optimal Foreign Investment and International Trade." Economic Record March 1973.

Ball, George. "Cosmocorp: The Importance of Being Stateless." Columbia Journal of World Business November/December 1967, pp. 25-30.

Barnes, Louie Burton, III. "State Regulation of Foreign Investment." (Note) Cornell International Law Journal Vol. 9, 1975, pp. 82-100.

Bauer, D. Foreign Direct Investment in the U.S.: A Profile by State and Industry. Conference Board Record, February 1974.

Bell, Harold F. "Australian Government Policy in Relation to Foreign Investment." Australian Quarterly Vol. 48, 1976, pp. 44-58.

Benvind, M.W. "Strategies for Entering Foreign Markets." Hastings International and Comparative Law Review Vol. 7, 1984, pp. 293-302.

Berger, R.G. "Applying Uniform Margin Requirements to Foreign Entities Attempting to Acquire U.S. Corporations." Virginia Journal of International Law Vol. 24, 1984, pp. 543-574.

Bergsten, C. Fred and Jeffrey J. Schott. New International Arrangements for Foreign Direct Investment. Washington, D.C.: Institute for International Economics, 1986.

Berle, Adolf A. Power without Property: A New Development in American Political Economy. London: Sidgwick & Jackson, 1960.

Berle, Adolf A. and Gardiner C. Means. The Modern Corporation and Private Property, revised ed. New York: Harcourt, Brace and World, 1968.

Brems, Hans. "A Growth Model of International Direct Investment." American Economic Review Vol. 60, 1970, pp. 320-331.

Brooke, M.Z. and H.L. Remmers. The International Firm: A Study of Management Across Frontiers - Trade and Investment. London: Pitman, 1977.

Bruck, N. and F. Lees. Foreign Investments, Capital Controls, and the Balance of Payments. New York University Graduate School of Business Administration, 1968.

Buckley, P.J. "Entry Strategy of Recent European Direct Investors in the United States of America." Journal of Comparative Corporate Law and Securities Regulations Vol. 3, 1981, pp. 169-191.

Campbell, Dennis, ed. International Handbook on Comparative Business Law. Boston: Kluwer, 1979.

Caves, R. "Benefits to Host Countries from Foreign Investment." Harvard Institute of Economic Research, Discussion Paper 294, May 1973.

Clagett, Brice M. "Protection of Foreign Investment under the Revised Restatement." Virginia Journal of International Law Vol. 25, 1984, pp. 73-98.

Clauser, H.R. "Foreign Investment and the Technology Drain." Research Management September 1976.

"Closing the Open Door to FDI." Cornell International Law Journal Vol. 16, Winter 1982, pp. 121-147.

Cohen, B.I. "An Alternative Theoretical Approach to the Impact of Foreign Investment on the Host Country." Yale Economic Growth Center, Discussion Paper 164, November 1972.

"Corporations Law - Defensive Tactics to Takeover Bids." 1984 Annual Survey of American Law 1984, pp. 669-691.

Dalebroux, Jeffrey M. "Foreign Investment - Mandamus Action to Enforce the Hickenlooper Amendment." Law and Policy in International Business Vol. 7, 1975, pp. 968-973.

Dunning, John H. Studies in International Investment. London: Allen & Unwin, 1970.

Dunning, John H., ed. International Investment. New York: Penguin Books, 1972.

Dunning, John H., ed. International Investment: Selected Readings. Harmondsworth: Penguin Modern Economics Readings, 1972.

Edwards, Corwin D. "The Internationality of Economic Interests." University of Pennsylvania Law Review Vol. III, 1962, pp. 183-193.

Ellis, Clarke N. "United States Multinational Corporations: The Impact of Foreign Direct Investment on United States Foreign Relations." San Diego Law Review Vol. 11, 1973, pp. 1-26.

Fanning, E.P. "U.S. Investment in Ireland." Journal of Transnational Law Vol. 17, 1984, pp. 563-630.

Flint, D. "The Legal Protection of Foreign Investment: Development and Fairness." Lawasia: Journal for the Law Association for Asia and the Western Pacific Vol. 2, 1984, pp. 155-170.

"Foreign Investment - Capital Controls, Termination of the Interest Equalization Tax, the Foreign Direct Investment Regulations and the Voluntary Foreign Credit Restraint Guidelines." Law and Policy in International Business Vol. 6, 1974, pp. 1263-1270.

"Foreign Investment in U.S. Real Property - the Withholding Requirements." Suffolk Transnational Law Journal Vol. 9, 1985, pp. 27-55.

Foreign Trade and Investment: Special Lead Articles Edition. Mercer Law Review Vol. 27, 1976, pp. 597-825.

Forry, John I. and M.J.A. Karlin. "Current Planning for Foreign Investors in U.S. Real Estate and Other Direct Investments." New York University Institute on Federal Taxation Vol. 38, 1986, sec. 21.1-21.55.

Giles, A. Patrick. "The Mandatory Investment Restriction Programme: Past, Present and Future." Miami Law Review Vol. 23, Winter-Spring 1969.

Goff, N.M. "Liquidating the Foreign Personal Holding Company: Alternative Considerations." New England Journal of International Law and Business Vol. 6, 1984, pp. 148-202.

Graham, E.M. "A Defensive Theory of Foreign Direct Investment and European Direct Investment in the United States." Massachusetts Institute of Technology: Sloan School of Management, 1976.

Gray, H.P. The Economics of Business Investment Abroad. New York: Macmillan, 1972.

Hawkins, Robert G., Richard M. Levich and Clas G. Wihlborg. The Internationalization of Financial Markets and National Economic Policy, Vol. 3 of H. Peter Gray, ed., Research in International Business and Finance. Greenwich, Connecticut: JAI Press, 1982.

Hofbauer, M.A. "Die Einbeziehung von Fremdkapitalzinsen in die Herstellungskosten nach geltenden und kuenftigem Bilanzrecht." Wallis Collection pp. 383-395.

Horn, Norbert and Clive M. Schmitthoff. The Transnational Law of International Commercial Transactions. Antwerp, Boston: Kluwer, 1982.

Horst, T. "Firm and Industry Determinants of the Decision to Invest Abroad: An Empirical Study." The Review of Economics and Statistics Vol. 54, 1972, pp. 258-266.

Hufbauer, Gary Clyde. "The Multinational Corporation and Direct Investment." Conference on Research in International Trade and Finance, Princeton, New Jersey, 30 March 1973.

"In Support of Azania: Divestiture of Public Pension Funds As One Answer to U.S. Private Investment in South Africa." Black Law Journal Vol. 9, 1985, pp. 167-188.

Jackson, John Howard. Legal Problems of International Economic Relations: Cases, Materials, and Text on the National and International Regulation of Transnational Economic Relations. St. Paul, Minnesota: West Publishing Company, 1977.

Jenkins, G.P. "Measurement of the Gains and Losses from Foreign Investment." Harvard Institute of Economic Research, Discussion Paper 283, March 1973.

Johnson, Gregg Allen. "Comment: The Foreign Direct Investment Regulations, 1973: Balance of Payments Remedy or Regulation of Multinational Corporations?" San Diego Law Review Vol. 11, 1973, pp. 267-285.

Kemp, Murray C. The Pure Theory of International Trade and Investment. New Jersey: Prentice-Hall, 1969.

Killick, T. "The Benefits of Foreign Direct Investment and Its Alternatives: An Empirical Exploration." Journal of Development Studies January 1973, pp. 301-316.

Kindleberger, Charles P. International Economics, 4th ed. Homewood, Illinois: Richard D. Irwin, 1968.

Kojima, K. "Direct Foreign Investment Between Advanced Industrialized Countries." Hitotsubashi Journal of Economics June 1977, pp. 1-18.

Kojima, K. "A Macroeconomic Approach to Foreign Direct Investment." Hitotsubashi Journal of Economics June 1973, pp. 1-21.

Kolde, Endel J. International Business Enterprise, 2d ed. Englewood Cliffs, New Jersey: Prentice-Hall, 1973.

Kronfol, Zouhair A. Protection of Foreign Investment: A Study in International Law. Leiden: Sijthoff, 1972.

Lalive, J.-F. "Unilateral Alteration or Abrogation by Either Party to a Contract Between a State and a Foreign National," in Rights and Duties of Private Investors Abroad. New York: Matthew Bender, 1965.

Langley, M. "International Investment Survey Act: The High Cost of Knowledge." Law and Policy in International Business Vol. 14, 1982, pp. 481-504.

Laszlo, A.P. "A Survey of Techniques Employed by State and Local Governments for the Promotion of Foreign Direct Investment." George Washington Journal of International Law and Economics Vol. 18, 1983-1984, pp. 155-182.

"Legislation - The Overseas Private Investment Corporation Amendment of 1974. OPIC's functions are to be gradually phased out and its programs are to be transferred to the private insurance industry. (22 U.S.C.A. Sec. 2191-2200a, as amended (- U.S.C.A. Sec. -)." (Note) Texas International Law Journal Vol. 10, 1975, pp. 402-410.

Liebman, John R. and Beth Levine. "Foreign Investors and Equal Protection." Mercer Law Review Vol. 27, 1976, pp. 615-628.

Lipsey, R.E. and M.Y. Weiss. "Analysing Direct Investment and Trade at the Company Level." American Statistical Association Meeting, Montreal, Canada, 14-17 August 1972.

Little, L.E. "Out of Woods [Woods v. Interstate Realty Co., 304 U.S. 64] and Into the Rules: The Relationship Between State Foreign Corporaton Door-Closing Statutes and Federal Rule of Civil Procedure 17(b). Virginia Law Review Vol. 72, 1986, pp. 767-809.

Lowenfeld, Andreas F. International Private Investment, 2d edition, Vol. 2. New York: Matthew Bender, 1982.

Lowenfeld, Andreas F. International Private Trade, 2d edition, Vol. 1. New York: Matthew Bender, 1981.

Ma, V.J. "Foreign Investment in the Troubled Waters of the East China Sea." Chinese Yearbook of International Law and Affairs, Chuo Law Review Vol. 18, 1981, pp. 35-73.

McNamara, D.E. "Foreign Direct Investment in the United States: Disclosure Regulations." Georgia Journal of International and Comparative Law Vol. 12, 1982, pp. 193-207.

Messmann, S. "Autogestion ouvrière et investissements étrangers." Annuaire de l'Association des Auditeurs et Anciens Auditeurs de l'Académie de Droit International de la Haye Vol. 47-48, 1977-1978, pp. 133-138.

Morgan, H.V., Jr. "Advising the Foreign Investor in the Southeastern U.S.: Perspectives on Foreign Investment in the Southeastern U.S. An Introduction." Other articles: "The U.S. Policy Toward Foreign Direct Investment." H.E. Bale, Jr.; "Determinants of Foreign Plant Start-ups in the U.S.: Lessons for Policymakers in the Southeast." M.I. Luger and S. Shetty; "An Evaluation of Current Trends in Foreign Direct Investment in the Southeastern U.S." C.L. Suzman and J.A. Heslin; "Federal Law and State Corporation Income Taxes." C.E. McLure, Jr.; "Attribution of a Multinational Corporation's Net Income: The Position of Unitary States Regarding Combined Reporting." W.D. Dexter; "The Foreign Investor: Current Approaches Towards U.S. Immigration Law." A.T. Fragomen, Jr. and G.M. Robosson; "Foreign Investment in the U.S.: A Survey of Current Legal Literature." I.I. Kavass. Vanderbilt Journal of Transnational Law Vol. 18, 1985, pp. 191-480.

Morgan Guaranty Trust Company. "Foreign Investment: The Two-Way Street." Morgan Guaranty Survey October 1970, pp. 3-7.

Nanda, Ved P., ed. The Law of Transnational Business Transactions. New York: C. Boardman Co., 1981.

New York University School of Law/Oceana Group. International Trade, Business, and Investment: The Source of Private and Public International Law: Research Methods: Pre-Conference Tapes: A Workshop for the Law Professional. Dobbs Ferry, New York: Condyne, 1981. (This comprises two sound cassettes.)

Nickel, Herman. "The Case for Doing Business in South Africa." Fortune 19 June 1978, pp. 60-74.

Nonnenmacher, G.-G. "Les investissements étrangers." Annuaire de l'Association des Auditeurs et Anciens Auditeurs de l'Académie de Droit International de la Haye Vol. 47-48, 1977-1978, pp. 7-11.

Organisation for Economic Co-operation and Development. Investing in Free Export Processing Zones. Paris: OECD Publications, 1984.

Organisation for Economic Co-operation and Development. Investment Incentives and Disincentives and the International Investment Process. Paris: OECD Publications, 1983.

Pengilley, W. "New England Commerce Legislation: The Likely Impact on Commercial Conduct in the Light of Australian Experience." 1986 New Zealand Law Journal 1986, pp. 111-118.

Penner, R.G. "Policy Reactions and the Benefit of Foreign Ownership." Canadian Journal of Economics May 1970, pp. 213-222.

Proceedings of the United Nations Conference on Trade and Development, Second Session, Vol. 1 and Corr. 1 & 3 and Add. 1 & 2, Report and Annexes. UN Sales No. E.68.II.D.14, New York, 1968.

"A Proposal for Uniform Regulation of Foreign Investment in American Real Estate." Cornell International Law Journal Vol. 18, 1985, pp. 147-178.

"Provisional Agenda for the Fifth Session of the United Nations Conference on Trade and Development." UNCTAD Document No. TD/220, 12 April 1979.

Ragazzi, G. "Theories of the Determinants of Direct Foreign Investment." IMF Staff Papers July 1973.

"Reaction Sanctions and Foreign Incorporated Subsidiaries: Between a Rock and a Hard Place." Temple International and Comparative Law Journal Vol. 1, 1985, pp. 35-68.

Richardson, J. David. "Theoretical Considerations in the Analysis of Foreign Direct Investments." University of Michigan, Discussion Paper 18, April 1970.

Richardson, J. David. "Theoretical Considerations in the Analysis of Foreign Direct Investment." Western Economic Journal March 1971, pp. 87-97.

Rolfe, Sidney E. and W. Damm, eds. The Multinational Corporation in the World Economy: Direct Investment in Perspective. New York: Praeger, 1972.

Rubin, Seymour J. Private Foreign Investment: Legal and Economic Realities. Baltimore: Johns Hopkins Press, 1956.

Rubin, Seymour J. and Gary Clyde Hufbauer. Emerging Standards of International Trade and Investment: Multinational Code and Corporate Conduct. Totowa, New Jersey: Rowman and Allanheld, 1984.

Ruckdeschel, F. "The Determinants of a Direct Investment Outflow with Emphasis on the Supply of Funds." Ph.D. dissertation, University of Pennsylvania, 1971.

Safarian, A.E. "Perspectives on Foreign Direct Investment from the Viewpoint of a Capital Receiving Country." Journal of Finance Vol. 28, 1973, pp. 419-438.

Sawadogo, F.M. and A. Watteyne. "La cotisation obligatoire au profit de la caisse autonome d'investissements." Revue Burdinabe de Droit No. 8, pp. 165-176.

Schmitz, A. "The Impact of Trade Blocs on Foreign Direct Investment." (Notes and Memoranda) Economic Journal Vol. 80, 1970, pp. 724-731.

Schwartz, Louis B. Free Enterprise and Economic Organization, 3d edition. Vol. 1: Concentration and Restrictive Practices; Vol. 2: Regulation of Entry, Rules and Discrimination. (University Casebook Series) Mineola, New York: Foundation Press, 1966.

Schwartzenberger, Georg. Foreign Investments and International Law, 8th edition. London: Stevens & Sons, 1969.

Shihata I.F.I. "International Responses to Investment Problems. Some Basic Comments." L'Egypte Contemporaine Vol. 64, 1973, pp. 169-176.

Shihata, I.F.I. "The Multilateral Investment Guarantee Agency (MIGA) and Its Role in the Promotion of Foreign Investment." Private Investors Abroad Vol. 11, 1985, pp. 1-17.

Simmonds, Kenneth R. "Foreign Investment, The International Law Standard, and the Multinational Corporation - An Overview," in K.R. Simmonds, ed., Legal Problems of Multinational Corporations. London: The British Institute of International and Comparative Law, 1977.

Singer, Stuart R. Regulation of Foreign Investments in the United States. New York: Practicing Law Institute, 1976.

"The South African Divestment Debate: Factoring 'Political Risk' Into the Prudent Investor Rule." University of Cincinnati Law Review Vol. 55, 1986, pp. 201-216.

Sparkman, John. "The Multinational Corporation and Foreign Investment." Mercer Law Review Vol. 27, 1976, pp. 381-389.

Starrels, A.J. "A Proposal for Uniform Regulation of Foreign Investment in American Real Estate." Cornell International Law Journal Vol. 18, 1985, pp. 147-178.

"State Securities Regulation: Merit Review of Foreign Equity Offerings." Virginia Journal of International Law Vol. 25, 1985, pp. 939-965.

Surrey, Walter Sterling, A Lawyer's Guide to International Business Transactions. Philadelphia: American Law Institute-American Bar Association Joint Committee on Continuing Legal Education, 1983.

Surrey, Walter Sterling and Don Wallace, Jr. A Lawyer's Guide to International Business Transactions. Philadelphia: American Law Institute-American Bar Association Joint Committee on Continuing Legal Education, 2d ed. 1977.

Sweezy, E., J. Baranson, and J. Hopper. _Field Survey to Assess Feasibility of Collection of Data for Analysis of Foreign Direct Investment and Technology Transfer_. Washington, DC: Institute of Public Administration, 14 October 1980.

Symposium of International Business in 1971 - Problems and Solutions of Private Investors Abroad. Dallas, Texas: International and Comparative Law Center of the Southwestern Legal Foundation, 16-18 June 1971.

Tedeschi, J.A.G. "Legal Controls on Foreign Participation in the Australian Economy." _Journal of World Trade Law_ Vol. 9, 1975, pp. 573-584.

Thoman, G. Richard. _Foreign Investment and Regional Development_. New York: Praeger, 1974.

Trumpy, T.B. "Analysis of Financial Regulations and Incentives Governing Foreign Private Direct Investments." _Annuaire de l'Association des Auditeurs et Anciens Auditeurs de l'Académie de Droit International de la Haye_ Vol. 47-48, 1977-1978, pp. 114-132.

"UNCTAD V Ends Session in Manila." UNCTAD Document No. TAD/INF/1079, UNCTAD Information Unit, 5 June 1979.

United Nations. Centre on Transnational Corporations. _Salient Features and Trends in Foreign Direct Investment_. UN Sales No. E.83.II.A.8.

United States Congress. _Hearings before the Senate Committee on Foreign Relations on Executives E, G, and H_. 84th Cong. 2d sess. 3-5, 1976.

United States Department of Commerce, International Trade Administration. "International Direct Investment: Global Trends and the U.S. Role." August, 1984.

United States Department of Commerce, International Trade Administration. Investment Climate in Foreign Countries. (Vol. 1: OECD and Other European Countries [includes Japan and Canada]; Vol. 2: Africa; Vol. 3: Asia [excluding Japan]; Vol. 4: Western Hemisphere [excluding Canada]) August 1985.

United States Department of Commerce, Office of International Finance, Investment and Services. Summary of Foreign Investment Policies: A Survey of 35 Countries' Inward Investment Policy and Outward Investment Policy. January 1981.

Vagts, Detlev F. "Coercion and Foreign Investment Rearrangements." American Journal of International Law Vol. 72, 1978, pp. 17-36.

Vernon, Raymond. "Perspectives on Foreign Direct Investment: Capital Exporting Country." Annual Meeting of American Economic Association, Toronto, Canada, 27-30 December 1972.

Vitanyi, B.K.J. "Quelques réflexions sur la Convention pour le règlement des différends relatifs aux investissements entre États et ressortissents d'autres États." Annuaire de l'Association des Auditeurs et Anciens Auditeurs de l'Académie de Droit International de la Haye Vol. 47-48, 1977-1978, pp. 139-216.

Wallace, Don, ed. Negotiating Foreign Investments. Washington, D.C.: The International Law Institute, 1982.

Weigel, Dale R. and Robert R. Miller. "Foreign Direct Investment in Economic Development." International Finance Corporation, Financial Policy and Analysis Department, June 1985.

Wilkinson, Theodore. "International Accounting: Harmony or Disharmony." Columbia Journal of World Business March-April, 1969, pp. 29-36.

Willey, H. David. "Direct Investment Controls and the Balance of Payments," in Charles P. Kindleberger, ed., The International Corporation: A Symposium. Cambridge, Massachusetts: MIT Press, 1970.

Williams, Harold R. "Exchange Rate Systems, the Marginal Efficiency of Investments and Foreign Direct Capital Movements." Kyklos Vol. 26, 1973, pp. 58-74.

Wilson, Donald T. International Business Transactions in a Nutshell. St. Paul, Minnesota: West Publishing Co., 1980.

Yelpaala, K. "The Efficacy of Tax Incentives within the Framework of the Neoclassical Theory of Foreign Direct Investment: A Legislative Policy Analysis." Texas International Law Journal Vol. 19, 1984, pp. 365-414.

Yelpaala, K. "In Search of Effective Policies for Foreign Direct Investment: Alternatives to Tax Incentive Policies." New England Journal of International Law and Business Vol. 7, 1985, pp. 208-266.

Yoshino, M.Y. "Toward a Concept of Managerial Control for a World Enterprise." Michigan Business Review Vol. 18, 1966, pp. 25-31.

11. INTERNATIONAL AGREEMENTS/TREATIES

Abrutyn, M. and N. Boidman. "The New Canada-United States Tax Convention." International Lawyer Vol. 20, 1986, pp. 125-152.

"Arbitration Clauses in International Contracts and the Extraterritorial Reach of the Securities Exchange Act of 1934 in Light of Scherk v. Alberto-Culver Co. (94 S.Ct. 2449)." Syracuse Law Review Vol. 26, 1975, pp. 995-1015.

Ault, H.J. "The Unitary Tax Controversy: Federalism, Treaties and International Tax Relationships." [in English and French] Revue de Droit des Affaires Internationales/ International Business Law Journal Vol. 1985, 1985, pp. 559-571.

Bartlett, J.W., III. "In re: Oil Spill by Amoco Cadiz [1984 A.M.C. 2123] - Choice of Law and A Pierced Corporate Veil Defeat the 1969 Civil Liability Convention." Maritime Law Vol. 10, 1985, pp. 1-23.

Bergman, M.S. "Bilateral Investment Protection Treaties: An Examination of the Evolution and Significance of the U.S. Prototype Treaty." New York University Journal of International Law and Politics Vol. 16, 1983, pp. 1-43.

Boidman, N. "Canada: New Legislation Respecting Treaty Interpretation." [Summaries in English, French, and German] Intertax 1983, pp. 383-389.

Boidman, N. "Canada: Supreme Court Interprets Canada-Germany Tax Treaty." [Summaries in English, French, and German] Intertax 1983, pp. 17-21.

Boidman, N. "Interpretation of Tax Treaties in Canada." Bulletin for International Fiscal Documentation Vol. 34, 1980, pp. 388-401.

Brown, J.T. "International Joint Venture Contracts in English Law." [Summary in French] Droit et Pratique du Commerce International Vol. 5, June 1979, pp. 193-243.

"The Canada-United States Memorandum of Understanding Regarding Application of National Antitrust Law: New Guidelines for Resolution of Multinational Antitrust Enforcement Disputes." New England Journal of International Law and Business Vol. 6, 1984/1985, pp. 1065-1095.

Carasco, E.F. "The Foreign Investment Review Agency and the General Agreement on Tariffs and Trade: Incompatible?" Georgia Journal of International and Comparative Law Vol. 13, 1983, pp. 441-463.

Clarizio, L. "International Agreements: Legal Status of Locally Incorporated Subsidiaries." Harvard International Law Journal Vol. 23, 1983, pp. 431-436.

Collins, C.J. "Antitrust: EEC Treaty: Joint-Venture Agreement." Vanderbilt Journal of Transnational Law Vol. 12, 1979, pp. 775-785.

"Comparison of the F.C.P.A. and the Draft International Agreement on Illegal Payments." Vanderbilt Journal of Transnational Law Vol. 13, 1980, pp. 795-823.

"Conflict of Laws: Discovery Abroad Under Provisions of the Hague Convention - Laker Airways Ltd. v. Pan American World Airways," et. al., Nos. 82-3362, 83-0416, 83-279] (D.D.C. June 26, 1984) reported in 23 International Legal Materials 748 (1984). Harvard International Law Journal Vol. 26, 1985, pp. 201-208.

"Convention on the Service Abroad of Judicial and Extrajudicial Documents in Civil or Commercial Affairs." Opened for signature February 10, 1969, 20 U.S.T. 361, T.I.A.S. No. 6638.

"Convention on Taking of Evidence Abroad in Civil or Commercial Matters." Opened for signature March 18, 1970, 23 U.S.T. 2555, T.I.A.S. No. 6638.

Cooper, M.J. and T.J. Rasmussen. "Tax Treaty Shopping." Bulletin of International Fiscal Documentation Vol. 36, July 1982, pp. 291-297.

DeVries, H.P. "The Enforcement of Economic Development Agreements With Foreign States." University of Detroit Law Review Vol. 62, 1984, pp. 1-22.

"Developing a Model Bilateral Investment Treaty." Law and Policy in International Business Vol. 15, 1983, pp. 273-301.

"The Economic Unity Doctrine in the EEC: A Limited Exemption to Article 85 of the Treaty of Rome." Fordham International Law Journal Vol. 9, 1985/1986, pp. 373-399.

Evans, Alona E. "Expropriation - Cuba - Extraterritorial Effect - Act of State - Trademark Infringement - Bretton Woods Agreement - Hickenlooper Amendment." American Journal of International Law Vol. 68, 1974, pp. 325-330.

Evans, Alona E. "Self-Executing Treaties in the United States of America." British Yearbook of International Law Vol. 30, 1953, pp. 178-205.

"An Examination of Compensation Terms in the U.S.-Egypt Bilateral Investment Treaty." Case Western Reserve Journal of International Law Vol. 16, 1984, pp. 287-302.

"Exchange of Information under the OECD and U.S. Model Tax Treaties." Loyola of Los Angeles International and Comparative Law Journal Vol. 5, 1982, pp. 129-142.

"Extraterritorial Discovery - Hague Evidence Convention - The Hague Convention Procedures Are Not Exclusive, and Courts May Issue Discovery Orders Using Alternative Means." Virginia Journal of International Law Vol. 25, Fall 1984, pp. 249-280.

"Extraterritorial Discovery Under the Hague Evidence Convention." Villanova Law Review Vol. 31, 1986, pp. 253-290.

Fox, D.W. "The EEC Treaty: 'Abusive Exploitation' and Provision of Discount." Solicitor's Journal Vol. 130, 18 April 1986, pp. 294-296.

"Further Attacks on Treaty Shopping." European Taxation Vol. 21, 1981, pp. 141-156.

Gann, P.B. "The U.S. Bilateral Investment Treaty Program." Stanford Journal of International Law Vol. 21, 1986, pp. 373-459.

"German-U.S. Tax Treaty: German Memorandum on the Questions of Dividend Taxation." [Summaries in English, French, and German] Intertax 1980, pp. 246-262.

Goldberg, H.L. "Conventions for the Elimination of International Double Taxation: Toward a Developing Country Model." Law and Policy in International Business Vol. 15, 1983, pp. 833-909.

Goldberg, S.H. "GATT and Export Tax Incentives: The Proposed Foreign Sales Corporation." New York University Institute on Federal Taxation Vol. 42, 1984, pp. 32.1-32.36.

Goldman, B. "Fusion des sociétés et le projet de convention sur la fusion internationale des sociétés anonymnes." Cahiers de Droit Européen Vol. 17, 1981, pp. 4-14, 57-69.

Gordon, William C. "Tests for Determining the Status of a Treaty Provision as Domestic Law." (Comment) Michigan Law Review Vol. 48, 1950, pp. 852-860.

Granwell, A.W. "Treaty Shopping: Recent United States Developments." [In French and English] Revue de Droit des Affaires Internationales/International Business Law Journal Vol. 13, 1985, pp. 103-120.

Gudgeon, K.S. "United States Bilateral Investment Treaties: Comments on Their Origin, Purposes, and General Treatment Standards." International Tax and Business Law Vol. 4, 1986, pp. 105-135.

Gyselen, L. and N. Kyriazis. "Artice 86 EEC: The Monopoly Power Measurement Issue Revisited." European Law Review Vol. 11, April 1986, pp. 134-148.

"Hague Evidence Convention: A Practical Guide to the Convention, United States Case Law, Convention-Sponsored Review Commissions (1978 and 1985), and Responses of Other Signatory Nations; with digest of cases and bibliography." Georgia Journal of International and Comparative Law Vol. 16, 1986, pp. 73-107.

Heck, A. "U.S. Misinterpretation of the Hague Evidence Convention." Columbia Journal of Transnational Law Vol. 24, 1986, pp. 231-278.

Horn, Norbert. "Vertragsbindung unter veraenderten Umstaenden." Neue Juristische Wochenschrift Vol. 38, 1985, pp. 1118-1125.

Hufbauer, Gary Clyde and others. "GATT Codes and the Unconditional Most-Favored-Nation-Principle." Law and Policy in International Business Vol. 12, 1980, pp. 59-93.

International Bank for Reconstruction and Development. "Convention on the Settlement of Investment Disputes between States and Nationals of Other States." IBRD, 18 March 1965.

International Bank for Reconstruction and Development. "Regional consultative meetings of legal experts on settlement of investment disputes; Chairman's report on issues raised and suggestions made with respect to the preliminary draft of a convention on the settlement of investment disputes between states and nationals of other states." Washington: IBRD Legal Department Report No. z-11, 1964.

International Chamber of Commerce. Bilateral Treaties for the Encouragement of International Private Investment. Paris: International Chamber of Commerce Brochure 266, 1970.

Jones, J.F.A., et al. "The Interpretation of Tax Treaties with Particular Reference to Article 3(2) of the OECD Model." British Tax Review Vol. 1984, 1984, pp. 14-54.

Kahn, P. "Contrats d'état et nationalisation." Journal du Droit International Vol. 109, 1982, pp. 844-909.

Kahn, P. "Standard Investment Agreement: Text and Comments." Georgia Journal of International and Comparative Law Vol. 4, 1974, pp. 39-73.

Kooiman, K. "Article 16: The U.S. Attitude to Treaty Shopping." Bulletin for International Fiscal Documentation Vol. 37, 1983, pp. 195-200.

Langer, S.H. "Israel-EEC Free Trade Agreement: An Analysis of the Agreement and Its Effect on Investments." Syracuse Journal of International Law and Commerce Vol. 9, Spring 1982, pp. 63-113.

LeGall, J.-P. "Règle de l'arm's length serait-elle incompatible avec le traité de Rome?" [Text in French and English] Droit et Pratique du Commerce International Vol. 8, July 1982, pp. 65-85.

Loumiet, Carlos. "Toward an International Commodity Agreement on Petroleum." Denver Journal of International Law and Policy Vol. 5, 1975, pp. 485-523.

Menck, T. "Qualifitsationsconflikt im neuen deutsch-kanadischen Doppelbesteuerungsabkommen." [Summaries in English, French, and German] Intertax 1982, pp. 417-423.

Modiano, G. "Contrats de Transfert de Technologie." Droit et Practique du Commerce International Vol. 9, 1983, pp. 553-591.

"Multinational Corporations and the Lesser Developed Countries - Foreign Investment, Transfer of Technology, and the Paris Convention: Caveat Investor." University of Dayton Law Review Vol. 5, 1980, pp. 105-154.

Olmstead, Cecil J., ed. Extraterritorial Application of Laws and Responses Thereto. (Various articles: "General Theory of State Jurisdiction and Limitations Under General International Law and Under International Agreements." Cecil J. Olmstead, Chairman; "Specific Extra-territorial Applications of Jurisdiction Resulting in Conflicts." Gunther Jaenicke, Chairman; "Securities Regulation: Extra-territorial Aspects." Maarten Bos, Chairman; "Corporate Governance: Responsibilities of Directors and Officers for Acts of Foreign Subsidiaries and Affiliates." A.E. von Overbeck, Chairman; "Discovery of Documentary and Other Evidence in a Foreign Country." Richard Bentham, Chairman; "Responses to Extra-territorial Exercises of Jurisdiction." Sir Francis Vallat Q.C., Chairman) Oxford: ESC Publishing, 1984.

Organisation for Economic Co-operation and Development. Draft Convention. Paris: OECD Publication No. 15636, 1962.

Organisation for Economic Co-operation and Development. Draft Convention on the Protection of Foreign Property and Resolution of the Council on the Draft Convention. Paris: OECD Publication No. 23081, November 1967.

Osborn, J.E. "Renegotiation of the United States-British Virgin Islands Tax Convention: Prelude to the End of Treaty Shopping?" Virginia Journal of International Law Vol. 22, 1982, pp. 381-412.

Osgood, R.K. "Interpreting Tax Treaties in Canada, the United States, and the United Kingdom." Cornell International Law Journal Vol. 17, 1984, pp. 255-297.

Oxman, B.H. "The Choice Between Direct Discovery and Other Means of Obtaining Evidence Abroad: The Impact of the Hague Evidence Convention." Univerisity of Miami Law Review Vol. 37, 1983, pp. 733-795.

Paterson, R.K. "The Economic Cooperation Agreement Between Canada and ASSAN: Charting a Foreign Investment Course in South East Asia." University of British Columbia Law Review Vol. 19, 1985, pp. 389-404.

Paterson, R.K. "The GATT and Restrictions on Foreign Investment: the U.S. Challenge to Canada's Foreign Investment Law." UCLA Pacific Basin Law Journal Vol. 1, 1985, pp. 224-246.

Pattison, J.E. "The United States-Egypt Bilateral Investment Treaty: A Prototype for Future Negotiation." Cornell International Law Journal Vol. 16, 1983, pp. 305-339.

Peter, Wolfgang. Arbitration and Renegotiation of International Investment Agreements. The Netherlands: Nijhoff, 1986.

Petersen, M. "Capital Movements and the Payments under the EEC Treaty after Casati." European Law Review Vol. 7, 1982, pp. 167-182.

Ramos, F. "First Application by the Spanish Supreme Court of the New York Convention of June 10, 1958 to the Exequatur of Foreign Arbitral Awards." [Summary in French] Droit et Pratique du Commerce International Vol. 10, 1984, pp. 95-116.

Ramsey, S.D. "The United States-Australia Antitrust Cooperation Agreement: A Step in the Right Direction." Virginia Journal of International Law Vol. 24, 1983, pp. 127-169.

Rosenbloom, H.D. "Tax Treaty Abuse: Policies and Issues." Law and Policy in International Business Vol. 15, 1983, pp. 763-831.

Rosenbloom, H.D. and S.I. Langbein. "United States Tax Treaty Policy: An Overview." Columbia Journal of Transnational Law Vol. 19, 1981, pp. 359-406.

Ruchelman, S.C. and K.K. Imamura. "Intercompany Transfer Pricing Including Tax Treaty Relief." New York University Institute on Federal Taxation Vol. 42, 1984, pp. 35.1-35.43.

Sadoff, M.J. "The Hague Evidence Convention: Problems at Home of Obtaining Foreign Evidence." The International Lawyer Vol. 20, 1986, pp. 659-676.

Salacuse, J.W. "Towards a New Treaty Framework for Direct Foreign Investment." Journal of Air Law and Commerce Vol. 50, 1985, pp. 969-1010.

Schroeter, H.R.B. "The Application of Art. 85 of the EEC Treaty to Exclusive Distribution Agreements." Fordham International Law Journal Vol. 8, 1984-1985, pp. 1-38.

"The Securities Acts and International Discovery: the Hague Evidence Convention After Anschuetz [754 F.2d. 602] and Messerschmitt Bolkow Blohm [757 F.2d. 729]." Syracuse Journal of International Law and Commerce Vol. 12, 1986, pp. 600-612.

Seidl-Hohenveldern, Ignaz. "Austrian Practice on Lump-Sum Compensation by Treaty." American Journal of International Law Vol. 70, 1976, pp. 763-777.

"Selective Distribution of Personal Computers in the EEC: Is Article 85 IBM Compatible?" Journal of Law and Commerce Vol. 5, 1985, pp. 505-534.

Shemanski, Donald R. "Obtaining Evidence in the Federal Republic of Germany: The Impact of the Hague Convention on German-American Judicial Cooperation." International Lawyer Vol. 17, 1983, pp. 465-487.

Slade, D.R. "Foreign Corrupt Payments: Enforcing a Multilateral Agreement." Harvard International Law Journal Vol. 22, 1981, pp. 117-155.

"Subsidiary Assertion of Foreign Parent Corporations' Rights Under Commercial Treaties to Hire Employees 'of their Choice'." Columbia Law Review Vol. 86, 1986, pp. 139-168.

"Taxation - Renegotiation of the United States-Netherlands Antilles Tax Treaty. Convention with Respect to Taxes on Income and Certain Other Taxes. April 29, 1948, United States-Netherlands, 62 Stat. 1757, T.I.A.S. No. 1855." Texas International Law Journal Vol. 18, 1983, pp. 400-407.

Timberg, Sigmund. "An International Antitrust Convention: A Proposal to Harmonize Conflicting National Policies Towards the Multinational Corporation." Journal of International Law and Economics Vol. 8, 1973, pp. 157-184.

Tomuschat, Christian. "Die Charta der wirtschaftlichen Rechte und Pflichten der Staaten. Zur Gestaltungskraft von Deklarationen der UN-Generalversammlung: Voelkerrecht als Rechtsordnung." Zeitschrift fuer auslaendisches oeffentliches Recht und Voelkerrecht Vol. 36, 1976, pp. 444-491.

"Transnational Discovery: The Balancing Act of American Trial Courts and the Northern District of Illinois' New Approach to the Hague Convention." Washington and Lee Law Review Vol. 42, 1985, pp. 1285-1310.

"A Treaty Exception to the Act of State Doctrine: A Framework for Judicial Application." Boston University International Law Journal Vol. 4, 1986, pp. 201-230.

"United States Bilateral Investment Treaties: Egypt and Panama." Georgia Journal of International and Comparative Law Vol. 13, 1983, pp. 491-514.

Vernon, Raymond. America's Foreign Trade Policy and the GATT. Princeton, New Jersey: Princeton University Press, 1954.

Vitanyi, B.K.J. "Quelques réflexions sur la Convention pour le règlement des différends relatifs aux investissements entre États et ressortissents d'autres États." Annuaire de l'Association des Auditeurs et Anciens Auditeurs de l'Académie de Droit International de la Haye Vol. 47-48, 1977-1978, pp. 139-216.

Vogel, K. "Double Tax Treaties and Their Interpretation." International Tax and Business Lawyer Vol. 4, 1986, pp. 1-85.

Vogelenzang, P. "Abuse of a Dominant Position in Article 86: The Problem of Causality and Some Applications." Common Market Law Review Vol. 13, 1976, pp. 61-78.

"Waiver of Rights Under the Hague Convention on the Taking of Evidence Abroad in Civil or Commercial Matters." Loyola of Los Angeles International and Comparative Law Journal Vol. 7, 1984, pp. 409-438.

Walker, Herman, Jr. "Modern Treaties of Friendship, Commerce and Navigation." Minnesota Law Review Vol. 42, 1958, pp. 805-824.

Wengler, Wilhelm. Die Mitbestimmung und das Voelkerrecht: Ein Gutachten ueber die Vereinbarkeit der Mitbestimmungs-gesetzgebung in der Bundesrepublik mit dem deutsch-amerikanischen Handelsvertrag. Baden-Baden: Nomos Verlaggesellschaft, 1975.

Whittaker, D.R. "An Examination of the OECD and UN Model Tax Treaties: History, Provisions and Application to U.S. Foreign Policy." North Carolina Journal of International Law and Commercial Regulation Vol. 8, 1982, pp. 39-60.

Wilson, Robert Renbert. "A Decade of New Commercial Treaties." (Editorial Comment) American Journal of International Law Vol. 50, 1956, pp. 927-933.

Wilson, Robert Renbert. The International Law Standard in Treaties of the United States. Cambridge, Massachusetts: Harvard University Press, 1953.

Wilson, Robert Renbert. United States Commercial Treaties and International Law. New Orleans, Louisiana: Hauser Press, 1960.

Wittman, Joseph I. "International Mergers under Section 7 of the Clayton Act and Article 86 of the Common Market Treaty of Rome: A Comparative Perspective." Washburn Law Journal Vol. 18, 1979, pp. 512-534.

Yusuf, A.A. "Differential and More Favourable Treatment: The GATT Enabling Clause." Journal of World Trade Law Vol. 14, 1980, pp. 488-507.

Zanon, DiValgiurata L. "Price Discrimination under Article 86 of the EEC Treaty: The *United Brands* Case." *International and Comparative Law Quarterly* Vol. 31, 1982, pp. 36-58.

12. INTERNATIONAL AND COMPARATIVE LAW

Abbott, Greg. "Act of State Doctrine - First National City Bank v. Banco Nacionale de Cuba, 406 U.S. 759 (1972) - Casenotes." Denver Journal of International Law and Policy Vol. 3, Spring 1973, pp. 117-132.

Abed, A. and H. Abed. "Motivations pour un droit international des investissements et expérience tunisienne." Annuaire de l'Association des Auditeurs et Anciens Auditeurs de l'Académie de Droit International de la Haye Vol. 47-48, 1977-1978, pp. 57-62.

Abi-Saab, Georges. "The International Law of Multinational Corporations." Annals of International Studies Vol. 2, 1971, pp. 97-122.

Abrams, Lee N., et al. "Litigating in an International Context." (Various articles) Proceedings of the Twenty-Ninth Annual Spring Meeting of the Section of Antitrust Law of the American Bar Association, Washington, D.C., 1981. Antitrust Law Journal Vol. 50, 1981, pp. 555-616.

"Act of State Doctrine - Anti-Trust Law." Denver Journal of International Law and Politics Vol. 3, 1973, pp. 133-140.

"The Act of State Doctrine: A Shield for Bribery and Corruption. Clayco Petroleum Corp. v. Occidental Petroleum Corp., 712 F.2d 404." University of Miami Inter-American Law Review Vol. 16, 1984, pp. 167-176.

Akehurst, Michael. "Jurisdiction in International Law." The British Yearbook of International Law Vol. 46, 1972-1973, pp. 145-257.

American Bar Associaton. Act of State and Extraterrritorial Reach: Problems of Law and Policy. Washington, D.C.: American Bar Association, 1983.

American Bar Association. Current Legal Aspects of Doing Business in Latin America. Washington, D.C.: American Bar Association, 1981.

Annuaire de L'Institut de Droit International Vol. 2, 1929.

"Antisuit Injunctions and International Comity." Virginia Law Review Vol. 71, 1985, pp. 1039-1070.

"Antitrust Law: Commission of the European Communities Suspends Proceedings Against International Business Machines Corporation - 3 Common Market Law Review 147 (1984)." Harvard International Law Journal Vol. 26, 1985, pp. 189-201.

"Arbitration: Public Policy Exception to Arbitration of Antitrust Issues - Mitsubishi Motors Corp. v. Soler Chrysler-Plymouth, Inc., 723 F.2d 155." Harvard International Law Journal Vol. 25, 1984, pp. 427-433.

Bartlett, J.W., III. "In re: Oil Spill by Amoco Cadiz [1984 A.M.C. 2123] - Choice of Law and A Pierced Corporate Veil Defeat the 1969 Civil Liability Convention." Maritime Law Vol. 10, 1985, pp. 1-23.

Beyer, Wayne. "Commercial Obligations under the Act of State Doctrine: A. Dunhill of London v. Republic of Cuba." Law and Policy in International Business Vol. 8, 1976, pp. 1093-1111.

Bishop, R.D. and S. Burnette. "United States Practice Concerning the Recognition of Foreign Judgments." International Lawyer Vol. 16, 1982, pp. 425-442.

Bishop, William W., Jr. International Law: Cases and Materials. Boston: Little, Brown & Co., 1962.

Blockmann, Albert. Grundgesetz und Voelkerrecht. Berlin: Duncker & Humbolt, 1975.

Blum, Y.Z. "Economic Boycotts in International Law." Texas International Law Journal Vol. 12, 1977, pp. 5-15.

Blumberg, Phillip I. The Law of Corporate Groups: Problems in the Bankruptcy or Reorganization of Parent and Subsidiary Corporations, Including the Law of Corporate Guaranties. Boston, Massachusetts: Little, Brown & Co., 1983.

Boorman, James A., III. "Economic Coercion in International Law: The Arab Oil Weapon and the Ensuing Juridicial Issues." Journal of International Law and Economics Vol. 8-9, 1973-1974, pp. 205-231.

Bowett, Derek W. The Law of International Institutions, 3d edition. London: Stevens, 1975.

Brewer, T.L. "International Regulation of Restrictive Business Practices." Journal of World Trade Law Vol. 16, 1982, pp. 108-118.

Brower, C.N. and J.B. Tepe, Jr. "Charter of Economic Rights and Duties of States: A Reflection or Rejection of International Law?" International Lawyer Vol. 9, April 1975, pp. 295-318.

Brown, R. "The Relationship Between the State and the Multinational Corporation in the Exploitation of Resources." International and Comparative Law Quarterly Vol. 33, January 1984, pp. 218-229.

Bryan, Greyson. "Overseas Investment: Liability of U.S. Government under Expropriation Insurance Contract - ITT Corporation, S.A. v. Overseas Private Investment Corp., 13 ILM 1307 (American Arbitration Association, 1974)." Harvard International Law Journal Vol. 16, 1975, pp. 721-739.

Burtis, David, et al., eds. MNC - Nation-State Interaction: An Annotated Bibliography. Philadelphia: Foreign Policy Research Institute, 1971.

Campbell, Dennis, ed. International Handbook on Comparative Business Law. Boston: Kluwer, 1979.

Campbell, Dennis, ed. Legal Aspects of Doing Business in Western Europe (International Business Series) St.Paul, Minnesota: West Publishing Co., 1983.

Campbell, Dennis, ed. Legal Aspects of Joint Ventures in Eastern Europe. London: Kluwer, 1981.

Charney, J.I. "Transnational Corporations and Developing Public International Law." Duke Law Journal Vol. 1983, 1983, pp. 748-788.

Cherol, R.L. and S. Zalduendo. "Legal Framework for Foreign Investment in the Caribbean and Central America." International Lawyer Vol. 57, 1984, pp. 957-982.

Christie, G.C. "What Constitutes a Taking of Property under International Law?" in British Yearbook of International Law: 1962. London: Oxford University Press, 1964.

Cole, P.E. "New Challenges to the U.S. Multinational Corporaton in the European Economic Community: Data Protection Laws." New York University Journal of International Law and Politics Vol. 17, 1985, pp. 893-947.

"Commercial Law Note." (Various Notes included in each issue) Australian Law Journal Vol. 52, 1978.

"Commercial Speech, Transborder Data Flows and the Right to Communicate under International Law." International Lawyer Vol. 17, 1983, pp. 87-95.

"Conflict of Laws: Discovery Abroad Under Provisions of the Hague Convention - Laker Airways Ltd. v. Pan American World Airways," et. al., Nos. 82-3362, 83-0416, 83-2791 (D.D.C. June 26, 1984) reported in 23 International Legal Materials 748 (1984)." Harvard International Law Journal Vol. 26, 1985, pp. 201-208.

Cooper, R.M. "Act of State Doctrine: Ethiopian Spice v. Kalamazoo Spice." Denver Journal of International Law and Politics Vol. 12, 1983, pp. 285-295.

D'Amato, A.A. The Concept of Custom in International Law. Ithaca: Cornell University Press, 1971.

"Daishowa International v. No. Coast Export [1982-Z Tr. Cas. (CCH) Para. 64,774]; An Alternative Approach in the Judicial Balancing of International Comity Considerations." Law and Policy in International Business Vol. 15, 1983, pp. 613-633.

de Visscher, Paul. "La Protection diplomatique des personnes morales." Receuil des Cours Vol. 102, 1961, pp. 399-513.

Dehner, W.J., Jr. "Multinational Enterprise and Racial Non-Discrimination: United States Enforcement of an International Human Right." Harvard International Law Journal Vol. 15, 1974, pp. 71-125.

"Determining the Arbitrability of International Antitrust Disputes." Journal of Comparative Business and Capital Market Law Vol. 8, 1986, pp. 197-218.

Dolzer, R. "Nationale Investitionsversicherung und voelkerrechtliches Enteignungsrecht." Zeitschrift fuer auslaendisches oeffentliches Recht und Voelkerrecht Vol. 42, 1982, pp. 480-507.

Dolzer, Rudolf. "New Foundations of Law of Expropriation of Alien Property." American Journal of International Law Vol. 75, 1981, pp. 553-589.

Domke, Martin. "Foreign Nationalizations: Some Aspects of Contemporary International Law." American Journal of International Law Vol. 55, 1961, pp. 585-616.

Ebenroth, C.T. and L.E. Teitz. "Winning (or Losing) by Default: The Act of State Doctrine, Sovereign Immunity and Comity in International Business Transactions." International Lawyer Vol. 19, 1985, pp. 225-258.

Evans, Alona E. "Expropriation - Cuba - Extraterritorial Effect - Act of State - Trademark Infringement - Bretton Woods Agreement - Hickenlooper Amendment." American Journal of International Law Vol. 68, 1974, pp. 325-330.

"Expropriated Property, Frozen Assets, and Sovereign Immunity: Legal Obstacles to United States-China Trade Regulations." Columbia Journal of Transnational Law Vol. 15, 1976, pp. 254-276.

"Extraterritoriality: Australian Limitations on Foreign Judgement and Discovery - Foreign Proceedings (Excess of Jurisdiction) Act 1984, No. 3 Australian Acts (1984)." Harvard International Law Journal Vol. 26, 1985, pp. 578-584.

Falk, R.A. and C.E. Black, eds. The Future of the International Legal Order. Princeton, New Jersey: Princeton University Press, 1970.

Feliciano, F.P. "Legal Problems of Private International Business Enterprises: An Introduction to the International Law of Private Business Associations and Economic Development." Receuil des Cours Vol. 118, 1966, pp. 209-312.

Fernandez Flores, G.L. "Sociedades supranacionales y derecho internacionál privado." Revista española de derecho internacional Vol. 25, 1972, pp. 151-162.

Fikentscher, Wolfgang. "United Nations Codes of Conduct: New Paths in International Law." American Journal of Comparative Law Vol. 30, 1982, pp. 577-604.

Fizman, S. "Foreign Investment Law: Encouragement vs. Restraint - Mexico, Cuba and the Caribbean Basin Initiative." Hastings International and Comparative Law Review Vol. 8, 1985, pp. 147-183.

Flint, D. "The Legal Protection of Foreign Investment: Development and Fairness." Lawasia: Journal for the Law Association for Asia and the Western Pacific Vol. 2, 1984, pp. 155-170.

1974 Fordham Corporate Law Institute - International Antitrust. New York: Matthew Bender and Co., 1975.

"Foreign Sovereign Compulsion and the Arab Boycott: A State Action Analogy." Georgetown Law Journal Vol. 65, 1976-1977, pp. 1001-1023.

Friedmann, W.G., et al., ed. Transnational Law in a Changing Society, Essays in honor of Philip C. Jessup. New York: Columbia University Press, 1972.

Garcia-Amador, F.V., Louis B. Sohn and R.R. Baxter. Recent Codification of the Law of State Responsibility for Injuries to Aliens. Dobbs Ferry, New York: Oceana, 1974.

Gavalda, C. "Les succursales bancaires en droit international et spécialement en droit communautaire." [Summary in English] Droit et Pratique du Commerce Vol. 11, 1985, pp. 425-440.

Gerber, D.J. "Beyond Balancing: International Law Restraints in the Reach of National Laws." Yale Journal of International Law Vol. 10, Fall 1984, pp. 185-221.

Given, T.C. and V.A. Vilaplana. "Comity Revisited: Multinational Bankruptcy Cases under Section 304 of the Bankruptcy Code." Arizona State Law Journal Vol. 1983, 1983, pp. 525-540.

Goldman, B. "Décisions du conseil constitutionnel relative aux nationalisations et le droit international." Journal du Droit International Vol. 109, 1982, pp. 275-345.

Gotlieb, A.E. "The Legal Aspects of International Investment: The Canadian-U.S. Experience." American Society of International Law Proceedings Vol. 76, 1982, pp. 47-55.

Greiff, T.E., C.R. Stevens and J. Leow. "Applicability of U.S. Employment Discrimination Laws to Foreign Corporations in the United States - the Circuit Court Decisions in Spress v. C. Itoh and Company (American), Inc., [643 F.2d. 353] and Avagliano v. Sumitomo Shogi American Inc. [638 F.2d. 552]." UCLA Pacific Basin Law Journal Vol. 1, 1982, pp. 153-61.

Grewlich, K.W. "Transnationale Unternehmen im Voelkerrecht der Kooperation." Recht der internationalen Wirtschaft Vol. 27, 1981 pp. 353-359.

Grippando, J.M. "Declining to Exercise Extraterritorial Antitrust Jurisdiction on Grounds of International Comity: An Illegitimate Extension of the Judicial Abstention Doctrine." Virginia Journal of International Law Vol. 23, 1983, pp. 395-428.

Grossfeld, B. and C.P. Rogers. "Shared Values Approach to Jurisdictional Conflicts in International Economic Law." International and Comparative Law Quarterly Vol. 32, 1983, pp. 931-947.

Hackworth, Green Haywood. Digest of International Law, Vol. 5 (1943). Washington, D.C.: U.S. Government Printing Office, 1940-1944.

Hadari, Y. "The Choice of National Law Applicable to the Multinational Enterprise and the Nationality of Such Enterprise." Duke Law Journal Vol. 1974, 1974, pp. 1-57.

"Harvard Draft No. 11." Proceedings, American Society of International Law, 1960.

Hauser, Rita. "International Law and Economic Interrelations: Policing a Two-Way Street." Panel discussion held at International Law Weekend, Association of the Bar, City of New York and International Law Association, American Branch, New York, 1975.

Hawk, Barry E., ed. International Antitrust: Annual Proceedings of the Fordham Corporate Law Institute (1978). New York: Law and Business, 1979.

Hawk, Barry E. International Anti-Trust Manual: U.S., Common Market, and International Antitrust: A Comparative Guide. New York: Law and Business, 1979.

Hawk, Barry E. "International Antitrust Policy and the 1982 Acts: The Continuing Need for Reassessment." Fordham Law Review Vol. 51, 1982, pp. 201-254.

Hermann, A.H. Conflicts of National Laws with International Business Activity: Issues of Extraterritoriality London: British-North American Committee, 1982.

Horn, Norbert. "Entwicklung des internationalen Wirtschaftsrechts durch Verhaltensrichtlinien." [Summary in English] Rabels Zeitschrift fuer auslaendisches und internationales Privatrecht Vol. 44, 1980, pp. 423-454.

Horn, Norbert, ed. Legal Problems of Codes of Conduct for Multinational Enterprises. Antwerp, Boston: Kluwer, 1980.

Horn, Norbert and Clive M. Schmitthoff. The Transnational Law of International Commercial Transactions. Antwerp, Boston: Kluwer, 1982.

Hornsby, S.B. "Public and Private Resale Price Maintenance Systems in the Publishing Sector: The Need for Equal Treatment in European Law." European Law Review Vol. 10, 1985, pp. 381-397.

Hossain, Kamal. Law and Policy in Petroleum Developments: Changing Relations Between Transnationals and Governments: A Comparative Study Sponsored by the Commonwealth Secretariat. New York: Nichols, 1979.

Hubbard, D. "International Law Commission and the New International Economic Order." German Yearbook of International Law Vol. 22, 1979, pp. 80-99.

Hufbauer, Gary Clyde, et al. "GATT Codes and the Unconditional Most-Favored-Nation-Principle." Law and Policy in International Business Vol. 12, 1980, pp. 59-93.

Institut de Droit International. Annuaire. Vol. 57, Tome II, Session d'Oslo 1977. Basel, Switzerland: S. Karger, 1978.

"International Law - Act of State Doctrine: An Emerging Corruption Exception in Antitrust Cases?" Notre Dame Law Review Vol. 59, 1984, pp. 455-470.

"The International Law of Compensation for Expropriation and International Debt: A Dangerous Uncertainty." Hastings International and Comparative Law Review Vol. 8, Winter 1985, pp. 223-247.

"The International Law of Expropriation of Foreign-Owned Property: The Compensation Requirement and the Role of the Taking State." Loyola of Los Angeles International and Comparative Law Journal Vol. 6, 1983, pp. 355-425.

International Legal Center. Law and Public Enterprise in Asia. London: Praeger, 1976.

International Law Association. Report on the 52nd Conference of the International Law Association 1966.

"Iran-United States Claims Tribunal: Case Concerning Starett Housing Corp., et al. and the Government of the Islamic Republic of Iran." International Legal Materials Vol. 23, 1984, pp. 1090-1142.

Issues of Transnational Legal Practice: The Michigan Yearbook of International Legal Studies Vol. VII. Ann Arbor, Michigan: Michigan Yearbook of International Legal Studies, 1985.

Jackson, John Howard. Legal Problems of International Economic Relations: Cases, Materials, and Text on the National and International Regulation of Transnational Economic Relations. St. Paul: West Publishing Company, 1977.

Jackson, John Howard, Richard O. Cunningham and Claude G.B. Fontheim. International Trade Policy: The Lawyer's Perspective. New York: Matthew Bender, 1985.

Jenks, C. Wilfred. "Multinational Entities in the Law of Nations," in W.G. Friedmann et al., eds., Transnational Law in a Changing Society. Essays in honor of Philip C. Jessup. New York: Columbia University Press, 1972.

Joelson, Mark R. "International Antitrust: Problems and Defenses." Law and Policy in International Business Vol. 15, 1983, pp. 1121-1134.

Joelson, Mark R. and Joseph P. Griffin. "Legal Status of Nation-State Cartels under United States Anti-Trust and Public International Law." International Lawyer Vol. 9, 1975, pp. 617-645.

Juncadella, S. "Foreign Investment Laws of Latin America: Present and Future." International Lawyer Vol. 16, 1982, pp. 463-472.

"Jurisdiction and the Conflicts of Law - the Bhopal Litigation." Harvard International Law Journal Vol. 26, 1985, pp. 637-645.

Kahale, G., III. "Characterizing Nationalizations for Purposes of the Foreign Sovereign Immunities Act and the Act of State Doctrine." Fordham International Law Journal Vol. 6, 1982-1983, pp. 391-420.

Kennet, Wayland, et al. Sovereignty and the Multinational Companies. London: Fabian Society Tract No. 409, 1971.

Kim, Chin. "Guide to International Trade and Investment Law in Japan." Journal of World Trade Law Vol. 9, 1975, pp. 553-567.

Kohler, Rainer M. "The New Corporate Laws in Germany (1966) and France (1967) and the Trend Towards a Uniform Corporation Law for the Common Market." Tulane Law Review Vol. 43, 1968, pp. 58-71.

Korah, Valentine. "The Control of Mergers under Article 86 of the Rome Treaty: Continental Can." Current Legal Proglems Vol. 26, 1973, pp. 82-113.

Koticha, K.C. "Comparative Analysis of Nationalization Laws: Objectives and Techniques." Comparative and International Law Journal of South Africa Vol. 8, 1975, pp. 87-99.

Kronfol, Zouhair A. Protection of Foreign Investment: A Study in International Law. Leiden: Sijthoff, 1972.

"Laker Airways v. Sabena [731 F.2d. 909]: Comity and Conflict." Law and Policy in International Business Vol. 17, 1985, pp. 157-176.

Lebedoff, G. and C. Raievski. "A French Perspective on the United States Ban on the Soviet Gas Pipeline Equipment." Texas International Law Journal Vol. 18, 1983, pp. 483-507.

Lee, O. "Formation of Contract and Contract Law through Multinational Joint Ventures: Indonesia, China and the Third World." International Lawyer Vol. 17, 1983, pp. 257-281.

Lipstein, Kurt. The Law of the European Economic Community. London: Butterworth, 1974.

Litvak, I.A. and C.J. Maule. "The Multinational Corporation: Some Economic and Political Legal Implications." Journal of World Trade Law Vol. 5, 1971, pp. 631-643.

Litvak, I.A. and C.J. Maule. "The Multinational Firm and Conflicting National Interests." Journal of World Trade Law Vol. 3, 1969, pp. 309-318.

Lowenfeld, A.F. "Jurisdiction to Prescribe: Some Contributions From an International Lawyer." Boston University International Law Journal Vol. 4, 1986, pp. 91-97.

Maier, H.G. "Extraterritorial Jurisdiction at a Crossroads: An Intersection Between Public and Private International Law." American Journal of International Law Vol. 76, 1982, pp. 280-320.

Maitland-Walker, J., ed. International Anti-Trust Law Oxford: ESC Publishing, 1984. (2 Vols.) Vol. 1: A review of national laws; Vol. 2: Recent developments in EEC and U.S. Anti-Trust Laws.

Mann, F.A. Studies in International Law. Oxford: Clarendon Press, 1973.

Mann, F.A. "The Doctrine of International Jurisdiction Revisited After 20 Years." Recueil des Cours Vol. 5, 1984, pp. 9-116.

Mann, F.A. "The Doctrine of Jurisdiction in International Law." Receuil des Cours Vol. 111, 1964, pp. 1-162.

Mannick, C.V. "Antitrust: British Restrictions on Enforcement of Foreign Judgments." Harvard International Law Journal Vol. 21, 1980, pp. 727-735.

Markert, Kurt E. "Recent Developments in International Antitrust Cooperation." Antitrust Bulletin Vol. 13, 1968, pp. 355-372.

Meal, D.H. "Governmental Compulsion as a Defense under United States and European Community Antitrust Law." Columbia Journal of Transnational Law Vol. 20, 1981, pp. 51-131.

Meesen, K.M. "Antitrust Jurisdiction under Customary International Law." American Journal of International Law Vol. 78, 1984, pp. 783-810.

Mendes, E.P. "Canadian National Energy Program: An Example of Assertion of Economic Sovereignty or Creeping Expropriation in International Law." Vanderbilt Journal of Transnational Law Vol. 14, 1981, pp. 475-507.

Metzger, Stanley D. "Cartels, Combines, Commodity Agreements and International Law." Texas International Law Journal Vol. 11, 1976, pp. 527-539.

Metzger, Stanley D. "The Individual and International Law: Property Interests," in Human Rights: Protection of the Individual under International Law, proceedings of the Fifth Summer Conference on International Law, Cornell Law School, Ithaca, NY, 18-20 June 1964. South Hackensack, New Jersey: Rothman, 1970, pp. 532-543.

Moore, John B. Digest of International Law, Vol. VI. Washington, D.C.: U.S. Government Printing Office, 1906.

Multinationals in the 1980s - Trends in European Regulation and International Control. Brussels: Agence Européen d'information, 1980.

Murase, S. "International Law Making for the New International Economic Order." Japan Annual of International Law Vol. 25, 1982, pp. 45-66.

Nanda, Ved P., ed. The Law of Transnational Business Transactions. New York: C. Boardman, 1981.

"Nationalization: Appropriate Standard of Compensation" - [U.S./Iran]. Harvard International Law Journal Vol. 25, 1984, pp. 491-500.

"Nationalization: The Dichotomy between Western and Third World Perspectives in International Law." Howard Law Journal Vol. 26, 1983, pp. 1547-1577.

"Nationalizations - Standard of Compensation - Nationalizing State Must Compensate Shareholders Based on Going Concern Value, Taking into Account Social and Economic Conditions." Virginia Journal of International Law Vol. 24, 1984, pp. 993-1012.

"The New International Economic Order and General Assembly Resolutions: The Debate Over the Legal Effects of General Assembly Resolutions Revisited." California Western International Law Journal Vol. 15, 1985, pp. 647-704.

New York University School of Law/Oceana Group. International Trade, Business, and Investment: The Source of Private and Public International Law: Research Methods: Pre-Conference Tapes: A Workshop for the Law Professional. Dobbs Ferry, New York: Condyne, 1981. (This comprises two sound cassettes.)

"Norm-Creating Effect of a General Assembly Resolution on Transnational Corporations." American Society of International Law International Law Journal Vol. 5, 1981, pp. 101-127.

Nowak, G.P. "The Multinational Corporation as a Challenge to the Nation-State: A Need to Coordinate National Competition Policies." Vanderbilt Law Review Vol. 23, 1969, pp. 65-103.

O'Connell, D.P. International Law, 2d ed., Vol. II. London: Stevens & Sons, 1970.

Olmstead, Cecil J., E.J. Krauland and D.F. Orentlicher. "Expropriation in the Energy Industry: Canada's Crown Share Provision as a Violation of International Law." McGill Law Journal Vol. 29, 1984, pp. 439-467.

Olmstead, Cecil J. Extraterritorial Application of Laws and Responses Thereto. (Various articles: "General Theory of State Jurisdiction and Limitations Under General International Law and Under International Agreements." Cecil J. Olmstead, Chairman; "Specific Extra-territorial Applications of Jurisdiction Resulting in Conflicts." Gunther Jaenicke, Chairman; "Securities Regulation: Extra-territorial Aspects." Maarten Bos, Chairman; "Corporate Governance: Responsibilities of Directors and Officers for Acts of Foreign Subsidiaries and Affiliates." A.E. von Overbeck, Chairman; "Discovery of Documentary and Other Evidence in a Foreign Country." Richard Bentham, Chairman; "Responses to Extraterritorial Exercises of Jurisdiction." Sir Francis Vallat, Q.C., Chairman) Oxford: ESC Publishing, 1984.

Organisation for Economic Co-operation and Development. National Treatment for Foreign-Controlled Enterprises. Paris: OECD Publications, 1985.

Painter, Therese Eve and Dianne Zomper. "A Bibliography of Current Issues in International Business Transactions: Investment Regulation, Antitrust, Acquisitions and Mergers, Transfer of Technology, Joint Ventures, Taxation, Dispute Resolution, Transnational Tort Claims, and Export Controls." Texas International Law Journal Vol. 21, 1985, pp. 165-197.

Paquet, G., ed. The Multinational Firm and the Nation State. Canada: Collier MacMillan, 1972.

Peay, T. Michael. "The Foreign Sovereign Immunities Act of 1975: Reflections on Old Problems in a New Bill." The Black Law Journal Vol. 5, pp. 270-279.

Pinto, R. "Some Legal Aspects of International Law and Multinational Enterprises." Friedman Collection pp. 241-248.

"Potential Havens from American Jurisdiction and Discovery Laws in International Antitrust Enforcement." Univerisity of Florida Law Review Vol. 33, 1981, pp. 240-271.

"Predictability and Comity: Toward Common Principles of Extraterritorial Jurisdiction." Harvard Law Review Vol. 98, 1985, pp. 1310-1330.

Preston, Leslie J. "The Defense of Coercive Foreign Legislation in Competition Proceedings before the Commission of the European Economic Community." Unpublished manuscript.

Raman, K.V. "The Role of the International Court of Justice in the Development of International Customary Law," in American Society of International Law, Proceedings of the 65th Annual Meeting, Washington, DC, 1965.

Rao, A. and M. Shakum. "A Normative Model for Negotiations between the Multinational Corporation and a Host Government." Project working paper, New York University Graduate School of Business Administration, October 1972.

Reese, Knut. "Multinational Companies and the Nation State." Studia Diplomatica Vol. 28, 1975, pp. 27-38.

Reicin, C.V. "Act of State Doctrine: Applicability of United States Antitrust Laws." Harvard International Law Journal Vol. 23, 1982, pp. 117-123.

Responses to Fedders ["Waiver by Conduct"]. Journal of Comparative Business and Capital Market Law Vol. 6, 1984, pp. 307-318.

Ridruejo, J.A. Pastor. "La faillite en droit international privé." Receuil des Cours Vol. 133, 1971, pp. 135-221.

Riedweg, A.J. "The Extra-Territorial Application of Restrictive Trade Legislation - Jurisdiction and International Law," in International Law Association, Report on the Fifty-First Conference, 1965.

Rodley, Nigel S. "Corporate Nationality and the Diplomatic Protection of Multinational Enterprises: The Barcelona Traction Case." Indiana Law Journal Vol. 47, 1971-1972, pp. 70-86.

Rosendahl, Roger W. Current Legal Aspects of Doing Business in the Pacific Basin. Washington, D.C.: American Bar Association, 1986.

Rothschild, L., Jr. and R.E. Anthony. "World-Wide Combined Reporting: Recent Legislative Developments." Bulletin of International Fiscal Documentation Vol. 37, 1983, pp. 59-64.

Rouhani, Tuad. "Renegociation des contrats entre Etats et investisseurs prives." Revue Juridique et Politique, Independance et Cooperation Vol. 1, 1975, pp. 93-99.

Rubin, Seymour J. "Multinational Enterprise and National Sovereignty: A Skeptic's Analysis." Law and Policy in International Business Vol. 83, 1971, pp. 1-41.

Rubin, Seymour J. "Transnational Corporations and International Chambers of Commerce: A Study of the Relationship Between International Legal Co-operation and Economic Development." American University Law Review Vol. 30, 1981, pp. 903-921.

Rubin, Seymour J. "Transnational Corporations and International Law: an Uncertain Partnership." Chinese Yearbook of International Law and Affairs; Chuo Law Review Vol. 4, 1984, pp. 39-49.

Sandrock, O. "Das Kollisionsrecht des unlauteren Wettbewerbs zwischen dem internationalen Immaterialguetterrecht und dem internationalen Kartellrecht." Gewerblicher Rechtsschutz und Urheberrecht, Internationaler Tiel 1985, pp. 507-522.

Sands, Jack E. "International Law - Act of State Doctrine." Washington Law Review Vol. 49, November 1973, pp. 213-230.

Sawyier, Michael T. "Encouraging Foreign Investment in the United States by Limiting the President's Emergency Authority under the Trading with the Enemy Act." Mercer Law Review Vol. 27, 1976, pp. 681-716.

Schachter, Oscar. "Compensation for Expropriation." American Journal of International Law Vol. 78, 1984, pp. 121-130.

Schwartz, Louis B. Free Enterprise and Economic Organization, 3d edition. Vol. 1: Concentration and Restrictive Practices; Vol. 2: Regulation of Entry, Rules and Discrimination. (University Casebook Series) Mineola, New York: Foundation Press, 1966.

Schwartzenberger, Georg. Foreign Investments and International Law, 8th edition. London: Stevens & Sons, 1969.

Schwarzenberger, Georg. The Principles and Standards of International Economic Law. Leiden: Sijthoff, 1967.

Seidel, G. "Das Verhaeltnis von Voelkerrecht und innerstaatlichem Recht im Lichte der Rechtspraxis der Bundesrepublik Deutschland." Neue Justiz Vol. 38, 1984, pp. 17-20.

Seidl-Hohenveldern, I. "The Impact of Public International Law on Conflict of Law Rules on Corporations." Receuil des Cours Vol. 123, 1968, pp. 1-113.

Shishkov, Y. "International Corporations and National Sovereignty." Co-existence Vol. 11, 1974, pp. 99-103.

"The Siberian Pipeline Dispute and the Export Administration Act: What's Left of Extraterritorial Limits and the Act of State Doctrine." Houston Journal of International Law Vol. 6, Autumn 1983, pp. 63-91.

Simma, Bruno. _Das Reziprozitaetselement in der Entstehung des Voelkergewohnheitsrechts_. Munich/Salzburg: Wilhelm Fink Verlag, 1970.

Simmonds, Kenneth R. "Foreign Investment, The International Law Standard, and the Multinational Corporation - An Overview," in K.R. Simmonds, ed., _Legal Problems of Multinational Corporations_. London: The British Institute of International and Comparative Law, 1977.

Simmonds, Kenneth R. "International Law and the New International Economic Order." _General Reports 1978_, pp. 677-688.

Sohn, L.B. and R.R. Baxter. "Responsibility of States for Injuries to the Economic Interests of Aliens." _American Journal of International Law_ Vol. 55, 1961, pp. 545-584.

Spofford, Charles M. "Third Party Judgment and International Economic Transactions." _Receuil des Cours_ Vol. 113, 1964, pp. 121-236.

Stein, Eric. _Harmonization of European Company Laws: National Reform and Transnational Coordination_. Indianapolis, Indiana: Bobbs-Merrill, 1971.

Stein, Eric and Peter Hay. _Cases and Materials on the Law and Institutions of the Atlantic Area_. Ann Arbor, Michigan: Overbeck, 1963.

Steiner, Henry and Detlev F. Vagts. _Transnational Legal Problems_, 2nd edition. Mineola, New York: Foundation Press, 1976.

Stephens, Richard A. "Reevaluation of Disclosure Requirements for Foreign Issuers: Securities Exchange Act of 1934." _George Washington Law Review_ Vol. 45, 1977, pp. 135-178.

Stephenson, Hugh. _The Coming Clash: The Impact of the International Corporation on the Nation State_. London: Weidenfeld & Nicolson, 1972.

Sundstroem, G.O. Zacharias. "Comparative Law in the Development of the Law of International Corporations." Mélanges de droit comparé en l'honneur du Doyen Ahe Malmstroem Stockholm: P.A. Norstedt & Soeners Foerlag, 1972.

Surrey, Walter Sterling, A Lawyer's Guide to International Business Transactions. Philadelphia: American Law Institute-American Bar Association Joint Committee on Continuing Legal Education, 1983.

Symons, R.H.N. "Australian Foreign Investment Law." Law Institute Journal Vol. 49, 1975, pp. 506-514.

"Symposium on International and Comparative Law." South Western University Law Review Vol. 9, 1977-1978, pp. 1-175.

"Taming the Transnationals: An Examination of Structural Solutions to Regulation of Transnational Enterprise and the Theoretic Problem of Sovereignty." Western State University Law Review Vol. 7, Spring 1980, pp. 187-203.

Thiesing, Jochen. "Antitrust and International Law as Viewed from the United States and the European Common Market." Record of the Association of the Bar of the City of New York Vol. 25, 1970, pp. 206-224.

Thirlway, H.W.A. International Customary Law and Codification. Leiden: Sijthoff, 1972.

Thompson, R.B. "United States Jurisdiction over Foreign Subsidiaries: Corporate and International Law Aspects." Law and Policy in International Business Vol. 15, 1983, pp. 319-400.

Timberg, Sigmund. "An International Antitrust Convention: A Proposal to Harmonize Conflicting National Policies Towards the Multinational Corporation." Journal of International Law and Economics Vol. 8, 1973, pp. 157-184.

Timberg, Sigmund. "International Combines and National Sovereigns." University of Pennsylvania Law Review Vol. 95, 1947, pp. 575-620.

"Toward More Adequate Diplomatic Protection of Private Claims: 'Aris Gloves,' 'Barcelona Traction,' and Beyond." Round Table with the Deutsche Gesellschaft fuer Voelkerrecht. American Society of International Law, *Proceedings of the 65th Annual Meeting* Vol. 65, 1971.

"A Treaty Exception to the Act of State Doctrine: A Framework for Judicial Application." *Boston University International Law Journal* Vol. 4, 1986, pp. 201-230.

United Nations Centre on Transnational Corporations. *Measures Strengthening the Negotiating Capacity of Governments in Their Relations with Transnational Corporations: Regional Integration Cum/Versus Corporations Integration. A Technical Paper*. UN Sales No. E.82.II.A.6.

United Nations Centre on Transnational Corporations. *Measures Strengthening the Negotiating Capacity of Governments in Their Relations with Transnational Corporations: Technology Transfer Through Transnational Corporations*. UN Sales No. E.79.II.A.6.

United Nations Centre on Transnational Corporations. *National Legislation and Regulations Relating to Transnational Corporations*. UN Sales No. E.78.II.A.3.

United Nations Centre on Transnational Corporations. *National Legislation and Regulations Relating to Transnational Corporations*. UN Sales No. E.83.II.A.7.

United Nations Centre on Transnational Corporations. *National Legislation and Regulations Relating to Transnational Corporations 1984: A Technical Paper*. UN Sales No. E.83.II.A.15.

United Nations Centre on Transnational Corporations. *Supplement to National Legislation and Regulations Relating to Transnational Corporations*. UN Sales No. E.80.II.A.5.

United Nations Commission on Transnational Corporations. *National Legislation and Regulations Relating to Transnational Corporations*. Report of the Second Session, Lima, 1-12 March 1976. UN Document No. E/C.10/8.

"United States Attitudes Towards Multinational Corporations." (Various articles: Vagts: control & protection; Tillinghast: tax; Ehrenhaft: anti-dumping; Surrey: Foreign Corrupt Practices Act; Loss: extraterritoriality in FSC) *Harvard International Law Journal* Vol. 20, 1979, pp. 233-330.

Vagts, Detlev F. "The Multinational Enterprise: A New Challenge for Transnational Law." *Harvard Law Review* Vol. 83, 1970, pp. 769-792.

van Hecke, G.A. "Nationality of Companies Analyzed." *Netherlands International Law Review* Vol. 8, 1961, pp. 223-239.

Varges, Gabe Shawn. *The New International Economic Order Legal Debate: Background, Status and Alternatives*. Frankfurt am Main: Peter Lang, 1983.

VerLoren van Themaat, Pieter. *The Changing Structure of International Economic Law: A Contribution of Legal History, of Comparative Law and of General Legal Theory to the Debate on a New International Economic Order*. The Hague, Boston, London: Nijhoff, 1981.

Vernon, Raymond, ed. *Big Business and the State: Changing Relations in Western Europe*. Cambridge, Massachusetts: Harvard University Press, 1974.

Vernon, Raymond. "Multinational Enterprise and the Nation State." *Journal of Common Market Studies* Vol. 8, December 1969, pp. 160-170.

Vernon, Raymond. "Multinational Enterprise and National Sovereignty." *Harvard Business Review* Vol. 45, March-April 1967, pp. 156-172.

Vernon, Raymond. "Progress Report: Multinational Enterprise and the Nation-State." Project, Harvard Business School, 1968.

Victor, A. Paul, et al. "International Acquisitions, Joint Ventures, and Other Agreements - The Applicable Substantive and Procedural Law." (Various articles) Proceedings of the Twenty-Ninth Annual Spring Meeting of the Section of Antitrust Law of the American Bar Association, Washington, D.C., 1981. Antitrust Law Journal Vol. 50, 1981, pp. 453-496

Victor, A. Paul. "Multinational Corporations: Anti-Trust Extraterritoriality and the Prospect of Immunity." Journal of International Law and Economics Vol. 8, 1973, pp. 11-29.

Vogelaar, T. "Multinational Corporations and International Law." Netherlands International Law Review Vol. 27, 1980, pp. 69-78.

Wallace, Cynthia Day. Legal Control of the Multinational Enterprise: National Regulatory Techniques and the Prospects for International Controls. The Hague: Nijhoff, 1982.

Waller, S.W. and A.M. Simon. "Analyzing Claims of Sovereignty in International Economic Disputes." Northwestern Journal of International Law and Business Vol. 7, Spring/Summer 1985, pp. 1-11.

Waller, S.W. "Redefining the Foreign Compulsion Defense in U.S. Antitrust Law: The Japanese Auto Restraints and Beyond." Law and Policy in International Business Vol. 14, 1982, pp. 747-817.

Wengler, Wilhelm. Die Mitbestimmung und das Voelkerrecht: Ein Gutachten ueber die Vereinbarkeit der Mitbestimmungsgesetzgebung in der Bundesrepublik mit dem deutsch-amerikanischen Handelsvertrag. Baden-Baden: Nomos, 1975.

Wengler, Wilhelm. "Parity Codetermination in West German Companies and International Law." Vanderbilt Journal of Transnational Law Vol. 9, 1976, pp. 1-56.

Weston, Burns H. "'Constructive Takings' under International Law: A Modest Foray into the Problem of 'Creeping Expropriation'." Virginia Journal of International Law Vol. 16, 1975, pp. 103-176.

Weston, Burns H. "International Law and the Deprivation of Foreign Wealth: A Framework for Future Inquiry," in R.A. Falk and C.E. Black, eds., The Future of the International Legal Order, Vol. II. Princeton, New Jersey: Princeton University Press, 1970.

Wildhaber, L. "Some Aspects of the Transnational Corporation in International Law." Netherlands International Law Review Vol. 27, 1980, pp. 79-88.

Wilson, Robert Renbert. The International Law Standard in Treaties of the United States. Cambridge, Massachusetts: Harvard University Press, 1953.

Wilson, Robert Renbert. United States Commercial Treaties and International Law. New Orleans, Louisiana: Hauser Press, 1960.

Wortley, B.A. Expropriation in Public International Law. Cambridge, Massachusetts: Cambridge University Press, 1959.

Yamauchi, K. "B. Grossfeld, Transnational Corporations and the Reorientation of International Economic Law." [In Japanese]. Hogaku Shimpo (The Chuo Law Review) Vol. 30, May 1985, pp. 81-104.

Young, C.K, "Defending Litigation Against a Foreign Airline Under the Foreign Sovereign Immunities Act." Journal of Air and Commerce Vol. 51, 1986, pp. 461-494.

Yusuf, A.A. "Differential and More Favourable Treatment: The GATT Enabling Clause." Journal of World Trade Law Vol. 14, 1980, pp. 488-507.

Zaphiriou, G.A. "The U.N. Economic Charter and U.S. Investment and Policy." Mercer Law Review Vol. 27, 1976, pp. 749-780.

Zinn, K.G. "Moeglichkeiten der Machtkontrolle von Superkonzernen durch internationale Organisationen und nationale Regierungen," in M. Krueper, ed., Investitionskontrolle gegen die Konzerne? Reinbek bei Hamburg: Rowholt, 1974.

13. INTERNATIONAL COMMERCIAL CASES

"The Act of State Doctrine: A Shield for Bribery and Corruption. Clayco Petroleum Corp. v. Occidental Petroleum Corp., 712 F.2d 404." University of Miami Inter-American Law Review Vol. 16, 1984, pp. 167-176.

"Antitrust - Foreign Import Cartels are Liable under the Sherman Act Although Domestic Export Competitors are Shielded within Webb-Pomerance Exemption; Daishowa International v. No. Coast Export Co. 1982-Z Tr.Cas. No. 64,774." Vanderbilt Journal of Transnational Law Vol. 16, 1983, pp. 645-665.

"Antitrust - Noerr-Pennington [Eastern R.R. Presidents Conf. v. Noerr Motor Freight, Inc., 81 S.Ct. 523] Extends Immunity from Sherman Act to Foreign Litigation and Foreign Acts that Result in Alleged Antitrust Violations. Coastal States Marketing, Inc. v. Hunt, 694 F.2d 1358." Vanderbilt Journal of Transnational Law Vol. 16, 1983, pp. 623-644.

"Arbitration Clauses in International Contracts and the Extraterritorial Reach of the Securities Exchange Act of 1934 in Light of Scherk v. Alberto-Culver Co. (94 S.Ct. 2449)." Syracuse Law Review Vol. 26, 1975, pp. 995-1015.

"Arbitration: Public Policy Exception to Arbitration of Antitrust Issues - Mitsubishi Motors Corp. v. Soler Chrysler-Plymouth, Inc., 723 F.2d 155." Harvard International Law Journal Vol. 25, 1984, pp. 427-433.

Bartlett, J.W., III. "In re: Oil Spill by Amoco Cadiz [1984 A.M.C. 2123] - Choice of Law and A Pierced Corporate Veil Defeat the 1969 Civil Liability Convention." Maritime Law Vol. 10, 1985, pp. 1-23.

Beyer, Wayne. "Commercial Obligations under the Act of State Doctrine: A. Dunhill of London v. Republic of Cuba." Law and Policy in International Business Vol. 8, 1976, pp. 1093-1111.

Binkowski, E.S. "Timberlane: Three Steps Forward, One Step Backwards." International Lawyer Vol. 15, 1981, pp. 419-431.

Bondurant, Ward S. "Extraterritorial Jurisdiction - Antitrust - The Impact of the British Protection of Trading Interests Act on the United States Antitrust Suit Brought by Laker Airways against British Airways and British Caledonian." (Recent Developments) Georgia Journal of International and Comparative Law Vol. 14, 1984, pp. 181-200.

Born, G.B. "Recent British Responses to the Extraterritorial Application of United States Law: The Midland Bank [Midland Bank v. Laker Airways, Slip Op. (C.A. July 30, 1985)] Decision and Retaliating Legislation Involving Unitary Taxation." Virginia Journal of International Law Vol. 26, 1985, pp. 91-108.

Briggs, Herbert W. "Barcelona Traction: The Jus Standi of Belgium." American Journal of International Law Vol. 65, 1971, pp. 327-345.

Bryan, Greyson. "Overseas Investment: Liability of U.S. Government under Expropriation Insurance Contract - ITT Corporation, S.A. v. Overseas Private Investment Corp., 13 ILM 1307 (American Arbitration Association, 1974)." Harvard International Law Journal Vol. 16, 1975, pp. 721-739.

Butler, E.B. "The Extraterritorial Reach of the U.S. Export Administration Act: Reflections on the Yamal Pipeline Controversy." Journal of Business Law Vol. 1983, 1983, pp. 275-283.

Caflisch, Lucius C. "The Protection of Corporate Investments Abroad in the Light of the Barcelona Traction Case." Zeitschrift fuer auslaendisches oeffentliches Recht und Voelkerrecht Vol. 31, 1971, p. 162.

Cairns, J.P. "Economics in Court: The Consumers Glass [R. v. Consumer Glass Co. Ltd. 124 D.L.R.3d 274] Case." Canadian Business Law Journal Vol. 11, 1986, pp. 212-220.

Campbell, Barry R. "Canadian Combines Law: A Perspective on the Current Combines Investigation Act and Recent Case Law." North Carolina Journal of International Law and Commercial Regulation Vol. 5, 1980, pp. 57-90.

Cary, W.L. and M.A. Eisenberg. Cases and Materials on Corporations, 5th edition. (University Casebook Series) Mineola, New York: Foundation Press, 1969.

"Civil Procedure - Class Action Jurisdiction Over Nonresident Plaintiffs - Shutts vs. Phillips Petroleum Co. [679 P.2d.1159 (Kan.)] ("Shutts II")". University of Kansas Law Review Vol. 33, 1985, pp. 525-545.

"Civil Procedure - in personam jurisdiction - Hall v. Helicopteros Nacionales de Colombia, SA. ("Hellicol") 638 S.W.2d 870 - (Tex)." St. Mary's Law Journal Vol. 14, 1982, pp. 79-94.

"Civil Procedure - Personal Jurisdiction - Mere Purchases, Even Occurring at Regular Intervals, Are Insufficient As Contacts and Do Not Justify a State's Claim of In Personam Jurisdiction Over a Nonresident Corporation in a Claim Not Related to the Purchase Transactions. Helicopteros Nacionales de Colombia v. Hall, 104 S.Ct. 1868." Journal of Air Law and Commerce Vol. 50, 1985, pp. 321-349.

"Continental Can [Europemballage Corp. and Continental Can Inc. v. EEC Commission]." Common Market Law Reports Vol. 12, 1973, p. 199-229.

Cooper, R.M. "Act of State Doctrine: Ethiopian Spice v. Kalamazoo Spice." Denver Journal of International Law and Politics Vol. 12, 1983, pp. 285-295.

Craig, William L. "Application of the Trading with the Enemy Act to Foreign Corporations Owned by Americans: Reflections on Fruehauf v. Massardy." Harvard Law Review Vol. 83, 1970, pp. 579-601.

"Daishowa International v. No. Coast Export [1982-Z Tr. Cas. (CCH) Para. 64,774]; An Alternative Approach in the Judicial Balancing of International Comity Considerations." Law and Policy in International Business Vol. 15, 1983, pp. 613-633.

de Smith, B. "The Laker Name Lives On: Litigation, Deregulation and the Airline Industry." Public Law Vol. 1985, 1985, pp. 22-32.

"Dow Jones and Co., Inc. v. Attorney General of Canada: The Canadian Foreign Investment Review Act." Law and Policy in International Business Vol. 14, 1982, pp. 505-519.

"Dresser Industries: The Failure of Foreign Policy Trade Controls Under the Export Administration Act." Maryland Journal of International Law and Trade Vol. 8, 1984, pp. 122-143.

Dunlop, B. "Bora Laskin and Competition." University of Toronto Law Journal Vol. 35, 1985, pp. 425-437.

"Economic Internationalism v. National Parochialism: Barcelona Traction." (Note) Law and Policy in International Business Vol. 3, 1971, pp. 544-563.

Ehlers, M.J. "The Marc Rich Case: Extension of Grand Jury Subpoena Power to Nonresident Alien Corporations." George Washington Journal of International Law and Economics Vol. 18, 1983-1984, pp. 97-128.

"Extraterritorial Application of U.S. Export Laws: Dresser Industries." Wisconsin International Law Journal Vol. 1983, 1983, pp. 138-159.

"Foreign Investment: International Chamber of Commerce Court of Arbitration - Southern Pacific Properties (Middle East) Ltd. v. Arab Republic of Egypt, reprinted in 22 International Legal Materials 752 (1983)." Harvard International Law Journal Vol. 25, 1984, pp. 463-470.

Friedman, A.S. "Laker Airways [Laker Airways, Ltd. v. Sabena, 731 F.2d. 909]: The Dilemma of Concurrent Jurisdiction and Conflicting National Policies." Brooklyn Journal of International Law Vol. 11, 1985, pp. 181-236.

Garner, S.S. "Hoffman-LaRoche and Dominant Position in the EEC." Journal of International Law and Economics Vol. 14, 1980, pp. 485-508.

"The G.M.-Toyota Joint Venture and Its Implications under the National Labor Relations Act." Detroit College Law Review Vol. 1984, 1984, pp. 647-685.

"The G.M.-Toyota Joint Venture: Legal Cooperation or Illegal Combination in the World Automobile Industry?" Texas International Law Journal Vol. 19, 1984, pp. 699-728.

Guyénot, Jean. "La décision 'Continental Can' de la Commission C.E.E. et la naissance du droit antitrust européen." Rivista della Societá Vol. 17, 1972, pp. 722-741.

"The Harvest of Sabbatino (Banco Nacional de Cuba v. Chase Manhattan Bank [660 F.2d 854]). North Carolina Journal of International Law and Commercial Regulation Vol. 8, 1982, pp. 87-101.

Haubert, William H., III. "Continental Can - New Strength for Common Market Anti-Trust." (Comment) San Diego Law Review Vol. 11, 1973, pp. 227-244.

Hay, P. "Judicial Jurisdiction over Foreign-Country Corporate Defendants - Comments on Recent Case Law." Oregon Law Review Vol. 63, 1984, pp. 431-454.

"Helicopteros Nacionales de Colombia, S.A. v. Hall [104 S.Ct. 1868]: Foreign Defendants and Minimum Contacts in the Real World." Rutgers Law Review Vol. 37, 1985, pp. 609-623.

Henne, D., M.J. Levine, W.J. Usery and H. Fishgold. "A Case Study in Cross-Cultural Mediation: the General Motors-Toyota Joint Venture." Arbitration Journal Vol. 41, 1986, pp. 5-15.

Honigsberg, C.C. "Uniform Foreign Money-Judgments Recognition Act: A Survey of the Case Law." Vanderbilt Journal of Transnational Law Vol. 14, 1981, pp. 171-196.

Hurwitz, James D. "The Impact of the Continental Can Case on Combinations and Concentrations within the Common Market." Hastings Law Journal Vol. 25, 1973-1974, pp. 469-517.

"The International Center for the Settlement of Investment Disputes: Selected Case Studies." International Trade Law and Practice Vol. 7, 1982-1983, pp. 306-326.

"International Joint Ventures and Antitrust Policy: FTC Puts GM and Toyota in the Driver's Seat." Wisconsin International Law Journal Vol. 4, 1985, pp. 64-85.

"International Joint Ventures in the United States: The GM-Toyota Deal." Columbia Journal of Transnational Law Vol. 22, 1984, pp. 505-540.

"International Mass Tort Litigation: Forum Non Conveniens and the Adequate Alternative Forum in Light of the Bhopal Disaster." Georgia Journal of International and Comparative Law Vol. 16, 1986, pp. 109-166.

"International Trade: Court of International Trade Disclosure of Confidential Information - American Spring Wire Corp. v. U.S." Harvard International Law Journal Vol. 24, 1983, pp. 219-225.

"Iran-United States Claims Tribunal: Case Concerning Starett Housing Corp., et al. and the Government of the Islamic Republic of Iran." International Legal Materials Vol. 23, 1984, pp. 1090-1142.

Jackson, John Howard. Legal Problems of International Economic Relations: Cases, Materials, and Text on the National and International Regulation of Transnational Economic Relations. St. Paul, Minnesota: West Publishing Company, 1977.

"Jurisdiction and the Conflicts of Law - the Bhopal Litigation." Harvard International Law Journal Vol. 26, 1985, pp. 637-645.

"Jurisdiction over a Foreign Corporation on the Basis of its Subsidiary's Activities in New York: Bulova Watch Co. v. K. Hattori & Co. [508 F.Supp. 1322]." Brooklyn Journal of International Law Vol. 9, 1983, pp. 91-113.

"Jurisdiction over Foreign Corporations - In re Marc Rich and Co. A.G., Marc Rich and Co., A.G. v. United States, 707 F.2d 663." Harvard International Law Journal Vol. 25, 1984, pp. 250-257.

"Jurisdiction: Personal Jurisdiction Over an Alien Corporation - Helicopteros Nacionales de Colombia v. Hall, 104 S.Ct. 1868." Harvard International Law Journal Vol. 26, 1985, pp. 630-636.

Korah, Valentine. "The Control of Mergers under Article 86 of the Rome Treaty: Continental Can." Current Legal Proglems Vol. 26, 1973, pp. 82-113.

"Laker Airways v. Sabena [731 F.2d. 909]: Comity and Conflict." Law and Policy in International Business Vol. 17, 1985, pp. 157-176.

"The Laker [British Airway Bd. v. Laker Airways, Ltd. (1984) 3 All E.R. 39] Jurisdictional Affair: The Judiciary Temporarily Avoids a Political Showdown." Wakeforest Law Review Vol. 20, 1984, pp. 951-974.

"The Laker [Laker Airways, Ltd. v. Sabena, Belgian World Airlines, 731 F.2d. 909] Antitrust Litigation: The Jurisdictional 'Rule of Reason' Applied to Transnational Injunctive Relief." Cornell Law Review Vol. 71, 1986, pp. 645-667.

Langbein, V. "U.S. Unitary Taxation Methode hier: Container Corp. of America v. (California) Franchise Tax Board." Recht der internationalen Wirtschaft Vol. 29, 1983, pp. 673-676.

LeBeau, C.P. and P.J. Dostart. "Offshore Tax Planning May Be Favorably Affected by Recent Hospital Corporation [81 T.C. 520] Decision." Journal of Taxation Vol. 60, 1984, pp. 294-301.

Lillich, R.B. "Two Perspectives on the Barcelona Traction Case: The Rigidity of Barcelona" (Editorial Comment). American Journal of International Law Vol. 65, 1971, pp. 522-532.

Mann, F.A. "The Dyestuffs Case in the Court of Justice of the European Communities." International and Comparative Law Quarterly Vol. 22, 1973, pp. 35-50.

"Marc Rich [Marc Rich and Co., A.G. v. U.S., 707 F.2d 663]: An Expansion of U.S. Criminal Jurisdiction Over Foreign Defendants." _New England Journal of International Law and Business_ Vol. 6, 1984, pp. 615-645.

McFadden, D.L. "A Selected Bibliography on Hazardous Activity, Technology and the Law: Bhopal and Beyond." _International Lawyer_ Vol. 19, 1985, pp. 1459-1475.

Merciai, P. "The Euro-Siberian Gas Pipeline Dispute - A Compelling Case for the Adoption of Jurisdictional Codes of Conduct." _Maryland Journal of International Law and Trade_ Vol. 8, 1984, pp. 1-52.

Merkin, R. "The Legality of Effective Competition in EEC Law: AEG Telefunken [AEG Telefunken v. Commission of European Communities, Case 107/82] in the European Court of Justice." _Liverpool Law Review_ Vol. 6, 1984, pp. 139-165.

Metzger, Stanley D. "Two Perspectives on the Barcelona Traction Case: Nationality of Corporate Investment under Investment Guaranty Schemes - The Relevance of Barcelona Traction." (Editorial Comment) _American Journal of International Law_ Vol. 65, 1971, pp. 532-541.

Mongoven, J.F. "Theory of Actual and Potential Competition: British Oxygen Co. v. Federal Trade Commission." _Columbia Journal of Transnational Law_ Vol. 18, 1979, pp. 289-307.

"The Multinational's Dilemma: The IBM [IBM Corp. v. Commission of European Communities (1981) _Common Market Law Reports_ Vol. 32 p. 93] Proceeding in Europe." _Dickinson Journal of International Law_ Vol. 3, 1985, pp. 255-280.

Norton, Joseph J. "European Court of Justice Judgment in _United Brands_: Extraterritorial Jurisdiction and Abuse of Dominant Position." _Denver Journal of International Law and Politics_ Vol. 8, 1979, pp. 379-414.

Oakley, L. "Laker Probe: Who Will Gain?" _Sunday Times_ (London) 3 July 1983, p. 20.

Parker, Paul S. "Foreign Relations Law." (Recent Decisions) Vanderbilt Journal of Transnational Law Vol. 8, 1974, pp. 223-230.

Petersen, M. "Capital Movements and the Payments under the EEC Treaty after Casati." European Law Review Vol. 7, 1982, pp. 167-182.

"Phillips Petroleum Company v. Shutts [105 S.Ct. 2965]: Multistate Plaintiff Class Actions: A Definite Forum, But Is It Proper?" The John Marshall Law Review Vol. 19, 1986, pp. 483-499.

"The Razor's Edge: The Doctrine of Forum Non Conveniens and the Union Carbide Methyl Isocyanate Gas Disaster at Bhopal, India." North Carolina Journal of International Law and Commercial Regulation Vol. 10, 1985, pp. 743-759.

"Reaching for Documents in a Foreign Country: Marc Rich & Company vs. United States." [707 F.2d. 663]. Houston Journal of International Law Vol. 8, 1985, pp. 119-130.

Ritomsky, B.A. and R.M. Jervis. "Doing Business in America: The Unfinished Work of Sumitomo Shoji America, Inc. v. Avagliano [102 S.Ct. 2374] Harvard International Law Journal Vol. 27, 1986, pp. 193-225.

Rodley, Nigel S. "Corporate Nationality and the Diplomatic Protection of Multinational Enterprises: The Barcelona Traction Case." Indiana Law Journal Vol. 47, 1971-1972, pp. 70-86.

Rogers, C.P. "Still Running Against the Wind: A Comment on Antitrust Jurisdiction and Laker Airways, Ltd. v. Sabena, Belgian World Airlines [731 F.2d. 909]." Journal of Air Law and Commerce Vol. 50, 1985, pp. 931-967.

Schmitthoff, Clive M. "Multinationals in Court." Journal of Business Law Vol. 1972, 1972, pp. 103-111.

"The Securities Acts and International Discovery: The Hague Evidence Convention After Anschuetz [754 F.2d. 602] and Messerschmitt Bolkow Blohm [757 F.2d. 729]." Syracuse Journal of International Law and Commerce Vol. 12, 1986, pp. 600-612.

"Securities Regulation - Exterritorial Application - Continental Grain (Australia) Pty. Ltd. v. Pacific Oilseeds, Inc. [592 F.2d 409]." New York Law School Journal of International and Comparative Law Vol. 4, 1982, pp. 187-204.

"Selective Distribution of Personal Computers in the EEC: Is Article 85 IBM Compatible?" Journal of Law and Commerce Vol. 5, 1985, pp. 505-534.

"The Siberian Pipeline Dispute and the Export Administration Act: What's Left of Extraterritorial Limits and the Act of State Doctrine." Houston Journal of International Law Vol. 6, Autumn 1983, pp. 63-91.

Simson, G.J. "Return of American Banana: A Contemporary Perspective on American Anti-Trust Abroad." Journal of International Law and Economics Vol. 9, 1974, pp. 233-265.

"Soviet Reaction to the U.S. Pipeline Embargo." Maryland Journal of International Law and Trade Vol. 8, 1984, pp. 144-155.

"State Unitary Tax: The 'Risk' of Container Corporation of America v. Franchise Tax Board [103 S.Ct. 2933]. Hastings International and Comparative Law Review Vol. 9, Fall 1985, pp. 59-76.

"State Unitary Taxes Imposed on Foreign Based Multinational Groups: A Post Container Analysis." Wayne Law Review Vol. 31, 1984-1985, pp. 219-246.

Steindorff, E. "Kapitalverkehrsfreiheit in EG nach Casati." Werner Collection pp. 877-891.

"The Supreme Court Upholds Worldwide Unitary Taxation by the States of Multinational Corporation Income: Container Corporation of America v. Franchise Tax Board [103 S.Ct. 2933]." Boston College Law Review Vol. 25, May 1984, pp. 645-683.

Swan, George S. "EEC United Brands Decision: Can Chiquita Banana Find Happiness in Europe?" California Western International Law Journal Vol. 7, 1977, pp. 385-417.

"Taxation - State Taxation of Multinational Corporations: Container Corporation of America v. Franchise Tax Board, 103 S.Ct. 2933." Creighton Law Review Vol. 17, 1983-1984, pp. 857-884.

"Taxation - State Taxation on Multinational Corporations - ASARCO, Inc. v. Idaho State Tax Commission, 102 S.Ct. 1303 (1982); F.W. Woolworth Co. v. Taxation and Revenue Dept., 102 S.Ct. 3128 (1982)." Harvard International Law Journal Vol. 23, 1983, pp. 480-487.

Terez, D.G. "The Misguided Helicopteros [Helicopteros Nacionales de Columbia, S.A.V. Hall, 104 S.Ct. 1868] Case: Confusion in the Courts Over Contracts." Baylor Law Review Vol. 37, 1984, pp. 1103-1124.

Thompson, Samuel C. Federal Income Taxation of Domestic and Foreign Business Transactions: Text, Cases and Problems. Indianapolis, Indiana: Bobbs-Merrill, 1980.

Tillotson, John. "The GKN-Sachs Affair: A Case Study in Economic Law." Journal of World Trade Law Vol. 14, 1980, pp. 39-67.

"Toward More Adequate Diplomatic Protection of Private Claims: 'Aris Gloves,' 'Barcelona Traction,' and Beyond," Round Table sponsored by American Society of International Law and Deutsche Gesellschaft fuer Voelkerrecht. American Society of International Law, Proceedings of the 65th Annual Meeting Vol. 65, 1971.

"United States Antitrust Law and Industrial Policy: International Joint Ventures and Global Competition After GM-Toyota [103 F.T.C. 374]." Fordham International Law Journal Vol. 9, 1985/1986, pp. 257-294.

Wallace, Cynthia Day. "Barcelona Traction Case," in Bernhardt, ed., Encyclopedia of Public International Law, Installment 2, 1981, pp. 30-33.

Weinberg, L. "The Helicopter Case [Helicopteros Nacionales de Colombia, S.A. v. Hall, 104 S.Ct. 1868] and the Jurisprudence of Jurisdiction." Southern California Law Review Vol. 58, 1985, pp. 913-946.

Wood, Jeffrey and Victor M. Carrera. "The International Uranium Cartel: Litigation and Legal Implications." Texas International Law Journal Vol. 14, 1979, pp. 59-114.

Young, C.K, "Defending Litigation Against a Foreign Airline Under the Foreign Sovereign Immunities Act." Journal of Air and Commerce Vol. 51, 1986, pp. 461-494.

Zanon, DiValgiurata L. "Price Discrimination and Hoffman-LaRoche." Journal of World Trade Law Vol. 15, 1981, pp. 305-322.

Zanon, DiValgiurata L. "Price Discrimination under Article 86 of the EEC Treaty: The United Brands Case." International and Comparative Law Quarterly Vol. 31, 1982, pp. 36-58.

Zaucha, J.J. "The Soviet Pipeline Sanctions: The Extraterritorial Application of U.S. Export Controls." Law and Policy in International Business Vol. 15, 1983, pp. 1169-1179.

"Zum Verhaeltnis der Monopol- und der Oligopol-vermutung in Nr. 22 Abs. 3 GWB: Kritische Anmerkungen zur Entscheidung des Kammergerichts in der Sache 'Blei- und Silber-huette Braubach' vom 16.1.1980." Betriebs-Berater Vol. 36, 1981, pp. 149-153.

14. INTERNATIONAL REGULATION/CODES AND GUIDELINES

Adler, F. Michael and Gary Clyde Hufbauer. "Foreign Investment Controls: Objective - Removal." Columbia Journal of World Business Vol. 4, May/June 1969, pp. 29-37.

Athos, E. "Antitrust Law: United Nations Guidelines." Harvard International Law Journal Vol. 22, 1981, pp. 405-411.

Atkesson, T.B. and D.G. Gill. "UNCTAD Restrictive Business Practices Code: A Step in the North-South Dialogue." International Lawyer Vol. 15, 1981, pp. 1-23.

"Auf dem Weg zu einem Verhaltenskodex fuer Multis: Tagung der UNO-Kommission fuer transnationale Gesellschaften." Neue Zuercher Zeitung 30 May 1979, p. 10.

Baade, Hans W. "Codes of Conduct for Multinational Enterprises: An Introductory Survey," in Norbert Horn and E.R. Lanier, eds., Legal Problems of Codes of Conduct for Multinational Enterprises Vol. 1., Frankfurt: Kluwer, 1980.

Baade, Hans W. "The Legal Effects of Codes of Conduct for Multinational Enterprises." German Yearbook of International Law Vol. 22, 1979, pp. 11-52.

Backstiegel and A. Catranis. "Verhaltenskodex der Vereinten Nationen fur multinationale Unternehmen: Illusion oder absehbare Realitaet." Neue Juristische Wochenschrift Vol. 33, August 1980, pp. 1823-1827.

Berhman, Jack, et al. International Control of Investment: The Dusseldorf Conference on Multinational Corporations. New York: Praeger, 1974.

Blake, David H. "International Labor and the Regulation of Multinational Corporations: Proposals and Prospects." San Diego Law Review Vol. 11, 1973, pp. 179-205.

Blanpain, R. The OECD Guidelines for Multinational Enterprises and Labour Relations: 1976-1979. Experience and Review. Deventer: Kluwer, 1979.

Blanpain, R.R. "Transnational Regulation of the Labor Relations of Multinational Enterprises." Chicago-Kent Law Review Vol. 58, 1982, pp. 909-947.

Brewer, T.L. "International Regulation of Restrictive Business Practices." Journal of World Trade Law Vol. 16, 1982, pp. 108-118.

Brusick, P. "UN Control of Restrictive Business Practices." Journal of World Trade Law Vol. 17, 1983, pp. 337-351.

"Comparison of the F.C.P.A. and the Draft International Agreement on Illegal Payments." Vanderbilt Journal of Transnational Law Vol. 13, 1980, pp. 795-823.

Coolidge, Philip, George C. Spina and Don Wallace, Jr., eds. The OECD Guidelines for Multinational Enterprises: A Business Appraisal. Washington, D.C.: Institute for International and Foreign Trade Law, Georgetown University Law Center, 1977.

Coombe, G.W., Jr. "Multinational Codes of Conduct and Corporate Accountability: New Opportunities for Corporate Counsel." Business Lawyer Vol. 36, 1980, pp. 11-43.

Czako, J.M. "Set of Multilaterally Agreed Equitable Principles and Rules for Restrictive Business Practices." Law and Policy in International Business Vol. 13, 1981, pp. 313-337.

Davidow, Joel. "UNCTAD Restrictive Business Practices Code." International Lawyer Vol. 13, 1979, pp. 587-617.

Dore, I.I. "Peaceful Settlement of International Trade Disputes: Analysis of the Scope of Application of the UNCITRAL Conciliation Rules." Columbia Journal of Transnational Law Vol. 21, 1983, pp. 339-352.

Eger, J.M. "Emerging Restrictions on Transnational Data Flows: Privacy Protection or Non-Tariff Trade Barriers?" Law and Policy in International Business Vol. 10, 1978, pp. 1055-1103.

Fatouros, A.-A. "Projet de code international de conduite sur les entreprises transnationales: essai préliminaire d'évaluation." Journal du Droit International Vol. 108, 1980, pp. 5-47.

Feld, Werner J. "UN Supervision over Multinational Corporations: Realistic Expectations or Exercise in Futility?" Orbis Vol. 19, 1976, pp. 1499-1518.

Fikentscher, Wolfgang (for the Max Planck Institute for Foreign and International Patent, Copyright, and Competition Law). The Draft International Code of Conduct on the Transfer of Technology. Weinheim: Chemie, 1980.

Fikentscher, Wolfgang and W. Straub. "Kodex der Vereinten Nationen Veltkartelrechtlinien." Gewerblicher Rechtsschutz und Urheberrecht, Internationaler Teil [I] Vol. 84, 1982, pp. 637-641; [II] Vol. 84, 1982, pp. 727-739.

Fikentscher, Wolfgang. "United Nations Codes of Conduct: New Paths in International Law." American Journal of Comparative Law Vol. 30, 1982, pp. 577-604.

Fleischhauer, C.A. "UNCITRAL and International Commercial Dispute Settlement." Arbitration Journal Vol. 38, 1983, pp. 9-13.

Frank, H. "International Code of Conduct on Transfer of Technology: Some Basic Observations from a Transnational Enterprise's Viewpoint and Some Related Conclusions." German Yearbook of International Law Vol. 24, 1981, pp. 367-376.

Fulda, Carl H. and Warren F. Schwartz. Regulation of International Trade and Investment. (University Casebook Series) Mineola, New York: Foundation Press, 1970.

Garcia-Amador, F.V., Louis B. Sohn and R.R. Baxter. Recent Codification of the Law of State Responsibility for Injuries to Aliens. Dobbs Ferry, New York: Oceana, 1974.

Gill, David. "The UNCTAD Restrictive Business Practices Code: A Code for Competition?" International Lawyer Vol. 13, 1979, pp. 607-617.

Greene, James. The Search for Common Ground. New York: The U.S. Conference Board, 1971.

Griffin, S. "UN Set of Multilaterally Agreed Equitable Principles and Rules for the Control of Restrictive Business Practices." Georgia Journal of International and Comparative Law Vol. 11, 1981, pp. 709-721.

Grigera Naón, Horacio A. "Reflexiones sobre los problemas suscitados por la adopción de una legislación uniforme sobre grupos multinacionales de sociedades in la C.E.E." Derecho de la Integración Vol. 8, 1975, pp. 323-341.

Grosse, R. "Codes of Conduct for Multinational Enterprises." Journal of World Trade Law Vol. 16, 1982, pp. 414-433.

Guenter, H. "International Labor Organisation Declaration of Multinational Enterprises and the International Code of Conduct Movement." Loyola of Los Angeles International and Comparative Law Journal Vol. 4, 1981, pp. 1-25.

Hawk, Barry E. International Anti-Trust Manual: U.S., Common Market, and International Antitrust: A Comparative Guide. New York: Law and Business, 1979.

Hawk, Barry E. "The OECD Guidelines for Multinational Enterprises: Competition." Fordham Law Review Vol. 46, 1978, pp. 241-276.

Hekrassow, Arkadi. "Transnationale Gesellschaften und zwischenstaatliche Kontrolle im Rahmen der UNO." Deutsche Aussenpolitik Vol. 20, 1975, pp. 84-95.

Horn, Norbert. "Entwicklung des internationalen Wirtschafts rechts durch Verhaltensrichtlinien." [Summary in English] Rabels Zeitschrift fuer auslaendisches und internationales Privatrecht Vol. 44, 1980, pp. 423-454.

Horn, Norbert, ed. Legal Problems of Codes of Conduct for Multinational Enterprises. Antwerp, Boston: Kluwer, 1980.

"Host-State Treatment of Transnational Corporations: Formulation of a Standard for the UN Code of Conduct on Transnational Corporations." Fordham International Law Journal Vol. 7, 1983-1984, pp. 467-500.

Houzhi, T. "UNCITRAL's Work on a Model Law on International Commercial Disputes." Pace Law Review Vol. 4, 1983-1984, pp. 519-627.

International Bar Association. Codes of Conduct for Transnational Corporations: Signals of Public Expectation? Berlin: International Bar Association, 1980.

International Chamber of Commerce. Guidelines for International Investment. Paris: ICC Publications, 1974.

International Labour Organisation. Tripartite Declaration of Principles concerning Multinational Enterprises and Social Policy. Geneva: International Labour Office, 1977.

Jackson, John Howard. Legal Problems of International Economic Relations: Cases, Materials, and Text on the National and International Regulation of Transnational Economic Relations. St. Paul, Minnesota: West Publishing Company, 1977.

Joelson, Mark R. "Proposed International Codes of Conduct as Related to Restrictive Business Practices." Law and Policy in International Business Vol. 8, 1976, pp. 837-874.

Jones, J.F.A. et al. "The Interpretation of Tax Treaties with Particular Reference to Article 3(2) of the OECD Model." British Tax Review Vol. 1984, pp. 14-54.

Keshane, Robert G. and Van Doom Ooms. "The Multinational Firm and International Regulation." International Organization Vol. 29, 1975, pp. 169-209.

Krueper, Manfred, ed. Investitionskontrolle gegen die Konzerne?. Reinbek bei Hamburg: Rowholt, 1974.

Langer, G. "Koennen multinationale Unternehmen international kontrolliert werden?" Aussenwirtschaftsdienst des Betriebs Beraters Contd. by Recht der Internationalen Wirtschaft Vol. 19, 1973, pp. 645-658.

Linde, Stephen A. "Regulation of Transfer Pricing in Multinational Corporations: An International Perspective." New York University Journal of International Law and Politics Vol. 10, 1977, pp. 67-123.

Lowenfeld, A.F., et al. "Extraterritoriality: Conflict and Overlap in National and International Regulation." American Society of International Law Proceedings 74th Meeting, 1980, pp. 30-48.

Merciai, P. "The Euro-Siberian Gas Pipeline Dispute - A Compelling Case for the Adoption of Jurisdictional Codes of Conduct." Maryland Journal of International Law and Trade Vol. 8, 1984, pp. 1-52.

Modiano, G. "Contrats de Transfert de Technologie." Droit et Pratique du Commerce International Vol. 9, 1983, pp. 553-591.

Morgenstern, F. "Déclaration de principes tripartite de l'O.I.T. sur les entreprises multinationales et la politique sociale: nouveaux problèmes, nouvelles méthodes." Journal du Droit International Vol. 110, 1983, pp. 61-75.

"Multinational Regulation of Multinational Enterprise Labor Relations." Boston College International and Comparative Law Review Vol. 4, 1981, pp. 409-451.

Nehemkis, P. "Supernational Control of the International Corporation: A Dissenting View." California Western Law Review Vol. 10, 1974, pp. 286-324.

"Norm-Creating Effect of a General Assembly Resolution on Transnational Corporations." American Society of International Law International Law Journal Vol. 5, 1981, pp. 101-127.

"OECD: Work on Tax Avoidance and Evasion." [Summaries in English, French, and German] Intertax 1980, pp. 9-16.

Oesterle, D.A. "United Nations Conference on Restrictive Business Practices." Cornell International Law Journal Vol. 14, 1981, pp. 1-55.

Organisation for Economic Co-operation and Development, Committee on International Investment and Multinational Enterprises. Review of the 1976 Declaration and Decisions on International Investment and Multinational Enterprises. Paris: OECD Publications, 1979.

Organisation for Economic Co-operation and Development. "Declaration on International Investment and Multinational Enterprises by the Governments of OECD Member Countries" 21 June 1976. International Investment and Multinational Enterprises Paris: OECD Publications, 1976.

Organisation for Economic Co-operation and Development. "The Draft Convention on the Protection of Foreign Property." Paris: OECD Publications, 1967.

Organisation for Economic Co-operation and Development. International Investment and Multinational Corporations: 1984 Review of the 1976 Declarations and Decisions. Paris: OECD Publications, 1984.

Organisation for Economic Co-operation and Development. OECD Guidelines. Paris: OECD Publications, 1986.

Organisation for Economic Co-operation and Development, Committee on International Investment and Multinational Enterprises. Review of the 1976 Declaration and Decisions on International Investment and Multinational Enterprises. Paris: OECD Publications, 1979.

Oyebode, Esq., Akendale Bobatunde. "International Regulation of the Multinational Corporation: A Look at Some Recent Proposals." Black Law Journal Vol. 5, 1977, pp. 231-248.

Perlmutter, Howard V. "Perplexing Routes to M.N.E. Legitimacy: Codes of Conduct for Technology Transfer." Stanford Journal of International Studies Vol. 11, pp. 169-199.

Planic, Daniel J. "The OECD Guidelines for Multinational Enterprises." International Lawyer Vol. 11, 1977, pp. 339-446.

Reynolds, T.H. "Clouds of Codes: The New International Economic Order through Codes of Conduct: A Survey." Law Library Journal Vol. 75, 1982, pp. 315-354.

Roffe, P. "Transfer of Technology: UNCTAD's Draft International Code of Conduct." International Lawyer Vol. 19, 1985, pp. 689-707.

Roffe, P. "UNCTAD Transfer of Technology Code - Fifth Session of the UN Conference." Journal of World Trade Law Vol. 18, 1984, pp. 176-182.

Rothschild, L., Jr. and R.E. Anthony. "World-Wide Combined Reporting: Recent Legislative Developments." Bulletin of International Fiscal Documentation Vol. 37, 1983, pp. 59-64.

Rubin, Seymour J. and Gary Clyde Hufbauer. Emerging Standards of International Trade and Investment: Multinational Code and Corporate Conduct. Totowa, New Jersey: Rowman & Allanheld, 1984.

Rubin, Seymour J. "Harmonization of Rules: A Perspective on the UN Commission on Transnational Corporations." Law and Policy in International Business Vol. 8, 1976, pp. 875-893.

Rubin, Seymour J. "Transnational Corporations and International Chambers of Commerce: A Study of the Relationship Between International Legal Co-operation and Economic Development." American University Law Review Vol. 30, 1981, pp. 903-921.

Rubin, Seymour J. "Report on the Dusseldorf Conference on International Controls on Foreign Investment." International Lawyer Vol. 7, 1973, pp. 825-829.

Sanders, P. "Implementing International Codes of Conduct for Multinational Enterprises." American Journal of Comparative Law Vol. 30, 1982, pp. 241-254.

Sanders, P. "Implementing International Codes of Conduct for Multinationals." International Law Review Vol. 28, 1981, pp. 318-332.

Sanz, F. Ortiz, et al. "Developing and Enforcing Guidelines for Multinational Enterprises." American Society of International Law Proceedings Vol. 70, 1976, pp. 16-34.

Stanley, T.W. "International Codes of Conduct for Multinational Corporations: A Skeptical View of the Process." American University Law Review Vol. 30, 1981, pp. 973-1008.

Starrels, A.J. "A Proposal for Uniform Regulation of Foreign Investment in American Real Estate." Cornell International Law Journal Vol. 18, 1985, pp. 147-178.

Stephanou, C.A. "Code des Nations Unies sur les Pratiques Commerciales Restrictives." Revue Hellenique de Droit International Vol. 34, 1981, pp. 21-47.

Stockman, K. "Reflections on Recent OECD Activities: Regulation of Multinational Corporation Conduct and Structure." Michigan Year Book of International Legal Studies Vol. 2, 1981, pp. 223-240.

Stoermann, W.E. "ILO Activities in the Field of Multinational Enterprises." Journal of International Law and Economics Vol. 10, 1975, pp. 347-353.

"Supranational Regulation of the Transnational Corporation: The UNCTAD and CTC Efforts." Michigan Year Book of International Legal Studies Vol. 2, 1981, pp. 268-279.

"Symposium: Codes of Conduct for Transnational Corporations." American University Law Review Vol. 30, 1981, pp. 903-1048.

Tharp, Paul A., Jr. "Transnational Enterprises and International Regulation: A Survey of Various Approaches in International Organizations." International Organization Vol. 30, 1976, pp. 47-73.

Thomas, B.S. "International Accounting and Reporting: Developments Leading to the Harmonization of Standards." New York University Journal of International Law and Politics Vol. 25, 1983, pp. 517-543.

Thomas, B.S. "International Harmonization - Recent Developments in the Pursuit of Comparability in General Purpose Reports of Multinational Enterprises." Business Lawyer Vol. 38, 1983, pp. 1397-1411.

Thompson, D. "UNCTAD: Model Law on Restrictive Business Practices." Journal of World Trade Law Vol. 14, 1980, pp. 444-449.

Timberg, S. "Impact on the Transnational Corporation of the International Code of Conduct on the Transfer of Technology." International Review of Industrial Property and Copyright Law Vol. 12, 1981, pp. 133-152.

"U.N. Set of Multilaterally Agreed Equitable Principles and Rules for the Control of Restrictive Business Practices. General Assembly Resolution 35/63 (1980)." Georgia Journal of International and Comparative Law Vol. 11, 1981, pp. 709-721.

United Nations. "Transnational Corporations: Issues Involved in the Formulation of a Code of Conduct." UN Document No. E/C.10/18.

United Nations. "Transnational Corporations: Texts Relevant to an Annotated Outline Suggested by the Chairman of the Intergovernmental Working Group on the Code of Conduct." Report of the Secretariat of the Commission on Transnational Corporations, Intergovernmental Working Group of the Whole on the Code of Conduct, Third Session, New York, 6-10 February 1978. UN Document No. E/C.10/AC.2/3.

United Nations Centre on Transnational Corporations. International Standards of Accounting and Reporting. Report of the Ad-Hoc Intergovernmental Working Group of Experts on International Standards of Accounting and Reporting. UN Sales No. E.84.II.A.2.

United Nations Centre on Transnational Corporations. International Standards of Accounting and Reporting for Transnational Corporations. UN Sales No. E.77.II.A.17. Reprint 1978.

United Nations Centre on Transnational Corporations. Towards International Standardization of Corporate Accounting and Reporting. UN Sales No. E.82.II.A.3.

United Nations Commission on Transnational Corporations, Intergovernmental Working Group on the Formulation of a Code of Conduct. "Transnational Corporations: Code of Conduct; Formulations by the Chairman." UN Document No. E/C.10/AC.2/8. 13 December 1978.

United Nations, Commission on Transnational Corporations, Intergovernmental Working Group. "Report on the Formulation of a Code of Conduct, Third Session, New York, 25 April-6 May 1977, Agenda item 5." UN Document No. E/C.10/31.

United Nations Conference on Trade and Development. "A Set of Multilaterally Agreed Equitable Principles and Rules for the Control of Restrictive Business Practices." UNCTAD Document No. TD/RBP/CONF/10. 2 May 1980. Also No. A/C.2/35/6.

Vagts, Detlev F. "Multinational Corporations and International Guidelines." Common Market Law Review Vol. 18, 1981, pp. 463-474.

Valdez, A.L. "The Andean Foreign Investment Code: An Analysis." The Journal of International Law and Economics Vol. 7, 1972, pp. 1-19.

van der Mensbrugghe, Y. "Codes de conduite pour sociétés multinationales: Quelques réflexions." *Revue de Droit. International et de Droit Comparé* Vol. 59, 1982, pp. 17-28.

Verma, S.K. "International Code of Conduct for Transnational Corporations." *Indian Journal of International Law* Vol. 20, 1980, pp. 20-46.

Vojnovic, M. "The New International Economic Order: 1. Principles and Theoretical Foundations; 2. International Regulation of the Behavior of Transnational Corporations." *Thesaurus Acroasium* Vol. 12, 1982, pp. 245-264.

Wallace, Cynthia Day. "International Codes and Guidelines for Multinational Enterprises: Update and Selected Issues." *International Lawyer* Vol. 17, 1983, pp. 435-463.

Wallace, Don, Jr. *International Control of Investment: The Duesseldorf Conference on Multinational Corporations*. New York: Praeger, 1974.

Wang, N.T. "Design of an International Code of Conduct for Transnational Corporations." *Journal of International Law and Economics* Vol. 10, 1975, pp. 319-336.

Watkins, Steven Lane. "Multinational Enterprises: The Need for an International Regime." Master of Law dissertation, London School of Economics, University of London, July 1975.

Wesley, R.G. "Problems in Regulating the Multinational Enterprise - An Overview." *International Lawyer* Vol. 10, 1976, pp. 613-622.

Wilkinson, Theodore. "International Accounting: Harmony or Disharmony." *Columbia Journal of World Business* March-April 1969, pp. 29-36.

Wilms-Wright, Carl. *Transnational Corporations: A Strategy for Control*. London: Fabian Society, 1977.

Wilner, G.M. "Applicable Law and Dispute Settlement in the Transfer of Technology Code." Journal of World Trade Law Vol. 17, 1983, pp. 389-396.

Zaphiriou, G.A. "International Code of Conduct on Transfers of Technology." International and Comparative Law Quarterly Vol. 26, 1977, pp. 210-218.

Zinn, K.G. "Moeglichkeiten der Machtkontrolle von Superkonzernen durch internationale Organisationen und nationale Regierungen," in M. Krueper, ed., Investitionskontrolle gegen die Konzerne? Reinbek bei Hamburg: Rowholt, 1974.

15. JAPAN

Alaska Department of Economic Development. Japanese Investment in Alaska. August 1974.

Ames, W.L. "Buying a Piece of Japan, Inc.: Foreign Acquisitions in Japan." Harvard International Law Journal Vol. 27, 1986, pp. 541-569.

"Antitrust Implications of Trade Law: Japan, the European Communities, and the United States: A Panel." American Society of International Law Proceedings Vol. 76, 1982, pp. 120-130.

Ariga, Michiko and Luvern V. Rieke. "The Antimonopoly Law of Japan and its Enforcement." Washington Law Review Vol. 39, 1964, pp. 437-478.

Ariga, Michiko. "International Trade of Japan and the Antimonopoly Act." Journal of International Law and Economics Vol. 8, 1973, pp. 185-202.

"Beyond the FCN Treaty: Japanese Multinationals under Title VII." Fordham Law Review Vol. 51, 1983, pp. 871-895.

Boston Consulting Group. The Prospect for Japanese Direct Investment in the United States 1974-80. January 1974.

Bruyneel, A. "Restrictions on Foreign Investment: Developments in Japanese Law." Journal of Comparative Corporate Law and Securities Regulation Vol. 3, 1981, pp. 357-372.

Burton, F.N. "Direct Investment by Sogo-Shasha in Europe." Journal of World Trade Law Vol. 17, 1983, pp. 249-258.

Calhoun, Alexander D., Jr. and George A. Brumder. "Japanese Laws Relating to Foreign Investment in Japan." Private Investors Abroad - Problems and Solutions in International Business in 1971. New York: Matthew Bender, 1971.

Casey, Thomas A. "Japanese Investments in Alaska." Alaska Seas and Coasts Vol. 4, 1976, pp. 5-7.

Columbia University, Conservation of Human Resources. _Economic Impact of the Japanese Business Community in the United States_. New York: The Japan Society, October 1979.

"Corporate Governance in Japan: The Position of Shareholders in Publicly Held Corporations." _University of Hawaii Law Review_ Vol. 5, 1983, pp. 135-206.

"The Costs of the Consensual Myth: Antitrust Enforcement and Institutional Barriers to Litigation in Japan." _Yale Law Journal_ Vol. 94, 1985, pp. 604-645.

Crampe, M.I. "Majority Ownership Strategies for Japan." _UCLA Pacific Basin Law Journal_ Vol. 1, 1982, pp. 41-82.

Deagen, James R. _Japanese Investment in Alaska_. Juneau: State of Alaska Division of Economic Enterprise, August 1974.

deKieffer, Donald E. "Antitrust and the Japanese Auto Quotas." _Antitrust Law Journal_ Vol. 50, 1981, pp. 779-790.

Dickey, W.L. "Aspects of the Legal, Political and Policy Issues That Will Confront the U.S.-Japan Trading Community During the Remainder of the 1980's." _Case Western Reserve Journal of International Law_ Vol. 15, 1983, pp. 445-468.

Directory of Japanese Companies in the U.S.A., 1979-1980. New York: Economic Salon, Ltd., 1980.

Foreign Direct Investment in the Southeast: West Germany, the United Kingdom and Japan. Atlanta, Georgia: Southern Center for International Studies, August 1979.

Fugate, Wilbur L. "Antitrust Aspects of U.S.-Japanese Trade." _Case Western Reserve Journal of International Law_ Vol. 15, 1983, pp. 505-525.

Glazer, Herbert. _The International Businessman in Japan_. Rutland, Vermont and Tokyo: C.E. Tuttle, 1968.

Grendell, Timothy J. "The Antitrust Legislation of the United States, the European Economic Community, Germany and Japan." International and Comparative Law Quarterly Vol. 29, 1980, pp. 64-86.

Haley, J.O. "Oil Cartel Cases: The End of an Era." Law in Japan: An Annual Vol. 15, 1982, pp. 1-11.

Hasebe, T. "Japan's Overseas Investment and Monetary Policy." Paper prepared for the Third Meeting of Japan-Hawaii Economic Council, Honolulu, Hawaii, 1974.

Heller, H. Robert and Emily E. Japanese Investment in the United States - with a Case Study of the Hawaiian Experience. New York: Praeger, 1974.

Helou, A. "Japan and the Tokyo Round." Journal of World Trade Law Vol. 15, 1981, pp. 450-455.

Henderson, Dan Fenno. Foreign Enterprise in Japan: Laws and Policies. Chapel Hill: The University of North Carolina Press, 1973.

Hiller, J.S. "Civil Rights Enforcement and Japanese Subsidiaries." American Business Law Journal Vol. 21, Winter 1984, pp. 463-474.

Honerman, L. "Japan's Direct Investment in California and the New Protectionism." Journal of World Trade Law Vol. 18, 1984, pp. 309-319.

Ishiyama, Y. "Anti-Tax Haven Legislation in Japan." [Summaries in English, French, and German] Intertax 1980, pp. 77-85.

"Japan: Federation of Economic Organizations versus Unitary Taxation." Bulletin for International Fiscal Documentation Vol. 38, 1984, pp. 99-120.

Japan Ministry of Finance and Foreign Department, International Finance Bureau, Bank of Japan. Manual of Foreign Investment in Japan. 1974.

Japan Ministry of Foreign Affairs. Hawaii's Reaction to Japanese Investments in the Islands. Hawaii International Services Agency, September 1973.

Japan Ministry of International Trade and Industry. "State of Overseas Investments Undertaken by Japanese Enterprises." Japan's Overseas Investments. Tokyo, Japan, 1974.

Japanese Investment in Alaska. Alaska Department of Economic Development: August 1974.

Japanese Investments in Hawaii. Honolulu, Hawaii: Economic Salon, Ltd., October 1973.

Johnson, Richard T. and W.C. Ouchi. "Made in America Under Japanese Management." Harvard Business Review Vol. 52, 1974, pp. 61-69.

Johnson, Richard T. "Success and Failure of Japanese Subsidiaries in America." Columbia Journal of World Business Vol. 12, Spring 1977, pp. 30-37.

Kim, Chin. "Guide to International Trade and Investment Law in Japan." Journal of World Trade Law Vol. 9, 1975, pp. 553-567.

Kotkin, Joel. "Japan is Building Economic Empire in American West." International Herald Tribune 3 August 1978, p. 1.

Kramer, Lee C. Japanese Investment in Alaska. Juneau: State of Alaska Department of Economic Development, April 1971.

Krause, Lawrence B. "Evolution of Direct Foreign Investment: The United States and Japan," in J.B. Cohen, ed., Pacific Partnerships: United States-Japan Trade. Lexington, Massachusetts: Heath & Co., 1972.

Lansing, P. and E.C. Rose. "The Japanese Industrial Policy Complex: An Appropriate Legal Model for the United States?" Brooklyn Journal of International Law Vol. 11, 1985, pp. 237-281.

Lindsay, Robert. "Japanese Beachhead in California." New York Times 21 August 1977, Section 3, p. 1.

Litvak, I.A. and C.J. Maule. "Japan's Overseas Investments." Pacific Affairs Vol. 46, 1973, pp. 254-268.

Macdonald, D.S. "The Pacific Basin: The View from Canada," in Private Investors Abroad - 1985, New York: Matthew Bender, 1985.

MacNaughton, B. "Japan's Trade and Currency Regulations: Do the Changes Put Japan in the Mainstream of World Commerce or Are They Merely an Illusion?" Texas International Law Journal Vol. 16, 1981, pp. 245-259.

Matsushita, M. "The Legal Framework of Trade and Investment in Japan." Harvard International Law Journal Vol. 27, 1986, pp. 361-388.

McArthur, P.A. "Joint Ventures in Japan." University of British Columbia Law Review Vol. 20, 1986, pp. 471-489.

Negandhi, Anant R. and Martin Welge. Global Rationalization Strategies of American, German and Japanese Multinational Companies Greenwich, Connecticut: JAI Press, 1984.

Oh, M.B.V. "The Pacific Basin: The View from Singapore," in Private Investors Abroad - 1985. New York: Matthew Bender, 1985.

Okita, S. and T. Miki. "Treatment of Foreign Capital: A Case Study of Japan," in J. Adler, ed., Capital Movements. New York: Macmillan, 1967.

Ozawa, Terutomo. "Japan's New Industrial Offensive in the United States." Michigan State University Business Topics Autumn 1972.

Ozawa, Terutomo. "Technology Imports and Direct Foreign Investment in Japan." Journal of World Trade Law Vol. 7, 1973, pp. 666-679.

Pritchard, R.L. "The Pacific Basin: The View from Australia." Private Investors Abroad - 1985. New York: Matthew Bender, 1985.

Ramseyer, J.M. "Japanese Antitrust Enforcement after the Oil Embargo." American Journal of Comparative Law Vol. 31, 1983, pp. 395-430.

Ramseyer, J.M. "Oil Cartel Criminal Cases: Translations and Postscript." Law in Japan: An Annual Vol. 15, 1982, pp. 57-78.

Reynolds, P. "Foreign Investment in Japan: The Legal and Social Climate." Texas International Law Journal Vol. 18, 1983, pp. 175-201.

Rhoades, R.V. "Tax Aspects of Financing the Pacific Basin Enterprise." UCLA Pacific Basin Law Journal Vol. 2, 1983, pp. 137-179.

Roemer, J.E. "Japanese Direct Foreign Investment in Manufactures: Some Comparisons with the U.S. Pattern." Quarterly Review of Economics and Business Vol. 16, Summer 1976, pp. 91-111.

Rosendahl, Roger W. Current Legal Aspects of Doing Business in the Pacific Basin. Washington, D.C.: American Bar Association, 1986.

Southern Center for International Studies. Foreign Direct Investment in the Southeast: West Germany, the United Kingdom and Japan. Atlanta, Georgia, August 1979.

Takitani, Kenji. "A Prototype for Japanese Investment in the United States?" Columbia Journal of World Business Vol. 8, Winter 1973, pp. 31-33.

Tarullo, D.K., M. Matsushita and W.L. Ames. "The Legal Framework of Trade and Investment in Japan." Harvard International Law Journal Vol. 27, 1986, pp. 343-569.

Toyama, K., N. Tateishi and J. Palenberg. "Trade Friction, Administrative Guidance and Antimonopoly Law in Japan." Case Western Reserve Journal of International Law Vol. 15, 1983, pp. 601-610.

Tsurumi, Yoshi. "The Best of Times and the Worst of Times: Japanese Management in America." Columbia Journal of World Business Vol. 13, Summer 1978, pp. 56-61.

Tsurumi, Yoshi. The Japanese Are Coming: A Multinational Spread of Japanese Firms. Cambridge, Massachusetts: Ballinger, 1976.

Tsurumi, Yoshi. "Japanese Multinational Firms." Journal of World Trade Law Vol. 7, 1973, pp. 74-90.

Tsurumi, Yoshi. "The Strategic Framework for Japanese Investments in the United States." Columbia Journal of World Business Vol. 8, Winter 1973, pp. 19-25.

Uesugi, Akinori. "Japanese Antimonopoly Policy - Its Past and Future." Antitrust Law Journal Vol. 50, 1981, pp. 709-720.

Uesugi, Akinori. "Japan's Cartel System and Its Impact on International Trade." Harvard International Law Journal Vol. 27, 1986, pp. 389-424.

United States Department of Commerce, International Trade Administration. Investment Climate in Foreign Countries. (Vol.1: OECD and Other European Countries [includes Canada and Japan]; Vol. 2: Africa; Vol. 3: Asia [excluding Japan]; Vol. 4: Western Hemisphere [excluding Canada]) August, 1985.

"United States and Japanese Government Procurement: The Impact on Trade Relations." Washington University Law Quarterly Vol. 62, Spring 1984, pp. 127-164.

"Verstaerkte Kapitalausfuhr aus Japan: Direktinvestitionen im Ausland auf Rekordhoehe." Neue Zuercher Zeitung 6 September 1979, p. 17.

Waller, S.W. "Redefining the Foreign Compulsion Defense in U.S. Antitrust Law: The Japanese Auto Restraints and Beyond." Law and Policy in International Business Vol. 14, 1982, pp. 747-817.

"West Germany Probes Alleged Japanese Cartel." International Herald Tribune 7-8 March 1981, p. 11.

Yamauchi, K. "B. Grossfeld, Transnational Corporations and the Reorientation of International Economic Law." [In Japanese]. Hogaku Shimpo (The Chuo Law Review) Vol. 30, May 1985, pp. 81-104.

Yoshikawa, Seichi. "Fair Trade Commission vs. MITI: History of the Conflicts Between the Antimonopoly Policy in the Post War Period of Japan." Case Western Reserve Journal of International Law Vol. 15, 1983, pp. 489-504.

Yoshino, M.Y. "Emerging Japanese Multinational Enterprises," in S.M. Davies, ed., Managing and Organizing Multinational Corporations. New York: Pergamon Press, 1979.

Yoshino, M.Y. Japan's Multinational Enterprises. Cambridge, Massachusetts: Harvard University Press, 1976.

Yoshino, M.Y. "Organization and Decision-Making in Emerging Japanese Multinational Enterprises." Ph.D. dissertation, Harvard Graduate School of Business Administration, 1972.

16. JOINT VENTURES

Alford, W.P. and D.E. Birenbaum. "Ventures in the China Trade: An Analysis of China's Emerging Legal Framework for the Regulation of Foreign Investment." Northwestern Journal of International Law and Business Vol. 3, 1981, pp. 56-102.

Archer, S.J. "The Role of Administrative Agencies in Regulating Joint Ventures in China." Stanford Journal of International Law Vol. 21, 1985, pp. 195-218.

Artisien, P.F.R. and P.J. Buckley. "Joint Ventures in Yugoslavia: Comment." Journal of World Trade Law Vol. 18, 1984, pp. 163-170. This is a discussion of C.C. Coughlin's "An Economic Analysis of Yugoslav Joint Ventures," in Journal of World Trade Law Vol. 17, 1983, pp. 12-33.

Bosco, D.M. "Law of the People's Republic of China on Joint Ventures Using Chinese and Foreign Investment." Brooklyn Journal of International Law Vol. 6, 1980, pp. 217-258.

Brown, J.T. "International Joint Venture Contracts in English Law." [Summary in French] Droit et Pratique du Commerce International Vol. 5, June 1979, pp. 193-243.

Campbell, Dennis, ed. Legal Aspects of Joint Ventures in Eastern Europe. London: Kluwer, 1981.

Chen, A. "To Open Wider, or to Close Again: China's Foreign Investment Policies and Laws." New York University Law School Journal of International and Comparative Law Vol. 6, 1984, pp. 1-53.

"China ebnet den Weg zu 'Joint Ventures': Gesetz gestattet Kapitalbeteiligungen und Transfer von Gewinnen." Sueddeutsche Zeitung 9 July 1979, p. 15.

"China's New Joint Venture Law: Analysis and Economic Overview." British Columbia International and Comparative Law Review Vol. 4, 1981, pp. 115-148.

Collins, C.J. "Antitrust: EEC Treaty: Joint-Venture Agreement." Vanderbilt Journal of Transnational Law Vol. 12, 1979, pp. 775-785.

Coughlin, C.C. "Economic Analysis of Yugoslav Joint Ventures." Journal of World Trade Law Vol. 17, 1983, pp. 12-33.

Crampe, M.I. "Majority Ownership Strategies for Japan." UCLA Pacific Basin Law Journal Vol. 1, 1982, pp. 41-82.

Davis, R.W. "Antitrust Analysis of Mergers, Acquisitions, and Joint Ventures in the 1980's: A Pragmatic Guide to Evaluation of Legal Risks." Delaware Journal of Corporate Law Vol. 11, 1986, pp. 25-133.

Eser, G. "Fusionskontrollrechtliche Problematik internationaler joint venture im Kartellrecht der Bundesrepublic Deutschland." Recht der internationalen Wirtschaft Vol. 28, March 1982, pp. 161-167.

1974 Fordham Corporate Law Institute - International Antitrust. New York: Matthew Bender, 1975.

"Foreign Investment in Cuba: A Preliminary Analysis of Cuba's New Joint Venture Law." Law and Policy in International Business Vol. 15, 1983, pp. 689-710.

"Foreign Investment in the People's Republic of China: Compensation Trade, Joint-Ventures, Industrial Property Protection and Dispute Settlement." Georgia Journal of International and Comparative Law Vol. 10, 1980, pp. 233-270.

Franko, Lawrence G. Joint Venture Survival in Multinational Corporations. New York: Praeger, 1971.

Garvey, G.E. "Transnational Joint Ventures and Antitrust Analysis." Stanford Journal of International Law Vol. 21, 1985, pp. 331-372.

"The G.M.-Toyota Joint Venture and Its Implications under the National Labor Relations Act." Detroit College Law Review Vol. 1984, 1984, pp. 647-685.

"The G.M.-Toyota Joint Venture: Legal Cooperation or Illegal Combination in the World Automobile Industry?" Texas International Law Journal Vol. 19, 1984, pp. 699-728.

Golden, E. "People's Republic of China: 1983 Joint Venture Implementing Regulations - the Supplement of Detail, in an Attempt to Attract Foreign Investment." Georgia Journal of International and Comparative Law Vol. 15, 1985, pp. 389-413.

Goldsweig, David N., ed. Joint Venturing Abroad: A Case Study. Washington, D.C.: American Bar Association, 1985.

Greenburg, D.A. "Joint Ventures in Poland: Polish Proposals Before the Joint American-Polish Trade Commission." George Washington Journal of International Law and Economics Vol. 16, 1982, pp. 377-399.

Henne, D., M.J. Levine, W.J. Usery and H. Fishgold. "A Case Study in Cross-Cultural Mediation: the General Motors-Toyota Joint Venture." Arbitration Journal Vol. 41, 1986, pp. 5-15.

Hsu, P.S.P., K.T. Li and S.L. Wang. "Joint Ventures in the People's Republic of China: A Study in International Business Cooperation." Denver Journal of International Law and Policy Vol. 3, 1973, pp. 59-93.

Hushon, John D. "Joint-Ventures Between Multinationals: Government Regulatory Aspects." North Carolina Journal of International Law and Commercial Regulation Vol. 6, 1981, pp. 207-233.

Hutcheson, N.L. and P.M. Kliger. "Current Antitrust Enforcement Policies Affecting Mergers and Joint Ventures." Michigan Bar Journal Vol. 64, 1985, pp. 55-58.

"International Joint Ventures and Antitrust Policy: FTC Puts GM and Toyota in the Driver's Seat." Wisconsin International Law Journal Vol. 4, 1985, pp. 64-85.

"International Joint Ventures and Section (1) of the Sherman Act: per se as the Meaningful Standard." American University Law Review Vol. 23, 1974, pp. 689-729.

"International Joint Ventures in the United States: The GM-Toyota Deal." Columbia Journal of Transnational Law Vol. 22, 1984, pp. 505-540.

Joelson, Mark R. and Joseph P. Griffin. "Multinational Joint Ventures and the U.S. Anti-Trust Laws." Virginia Journal of International Law Vol. 15, 1975, pp. 487-538.

Kitch, E.W. "The Antitrust Economics of Joint Ventures." Antitrust Law Journal Vol. 54, 1985, pp. 957-966.

Klitgaard, T.J. "People's Republic of China Joint Venture Dispute Resolution Procedures." UCLA Pacific Basin Law Journal Vol. 1, 1982, pp. 1-40.

Kozyris, P. John. "Equal Joint-Venture Corporations in France: Problems of Control and Resolution of Deadlocks." American Journal of Comparative Law Vol. 17, 1969, pp. 503-528.

Lee, O. "Formation of Contract and Contract Law through Multinational Joint Ventures: Indonesia, China and the Third World." International Lawyer Vol. 17, 1983, pp. 257-281.

Lussenburg, S.M. "Joint Venture Investment in People's Republic of China: A Continuing Challenge." Canadian Business Review Vol. 63, 1985, pp. 545-596.

McArthur, P.A. "Joint Ventures in Japan." University of British Columbia Law Review Vol. 20, 1986, pp. 471-489.

Miranda, F.R. "Problems of Joint International Business Ventures." International Lawyer Vol. 4, 1970, pp. 550-555.

Muenzel, F. "Neues Chinesisches Vertrags und Wettbewerbsrecht." Recht der internationalen Wirtschaft Vol. 27, 1981, pp. 218-224.

Painter, Therese Eve and Dianne Zomper. "A Bibliography of Current Issues in International Business Transactions: Investment Regulation, Antitrust, Acquisitions and Mergers, Transfer of Technolgy, Joint Ventures, Taxation, Dispute Resolution, Transnational Tort Claims, and Export Controls." Texas International Law Journal Vol. 21, 1985, pp. 165-197.

Pattison, J.E. "China's Developing Legal Framework for Foreign Investment: Experience and Expectations." Law and Policy in International Business Vol. 13, 1981, pp. 89-175.

"People's Republic of China - 1983 Joint Venture Implementing Regulations - the Supplement of Detail in an Attempt to Attract Foreign Investment." Georgia Journal of International and Comparative Law Vol. 15, 1985, pp. 389-413.

"Pros and Cons of Joint Ventures Abroad." Management Monographs, No. 18. New York: Business International, 1964.

"Recent Legal Developments in U.S.-China Economic Relations." Business Lawyer Vol. 36, 1981, pp. 1699-1732.

"Riding a Tiger: Joint Ventures Under South Korea's New Foreign Capital Inducement Act." New York University Journal of International Law and Policy Vol. 17, 1985, pp. 1023-1050.

Rowe, Frederick M. "Antitrust Aspects of European Acquisitions or Joint Ventures in the United States." Paper presented at a conference on the "U.S. Antitrust Laws/Die U.S. Antitrust Gesetze: the legal implications for those entering or operating in the U.S. market." Practising Law Institute, (New York)/German-American Lawyers Association (Bonn), Cologne, June, 1979.

Rule, C.F. "The Administration's Views on Joint Ventures." Antitrust Law Journal Vol. 54, 1985, pp. 1121-1136.

Scriven, J.G. "Joint Venture Legislation in Eastern Europe: A Practical Guide." Harvard International Law Journal Vol. 21, 1980, pp. 633-665.

Shiao-Ming, S. "China's New Law on Joint Ventures Using Chinese and Foreign Investment." Southwestern Law Journal Vol. 34, 1981, pp. 1183-1197.

Straube, M. "Joint-Venture Groups." International Business Lawyer Vol. 13, 1985, pp. 131-133.

Torbert, Preston M. "China's Joint Venture Law: A Preliminary Analysis." Vanderbilt Journal of Transnational Law Vol. 12, 1979, pp. 819-895.

United Nations Centre on Transnational Corporations. Measures Strengthening the Negotiating Capacity of Governments in Their Relations with Transnational Corporations. Joint Ventures Among Firms in Latin America: A Technical Paper. UN Sales No. E.83.II.A.19.

"United States Antitrust Law and Industrial Policy: International Joint Ventures and Global Competition After GM-Toyota [103 F.T.C. 374]." Fordham International Law Journal Vol. 9, 1985/1986, pp. 257-294.

Victor, A. Paul, et al. "International Acquisitions, Joint Ventures, and Other Agreements - The Applicable Substantive and Procedural Law." (Various articles) Proceedings of the Twenty-Ninth Annual Spring Meeting of the Section of Antitrust Law of the American Bar Association, Washington, D.C., 1981. Antitrust Law Journal Vol. 50, 1981, pp. 453-496.

Walmsley, J. Handbook of International Joint Ventures. London: Graham & Trotman, 1982.

Wilson, P.J. "The Legal Structures Governing Technology Transfers and Joint Ventures with the People's Republic of China." International Tax and Business Lawyer Vol. 3, 1985, pp. 1-51.

Zhang, Xiangyu. "A Survey of the Chinese Legal System of Foreign Investments." ASILS International Law Journal Vol. 9, 1985, pp. 37-60.

Zorn, J.G. and H.A. Mayerson. Cuba's Joint Venture Law: New Rules for Foreign Investment." Columbia Journal of Transnational Law Vol. 21, 1983, pp. 27-303.

17. JURISDICTION

Abrams, Lee N., et al. "Litigating in an International Context." (Various articles) Proceedings of the Twenty-Ninth Annual Spring Meeting of the Section of Antitrust Law of the American Bar Association, Washington, D.C., 1981. Antitrust Law Journal Vol. 50, 1981, pp. 555-616.

Adisert, R.J. "Federal Courts and Extraterritorial Antitrust Law: Enlightened Self-Interest or Yankee Imperialism?" Journal of Law and Commerce Vol. 5, 1985, pp. 415-432.

Akehurst, Michael. "Jurisdiction in International Law." The British Yearbook of International Law Vol. 46, 1972-1973, pp. 145-257.

"Alien Corporations and Federal Diversity Jurisdiction." Columbia Law Review Vol. 84, 1984, pp. 177-197.

Amerasinghe, C.F. "Submissions and the Jurisdiction of the International Center for the Settlement of Investment Disputes." Journal of Maritime Law Vol. 5, 1974, pp. 211-250.

American Bar Associaton. Act of State and Extraterrritorial Reach: Problems of Law and Policy. Washington, D.C.: American Bar Association, 1983.

"Arbitration Clauses in International Contracts and the Extraterritorial Reach of the Securities Exchange Act of 1934 in Light of Scherk v. Alberto-Culver Co. (94 S.Ct. 2449)." Syracuse Law Review Vol. 26, 1975, pp. 995-1015.

"Bank of Nova Scotia II: The American Subpoena and the Multinational Enterprise." Canadian Business Law Journal Vol. 9, 1984, pp. 497-511.

Bartlett, J.W., III. "In re: Oil Spill by Amoco Cadiz [1984 A.M.C. 2123] - Choice of Law and A Pierced Corporate Veil Defeat the 1969 Civil Liability Convention." Maritime Law Vol. 10, 1985, pp. 1-23.

Behrens, Peter. "Durchgriff ueber die Grenze." Rabels Zeitschrift fuer auslaendisches und internationales Privatrecht Vol. 46, 1982, pp. 308-356.

Bierman, J.N. "The 1983 Export Administration Act Legislation: The Extraterritoriality Issue." Law and Policy in International Business Vol. 15, 1983, pp. 1181-1185.

Bishop, R.D. and S. Burnette. "United States Practice Concerning the Recognition of Foreign Judgments." International Lawyer Vol. 16, 1982, pp. 425-442.

Blechman, Michael D. "Antitrust Jurisdiction, Discovery and Enforcement in the International Sphere: An Appraisal of American Developments and Foreign Reactions." Antitrust Law Journal Vol. 49, 1980, pp. 1197-1206.

Blythe, M.A. "Extraterritorial Impact of the Anti-Trust Laws: Protecting British Trading Interests." American Journal of Comparative Law Vol. 31, 1983, pp. 99-129.

Bondurant, Ward S. "Extraterritorial Jurisdiction - Antitrust - The Impact of the British Protection of Trading Interests Act on the United States Antitrust Suit Brought by Laker Airways against British Airways and British Caledonian." (Recent Developments) Georgia Journal of International and Comparative Law Vol. 14, 1984, pp. 181-200.

Born, G.B. "Recent British Responses to the Extraterritorial Application of United States Law: The Midland Bank [Midland Bank v. Laker Airways, Slip Op. (C.A. July 30, 1985)] Decision and Retaliating Legislation Involving Unitary Taxation." Virginia Journal of International Law Vol. 26, 1985, pp. 91-108.

Bridge, J.W. "The Law and Politics of United States Foreign Policy Export Controls." Legal Studies Vol. 4, 1984, pp. 2-29.

Briggs, Herbert W. "Barcelona Traction: The Jus Standi of Belgium." American Journal of International Law Vol. 65, 1971, pp. 327-345.

Bringezu, Volker. "Parent-Subsidiary Relations under German Law." International Lawyer Vol. 7, 1973, pp. 138-157.

Butler, E.B. "The Extraterritorial Reach of the U.S. Export Administration Act: Reflections on the Yamal Pipeline Controversy." Journal of Business Law Vol. 1983, 1983, pp. 275-283.

Buxbaum, R.M. "Extension of Parent Company Shareholders' Rights to Participate in the Governance of Subsidiaries." American Journal of Comparative Law Vol. 31, 1983, pp. 511-519.

Caflisch, Lucius C. "The Protection of Corporate Investments Abroad in the Light of the Barcelona Traction Case." Zeitschrift fuer auslaendisches oeffentliches Recht und Voelkerrecht Vol. 31, 1971, pp. 162-196.

Calabrese, M.R. "Jurisdiction: Limitations on Concurrent Jurisdiction." Virginia Journal of International Law Vol. 20, 1980, pp. 925-941.

Carnulutti, A. and F. Delon. "États face aux éffets extraterritoriaux du droit de la concurrence des États-Unis d'Amérique: l'exemple de la France." Revue Française de Droit Aérien Vol. 36, 1982, pp. 15-41.

"Civil Procedure - Class Action Jurisdiction Over Nonresident Plaintiffs - Shutts vs. Phillips Petroleum Co. [679 P.2d.1159 (Kan.)] ("Shutts II")". University of Kansas Law Review Vol. 33, 1985, pp. 525-545.

"Civil Procedure - in personam jurisdiction - Hall v. Helicopteros Nacionales de Colombia, SA. ("Hellicol") 638 S.W.2d 870 - (Tex)." St. Mary's Law Journal Vol. 14, 1982, pp. 79-94.

"Civil Procedure - Personal Jurisdiction - Mere Purchases, Even Occurring at Regular Intervals, Are Insufficient As Contacts and Do Not Justify a State's Claim of In Personam Jurisdiction Over a Nonresident Corporation in a Claim Not Related to the Purchase Transactions. Helicopteros Nacionales de Colombia v. Hall, 104 S.Ct. 1868." Journal of Air Law and Commerce Vol. 50, 1985, pp. 321-349.

Cohen, B.E. "In Personam Jurisdiction in Federal Courts Over Foreign Corporations: The Need for a Federal Long-Arm Statute." *Denver Journal of International Law and Policy* Vol. 14, 1985, pp. 59-73.

"Conference on Extraterritoriality for the Businessman and the Practicing Lawyer." *Law and Policy in International Business* Vol. 15, 1983, pp. 1095-1221.

"Conflict of Laws: Discovery Abroad Under Provisions of the Hague Convention - Laker Airways Ltd. v. Pan American World Airways," et. al., Nos. 82-3362, 83-0416, 83-2791 (D.D.C. June 26, 1984) reported in 23 *International Legal Materials* 748 (1984)." *Harvard International Law Journal* Vol. 26, 1985, pp. 201-208.

"Continental Can [Europemballage Corp. and Continental Can Inc. v. EEC Commission]." *Common Market Law Reports* Vol. 12, 1973, pp. 199-229.

Dachs, R.A. "Enforcement of Foreign Tax Judgments in the United States." *George Washington Journal of International Law and Economics* Vol. 14, 1980, pp. 281-299.

"Daishowa International v. No. Coast Export [1982-Z Tr. Cas. (CCH) Para. 64,774]; An Alternative Approach in the Judicial Balancing of International Comity Considerations." *Law and Policy in International Business* Vol. 15, 1983, pp. 613-633.

Dam, K.W. "Economic and Political Aspects of Extraterritoriality." *International Lawyer* Vol. 19, 1985, pp. 887-896.

"Diversity Jurisdiction over Alien Corporations." *Univeristy of Chicago Law Review* Vol. 50, 1983, pp. 1458-1480.

"Dresser Industries: The Failure of Foreign Policy Trade Controls Under the Export Administration Act." *Maryland Journal of International Law and Trade* Vol. 8, 1984, pp. 122-143.

Dunfee, T.W. and A.S. Friedman. "The Extraterritorial Application of United States Antitrust Laws: A Proposal for an Interim Solution." Ohio State Law Journal Vol. 45, 1984, pp. 883-932.

Eaton, T. "Illinois Replaces 'Profit' for 'Presence' in Determining Long-Arm Jurisdiction over Foreign Corporations." Illinois Bar Journal Vol. 69, 1981, pp. 676-682.

Eaton, T. "New Jurisdictional Ground Since World-Wide Volkswagen." Trade Law Guide Vol. 25, 1982, pp. 549-567.

"Economic Internationalism v. National Parochialism: Barcelona Traction." (Note) Law and Policy in International Business Vol. 3, 1971, pp. 544-563.

Ehlers, M.J. "The Marc Rich Case: Extension of Grand Jury Subpoena Power to Nonresident Alien Corporations." George Washington Journal of International Law and Economics Vol. 18, 1983-1984, pp. 97-128.

Ellicott, J. "Extraterritorial Trade Controls - Law, Policy, and Business." Private Investor Abroad Vol. 1983, 1983, pp. 1-35.

Ellicott, J. "Trends in Export Control Regulation." Business Lawyer Vol. 38, 1983, pp. 533-553.

Evans, Alona E. "Expropriation - Cuba - Extraterritorial Effect - Act of State - Trademark Infringement - Bretton Woods Agreement - Hickenlooper Amendment." American Journal of International Law Vol. 68, 1974, pp. 325-330.

"The Expanding Extraterritorial Jurisdiction of the Sherman Antitrust Act: Intent and Effects in the Balance?" Loyola of Los Angeles International and Comparative Law Journal Vol. 6, 1983, pp. 463-482.

"Extraterritorial Application of the Sherman Act to Foreign Corporations." Delaware Journal of Corporate Law Vol. 11, 1986, pp. 513-534.

"Extraterritorial Application of U.S. Export Laws: Dresser Industries." Wisconsin International Law Journal Vol. 1983, 1983, pp. 138-159.

"Extraterritorial Discovery: An Analysis Based on Good Faith." Columbia Law Review Vol. 83, 1983, pp. 1320-1350.

"Extraterritorial Discovery - Hague Evidence Convention - The Hague Convention Procedures Are Not Exclusive, and Courts May Issue Discovery Orders Using Alternative Means." Virginia Journal of International Law Vol. 25, Fall 1984, pp. 249-280.

"Extraterritorial Discovery Under the Hague Evidence Convention." Villanova Law Review Vol. 31, 1986, pp. 253-290.

"The Extraterritorial Enforcement of U.S. Antitrust Laws and Retaliatory Legislation in the United Kingdom and Australia. Denver Journal of International Law and Policy Vol. 13, 1984, pp. 377-386.

"Extraterritoriality: Australian Limitations on Foreign Judgement and Discovery - Foreign Proceedings (Excess of Jurisdiction) Act 1984, No. 3 Australian Acts (1984)." Harvard International Law Journal Vol. 26, 1985, pp. 578-584.

"Extraterritoriality: Current Policy of the United States." Syracuse Journal of International Law and Commerce Vol. 12, 1986, pp. 493-519.

"Federal Courts: Jurisdiction over Foreign Corporations." Harvard International Law Journal Vol. 22, 1981, pp. 688-693.

Feldman, M.B. "The Restructuring of National Security Controls Under the 1985 Amendments to the Export Administration Act: Multilateral Diplomacy and the Extraterritorial Application of United States Law." Stanford Journal of International Law Vol. 21, 1985, pp. 235-279.

"Foreign Statutory Response to Extraterritorial Application of United States Antitrust Law." Dickinson International Law Annual Vol. 1, 1982, pp. 125-155.

"Forum Non Conveniens and the Extraterritorial Application of United States Antitrust Law." Yale Law Journal Vol. 94, 1985, pp. 1693-1714.

Friedman, A.S. "Laker Airways [Laker Airways, Ltd. v. Sabena, 731 F.2d. 909]: The Dilemma of Concurrent Jurisdiction and Conflicting National Policies." Brooklyn Journal of International Law Vol. 11, 1985, pp. 181-236.

Gerber, D.J. "Beyond Balancing: International Law Restraints in the Reach of National Laws." Yale Journal of International Law Vol. 10, Fall 1984, pp. 185-221.

Gerber, D.J. "The Extraterritorial Application of the German Antitrust Laws." American Journal of International Law Vol. 77, 1983, pp. 756-783.

Gordon, Edward. "Extraterritorial Application of United States Economic Law: Britain Draws the Line." International Lawyer Vol. 14, 1980, pp. 151-166.

Gotlieb, A.E. "Extraterritoriality: A Canadian Perspective." Northwestern Journal of International Law and Business Vol. 5, 1983, pp. 449-461.

Graham, W.C. "The Foreign Extraterritorial Measures Act." The Canadian Business Law Journal Vol. 11, 1986, pp. 410-444.

Griffin, Joseph P. "The Power of the Host Countries over the Multinational: Lifting the Veil in the European Economic Community and the United States." Law and Policy in International Business Vol. 6, 1974, pp. 375-435.

Grippando, J.M. "Declining to Exercise Extraterritorial Antitrust Jurisdiction on Grounds of International Comity: An Illegitimate Extension of the Judicial Abstention Doctrine." Virginia Journal of International Law Vol. 23, 1983, pp. 395-428.

Grossfeld, B. and C.P. Rogers. "Shared Values Approach to Jurisdictional Conflicts in International Economic Law." International and Comparative Law Quarterly Vol. 32, 1983, pp. 931-947.

Guyénot, Jean. "La décision 'Continental Can' de la Commission C.E.E. et la naissance du droit antitrust européen." Rivista della Società Vol. 17, 1972, pp. 722-741.

Hammesfahr, R.W. and R.L. Blatt. "Extraterritorial Application of American Antitrust Laws: An Overview." Chicago Bar Record Vol. 65, 1983, pp. 106-112.

Harding, C.D.P. "Jurisdiction in EEC Competition Law: Some Recent Developments." Journal of World Trade Law Vol. 2, 1977, pp. 422-440.

Haubert, William H., III. "Continental Can - New Strength for Common Market Anti-Trust." (Comment) San Diego Law Review Vol. 11, 1973, pp. 227-244.

Hay, P. "Judicial Jurisdiction over Foreign-Country Corporate Defendants - Comments on Recent Case Law." Oregon Law Review Vol. 63, 1984, pp. 431-454.

"Helicopteros Nacionales de Colombia, S.A. v. Hall [104 S.Ct. 1868]: Foreign Defendants and Minimum Contacts in the Real World." Rutgers Law Review Vol. 37, 1985, pp. 609-623.

Hermann, A.H. Conflicts of National Laws with International Business Activity: Issues of Extraterritoriality. London: British-North American Committee, 1982.

Honigsberg, C.C. "Uniform Foreign Money-Judgments Recognition Act: A Survey of the Case Law." Vanderbilt Journal of Transnational Law Vol. 14, 1981, pp. 171-196.

Hurwitz, James D. "The Impact of the Continental Can Case on Combinations and Concentrations within the Common Market." Hastings Law Journal Vol. 25, 1973-1974, pp. 469-517.

International Bar Association, Committee C - Antitrust Law and Monopolies. Enforcing Antitrust Against Foreign Enterprises: Procedural Problems in the Extraterritorial Application of Antitrust Laws. Boston: Kluwer, 1981.

"International Mass Tort Litigation: Forum Non Conveniens and the Adequate Alternative Forum in Light of the Bhopal Disaster." Georgia Journal of International and Comparative Law Vol. 16, 1986, pp. 109-166.

"International Transactions: Jurisdictional Developments; Applicability of American Employment Discrimination Legislation to Domestically Based Foreign Companies; and Governmental Restrictions on International Economic Transactions." 1985 Annual Survey of American Law Vol. 1985, 1986, pp. 409-438.

Jennings, R.Y. "Extraterritorial Jurisdiction and the United States Anti-Trust Laws." British Yearbook of International Law Vol. 33, 1957, pp. 146-175.

Jones, Robert T. "Extraterritoriality in U.S. Antitrust: An International 'Hot Potato'." International Lawyer Vol. 11, 1977, pp. 415-435.

"Jurisdiction and the Conflicts of Law - the Bhopal Litigation." Harvard International Law Journal Vol. 26, 1985, pp. 637-645.

"Jurisdiction over a Foreign Corporation on the Basis of its Subsidiary's Activities in New York: Bulova Watch Co. v. K. Hattori & Co. [508 F.Supp. 1322]." Brooklyn Journal of International Law Vol. 9, 1983, pp. 91-113.

"Jurisdiction over Alien Corporations Based on the Activities of Their Subsidiaries in the Forum: Whither the Doctrine of Corporate Separateness?" Fordham International Law Journal Vol.9, 1985/1986, pp. 540-595.

"Jurisdiction over Foreign Corporations - In re Marc Rich and Co. A.G., Marc Rich and Co., A.G. v. United States, 707 F.2d 663." Harvard International Law Journal Vol. 25, 1984, pp. 250-257.

"Jurisdiction: Personal Jurisdiction Over an Alien Corporation - Helicopteros Nacionales de Colombia v. Hall, 104 S.Ct. 1868." Harvard International Law Journal Vol. 26, 1985, pp. 630-636.

"Jurisdiction to Expropriate and the Shell Game of Intangible Assets." California Western International Law Journal Vol. 16, 1986, pp. 373-392.

Kestenbaum, L. "Antitrust's 'Extraterritorial' Jurisdiction: A Progress Report on the Balancing of Interests Test." Stanford Journal of International Law Vol. 18, 1982, pp. 311-346.

Kleinberg, J.P. "The Extraterritorial Application of the United States." Hastings International and Comparative Law Review Vol. 8, 1985, pp. 187-195.

Korah, Valentine. "The Control of Mergers under Article 86 of the Rome Treaty: Continental Can." Current Legal Problems Vol. 26, 1973, pp. 82-113.

Kuyper, P.J. "European Community Law and Extraterritoriality: Some Trends and New Developments." International and Comparative Law Quarterly Vol. 33, 1984, pp. 1013-1021.

"Laker Airways v. Sabena [731 F.2d. 909]: Comity and Conflict." Law and Policy in International Business Vol. 17, 1985, pp. 157-176.

"The Laker [British Airway Bd. v. Laker Airways, Ltd. (1984) 3 All E.R. 39] Jurisdictional Affair: The Judiciary Temporarily Avoids a Political Showdown." Wakeforest Law Review Vol. 20, 1984, pp. 951-974.

"The Laker [Laker Airways, Ltd. v. Sabena, Belgian World Airlines, 731 F.2d. 909] Antitrust Litigation: The Jurisdictional 'Rule of Reason' Applied to Transnational Injunctive Relief." Cornell Law Review Vol. 71, 1986, pp. 645-667.

Larose, L.A. "Conflicts, Contacts, and Cooperation: Extraterritorial Application of the United States Securities Laws." Securities Regulation Law Journal Vol. 12, Summer 1984, pp. 99-137.

Lazarski, H. "System of 'Territoriality': The Present Situation Possible Uses, Anti-Avoidance Measures." European Taxation Vol. 22, 1982, pp. 175-182.

Lebedoff, G. and C. Raievski. "A French Perspective on the United States Ban on the Soviet Gas Pipeline Equipment." Texas International Law Journal Vol. 18, 1983, pp. 483-507.

LeGall, J.-P. "Règle de l'arm's length serait-elle incompatible avec le traité de Rome?" [Text in French and English] Droit et Pratique du Commerce International Vol. 8, July 1982, pp. 65-85.

Lillich, R.B. "Two Perspectives on the Barcelona Traction Case: The Rigidity of Barcelona." (Editorial Comment) American Journal of International Law Vol. 65, 1971, pp. 522-532.

Lopez-Balboa, V.M. and J. Myers. "Jurisdictional Standards Under EEC Competition Law: The Evolution of the Economic Entity Test." Journal of Comparative Business and Capital Market Law Vol. 6, 1984, pp. 383-407.

Lowe, A.V. "Blocking Extraterritorial Jurisdiction: The British Protection of Trading Interests Act, 1980." American Journal of International Law Vol. 75, 1981, pp. 257-282.

Lowe, A. V. "The Problems of Extraterritorial Jurisdiction: Economic Sovereignty and the Search for a Solution. International and Comparative Law Quarterly Vol. 34, 1985, pp. 724-746.

Lowenfeld, A.F. "Jurisdiction to Prescribe: Some Contributions From an International Lawyer." Boston University International Law Journal Vol. 4, 1986, pp. 91-97.

Lowenfeld, A.F., et al. "Extraterritoriality: Conflict and Overlap in National and International Regulation." American Society of International Law Proceedings 74th Meeting, 1980, pp. 30-48.

Lowenfeld, A.F. "Sovereignty, Jurisdiction and Reasonableness: A Reply to A.V. Lowe." American Journal of International Law Vol. 75, 1981, pp. 629-638.

Maier, H.G. "Extraterritorial Jurisdiction at a Crossroads: An Intersection Between Public and Private International Law." American Journal of International Law Vol. 76, 1982, pp. 280-320.

Maier, H.G. "Interest Balancing and Extraterritorial Jurisdiction." American Journal of Comparative Law Vol. 31, 1983, pp. 579-597.

Mann, F.A. "The Doctrine of International Jurisdiction Revisited After 20 Years." Recueil des Cours Vol. 5, 1984, pp. 9-116.

Mann, F.A. "The Doctrine of Jurisdiction in International Law." Receuil des Cours Vol. 111, 1964, pp. 1-162.

Mann, F.A. "The Dyestuffs Case in the Court of Justice of the European Communities." International and Comparative Law Quarterly Vol. 22, 1973, pp. 35-50.

"Marc Rich [Marc Rich and Co., A.G. v. U.S., 707 F.2d 663]: An Expansion of U.S. Criminal Jurisdiction Over Foreign Defendants." New England Journal of International Law and Business Vol. 6, 1984, pp. 615-645.

Marcuss, S.J. and E.L. Richard. "Extraterritorial Jurisdiction in United States Trade Law: The Need for a Consistent Theory." Columbia Journal of Transnational Law Vol. 20, 1981, pp. 411-479.

Meesen, K.M. "Antitrust Jurisdiction under Customary International Law." American Journal of International Law Vol. 78, 1984, pp. 783-810.

Meng, Werner. "Neuere Entwicklungen im Streit um die Jurisdiktionshoheit der Staaten im Bereich der Wettbewerbsbeschraenkungen." Zeitschrift fuer auslaendisches oeffentliches Recht und Voelkerrecht Vol. 41, 1981, pp. 469-513.

Merciai, P. "The Euro-Siberian Gas Pipeline Dispute - A Compelling Case for the Adoption of Jurisdictional Codes of Conduct." Maryland Journal of International Law and Trade Vol. 8, 1984, pp. 1-52.

Metzger, Stanley D. "Two Perspectives on the Barcelona Traction Case: Nationality of Corporate Investment under Investment Guaranty Schemes - The Relevance of Barcelona Traction." (Editorial Comment) American Journal of International Law Vol. 65, 1971, pp. 532-541.

Millstein, Ira M., et al. "Extraterritorial Application of U.S. Antitrust Law (Economic Imperialism or Protecting Competition Against Foreign Invasion?)." (Debate) Proceedings of the Twenty-Ninth Annual Spring Meeting of the Section of Antitrust Law of the American Bar Association, Washington, D.C., 1981. Antitrust Law Journal Vol. 50, 1981, pp. 617-644.

Murphy, D.T. "Moderating Antitrust Subject Matter Jurisdiction: The Foreign Trade Antitrust Improvements Act and the Restatement of Foreign Relations Law (Revised)." University of Cincinnati Law Review Vol. 54, 1986, pp. 779-827.

Nixon, J.B. and J.H. Burns. "An Examination of the Legality of the Use of the Foreign Investment Review Act by the Government of Canada to Control Intra- and Extraterritorial Commercial Activity by Aliens." International and Comparative Law Quarterly Vol. 33, 1984, pp. 57-80.

Norton, Joseph J. "European Court of Justice Judgment in United Brands: Extraterritorial Jurisdiction and Abuse of Dominant Position." Denver Journal of International Law and Politics Vol. 8, 1979, pp. 379-414.

Nothstein, G.Z. "Multinational Corporations and the Extraterritorial Application of the Labor Management Relations Act." Cornell International Law Journal Vol. 10, 1976, pp. 1-58.

Novicoff, M.L. "Blocking and Clawing Back in the Name of Public Policy: The United Kingdom's Protection of Private Economic Interests Against Adverse Foreign Adjudications." New England Journal of International Law and Business Vol. 7, 1985, pp. 12-36.

Olmstead, Cecil J., ed. Extraterritorial Application of Laws and Responses Thereto. (Various articles: "General Theory of State Jurisdiction and Limitations Under General International Law and Under International Agreements." Cecil J. Olmstead, Chairman; "Specific Extra-territorial Applications of Jurisdiction Resulting in Conflicts." Gunther Jaenicke, Chairman; "Securities Regulation: Extra-territorial Aspects." Maarten Bos, Chairman; "Corporate Governance: Responsibilities of Directors and Officers for Acts of Foreign Subsidiaries and Affiliates." A.E. von Overbeck, Chairman; "Discovery of Documentary and Other Evidence in a Foreign Country." Richard Bentham, Chairman; "Responses to Extra-territorial Exercises of Jurisdiction." Sir Francis Vallat, Q.C., Chairman) Oxford: ESC Publishing, 1984.

Ongman, John Will. "Be No Longer a Chaos: Constructing a Normative Theory of the Sherman Act's Extraterritorial Jurisdictional Scope." Northwestern University Law Review Vol. 6, 1977, pp. 733-766.

Onkelinx, Ivo T. "Conflict of International Jurisdiction: Ordering the Production of Documents in Violation of the Law of the Situs." Northwestern University Law Review Vol. 64, 1969-1970, pp. 487-533.

Organisation for Economic Co-operation and Development. "Responsibility of Parent Companies for their Subsidiaries." Paris: OECD Publications, 1980.

"The Outer Limits of in Personam Jurisdiction over Alien Corporations: The National Contacts Theory." George Washington Journal of International Law and Economics Vol. 16, 1982, pp. 637-658.

Painter, Therese Eve and Dianne Zomper. "A Bibliography of Current Issues in International Business Transactions: Investment Regulation, Antitrust, Acquisitions and Mergers, Tranfer of Technology, Joint Ventures, Taxation, Dispute Resolution, Transnational Tort Claims, and Export Controls." Texas International Law Journal Vol. 21, 1985, pp. 165-197.

Park, J.G. "Extraterritorial Impact of United States Antitrust Laws and Commercial Bribery Considerations." Dickinson International Law Annual Vol. 1, 1982, pp. 105-124.

"Phillips Petroleum Company v. Shutts [105 S.Ct. 2965]: Multistate Plaintiff Class Actions: A Definite Forum, But Is It Proper?" The John Marshall Law Review Vol. 19, 1986, pp. 483-499.

"Potential Havens from American Jurisdiction and Discovery Laws in International Antitrust Enforcement." Univerisity of Florida Law Review Vol. 33, 1981, pp. 240-271.

"Predictability and Comity: Toward Common Principles of Extraterritorial Jurisdiction." Harvard Law Review Vol. 98, 1985, pp. 1310-1330.

"The Razor's Edge: The Doctrine of Forum Non Conveniens and the Union Carbide Methyl Isocyanate Gas Disaster at Bhopal, India." North Carolina Journal of International Law and Commercial Regulation Vol. 10, 1985, pp. 743-759.

"Reasonableness as a Limit to Extraterritorial Jurisdiction." Washington University Law Quarterly Vol. 62, 1985, pp. 681-706.

Riedweg, A.J. "The Extra-Territorial Application of Restrictive Trade Legislation - Jurisdiction and International Law," in International Law Association, _Report on the Fifty-First Conference_. 1965.

Robinson, D.R. "Conflicts of Jurisdiction and the Draft Restatement." _Law and Policy in International Business_ Vol. 15, 1983, pp. 1147-1155.

Rodley, Nigel S. "Corporate Nationality and the Diplomatic Protection of Multinational Enterprises: The _Barcelona Traction_ Case." _Indiana Law Journal_ Vol. 47, 1971-1972, pp. 70-86.

Rogers, C.P. "Still Running Against the Wind: A Comment on Antitrust Jurisdiction and Laker Airways, Ltd. v. Sabena, Belgian World Airlines [731 F.2d. 909]." _Journal of Air Law and Commerce_ Vol. 50, 1985, pp. 931-967.

Rubin, Seymour J. "The International Firm and National Jurisdiction," in Charles P. Kindleberger, ed., _The International Corporation: A Symposium_. Cambridge, Massachusetts: MIT Press, 1970.

Schmidt, H.R. "The Extraterritorial Application of the United States Antitrust Laws." _Journal of Law and Commerce_ Vol. 5, 1985, pp. 321-345.

"Securities Regulation - Exterritorial Application - Continental Grain (Australia) Pty. Ltd. v. Pacific Oilseeds, Inc. [592 F.2d 409]." _New York Law School Journal of International and Comparative Law_ Vol. 4, 1982, pp. 187-204.

Sennett, M. and A.I. Gavil. "Antitrust Jurisdiction, Extraterritorial Conduct and Interest-Balancing." _International Lawyer_ Vol. 19, 1985, pp. 1185-1214.

"The Sham Exception to the Noerr-Pennington Doctrine: A Commercial Speech Interpretation." _Brooklyn Law Review_ Vol. 49, 1983, pp. 573-603.

Shenefeld, J.H. "Extraterritoriality in Antitrust." Law and Policy in International Business Vol. 15, 1983, pp. 1109-1120.

Shenefeld, J.H. "Thoughts on Extraterritorial Application of the United States Antitrust Laws." Fordham Law Review Vol. 52, 1983, pp. 350-373.

Sheriden, S.D. "Extraterritorial Application of NEPA under Executive Order 12,114." Vanderbilt Journal of Transnational Law Vol. 13, 1980, pp. 173-218.

"Shortening the Long Arm of American Antitrust Jurisdiction: Extraterritoriality and the Foreign Blocking Statutes." Loyola Law Review Vol. 28, 1982, pp. 213-280.

Shulz, George P. "Trade, Interdependence, and Conflicts of Jurisdiction." South Carolina Law Review Vol. 36, 1985, pp. 295-307.

"The Siberian Pipeline Dispute and the Export Administration Act: What's Left of Extraterritorial Limits and the Act of State Doctrine." Houston Journal of International Law Vol. 6, Autumn 1983, pp. 63-91.

Skol, A.G. and C.H. Peterson. "Export Control Laws and Multinational Enterprises." International Lawyer Vol. 11, 1977, pp. 29-44.

Sornarajah, M. "Extraterritorial Enforcement of U.S. Antitrust Laws: Conflict and Compromise." International and Comparative Law Quarterly Vol. 31, 1982, pp. 127-149.

"Soviet Reaction to the U.S. Pipeline Embargo." Maryland Journal of International Law and Trade Vol. 8, 1984, pp. 144-155.

"Specific Jurisdiction Time for a 'Related to' Analysis." The Review of Litigation Vol. 4, 1985, pp. 341-365.

"Stapled Stock and I.R.C. Section 269b: Ill-Conceived Change in the Rules of International Tax Jurisdiction." Cornell Law Review Vol. 71, 1986, pp. 1066-1094.

"Strict Enforcement of Extraterritorial Discovery." Stanford Law Review Vol. 38, 1986, pp. 841-890.

Stuermer, U. "Neuere Entwicklung der extraterritorialen Anwendung amerikanischen Securities Regulations." Recht der internationalen Wirtschaft Vol. 29, 1983, pp. 641-646.

"Subject Matter Jurisdiction in Transnational Securities Frauds." Ohio Northern University Law Review Vol. 3, 1976, pp. 1305-1331.

"Subsidiary Assertion of Foreign Parent Corporations' Rights Under Commercial Treaties to Hire Employees 'of their Choice'." Columbia Law Review Vol. 86, 1986, pp. 139-168.

Terez, D.G. "The Misguided Helicopteros [Helicopteros Nacionales de Colombia, S.A. v. Hall 104 S.Ct. 1868] Case: Confusion in the Courts Over Contracts." Baylor Law Review Vol. 37, 1984, pp. 1103-1125.

Thomas, B.S. "Extraterritoriality in an Era of Internationalization of the Securities Markets: The Need to Revisit Domestic Policies." Rutgers Law Review Vol. 35, 1983, pp. 453-471.

Thompson, R.B. "United States Jurisdiction over Foreign Subsidiaries: Corporate and International Law Aspects." Law and Policy in International Business Vol. 15, 1983, pp. 319-400.

Tittman, H.H. "Extraterritorial Application of U.S. Export Control Laws on Foreign Subsidiaries of U.S. Corporations: An American Lawyer's View from Europe." International Lawyer Vol. 16, 1982, pp. 730-737.

Toms, B.C., III. "French Response to the Extraterritorial Application of U.S. Antitrust Laws." International Lawyer Vol. 15, 1981, pp. 585-614.

"United States Attitudes Towards Multinational Corporations." (Various articles: Vagts: control & protection; Tillinghast: tax; Ehrenhaft: anti-dumping; Surrey: Foreign Corrupt Practices Act; Loss: Extraterritoriality in FSC) Harvard International Law Journal Vol. 20, 1979, pp. 233-330.

"United States v. First National City Bank of Chicago [699 F.2D 34]: Limiting American Extraterritorial Authority to Order the Production of Documents in Violation of Foreign Law." DePaul Law Review Vol. 33, Fall 1983, pp. 183-206.

Veltius, M.A. "Neueste Entwicklungen der extraterritorialen Anwendung des U.S. Antitrust-Rechts." Recht der internationalen Wirtschaft Vol. 28, 1982, pp. 157-161.

Victor, A. Paul. "Multinational Corporations: Anti-Trust Extraterritoriality and the Prospect of Immunity." Journal of International Law and Economics Vol. 8, 1973, pp. 11-29.

Wallace, Don, Jr. "Extraterritorial Jurisdiction." Law and Policy in International Business Vol. 15, 1983, pp. 1099-1107.

Waller, S.W. and A.M. Simon. "Analyzing Claims of Sovereignty in International Economic Disputes." Northwestern Journal of International Law and Business Vol. 7, Spring/Summer 1985, pp. 1-11.

Watson, J. Shand. "Jurisdiction and Control over the Multinational Enterprise: De Maximis Non Curat Lex." Mercer Law Review Vol. 27, 1976, pp. 493-518.

Weinberg, L. "The Helicopter Case [Helicopteros Nacionales de Colombia, S.A. v. Hall, 104 S.Ct. 1868] and the Jurisprudence of Jurisdiction." Southern California Law Review Vol. 58, 1985, pp. 913-946.

Wood, Jeffrey and Victor M. Carrera. "The International Uranium Cartel: Litigation and Legal Implications." Texas International Law Journal Vol. 14, 1979, pp. 59-114.

Young, C.K, "Defending Litigation Against a Foreign Airline Under the Foreign Sovereign Immunities Act." _Journal of Air and Commerce_ Vol. 51, 1986, pp. 461-494.

Zaucha, J.J. "The Soviet Pipeline Sanctions: The Extraterritorial Application of U.S. Export Controls." _Law and Policy in International Business_ Vol. 15, 1983, pp. 1169-1179.

Zwarensteyn, Hendrik. _Some Aspects of the Extraterritorial Reach of the American Antitrust Laws_. Deventer: Kluwer, 1970.

18. LDCs/NICs/NON-MARKET ECONOMIES

Abed, A. and H. Abed. "Motivations pour un droit international des investissements et expérience tunisienne." Annuaire de l'Association des Auditeurs et Anciens Auditeurs de l'Académie de Droit International de la Haye Vol. 47-48, 1977-1978, pp. 57-62.

Akinsauya, A. and A. Davies. "Third World Quest for a New International Economic Order: An Overview." International and Comparative Law Quarterly Vol. 33, 1984, pp. 208-217.

Alford, W.P. and D.E. Birenbaum. "Ventures in the China Trade: An Analysis of China's Emerging Legal Framework for the Regulation of Foreign Investment." Northwestern Journal of International Law and Business Vol. 3, 1981, pp. 56-102.

American Bar Association. Current Legal Aspects of Doing Business in Latin America. Washington, D.C.: American Bar Association, 1981.

Arab Investments in the United States: General Outlook Plus Special Report on Kuwait. Atlanta, Georgia: Conway Research, Inc., 1974.

Archer, S.J. "The Role of Administrative Agencies in Regulating Joint Ventures in China." Stanford Journal of International Law Vol. 21, 1985, pp. 195-218.

Artisien, P.F.R. and P.J. Buckley. "Joint Ventures in Yugoslavia: Comment." Journal of World Trade Law Vol. 18, 1984, pp. 163-170. This is a discussion of C.C. Coughlin's "An Economic Analysis of Yugoslav Joint Ventures," in Journal of World Trade Law Vol. 17, 1983, pp. 12-33.

Atkesson, T.B. and D.G. Gill. "UNCTAD Restrictive Business Practices Code: A Step in the North-South Dialogue." International Lawyer Vol. 15, 1981, pp. 1-23.

Baloro, John. "Legal Aspects of the New International Economic Order." Ph.D. (Laws) dissertation, London School of Economics, 1982.

Bettwy, S.W. "Mexico's Development: Foreign Trade Zones and Direct Foreign Investment." Comparative Juridical Review Vol. 22, 1985, pp. 49-86.

Bilder, R.B. "Comments on the Legality of the Arab Oil Boycott." Texas International Law Journal Vol. 12, 1977, pp. 41-46.

Billerbeck, K. and Y. Yasugi. Private Direct Foreign Investment in Developing Countries. World Bank Staff Working Paper No. 348, 1979.

Boorman, James A., III. "Economic Coercion in International Law: The Arab Oil Weapon and the Ensuing Juridicial Issues." Journal of International Law and Economics Vol. 8-9, 1973-1974, pp. 205-231.

Bosco, D.M. "Law of the People's Republic of China on Joint Ventures Using Chinese and Foreign Investment." Brooklyn Journal of International Law Vol. 6, 1980, pp. 217-258.

Brower, C.N. and J.B. Tepe, Jr. "Charter of Economic Rights and Duties of States: A Reflection or Rejection of International Law?" International Lawyer Vol. 9, April 1975, pp. 295-318.

Brown, R. "The Relationship Between the State and the Multinational Corporation in the Exploitation of Resources." International and Comparative Law Quarterly Vol. 33, 1984, pp. 218-229.

Burton, F.N. and H. Inoue. "Expropriations of Foreign-Owned Firms in Developing Countries." Journal of World Trade Law Vol. 18, 1984, pp. 396-414.

Campbell, Dennis, ed. Legal Aspects of Joint Ventures in Eastern Europe. London: Kluwer, 1981.

Chao, H. and Yang Xiaoping. "Private Enterprise in China: The Developing Law of Collective Enterprises." International Lawyer Vol. 19, 1985, pp. 1215-1237.

Chen, A. "To Open Wider, or to Close Again: China's Foreign Investment Policies and Laws." New York University Law School Journal of International and Comparative Law Vol. 6, 1984, pp. 1-53.

Cherol. R.L. and N. Nuñez del Arco. "Empresas multinacionales andinas: un nuevo envoque de la inversión multinacionál en el Grupo Andino." International Lawyer Vol. 17, 1983, pp. 309-332.

Cherol, R.L. and S. Zalduendo. "Legal Framework for Foreign Investment in the Caribbean and Central America." International Lawyer Vol. 57, 1984, pp. 957-982.

"Chile Formally Quits Andean Market Pact." International Herald Tribune 1 November 1976, p. 4.

"China ebnet den Weg zu 'Joint Ventures': Gesetz gestattet Kapitalbeteiligungen und Transfer von Gewinnen." Sueddeutsche Zeitung 9 July 1979, p. 15.

"China's New Joint Venture Law: Analysis and Economic Overview." British Columbia International and Comparative Law Review Vol. 4, 1981, pp. 115-148.

Chrysostomides, K. "The Legal Aspects of Foreign Investments in Cyprus." Annuaire de l'Association des Auditeurs et Anciens Auditeurs de l'Académie de Droit International de la Haye Vol. 47-48 1977-1978, pp. 63-86.

"Closing the Open Door: A Reappraisal of Foreign Investment in Egypt." Brigham Young University Law Review Vol. 1985, 1985, pp. 537-558.

"Commercial Dispute Settlement in China-United States Trade: Conciliation in Perspective." Fordham International Law Journal Vol. 6, 1982-1983, pp. 172-201.

Coronna, M. E. "The Concept of Social Property and the Rights of the Foreign Investor in Yugoslavia." Review of Socialist Law Vol. 11, 1985, pp. 227-247.

Coughlin, C.C. "Economic Analysis of Yugoslav Joint Ventures." Journal of World Trade Law Vol. 17, 1983, pp. 12-33.

deBauw, F. and B. Dewit. "Formes d'investissement étranger en République populaire de Chine." Droit et Pratique du Commerce International Vol. 9, 1983, pp. 511-552.

de Belder, R. and M.A. Khan. "Legal Aspects of Doing Business in Pakistan." International Lawyer Vol. 20, 1986, pp. 535-562.

Evans, Alona E. "Expropriation - Cuba - Extraterritorial Effect - Act of State - Trademark Infringement - Bretton Woods Agreement - Hickenlooper Amendment." American Journal of International Law Vol. 68, 1974, pp. 325-330.

"An Examination of Compensation Terms in the U.S.-Egypt Bilateral Investment Treaty." Case Western Reserve Journal of International Law Vol. 16, 1984, pp. 287-302.

"Expropriated Property, Frozen Assets, and Sovereign Immunity: Legal Obstacles to United States-China Trade Regulations." Columbia Journal of Transnational Law Vol. 15, 1976, pp. 254-276.

Fizman, S. "Foreign Investment Law: Encouragement vs. Restraint - Mexico, Cuba and the Caribbean Basin Initiative." Hastings International and Comparative Law Review Vol. 8, 1985, pp. 147-183.

Flint, D. "The Legal Protection of Foreign Investment: Development and Fairness." Lawasia: Journal for the Law Association for Asia and the Western Pacific Vol. 2, 1984, pp. 155-170.

Focke, Katharina. "From Lome 1 towards Lome 2." Texts of the Report and Resolution Adopted on 26 September 1980 by the APC-EEC Consultative Assembly. Luxembourg: Office for Official Publications of the European Communities, 1980.

"Foreign Investment: Foreign Economic Contract Law - the Foreign Economic Contract Law of the People's Republic of China, reprinted in 24 ILM 799 (1985) (unofficial transcript); and The Regulation of the People's Republic of China Governing Contracts for the Imports of Technology, reprinted in 24 ILM 801 (1985) (unofficial transcript)." Harvard International Law Journal Vol. 27, 1986, pp. 275-283.

"Foreign Investment in Cuba: A Preliminary Analysis of Cuba's New Joint Venture Law." Law and Policy in International Business Vol. 15, 1983, pp. 689-710.

"Foreign Investment in Industries Which Do Not Need Foreign Technology Has Been Stopped." Financial Times 15 March 1985, p. 4. Reported in Bulletin of Legal Developments, 10 April 1985, p. 59.

"Foreign Investment in the People's Republic of China: Compensation Trade, Joint-Ventures, Industrial Property Protection and Dispute Settlement." Georgia Journal of International and Comparative Law Vol. 10, 1980, pp. 233-270.

"Foreign Sovereign Compulsion and the Arab Boycott: A State Action Analogy." Georgetown Law Journal Vol. 65, 1976-1977, pp. 1001-1023.

Gelatt, T.A. and R.D. Pomp. "Tax Aspects of Doing Business with the People's Republic of China." Columbia Journal of Transnational Law Vol. 22, 1984, pp. 421-504.

"Gesetzentwuerfe in chinesischen Volkskongress." Frankfurter Allgemeine Zeitung 28 June 1979, p. 3.

Goldberg, H.L. "Conventions for the Elimination of International Double Taxation: Toward a Developing Country Model." Law and Policy in International Business Vol. 15, 1983, pp. 833-909.

Golden, E. "People's Republic of China: 1983 Joint Venture Implementing Regulations - the Supplement of Detail, in an Attempt to Attract Foreign Investment." Georgia Journal of International Law Vol. 15, 1985, pp. 389-413.

Gordon, Michael W. "The Impact of the Multinational Corporation in the Third World," in K.R. Simmonds, ed., Legal Problems of Multinational Corporations. London: The British Institute of International and Comparative Law, 1977.

Gordon, Michael W. "Of Aspirations and Operation: the Governance of Multinational Enterprises by Third World Nations." Legal Issues of European Integration Vol. 16, 1984, pp. 301-353.

Greenburg, D.A. "Joint Ventures in Poland: Polish Proposals Before the Joint American-Polish Trade Commission." George Washington Journal of International Law and Economics Vol. 16, 1982, pp. 377-399.

Grzybowski, K. "Arbitral Tribunals for Foreign Trade in Socialist Countries." Law and Contemporary Problems Vol. 37, 1972, pp. 592-610.

Haight, G.W. "The New International Economic Order and the Charter of Economic Rights and Duties of States." International Lawyer Vol. 9, 1975, pp. 591-604.

Han, A.M. "People's Republic of China's Foreign Enterprises Income Tax Law and Regulations." Hasting's International and Comparative Law Review Vol. 6, 1983, pp. 689-717.

Hsu, P.S.P., K.T. Li and S.L. Wang. "Joint Ventures in the People's Republic of China: A Study in International Business Cooperation." Denver Journal of International Law and Policy Vol. 3, 1973, pp. 59-93.

Hubbard, D. "International Law Commission and the New International Economic Order." German Yearbook of International Law Vol. 22, 1979, pp. 80-99.

Hushon, John D. "Joint-Ventures Between Multinationals: Government Regulatory Aspects." North Carolina Journal of International Law and Commercial Regulation Vol. 6, 1981, pp. 207-233.

International Legal Center. Law and Public Enterprise in Asia. London: Praeger, 1976.

International Monetary Fund, Research Department. Foreign Private Investment in Developing Countries. Occasional Paper series (ISSN 0251-6365) No. 33; International Monetary Fund, Washington, D.C., 1985.

Jadaen, C.L. "Ownership and Investment in Poland." Cornell International Law Journal Vol. 18, 1985, pp. 63-97.

Jakubowski, J. "Entreprises Internationales des pays du C.A.E.M.: Quelques aspects juridiques." Journal du Droit International Vol. 107, 1980, pp. 829-851.

Juncadella, S. "Foreign Investment Laws of Latin America: Present and Future." International Lawyer Vol. 16, 1982, pp. 463-472.

Klitgaard, T.J. "People's Republic of China Joint Venture Dispute Resolution Procedures." UCLA Pacific Basin Law Journal Vol. 1, 1982, pp. 1-40.

Knox, G.R., S.E. Alley, and D.B. Person. "The U.S. Tax Regime Affecting Mexican Nationals Who Desire to Conduct Business or Invest Within the United States." Houston Journal of International Law Vol. 8, 1985, pp. 87-118.

Krishnamurti, R. "The Developing Countries Point of View II," in Don Wallace, ed., International Control of Investment. Dusseldorf Conference on Multinational Corporations. New York: Praeger, 1974.

Lahoud, N.J. "'Non-discriminatory' United States Generalized System of Preferences: De Facto Discrimination Against the Least Developed Developing Countries." Harvard International Law Journal Vol. 23, 1982, pp. 1-47.

Langer, S.H. "Israel-EEC Free Trade Agreement: An Analysis of the Agreement and Its Effect on Investments." Syracuse Journal of International Law and Commerce Vol. 9, 1982, pp. 63-113.

Lee, O. "Formation of Contract and Contract Law through Multinational Joint Ventures: Indonesia, China and the Third World." International Lawyer Vol. 17, 1983, pp. 257-281.

"Legal Framework for American Direct Investment in Eastern Europe: Romania, Hungary, and Yugoslavia." Cornell International Law Journal Vol. 7, 1974, pp. 187-203.

Lippman, M. "Transnational Corporations and Repressive Regimes: the Ethical Dilemma." Western California International Law Journal Vol. 15, 1985, pp. 542-551.

Lizares, E.P. "New International Economic Order and the International Center for the Settlement of Investment Disputes." Philippine Law Journal Vol. 55, 1980, pp. 298-326.

Lussenburg, S.M. "Joint Venture Investment in People's Republic of China: A Continuing Challenge." Canadian Business Review Vol. 63, 1985, pp. 545-596.

Ma, R. "China Opens for Business." California Lawyer Vol. 5, August 1985, pp. 34-71.

Ma, V.J. "Foreign Investment in the Troubled Waters of the East China Sea." Chinese Yearbook of International Law and Affairs, Chuo Law Review Vol. 18, 1981, pp. 35-73.

Machowski, H. "Multinationale Unternehmen sozialistischer Laender." Neue Zuercher Zeitung 15 May 1979, p. 10.

Maviglia, S.F. "Mexico's Guidelines for Foreign Investment: The Selective Promotion of Necessary Industries." American Journal of International Law Vol. 80, 1986, pp. 281-304.

McNair, Lord. "The Seizure of Property and Enterprises in Indonesia." Nederlands Tijdschrift voor International Recht Vol. 6, 1959, pp. 217-256.

"Mexico's Maquiladoras Examined: Are In-Bond Production Plants the Wave of the Future?" Pepperdine Law Review Vol. 13, 1986, pp. 357-385.

Mierzwa, A.M. and A.K.P. Drab. "New Legislation on Foreign Private Firms in Poland." Review of Socialist Law Vol. 10, 1984, pp. 119-128.

Moxon, Richard W., Thomas W. Roehl and J. Frederick Truitt. International Business Strategies in the Asia-Pacific Region, Vol 4 of H. Peter Gray, ed., Research in International Business and Finance. Greenwich, Connecticut: JAI Press, 1984.

Muenzel, F. "Neues Chinesisches Vertrags und Wettbewerbsrecht." Recht der internationalen Wirtschaft Vol. 27, 1981, pp. 218-224.

"Multinational Corporations and the Lesser Developed Countries - Foreign Investment, Transfer of Technology, and the Paris Convention: Caveat Investor." University of Dayton Law Review Vol. 5, 1980, pp. 105-154.

Murase, S. "International Law Making for the New International Economic Order." Japan Annual of International Law Vol. 25, 1982, pp. 45-66.

"Nationalization: The Dichotomy between Western and Third World Perspectives in International Law." Howard Law Journal Vol. 26, 1983, pp. 1547-1577.

Negandhi, Anant R., ed. China's Trade with the Industrialized Countries: Socio-Economic and Political Perspectives, Vol 2 in his Research in International Business and International Relations. Greenwich, Connecticut: JAI Press, 1986.

"New International Economic Order." Workshop, The Hague, October, 1980.

"The New International Economic Order and General Assembly Resolutions: The Debate Over the Legal Effects of General Assembly Resolutions Revisited." California Western International Law Journal Vol. 15, 1985, pp. 647-704.

Oh, M.B.V. "The Pacific Basin: The View from Singapore." in Private Investors Abroad - 1985. New York: Matthew Bender, 1985.

Oh, Moonsong David. The Role of International Corporations in the Transfer of Technology of Developing Countries. Ann Arbor, Michigan: University Microfilms, 1970.

Oman, Charles. New Forms of International Investment in Developing Countries. Organisation for Economic Co-operation and Development. Washington, D.C.: OECD Publications and Information Center, 1984.

Orbe, L.F., III. "The Multinational in Yugoslavia." International Lawyer Vol. 19, 1985, pp. 623-638.

Parsky, G.L. "OPEC Investment in the U.S." Middle East Economic Survey Vol 18, 21 March 1975, Supplement.

Paterson, R.K. "The Economic Cooperation Agreement Between Canada and ASSAN: Charting a Foreign Investment Course in South East Asia." University of British Columbia Law Review Vol. 19, 1985, pp. 389-404.

Pattison, J.E. "China's Developing Legal Framework for Foreign Investment: Experience and Expectations." Law and Policy in International Business Vol. 13, 1981, pp. 89-175.

Pattison, J.E. "The United States-Egypt Bilateral Investment Treaty: A Prototype for Future Negotiation." Cornell International Law Journal Vol. 16, 1983, pp. 305-339.

"People's Republic of China - 1983 Joint Venture Implementing Regulations - the Supplement of Detail in an Attempt to Attract Foreign Investment." Georgia Journal of International and Comparative Law Vol. 15, 1985, pp. 389-413.

Perry, F.V. "The Foreign Investment Transaction in Mexico." Loyola of Los Angeles International and Comparative Law Journal Vol. 8, 1985, pp. 67-94.

"Promises, Promises: A Critical Analysis of Lome III's Private Investment Provisions." Fordham International Law Journal Vol. 9, 1985/1986, pp. 634-679.

Rajsky, J. "Le nouveau régime juridique des petits investissements étranger en Pologne." [In French and English] _Revue de Droit des Affaires Internationales/ International Business Law Journal_ Vol. 1985, 1985, pp. 217-227.

"Recent Legal Developments in U.S.-China Economic Relations." _Business Lawyer_ Vol. 36, 1981, pp. 1699-1732.

Reynolds, T.H. "Clouds of Codes: The New International Economic Order through Codes of Conduct: A Survey." _Law Library Journal_ Vol. 75, 1982, pp. 315-354.

"Riding a Tiger: Joint Ventures Under South Korea's New Foreign Capital Inducement Act." _New York University Journal of International Law and Policy_ Vol. 17, 1985, pp. 1023-1050.

Robinson, Richard D. "The Developing Countries, Development, and the Multinational Corporation," in D.H. Blake, ed., "The Multinational Corporation." _Annals of the American Academy of Political and Social Science_ Vol. 403, September 1972, pp. 67-79.

Rosendahl, Roger W. _Current Legal Aspects of Doing Business in the Pacific Basin._ Washington, D.C.: American Bar Association, 1986.

Rudway, R.J. and F.T. Hoet-Linares. "Venezuela Revisited: Foreign Investment, Technology and Related Issues." _Vanderbilt Journal of Transnational Law_ Vol. 15, 1982, pp. 1-45.

Scriven, J.G. "Joint Venture Legislation in Eastern Europe: A Practical Guide." _Harvard International Law Journal_ Vol. 21, 1980, pp. 633-665.

Scriven, J.G. "Structural Aspects of Multinational Corporation Trade with the Nonmarket Economies of Eastern Europe: An MNC Perspective on Domestic and Foreign Relations." _Michigan Year Book of International Legal Studies_ Vol. 2, 1981, pp. 201-219.

Seidl-Hohenveldern, Ignaz. "Chilean Copper Nationalization Cases before German Courts." American Journal of International Law Vol. 69, 1975, pp. 110-119.

Shiao-Ming, S. "China's New Law on Joint Ventures Using Chinese and Foreign Investment." Southwestern Law Journal Vol. 34, 1981, pp. 1183-1197.

Shihata, I.F.I. "The Multilateral Investment Guarantee Agency (MIGA) and Its Role in the Promotion of Foreign Investment." Private Investors Abroad Vol. 11, 1985, pp. 1-17.

Shillinglaw, T.L. and D.D. Stein. "Doing Business in the Soviet Union." Law and Policy in International Business Vol. 13, 1981, pp. 1-87.

Simmonds, Kenneth R. "International Law and the New International Economic Order." General Reports 1978, pp. 677-688.

Tobi, N. "Legal Aspects of Foreign Investment in Nigeria." Annuaire de l'Association des Auditeurs et Anciens Auditeurs de l'Académie de Droit International de la Haye Vol 47-48, 1977-1978, pp. 31-56.

Tomuschat, Christian. "Die Charta der wirtschaftlichen Recht und Pflichten der Staaten. Zur Gestaltungskraft von Deklarationen der UN-Generalversammlung." Zeitschrift fuer auslaendischer oeffentliches Recht und Voelkerrecht Vol. 36, 1976, pp. 444-491.

Torbert, Preston M. "China's Joint Venture Law: A Preliminary Analysis." Vanderbilt Journal of Transnational Law Vol. 12, 1979, pp. 819-895.

"Transfer of Technology in the International Marketplace: A Symposium." British Columbia International and Comparative Law Review Vol. 7, 1984, pp. 235-352.

Tsur, Y.A. "Some Aspects of Private Foreign Investment in Relation to Developing Countries." Annuaire de l'Association des Auditeurs et Anciens Auditeurs de l'Academie de Droit International de la Haye Vol. 47-48, 1977-1978, pp. 87-113.

Turner, Louis. Multinational Companies and the Third World. New York: Hill & Wang, 1973.

Tyler, M.R. "Legal Aspects of Investing in Ghana." Loyola of Los Angeles International and Comparative Law Journal Vol. 7, 1984, pp. 165-192.

"UNCTAD V Ends Session in Manila." UNCTAD Document No. TAD/INF/1079, UNCTAD Information Unit, 5 June 1979.

United Nations Centre on Transnational Corporations. The Acquisition of Technology from Multinational Corporations by Developing Countries. UN Sales No. E.74.II.A.7.

United Nations Centre on Transnational Corporations. Measures Strengthening the Negotiating Capacity of Governments in Their Relations with Transnational Corporations. Joint Ventures Among Firms in Latin America: A Technical Paper. UN Sales No. E.83.II.A.19.

United Nations Centre on Transnational Corporations. Transborder Data Flows and Brazil. UN Sales No. E.83.II.A.3.

United Nations Centre on Transnational Corporations. Transnational Corporations in Southern Africa: Update on Financial Activities and Employment Practices. UN Sales No. E.82.II.A.12.

United Nations Centre on Transnational Corporations. Transnational Corporations Linkages in Developing Countries. The Case of Backward Linkages Via Subcontracting. UN Sales No. E.81.II.A.4.

United Nations Centre on Transnational Corporations. Transnational Corporations: Activities of Transnational Corporations in Southern Africa: Impact of Financial and Social Structure. UN Sales No. E.78.II.A.6.

"United States Bilateral Investment Treaties: Egypt and Panama." Georgia Journal of International and Comparative Law Vol. 13, 1983, pp. 491-514.

United States Department of Commerce, International Trade Administration. Investment Climate in Foreign Countries. (Vol.1: OECD and other European countries [includes Canada and Japan]; Vol. 2: Africa; Vol. 3: Asia [excluding Japan]; Vol. 4: Western Hemisphere [excluding Canada]) August, 1985.

United States Department of Commerce, Office of Foreign Investment in the U.S. OPEC Direct Investments, 1974-1979. December 1980.

United States General Accounting Office. Are OPEC Financial Holdings a Danger to U.S. Banks or the Economy? 11 June 1979.

United States General Accounting Office. Changes Needed to Improve Government's Knowledge of OPEC Financial Influence in the U.S. 19 December 1979.

Valdez, A.L. "The Andean Foreign Investment Code: An Analysis." The Journal of International Law and Economics Vol. 7, 1972, pp. 1-19.

Varges, Gabe Shawn. The New International Economic Order Legal Debate: Background, Status and Alternatives. Frankfurt am Main: Peter Lang, 1983.

VerLoren van Themaat, Pieter. The Changing Structure of International Economic Law: A Contribution of Legal History, of Comparative Law and of General Legal Theory to the Debate on a New International Economic Order. The Hague, Boston, London: Nijhoff, 1981.

Vernon, Raymond, ed. Public Policy and Private Enterprise in Mexico. Cambridge, Massachusetts: Harvard University Press, 1964.

Vojnovic, M. "The New International Economic Order: 1. Principles and Theoretical Foundations; 2. International Regulation of the Behavior of Transnational Corporations." Thesaurus Acroasium Vol. 12, 1982, pp. 245-264.

Weston, Burns H. "Charter of Economic Rights and Duties of States and the Deprivation of Foreign-Owned Wealth." American Journal of International Law Vol. 75, 1981, pp. 437-475.

Wilson, P.J. "The Legal Structures Governing Technology Transfers and Joint Ventures with the People's Republic of China." International Tax and Business Lawyer Vol. 3, 1985, pp. 1-51.

Zagris, B. "Financing Participation in Caribbean Basin Investments and Trade." The University of Miami Inter-American Law Review Vol. 17, Fall 1985, pp. 97-130.

Zhang, Xiangyu. "A Survey of the Chinese Legal System of Foreign Investments." ASILS International Law Journal Vol. 9, 1985, pp. 37-60.

Zorn, J.G. and H.A. Mayerson. Cuba's Joint Venture Law: New Rules for Foreign Investment." Columbia Journal of Transnational Law Vol. 21, 1983, pp. 27-303.

19. MULTINATIONAL ENTERPRISES - GENERAL

Aharoni, Yair. "On the Definition of a Multinational Corporation." Quarterly Review of Economics and Business Autumn 1971, pp. 27-37.

Alger, Chadwick F. "The Multinational Corporation and the Future International System," in D.H. Blake, ed., "The Multinational Corporations." The Annals of the American Academy of Political Science Vol. 403, 1972, pp. 104-115.

"Amenability of Foreign Corporations to United States Employment Discrimination Laws." Vanderbilt Journal of Transnational Law Vol. 14, 1981, pp. 197-221.

Angelo, Homer G. "Multinational Enterprise." Receuil des Cours Vol. 125, 1968, pp. 443-607.

Baade, H.W. "Multinationale Gesellschaft im americanen Kollisionsrecht." [Summary in English] Rabels Zeitschrift fuer auslaendisches und internationales Privatrecht Vol. 37, 1973, pp. 5-35.

Backman, Jules and Ernest Block, eds. Multinational Companies, Trade and the Dollar in the Seventies. New York: New York University Press, 1974.

Baker, James C. and Thomas H. Bates. Financing International Business Operations. Scranton, Pennsylvania: Intext Educations Publishers, 1971.

Ballantine, H.W. "Parent and Subsidiary Corporations." California Law Review Vol. 14, 1925, p. 12-21.

Barnet, Richard J. and Ronald E. Mueller. Global Reach: The Power of the Multinationals. London: Jonathan Cape, 1975.

Behrman, Jack N. "Industrial Integration and the Multinational Enterprise," in D.H. Blake, ed., "The Multinational Corporation." The Annals of the American Academy of Political and Social Science Vol. 403, 1972, pp. 46-57.

Behrman, Jack N. *National Interests and the Multinational Enterprise: Tensions Among the North Atlantic Countries*. Englewood Cliffs, New Jersey: Prentice-Hall, 1970.

Behrman, Jack N. *Some Patterns in the Rise of the Multinational Enterprise*. (Research Paper 18) Chapel Hill: Graduate School of Business Administration, University of North Carolina, 1969.

Bertrandon, J. "La succursale internationale: statut fiscal." [Summary in English] *Droit et Pratique du Commerce* Vol. 11, 1985, pp. 385-400.

Blake, David H., ed. "The Multinational Corporation." *The Annals of the American Academy of Political and Social Science* Vol. 403, 1972 (Entire volume).

Blanpain, R. *The OECD Guidelines for Multinational Enterprises and Labour Relations: 1976-1979. Experience and Review*. Deventer: Kluwer, 1979.

Borton, Richard C. and James M. Goss. "Control of MNCs' Foreign Activities." *Washburn Law Journal* Vol. 15, 1976, pp. 435-456.

Borts, G.H. "The International Firm, the Tariff, and Long-Run Capital Movements." Paper presented at a Conference on the Multinational Firm and Economic Analysis, Bellagio, Italy, July 1972.

Brooke, Michael Z. and H. Lee Remmers, eds. *Multinational Firms*. New York: Penguin, 1974.

Brooke, Michael Z. and H. Lee Remmers, eds. *The Strategy of Multinational Enterprise: Organization and Finance*. London: Longman, 1970.

Brown, R. "The Relationship Between the State and the Multinational Corporation in the Exploitation of Resources." *International and Comparative Law Quarterly* Vol. 33, January 1984, pp. 218-229.

Burtis, David, et al., eds. MNC - Nation-State Interaction: An Annotated Bibliography. Philadelphia: Foreign Policy Research Institute, 1971.

Canada. Department of Industry, Trade and Commerce, Foreign Investment Division. "Notes on Some Definitions of the MNE." Ottawa, 1971.

Caves, R. "International Corporations: The Industrial Economics of Foreign Investment." Economica Vol. 38, 1971, pp. 1-27.

Caves, R. "Multinational Enterprise and Industrial Organization." Paper presented at a Conference on the Multinational Firm and Economic Analysis, Bellagio, Italy, July 1972.

Church, Frank. "The Multinational Enterprise." (Forward) San Diego Law Review Vol. 11, 1973, pp. 1-285.

Clausen, A.W. "The Internationalized Corporation: An Executive's View," in D.H. Blake, ed., "The Multinational Corporation." The Annals of the American Academy of Political and Social Science Vol. 403, 1972, pp. 12-21.

Cole, P.E. "New Challenges to the U.S. Multinational Corporation in the European Economic Community: Data Protection Laws." New York University Journal of International Law and Politics Vol. 17, 1985, pp. 893-947.

Cornell, R.A. "Trade of Multinational Corporations and Nations' Comparative Advantage." Paper presented at CIB-UCLA Conference on Multinational Corporations and Governments, 15-17 November 1973.

de Richmont, Jean. "L'épineaux problème du contrôle des firmes multinationales." Revue du Marché Commun, 1974, pp. 497-506.

Dehner, W.J. Jr. "Multinational Enterprise and Racial Non-Discrimination: United States Enforcement of an International Human Right." Harvard International Law Journal Vol. 15, 1974, pp. 71-125.

Deppe, F. "Wissenschaftlich-technischer Fortschritt, internationale Konzerne und Supranationalitaet," in Manfred Krueper, ed., _Investitionskontrolle gegen die Konzerne?_ Reinbek bei Hamburg: Rowholt, 1974.

de Vries, Henry P. "Business Organization: The Form of the Affiliate." _Columbia Journal of World Business_ Vol. 4, May-June 1969, pp. 91-92.

Domke, Martin. "The Control of Corporations." _International Law Quarterly_ Vol. 3, 1950, pp. 52-59.

Dueren, A. "Multinational Companies as a Political Problem." _The World Today_ Vol. 28, 1972, pp. 473-482.

Duerr, M.G. and J.M. Roach. _Organization and Control of International Operations_. New York: The Conference Board, 1973.

Dunning, John H., ed. _Economic Analysis and the Multinational Enterprise_. London: Allen & Unwin, 1974.

Dunning, John H. "The Future of the Multinational Enterprise." _Lloyd's Bank Review_ No. 113, July 1974, pp. 15-32.

Dunning, John H. _International Production and the Multinational Enterprise_. London: Allen & Unwin, 1981.

Dunning, John H. "Multinational Enterprises and Domestic Capital Formations." Manchester School of Economics and Social Studies, September 1973.

Dymsza, W. _Multinational Business Strategy_. New York: McGraw Hill, 1972.

The Economic Effects of Multinational Corporations, Vol. I of H. Peter Gray, ed., _Research in International Business and Finance_. Greenwich, Connecticut: JAI Press, 1979.

Eells, Richard. _Global Corporations_. New York: Interbook, 1972.

Eells, Richard. Global Corporations: The Emerging System of World Economic Power. New York: Free Press, 1976.

Eiteman, David K. and Arthur I. Stonehill. Multinational Business Finance. Reading, Massachusetts: Addison-Wesley Publishing Co., 1973.

L'Entreprise multinationale. Etude accompagnant le 35me Rapport annuel de la Kredietbank S.A. 1971.

Escobar, Luis. "Rules of the Game for MNCs." Worldview Vol. 17, 1974, pp. 25-30.

Ewing. "MNCs on Trial." Harvard Business Review May-June 1972, pp. 130-138.

Fatouros, A.A. "Problemes et Methodes d'une reglementation des entreprises multinationales." Journal du Droit International Vol. 101, 1974, pp. 495-521.

Fayerweather, John. "The Internationalization of Business," in D.H. Blake, ed., "The Multinational Corporation." The Annals of the American Academy of Political and Social Science Vol. 403, 1972, pp. 1-11.

Fayerweather, John. "Variables Influencing Elite Attitudes Toward Foreign Firms." (Working Paper Series 72-50) New York University, Graduate School of Business Administration, 1972.

Fligler, Carlos. Multinational Public Enterprise. London: Her Majesty's Stationery Office, 1963.

"Foreign Subsidiaries Are Not Immune to Employment Discrimination Laws." Washington University Law Quarterly Vol. 60, 1982, pp. 663-674.

Franko, Lawrence G. "Multinationals: The End of U.S. Dominance." Harvard Business Review Vol. 56, November-December 1978, pp. 93-101.

Gabriel, Peter P. "Management of Public Interests by the Multinational Corporation." Journal of World Trade Law Vol. 11, 1977, pp. 15-36.

Galloway, Jonathan F. "Labor and the Multinational Challenge." Stanford Journal of International Studies Vol. 11, pp. 102-121.

Gavalda, C. "Le profit de loi sur le règlement judiciaire des entreprises en difficultés." Recueil Dalloz Sirey 1984, pp. C13-C20.

Gordon, M.W. "The Multinational Corporation and International Trade Theory." Paper presented at a Conference on the Multinational Firm and Economic Analysis, Bellagio, Italy, September 1972.

Graham, E.M. "Transatlantic Investment by Multinational Firms: A Private Phenomenon?" Journal of Post-Keynesian Economics Vol. 28, September 1978, pp. 82-99.

Grisoli, Angelo. "Problems in the Legal Regulation of Multinational Corporations." Politico Vol. 40, 1975, pp. 373-381.

Grunberg, Leon. Failed Multinational Ventures: The Political Economy of International Divestments. Lexington, Massachusetts: Lexington Books, 1981.

Gunter, H. "Erosion of Trade Union Power through Multinational Enterprises?" Vanderbilt Journal of Transnational Law Vol. 9, 1976, pp. 771-793.

Gyorgy, Adam. The World Corporation Problematics; Apologetics and Critique. Budapest: Hungarian Scientific Council for World Economy, 1971.

Hadden, Tom. Company Law and Capitalism. London: Weidenfeld & Nicolson, 1972.

Hahlo, H.R., ed. Nationalism and the Multinational Enterprise: Legal, Economic and Managerial Aspects. Dobbs Ferry, New York: Oceana, 1973.

Hahn, M. "Functional Limits of Multinational Enterprises." New York University Journal of International Law and Politics Vol. 7, 1974, pp. 475-492.

Hays, Richard D., Christopher M. Korth and Mauncher Roudiani. International Business: An Introduction to the World of the Multinational Firm. Englewood Cliffs, New Jersey: Prentice-Hall, 1972.

Hellman, Rainer. The Challenge to U.S. Dominance of the International Corporations. New York: Dunellen, 1970.

Hellman, Rainer. "Countervailing Powers to the Multinational Corporation," in Don Wallace, ed., International Control of Investment: The Dusseldorf Conference on Multinational Corporations. New York: Praeger, 1974.

Hermann, Don H.J. "Criminal Prosecutions of U.S. Multinational Corporations." Loyola University of Chicago Law Review Vol. 8, 1976-1977, pp. 465-498, 619-641.

Hochmuth, M.S. Organizing the Transnational: The Experience with Transnational Enterprise in Advanced Technology. Leiden: Sijthoff, 1974.

Hofbauer, M.A. "Die Einbeziehung von Fremdkapitalzinsen in die Herstellungskosten nach geltenden und Kunftigem Bilanzrecht." Wallis Collection pp. 383-395.

Hopt, Klaus J., ed. Legal and Economic Analyses on Multinational Enterprises. New York: Walter de Gruyter, 1982. (2 Vols.) Vol. 1: European Merger Control; Vol. 2: Groups of Companies in European Laws.

Horst, T. "Multinational Enterprise and the Theory of the Firm." Paper presented at a Conference on the Multinational Firm and Economic Analysis, Bellagio, Italy, July 1972.

Hossain, Kamal. Law and Policy in Petroleum Developments: Changing Relations Between Transnationals and Governments: A Comparative Study Sponsored by the Commonwealth Secretariat. New York: Nichols, 1979.

Hufbauer, Gary Clyde. "The Multinational Corporation and Direct Investment." Paper presented at a Conference on Research in International Trade and Finance, Princeton, New Jersey, 30 March 1973.

Hymer, Stephen H. "The Efficiency Contradictions of Multinational Corporations," in Gilles Paguet, ed., The Multinational Firm and the Nation-State. Canada: Collier-MacMillan, 1972.

Hymer, Stephen H. "The MNE and the Law of Uneven Development," in Jagdish N. Bhagwati, ed., Economics and World Order from the 1970's to the 1990's. New York: Macmillan, 1972.

Hymer, Stephen H. and Robert Rowthorn. "Multinational Corporations and International Oligopoly: The Non-American Challenge," in Charles P. Kindleberger, ed., The International Corporation: A Symposium. Cambridge, Massachusetts: MIT Press, 1970.

International Chamber of Commerce. The International Corporation, with an Epilogue on Rights and Responsibilities, from the 22nd Congress, 1969. Paris: International Chamber of Commerce, 1969.

International Chamber of Commerce. "International Economic Growth: The Role, Rights and Responsibilities of the International Corporation," from the 22nd Congress, 1969. Paris: International Chamber of Commerce, 1969.

International Chamber of Commerce. Realities: Multinational Enterprises Respond on Basic Issues. Paris: International Chamber of Commerce, 1974.

International Chamber of Commerce, Special Committee on Multinational Enterprises. "Multinational Enterprises and their Role in Economic Developemnt." ICC Document No. 191/81.

International Labor Organization. Multinational Enterprises and Social Policy. Geneva: International Labor Office, 1973.

Jakubowski, J. "Le droit applicable aux entreprises multinationales." Rapports polonais présentés au 9e congrès international du droit comparé, Varsovie, 1974, pp. 75-86.

Jayagovinda, A. "Report on the Group of Eminent Persons on Multinational Corporations: An Analysis." Indian Journal of International Law Vol. 15, 1975 pp. 521-525.

Jenks, C. Wilfred. "Multinational Entities in the Law of Nations," in W.G. Friedmann et al., eds., in Transnational Law in a Changing Society. Essays in honor of Philip C. Jessup. New York: Columbia University Press, 1972.

Johnson, Harry G. "The MNC as an Agency of Economic Development; Some Exploratory Observations," in James Ward et al., The Widening Gap; Development in the 1970s - A Report on the Columbia Conference on International Economic Development, 1970. New York: Columbia University Press, 1971.

Judge, A.J.N. "Multinational Business Enterprises." Yearbook of International Organizations 1968-1969, pp. 1189-1214.

Kapoor, Ashok and P.D. Grub, eds. The Multinational Enterprise in Transition: Selected Readings and Essays. Princeton, New Jersey: Darwin Press, 1972.

Kendall, Donald. "Corporate Ownership: The International Dimension." Columbia Journal of World Business Vol 4, July-August 1969, pp. 59-65.

Kindleberger, Charles P., ed. The International Corporation: A Symposium. Cambridge, Massachusetts: MIT Press, 1970.

Kirchner, D. "Now the Transnational Enterprise." Harvard Business Review Vol. 10, 1964, pp. 6-11.

Knickerbocker, Frederick T. _Oligopolistic Reaction and Multinational Enterprise_. Boston: Harvard Graduate School of Business Administration, 1973.

Kolde, Endel J. "The Administrative Structure of International Business with Special Reference to Foreign-Based Affiliates." _University of Washington Business Review_ Vol. 22, 1963.

Kolde, Endel J. _The Multinational Company_. Lexington, Massachusetts: D.C. Heath & Co., 1974.

Krainer, R.E. "The Valuation and Financing of the Multinational Firm." _Kyklos_ Vol. 25, 1972, pp. 553-574.

Krauthoff, Louis. "The Practical Implications of International Economic Regulation of Multinational Corporations and Business as Seen from Capitol Hill." _International Lawyer_ Vol. 11, 1977, pp. 347-354.

Lalive, P. "Les entreprises multinationales," in _Le Droit international demain/International Law Tomorrow_. Neuchatel, 1974.

Lall, Sanjaya. _Foreign Private Manufacturing Investment and Multinational Corporations: An Annotated Bibliography_. New York: Praeger, 1975.

Lall, Sanjaya. _The Multinational Corporation_. London: MacMillan, 1980.

Latty, Elvin. _Subsidiaries and Affiliated Corporations. A Study in Stockholders' Liability_. Chicago: Foundation Press, 1936.

Layne, C. "Multinational Enterprises in the International Political System: A Theoretical Consideration." _New York University Journal of International Law and Policy_ Vol. 13, 1980, pp. 27-61.

Lea, Sperry and Simon Webley. _Multinational Corporations in Developed Countries: A Review of Recent Research and Policy Thinking_. Washington, D.C.: British-North American Committee, 1973.

Levinson, Charles. Capital, Inflation and the Multinationals. New York: MacMillan, 1972.

Libbrecht, Emmanuel. Entreprises à caractère juridiquement international. Leiden: Sijthoff, 1972.

Linde, Stephen A. "Regulation of Transfer Pricing in Multinational Corporations: An International Perspective." Journal of International Law and Politics Vol. 10, 1977.

Lions, Earl Perry. The Anational Corporation. Lausanne: Imprimerie Reunies S.A., 1972.

Litvak, I.A. and C.J. Maule. "The Multinational Corporation: Some Economic and Political Legal Implications." Journal of World Trade Law Vol. 5, 1971, pp. 631-643.

Litvak, I.A. and C.J. Maule. "The Multinational Firm and Conflicting National Interests." Journal of World Trade Law Vol. 3, 1969, pp. 309-318.

Lombardi, R. "Multinational Enterprises." International Chamber of Commerce Information Vol. 39, 1973, pp. 1-2.

Loussouarn, Y. "La succursale, technique juridiuqe du commerce international." [Summary in English] Droit et Pratique du Commerce Vol. 11, 1985, pp. 359-369.

Manser, W.A. The Financial Role of Multinational Enterprises. New York: J. Wiley, 1973.

Mansfield, E. "The Multinational Firm and Technological Change." Paper presented at a Conference on the Multinational Firm and Economic Analysis, Bellagio, Italy, September 1972.

Martyn, Howe. Multinational Business Management. Lexington, Massachusetts: D.C. Heath & Co., 1970.

Maynard, Geoffrey. "Multinational Enterprises and Monetary Analysis." Paper presented at a Conference on Multinational Firm and Economic Analysis, Bellagio, Italy, September 1972.

Merle, M. "Firmes multinationales et relations internationales." Revue égyptienne de droit international Vol. 27, 1971, pp. 1-12.

Miller, Arthur S. "The Corporation as a Private Government in the World Community." Virginia Law Review Vol. 46, 1960, pp. 1539-1572.

Miller, Arthur S. "Toward the 'Techno-Corporate' State? - An Essay in American Constitutionalism." Villanova Law Review Vol. 14, 1968, pp. 1-73.

Miller, J. Irwin. "Multinational Corporations: The UN Report." Business Horizons Vol. 17, December 1974, pp. 17-24.

Modelski, George. "The Corporation in World Society." Yearbook of World Affairs Vol. 22, 1968, pp. 64-79.

Modelski, George, ed. "Multinational Corporations and World Order." International Studies Quarterly Vol. 16, 1972, pp. 407-432.

Moran, Theodore. Multinational Corporations and the Politics of Dependence: Copper in Chile. Princeton, New Jersey: Princeton University Press, 1975.

Multinational Companies. Brussels: Europe Information Service, 1979.

The Multinational Corporation, Report of conference held at U.S. Department of State, 14 February 1969. Washington, DC: U.S.Government Printing Office, 1969.

"Multinational Corporations and Employment Discrimination: A Strategy for Litigation." University of San Francisco Law Review Vol. 16, 1982, pp. 491-516.

"Multinational Firms Face a Growing Power: Multinational Unions." Wall Street Journal 23 April 1973, pp. 1, 14.

"Multinationals and the Antiquities of Company Law." Modern Law Review Vol. 47, 1984, pp. 87-92.

"Multinationals: Bad Guys Do Good." The Economist 22 November 1975, p. 81.

"Multinationals: ICC Speaks to UN Session in Peru." Information (ICC Members' Bulletin) No. 2, 1976, p. 3.

Nadelmann, K.H. "The Lure in 'International Bankruptcies' of Assets Located Abroad." International and Comparative Law Quarterly Vol. 33, 1984, pp. 431-436.

Negandhi, Anant R., Howard Thomas and K.L.K. Rao, eds. Multinational Corporations and State-Owned Enterprises: A New Challenge in International Business, Vol. I of Anant R. Negandhi, ed, Research in International Business and International Relations. Greenwich, Connecticut: JAI Press, 1986.

"New Era for the Multinationals." Business Week 6 July 1974, pp. 73-74.

Ocran, Tawia Modibo. "Negotiations with Multinational Corporations." Akron Law Review Vol. 18, 1985, pp. 405-434.

Organisation for Economic Co-operation and Development, Committee on International Investment and Multinational Enterprises. Review of the 1976 Declaration and Decisions on International Investment and Multinational Enterprises. Paris: OECD Publications, 1979.

Organisation for Economic Co-operation and Development. "Declaration on International Investment and Multinational Enterprises by the Governments of OECD Member Countries" 21 June 1976. International Investment and Multinational Enterprises Paris: OECD Publications, 1976.

Organisation for Economic Co-operation and Development. International Investment and Multinational Enterprises Paris: OECD Publications, 1976.

Organisation for Economic Co-operation and Development. International Investment and Multinational Corporations: 1984 Review of the 1976 Declarations and Decisions. Paris: OECD Publications, 1984.

Organisation for Economic Co-operation and Development. Structural Adjustment and Multinational Corporations. Paris: OECD Publications, 1985.

Osterberg, D. and F. Ajami. "The Multinational Corporation: Expanding the Frontiers of World Politics." The Journal of Conflict Resolution Vol. 15, 1971, pp. 457-470.

Paquet, G., ed. The Multinational Firm and the Nation State. Canada: Collier MacMillan, 1972.

Perlmutter, Howard V. "L'entreprise internationale - trois conceptions." Revue économique et sociale Vol. 16, 1965, pp. 151-156.

Perlmutter, Howard V. "Some Architectural Problems of the Multinational Firm." Quarterly Journal of AISEC International Vol. 3, August 1967, pp. 33-44.

Perlmutter, Howard V. "The Tortuous Evolution of Multinational Corporations." Columbia Journal of World Business Vol. 3, 1969, pp. 9-18.

Phatak, Arvind V. Evolution of World Enterprises. New York: American Management Association, 1971.

Phatak, Arvind V. Managing Multinational Corporations. New York: Praeger, 1974.

Rangarajan, S. "Structure of and Legal Control over Multinational Corporations in a Mixed Economy." Indian Journal of International Law Vol. 15, 1975, pp. 521-525.

Ray, Dennis M. "Corporations and American Foreign Relations," in D.H. Blake, "The Multinational Corporation." The Annals of the American Academy of Political and Social Science Vol. 403, 1972, pp. 80-92.

Reese, Knut. "Multinational Companies and the Nation State." Studia Diplomatica Vol. 28, 1975, pp. 27-38.

Robbins, Sidney M. and Robert B. Stobaugh. Money in the Multinational Enterprise: A Study of Financial Policy. New York: Basic Books, 1973.

Robinson, E.A.G. The Structure of Competitive Industry. Cambridge, Massachusetts: James Nisbet & Co./Cambridge University Press, 1958.

Robinson, Richard D. "Beyond the Multinational Corporation," in John Fayerweather, ed., International Business-Government Affairs, Toward an Era of Accommodation. Cambridge, Massachusetts: Ballinger, 1973.

Robinson, Richard D. International Management. New York, London: Holt, Rhinehart & Winston, 1967.

Rodriguez Sastre, Antonio. "Problemas jurídicos de las empresas multinacionales." Revista de Estudios Políticos Vol. 202, 1975, pp. 97-143.

Rolfe, Sidney E. The Multinational Corporation. New York: Foreign Policy Association (Headline Series, 199), 1970.

Rolfe, Sidney E. and W. Damm, eds. The Multinational Corporation in the World Economy: Direct Investment in Perspective. New York: Praeger, 1972.

Rolfe, Sidney E. "Special Study of the Transnational Corporation." U.S. Council of the International Chamber of Commerce Inc., Document No. 191/10, 28.III, 1968.

Rosenberg, Herman. "Weighing the Power of the Multinationals." Stanford Journal of International Studies Vol. 11, 1976. (This is a book review of A.A. Said and L.R. Simmons, The New Sovereigns: Multinational Corporations as World Powers. Englewood Cliffs, New Jersey: Prentice-Hall, 1975.)

Ross, Howard. "An Attempted Summing Up," in H.R. Hahlo, ed., Nationalism and the Multinational Enterprise: Legal, Economic and Managerial Aspects. Dobbs Ferry, New York: Oceana, 1973.

Rubin, Seymour J. "Multinational Enterprise and National Sovereignty: A Skeptics Analysis." Law and Policy in International Business Vol. 83, 1971, pp. 1-41.

Rubin, Seymour J. "The Multinational Enterprise at Bay." American Journal of International Law Vol. 68, 1974. pp. 475-488.

Sacerdoti, G. "Questions de responsabilité envers les tiers dans les groupes multinationaux de sociétés." Rivista delle Societá Vol. 30, 1984, pp. 976-994.

Safarian, Albert. "Country of Ownership and Performance of the Firm." Economic Record Vol. 44, 1968, pp. 82-96.

Said, Abdul A. and Luiz R. Simmons, eds. The New Sovereigns: Multinational Corporations as World Powers. Englewood Cliffs, New Jersey: Prentice-Hall, 1975.

Salera, Virgil. Multinational Business. Boston: Houghton Mifflin, 1969.

Salter, L.M. "The Dynamics of the Multinational Enterprise: Exemplar for World Government." International Lawyer Vol. 8, 1974, pp. 11-19.

Sauvant, Karl P. and Farid G. Lavifour, eds. Controlling Multinational Enterprises: Problems, Strategies, Counter-strategies. Boulder, Colorado: Westview Press, 1976.

Schaffner, Hans. Die Multinationalen - Ausbeuter oder Triebkraft der Weltwirtschaft? Zurich: Edition Interfrom, 1974.

Schmidt, Dominique. "La Protection des entreprises nationales contre les prises de contrôle par des sociétés multinationales étrangères." Rivista della Societá Vol. 21, 1976, pp. 621-631.

Schmitthoff, Clive M. "Group Liability of Multinationals," in K.R. Simmonds, ed., Legal Problems of Multinational Corporations. London: British Institute of International and Comparative Law, 1977.

Schmitthoff, Clive M. "Multi-national Companies." Journal of Business Law Vol. 1970, 1970, pp. 177-184.

Schmitthoff, Clive M. "Multi-National Enterprises." New Law Journal Vol. 121, 1971, pp. 1053-1054.

Schmitthoff, Clive M. "Multinationals in Court." Journal of Business Law Vol. 1972, 1972, pp. 103-111.

Schollhammer, Hans. Locational Strategies of Multinational Firms. Los Angeles, California: Center for International Business, Pepperdine University, 1974.

Schwindiman, John S. Strategic and Long Range Planning for the Multinational Corporation. New York: Praeger Special Studies Service, 1973.

Seidl-Hohenfeldern, Ignaz. "The United Nations and Transnational Corporations," in K.R. Simmonds, ed., Legal Problems of Multinational Corporations. London: British Institute of International and Comparative Law, 1977.

Servan-Schreiber, Jean-Jacques. The American Challenge. London: Hamish Hamilton, 1968.

Sethi, S.P. and J.N. Sheth, eds. Multinational Business Operations. Pacific Palisades, California: Goodyear Publishing Company, 1973.

Simmonds, Kenneth R. "Foreign Investment, The International Law Standard, and the Multinational Corporation - An Overview," in K.R. Simmonds, ed., Legal Problems of Multinational Corporations. London: British Institute of International and Comparative Law, 1977.

Simmonds, Kenneth R. "Is the World Going More Multinational?" Paper prepared for an Internationalization of Business Conference, Society of Business Economists, Churchill College, Cambridge, 1971.

Simmonds, Kenneth R., ed. Legal Problems of Multinational Corporations. London: British Institute of International and Comparative Law, 1977.

Skol, A.G. and C.H. Peterson. "Export Control Laws and Multinational Enterprises." International Lawyer Vol. 11, 1977, pp. 29-44.

Solomon, L.D. "Multinational Corporations and the Emerging World Order." Case Western Reserve Journal of International Law Vol. 8, 1976, pp. 329-428.

Sparkman, John. "The Multinational Corporation and Foreign Investment." Mercer Law Review Vol. 27, 1976, pp. 381-389.

Stauffer, Robert B. Nation Building in a Global Economy; the Role of the Multinational Corporation. Beverly Hills, California: Sage Publications (Paper in Comparative Politics 01-039), 1973.

Steindorff, E. "Gemeinschaftsunternehmen mit zwei paritaetisch beteiligten Gesellschaftern." Neue Juristische Wochenschrift Vol. 33, 1980, pp. 1921-1924.

Stevens, Guy. "The Multinational Firm and the Determinants of Investment." Paper presented at a Conference on the Multinational Firm and Economic Analysis, Bellagio, Italy, September 1972.

Stopford, John M. and Louis T. Wells, Jr. Managing the Multinational Enterprises: Organization of the Firm and Ownership of the Subsidiaries. London: Longman, 1972.

Supiot, A. "Groupes de sociétés et paradigme de l'entreprise." Revue Trimestrielle de Droit Commercial et de Droit Économique Vol. 38, 1985, pp. 621-644.

Thomas, B.S. "International Harmonization - Recent Developments in the Pursuit of Comparability in General Purpose Reports of Multinational Enterprises." Business Lawyer Vol. 38, 1983, pp. 1397-1411.

Tindall, Robert E. Multinational Enterprises: Legal and Management Structures and Interrelationship with Ownership, Control, Antitrust, Labor, Taxation and Disclosure. Dobbs Ferry, New York: Oceana, 1975.

"Title VII of the Civil Rights Act of 1964 and the Multinational Enterprise." Georgia Law Journal Vol. 73, 1985, pp. 1465-1498.

Trotier, B. "Le contrôle juridique des entreprises multinationales." Cahiers de Droit Vol. 27, 1986, pp. 419-435.

Tugendhat, Christopher. The Multinationals. New York: Random House, 1972.

Turner, Louis. Invisible Empires: Multinational Companies and the Modern World. London: Hamish Hamilton, 1970.

United Nations. The Impact of Multinational Corporations on Development and on International Relations UN Publication E/5500/Rev.1; ST/ESA/6, Sales No. E.74.II.A.5. New York, 1974.

United Nations. Multinational Corporations in World Development. UN Publication E/500/REV.1; St/ESA/6, Sales No. E.74.II.A.5. New York, 1974.

United Nations. Multinational Corporations in World Development. UN Publication ST/ECA/190, Sales No. E.73.II.A.11. New York, 1973.

United Nations. Summary of the Hearings Before the Group of Eminent Persons to Study the Impact of Multinational Corporations on Development and on International Relations. UN Publication ST/ESA/15, Sales No. 1975.I.5. New York, 1979.

United Nations. Summary of the Hearings Before the Group of Eminent Persons to Study the Impact of Multinational Corporations on Development and on International Relations. New York: UN Publication No. ST/ESA/15, Sales No. E.74.II.A.9, 1974.

United Nations Centre on Transnational Corporations. The Activities of Transnational Corporations in the Industrial, Mining and Military Sectors of Southern Africa. UN Sales No. E.80.II.A.3.

United Nations Centre on Transnational Corporations. Transnational Corporations in Advertising: A Technical Paper. UN Sales No. E.79.II.A.2.

United Nations Centre on Transnational Corporations. Transnational Corporations in the Agricultural Machinery and Equipment Industry. UN Sales No. E.83.II.A.4.

United Nations Centre on Transnational Corporations. Transnational Corporations in the Bauxite/Aluminum Industry. UN Sales No. E.81.II.A.5.

United Nations Centre on Transnational Corporations. Transnational Corporations and Contractual Relations in the World Uranium Industry: A Technical Paper. UN Sales No. E.83.II.A.17.

United Nations Centre on Transnational Corporations. Transnational Corporations in the Copper Industry. UN Sales No. E.81.II.A.3.

United Nations Centre on Transnational Corporations. Transnational Corporations in the Fertilizer Industry. UN Sales No. E.82.II.A.10.

United Nations Centre on Transnational Corporations. Transnational Corporations in Food and Beverage Processing. UN Sales No. E.81.II.A.12.

United Nations Centre on Transnational Corporations. *Transnational Corporations in the International Auto Industry*. UN Sales No. E.83.II.A.6.

United Nations Centre on Transnational Corporations. *Transnational Corporations in International Tourism*. UN Sales No. E.82.II.A.9.

United Nations Centre on Transnational Corporations. *Transnational Corporations in the Pharmaceutical Industry*. UN Sales No. E.79.II.A.3.

United Nations Centre on Transnational Corporations. *Transnational Corporations in the Power Equipment Industry*. UN Sales No. E.82.II.A.11.

United Nations Centre on Transnational Corporations. *Transnational Corporations in World Development, 3rd Survey*. UN Sales No. E.83.II.A.14.

United Nations Centre on Transnational Corporations. *Transnational Reinsurance Operations: A Technical Paper*. UN Sales No. E.80.II.A.10.

United Nations Centre on Transnational Corporations. *Users Guide to the Information System on Transnational Corporations: A Technical Paper*. UN Sales No. E.80.II.A.6.

United Nations Commission on Transnational Corporations. *National Legislation and Regulations Relating to Transnational Corporations*. Report of the Second Session, Lima, 1-12 March 1976. UN Document No. E/C.10/8.

United Nations Commission on Transnational Corporations. "Report on the First Session 17-28 March 1975 of the Economic and Social Council." 59th Session, Supplement No. 12. UN Document No. E/5655, E./C.10/6.

United Nations Commission on Transnational Corporations. "Report on the Second Session 1-12 March 1976." UN Document No. E/5782, E/C.10/16.

Vagts, Detlev F. "The Host Country Faces the Multinational Enterprise." Boston University Law Review Vol. 53, 1973, pp. 261-277.

Vagts, Detlev F. "Law and Accounting in Business Associations," in Vol. XIII "Business and Private Organizations," International Encyclopedia of Comparative Law. Dobbs Ferry, New York: Oceana, 1972.

Vagts, Detlev F. "The Multinational Enterprise: A New Challenge for Transnational Law." Harvard Law Review Vol. 83, 1970, pp. 769-792.

van Hecke, G.A. "Nationality of Companies Analyzed." Netherlands International Law Review Vol. 8, 1961, pp. 223-239.

Vaupel, J.W. and J.P. Curhan. The Making of Multinational Enterprise. Boston: Harvard Business School, 1969.

Vaupel, J.W. and J.P. Curhan. The World's Multinational Enterprises. Boston: Harvard University Press, 1974.

Vernon, Raymond. The Economic and Political Consequences of Multinational Enterprise: An Anthology. Cambridge, Massachusetts: Harvard Business School, 1972.

Vernon, Raymond. "Economic Sovereignty at Bay." Foreign Affairs Vol. 47, October 1968, pp. 110-122.

Vernon, Raymond. "Future of the Multinational Enterprise," in Charles P. Kindleberger, ed., The International Corporation: A Symposium. Cambridge, Massachusetts: MIT Press, 1970.

Vernon, Raymond. "Multinational Business and National Economic Goals." International Organization Vol. 25, 1971, pp. 693-705.

Vernon, Raymond. Multinational Enterprises and National Security. London: Institute for Strategic Studies, 1971.

von Mehren, Robert B. and Martin E. Gold. "Multinational Corporations: Conflicts and Controls." Stanford Journal of International Studies Vol. 11, 1976, pp. 1-41.

Wallace, Don, Jr. International Control of Investment: The Dusseldorf Conference on Multinational Corporations. New York: Praeger, 1974.

Watkins, Steven Lane. "Multinational Enterprises: The Need for an International Regime." Master of Law dissertation, London School of Economics, University of London, July 1975.

Wesley, R.G. "Problems in Regulating the Multinational Enterprise - An Overview." International Lawyer Vol. 10, 1976, pp. 613-622.

Wilms-Wright, Carl. Transnational Corporations: A Strategy for Control. London: Fabian Society, 1977.

Winqwist, Carl-Henrik. "Multinationals." International Chamber of Commerce Information (ICC bulletin) Vol. 40, July-August 1974, p. 1.

Witherspoon, R.A. "Multinational Corporations - Governmental Regulation of Business Ethics under the Foreign Corrupt Practices Act of 1977: An Analysis." Dickinson Law Review Vol. 87, 1983, pp. 531-593.

Wriston, W.B. "World Corporations - New Weight in an Old Balance." New York School of Business Journal Vol. 46, February 1974, pp. 77-83.

20. TAXATION

Abrutyn, M. and N. Boidman. "The New Canada-United States Tax Convention." International Lawyer Vol. 20, 1986, pp. 125-152.

"Alternatives to Worldwide Unitary Apportionment - An Analysis." University of Florida Law Review Vol. 36, 1984, pp. 1051-1080.

"America's Reliance on Foreign Funds to Fight the Deficit: Repeal of the 30% Withholding Tax." Brooklyn Journal of International Law Vol. 12, 1986, pp. 127-159.

Arnold, B.J. and C.F.L. Young. "International Taxation and Federalism: The Canadian Perspective." [In English and French] Revue de Droit des Affaires Internationales/ International Business Law Journal Vol. 1985, 1985, pp. 541-558.

Arnold, B.J. "The Taxation of Controlled Foreign Corporations: Defining and Designating Tax Havens." Canadian Tax Journal Vol. 33, 1985, pp. 445-489.

Arpan, Jeffrey S. International Intracorporate Pricing: Non-American Systems and Views. New York: Praeger, 1972.

Augustyn, F.M. "A Primer for Incorporating Under the Income Tax Laws of France, Germany, or the United Kingdom." New England Journal of International Law and Business Vol. 7, 1985, pp. 267-317.

Ault, H.J. "The Unitary Tax Controversy: Federalism, Treaties and International Tax Relationships." [In English and French] Revue de Droit des Affaires Internationales/ International Business Law Journal Vol. 1985, 1985, pp. 559-571.

Baker, M.B. "Redefining Taxation of International Entities: The Unitary Controversy (A Constitutional Approach)." Denver Journal of International Law and Policy Vol. 14, 1985, pp. 35-37.

Ball, G.T., et al. "Unilateral Measures to Prevent Double Taxation: National Report." International Fiscal Association Cahiers de Droit Fiscal International No. 66B, 1981: U.S. pp. 301-328; U.K. pp. 413-428.

Baxter, I.F.G. "The United Kingdom and Tax Havens: A Comparative Comment." American Journal of Comparative Law Vol. 33, 1985, pp. 707-719.

Berberian, D. and Menck, T. "Comparison of U.S. and German Intercompany Pricing Regulations." [Summaries in English, French and German] Intertax 1981, pp. 410-420.

Block, N.J., et al. "Transition from DISC to a Foreign Sales Corporation: Tax and Other Considerations." International Lawyer Vol. 19, 1985, pp. 343-359.

Boehme, R. "Current Issues in U.S.-German Financial and Economic Relations." [Summaries in English, French, and German] Intertax 1982, pp. 129-135.

Boidman, N. "Canada: New Legislation Respecting Treaty Interpretation." [Summaries in English, French, and German] Intertax 1983, pp. 383-389.

Boidman, N. "Canada: Supreme Court Interprets Canada-Germany Tax Treaty." [Summaries in English, French, and German] Intertax January 1983, pp. 17-21.

Boidman, N. "International Tax Avoidance: The Impact on Legal Systems." Bulletin for International Fiscal Documentation Vol. 35, 1981, pp. 435-447.

Boidman, N. "Interpretation of Tax Treaties in Canada." Bulletin for International Fiscal Documentation Vol. 34, 1980, pp. 388-401.

Born, G.B. "Recent British Responses to the Extraterritorial Application of United States Law: The Midland Bank [Midland Bank v. Laker Airways, Slip Op. (C.A. July 30, 1985)] Decision and Retaliating Legislation Involving Unitary Taxation." Virginia Journal of International Law Vol. 26, Fall 1985, pp. 91-108.

Bowen, S. "Defenses Against Takeovers - Selected Tax Problems." Taxes Vol. 64, 1986, pp. 835-845.

Brean, Donald J.S. International Issues on Taxation: The Canadian Perspective Toronto: Canadian Tax Foundation, 1984.

Brown, R.D. "Tax Aspects of Technology Transfers Between the United States and Canada: A Canadian Viewpoint." Canada-United States Law Journal Vol. 11, 1986, pp. 227-246.

"CFC-FPHC Coordination - A Better Way." University of Florida Law Review Vol. 36 1984, pp. 1103-1125.

"CFE: Opinion on the Proposal for a Directive on the Common System of Taxation Applicable to Mergers, Divisions and Contributions of Assets Occurring Between Companies of Different Member States." [Summaries in English, French, and German] Intertax 1980, pp. 314-320.

Cabanellas, G. and L. Bertone. "Host Country Taxation of Transfer of Technology Transactions." Georgia Journal of International and Comparative Law Vol. 1981, 1981, pp. 495-516.

"Canada-United States Transnational Business Activities: Current Tax and Other Developments." (Various articles) Canada-United States Law Journal Vol. 4, 1981, pp. 90-173.

Carroll, Mitchell B. "Taxation of U.S.-Based Transnational Corporations." Mercer Law Review Vol. 27, 1976, pp. 441-468.

Chilton, F.R., Jr. "United States Tax Developments during 1983 That Can Affect International Transactions." Hasting's International and Comparative Law Review Vol. 1984, 1984, pp. 333-375.

Choate, Alan G. "U.S. Taxation of Foreign Direct Investment." Dickinson International Law Annual Vol. 1, 1982, pp. 35-58.

Chown, J.F. and W. Hopper. "Company Tax Harmonization in the European Economic Community." [Summaries in English, French, and German] Intertax 1982, pp. 275-284.

Chown, J.F. "European Tax Treatment of Foreign Investment." Boston University International Law Journal Vol. 4, 1986, pp. 55-65.

"Colloquy on International Tax Avoidance and Evasion, Strasbourg. March 5-7, 1980." European Taxation Vol. 20, 1980, pp. 133-233.

Conway, J.D. "The Proposed Tax Straddle Reform Act of 1983 - Unjust Treatment for Many United States-Owned Foreign Corporations." Taxes Vol. 62, 1984, pp. 256-270.

Cooper, M.J. and T.J. Rasmussen. "Tax Treaty Shopping." Bulletin of International Fiscal Documentation Vol. 36, July 1982, pp. 291-297.

"Corporate Tax - Part II." New York University Institute of Federal Taxation Vol. 42, 1984, pp. 13.1-16.20.

Crowley, C. and P. McGowan. "Irish Tax Law and the Foreign Investor." Vanderbilt Journal of Transnational Law Vol. 17, 1984, pp. 631-664.

Dachs, R.A. "Enforcement of Foreign Tax Judgments in the United States." George Washington Journal of International Law and Economics Vol. 14, 1980, pp. 281-299.

Davies, A.G. "Some Taxation Problems of Large Multinational Firms." [Summaries in English, French, and German] Intertax 1975, pp. 161-168.

Davies, David R. Principles of International Double Taxation Relief. Ontario, Canada: Carswell, 1986.

Davies, David R. "United Kingdom: Inland Revenue Guidance Notes on Transfer Pricing and Multinational Enterprises." [Summaries in English, French, and German] Intertax 1982, pp. 12-18.

Davies, David R. "United Kingdom: Recent Tax Cases Concerning Parent Company and Subsidiary Branch Operations." [Summaries in English, French, and German] Intertax 1983, pp. 301-306.

Degnan, T.E. and K.A. Coyle. "Final Regulations for FIRPTA Code Section 897." Oil and Gas Tax Quarterly Vol. 35, September 1986, pp. 50-72.

de Vries, E. "Intercompany Pricing Provisions in the United Kingdom." [Summaries in English, French, and German] Intertax 1980, pp. 294-300.

Dexter, W.D. "Attribution of a Multinational Coporation's Net Income: The Position of Unitary States Regarding Combined Reporting." Vanderbilt Journal of Transnational Law Vol. 18, 1985, pp. 311-334.

Dinur, D.D. and C.H. Coffin. "FIRPTA: An Update on Substance and Procedure." New York University Institute on Federal Taxation Vol. 42, 1984, pp. 30.1-30.44.

"Domestication of Foreign Corporations: Tax Planning in the Net of Internal Revenue Code Section 7701 (b)." North Carolina Journal of International Law and Commercial Regulation Vol. 11, 1986, pp. 131-146.

Dunn, R.R. "Taxation: Foreign Corrupt Practices Act." Texas International Law Journal Vol. 18, 1983, pp. 407-412.

"EC: Tax and Financial Measures in Favour of Investment." [Summaries in English, French, and German] Intertax 1983, pp. 350-362.

"Exchange of Information under the OECD and U.S. Model Tax Treaties." Loyola of Los Angeles International and Comparative Law Journal Vol. 5, 1982, pp. 129-142.

Farnsworth, Clyde H. "Tax Loophole for Multinationals." New York Times, 21 August 1977, Section 3, p. 1.

Fischer, Bart S. "The Multinationals at Bay: The Foreign Taxation Provisions of the Tax Reduction Act of 1975." Journal of International Law and Economics Vol. 10, April 1975, pp. 61-88.

Fordham Corporate Law Institute. International Taxation and Transfer Pricing. (Proceedings of 3d Meeting, New York, 1976) New York: Matthew Bender, 1976.

"Foreign Investment - Capital Controls, Termination of the Interest Equalization Tax, the Foreign Direct Investment Regulations and the Voluntary Foreign Credit Restraint Guidelines." Law and Policy in International Business Vol. 6, 1974, pp. 1263-1270.

"Foreign Investment in the United States: A Symposium." "United States Taxation of Foreign Nationals." C.R. Irish, M.G. Reinecke; Other articles: "Foreign Acquisitions of U.S. Banking Institutions: The Current Climate." T.J. Sheehan; "Foreign Direct Investment in the United States; a Legal Analysis." R.W. Shepro. Wisconsin International Law Journal Vol. 4, 1985, pp. 1-63.

Funck-Brentano, L. "EWG: Harmonisierung der Besteuerung und Kooperation Zwischen den nationalen Steuerbehoerden." Recht der internationalen Wirtschaft Vol. 28, 1982, pp. 816-820.

Furr, D.M. "The FIRPTA Withholding Rules: A Review of Internal Code Section 1445 (a) and the Temporary Regulations." North Carolina International Law and Commercial Regulation Vol. 11, 1986, pp. 67-80.

"Further Attacks on Treaty Shopping." European Taxation Vol. 21, 1981, pp. 141-156.

Gans, J.L. "New Tax Twists for FIC's." International Taxation and Business Law Vol. 3, 1985, pp. 154-173.

Gelatt, T.A. and R.D. Pomp. "Tax Aspects of Doing Business with the People's Republic of China." Columbia Journal of Transnational Law Vol. 22, 1984, pp. 421-504.

"German-U.S. Tax Treaty: German Memorandum on the Questions of Dividend Taxation." [Summaries in English, French, and German] Intertax 1980, pp. 246-262.

Glazer, D.B. "Taxation: State Taxation of Multinational Corporations." Harvard International Law Journal Vol. 23, 1983, pp. 480-487.

Goldberg, H.L. "Conventions for the Elimination of International Double Taxation: Toward a Developing Country Model." Law and Policy in International Business Vol. 15, 1983, pp. 833-909.

Goldberg, S.H. "GATT and Export Tax Incentives: The Proposed Foreign Sales Corporation." New York University Institute on Federal Taxation Vol. 42, 1984, pp. 32.1-32.36.

Gonzales, J.M., et al. "Tax Treatment of Interest on International Economic Transactions: National Reporters." International Fiscal Association Cahiers de Droit Fiscal International. Japan: No. 67B, 1982, pp. 329-341; United Kingdom: No. 67A, 1982, pp. 593-612; United States: No. 67A 1982, pp. 405-422; West Germany: No. 67A, 1982, pp. 228-258.

Goodrich, G.G. "U.S. Tax Aspects of Technology Transfers Between the United States and Canada." Canada-United States Law Journal Vol. 11, 1986, pp. 213-226.

Granwell, A.W. "Current United States International Tax Developments." Canada-United States Law Journal Vol. 8, 1984, pp. 43-60.

Great Britain Board of Internal Revenue, International Tax Avoidance. London: Board of Inland Revenue, 1981.

Greenhill, C.R. and E.O. Herbolzheimer. "International Transfer Pricing: The Restrictive Business Practices Approach." Journal of World Trade Law Vol. 1980, 1980, pp. 232-241.

Gustafson, K. "Proposed Congressional Limitations on State Taxation of Multinational Corporations." Georgia Journal of International and Comparative Law Vol. 11, 1981, pp. 343-363.

Hadari, Y.I. "Tax Treaties and Their Role in the Financial Planning of the Multinational Enterprise." The American Journal of Comparative Law Vol. 20, 1972, pp. 111-145.

Han, A.M. "People's Republic of China's Foreign Enterprises Income Tax Law and Regulations." Hasting's International and Comparative Law Review Vol. 6, 1983, pp. 689-717.

Harter, P.R. "Taxation Summons to Secure Business Records of a Foreign Subsidiary." Harvard International Law Journal Vol. 22, 1981, pp. 704-710.

Helmers, D. "BIAC's Response to the OECD Report on Transfer Pricing and Multinational Enterprises." [Summaries in English, French, and German] Intertax 1980, pp. 286-293.

Henrey, R.J.E. "Impact of New Tax Legislation on International Operations: TEFRA; Possessions Companies; DISCs". New York University Institute on Federal Taxation Vol. 42, 1984, pp. 34.1-34.45.

Henszey, B.N. "Proposed Federal Unitary Tax Legislation (Information Disclosure): An Overview." Taxes Vol. 64, 1986, pp. 513-517.

Hilinski, C.C. "U.S. Tax Aspects of European Direct Investment in the U.S." Commerce in Belgium September 1975.

Hoeppner, H.-D. "German Regulations on Transfer Pricing: A Tax Administrator's Point of View." [Summaries in English, French, and German] Intertax 1983, pp. 208-223.

Hogg, R.D. "Intercompany Pricing: A Canadian Tax Overview." [Summaries in English, French, and German] Intertax 1983, pp. 224-238.

Holtz, R.E. "An Analysis of IRC Sec. 1445." (Tax ramifications of foreign investment in U.S. real estate) Wisconsin Bar Bulletin Vol. 59, September 1986, pp. 23-25.

Hughes, Kent M. Trade, Taxes, and Transnationals: International Economic Decision Making in Congress. New York: Praeger, 1979.

International Bureau of Fiscal Documentation, International Tax Avoidance and Evasion. From the colloquy held in Strasbourg, 5-7 March 1980. Amsterdam: International Bureau of Fiscal Documentation, 1981.

International Chamber of Commerce, Commission on Taxation. ICC Report. Document No. 180/136, 30.I.1974.

International Fiscal Association, "Recourse to Tax Havens: Use and Abuse." Proceedings of the 34th International Fiscal Association Congress Paris, 1980. Deventer: Kluwer, 1981.

Irish, C.R. "Tax Havens." Vanderbilt Journal of International Law Vol. 15, 1982, pp. 449-510.

Ishiyama, Y. "Anti-Tax Haven Legislation in Japan." [Summaries in English, French, and German] Intertax 1980, pp. 77-85.

Jacob, F. "Unitary Approaches in International Taxation." Bulletin for International Fiscal Documentation Vol. 38, 1984, pp. 99-120.

"Japan: Federation of Economic Organizations versus Unitary Taxation." Bulletin for International Fiscal Documentation Vol. 38, 1984, pp. 255-258.

Johnson, Alan R. "The Initial FIRPTA Regulations." Tax Lawyer Vol. 36, 1983, pp. 713-749.

Jonas, B. "New Directive on Intercompany Pricing." European Taxation Vol. 23, 1983, pp. 107-116.

Jones, J.F.A., et al. "The Interpretation of Tax Treaties with Particular Reference to Article 3(2) of the OECD Model." British Tax Review Vol. 1984, 1984, pp. 14-54.

Kaden, L.B. "State Taxation of Multinational Corporations." Catholic University Law Review Vol. 32, 1983, pp. 829-849.

Kaplan, P.T. "The Unitary Tax Debate, The United States Supreme Court, and Some Plain English." British Tax Review Vol. 1983, 1983, pp. 203-220.

Kaplan, P.T. "U.S. Tax Act 1982: Provisions of Special Interest to Firms Doing Business Internationally." [Summaries in English, French, and German] Intertax 1982, pp. 463-475.

Karzon, A.U. "International Tax Evasion: Spawned in the United States and Nurtured by Secrecy Havens." Vanderbilt Journal of Transnational Law Vol. 16, 1983, pp. 757-832.

Kessler, S.A. "Adjusting to FIRPTA." Taxes Vol. 61, 1983, pp. 960-971.

Knox, G.R., S.E. Alley, and D.B. Person. "The U.S. Tax Regime Affecting Mexican Nationals Who Desire to Conduct Business or Invest Within the United States." Houston Journal of International Law Vol. 8, 1985, pp. 87-118.

Kooiman, K. "Article 16: The U.S. Attitude to Treaty Shopping." Bulletin for International Fiscal Documentation Vol. 37, 1983, pp. 195-200.

Kopits, G.F. "Tax Provisions to Boost Capital Formation Vary Widely in Industrial Nations." [Summaries in English, French, and German] Intertax 1981, pp. 96-101.

Langbein, V. "U.S. Unitary Taxation Methode hier: Container Corp. of America v. (California) Franchise Tax Board." Recht der internationalen Wirtschaft Vol. 29, 1983, pp. 673-676.

Law Society, Standing Committee on Revenue Law. "Taxation of International Business: Memorandum by the Committee." London: Law Society, 1983.

LeBeau, C.P. and P.J. Dostart. "Offshore Tax Planning May Be Favorably Affected by Recent Hospital Corporation [81 T.C. 520] Decision." Journal of Taxation Vol. 60, 1984, pp. 294-301.

LeGall, J.-P. "Règle de l'arm's length serait-elle incompatible avec le traité de Rome?" [Text in French and English] Droit et Pratique du Commerce International Vol. 8, July 1982, pp. 65-85.

Liebman, Howard M. "Taxation of Foreign Source of Income: Implications of CCA, Inc." Harvard International Law Journal Vol. 17, 1976, pp. 335-358.

Linde, Stephen A. "Regulation of Transfer Pricing in Multinational Corporations: An International Perspective." New York University Journal of International Law and Politics Vol. 10, 1977, pp. 67-123.

Lindencrona, G. and N. Mattson. "Arbritration in Taxation." [Summaries in English, French, and German] Intertax 1982, pp. 76-82.

List, H. "Recent Cases of the German Supreme Tax Court on International Tax Law." Bulletin for International Fiscal Documentation. Vol. 35, 1981, pp. 348-355.

Maiers, J.D. "New Tax Withholding Rules for Foreign-Owned U.S. Real Estate." Georgia Journal of International and Comparative Law Vol. 15, 1985, pp. 29-37.

Maktouf, L, and M. Milliet-Einbinder. "Grandeur et décadence de la taxation unitaire aux États-Unis." [In French and English] Revue de Droit des Affaires Internationales/ International Business Law Journal Vol 13, 1985, pp. 573-601.

Maskall, M.E. "United Kingdom: Tax Consequences of the Abolition of Exchange Controls." [Summaries in English, French, and German] Intertax 1981, pp. 32-38.

McClure, C.E. "Federal Law and State Corporate Income Taxes." Vanderbilt Journal of Transnational Law Vol. 18, 1985, pp. 275-310.

Menck, T. "Qualifitsationsconflikt im neuen deutsch-kanadischen Doppelbesteuerungsabkommen." [Summaries in English, French, and German] Intertax 1982, pp. 417-423.

Miles, A. "Germany: Intercompany Prices and Charges." [Summaries in English, French, and German] Intertax 1985, pp. 335-340.

Morgan, H.V., Jr. "Advising the Foreign Investor in the Southeastern U.S.: Perspectives on Foreign Investment in the Southeastern U.S. An Introduction." Other articles: "The U.S. Policy Toward Foreign Direct Investment." H.E. Bale, Jr.; "Determinants of Foreign Plant Start-Ups in the U.S.: Lessons for Policymakers in the Southeast." M.I. Luger and S. Shetty; "An Evaluation of Current Trends in Foreign Direct Investment in the Southeastern U.S." C.L. Suzman and J.A. Heslin; "Federal Law and State Corporation Income Taxes." C.E. McLure, Jr.; "Attribution of a Multinational Corporation's Net Income: The Position of Unitary States Regarding Combined Reporting." W.D. Dexter; "The Foreign Investor: Current Approaches Towards U.S. Immigration Law." A.T. Fragomen, Jr. and G.M. Robosson; "Foreign Investment in the U.S.: A Survey of Current Legal Literature." I.I. Kavass. Vanderbilt Journal of Transnational Law Vol. 18, 1985, pp. 191-480.

Mueller-Dott, J.P. "California Franchise Tax und Unitary Tax Concept." Recht der internationalen Wirtschaft Vol. 26, Fall 1980, pp. 109-116.

"Multinational Enterprises: Charges for Intra-Group Services." [Summaries in English, French, and German] Intertax 1980, pp. 113-119.

Newmark, M.N. and D.M. Lang. "Subchapter S Revision Act of 1982." Tax Lawyer Vol. 37, 1983, pp. 93-132.

Olson, T.H. "Tax Considerations in Structuring Foreign Investment in the United States." Brigham Young University Law Review Vol. 1983, 1983, pp. 713-754.

"OECD: Work on Tax Avoidance and Evasion." [Summaries in English, French, and German] Intertax 1980, pp. 9-16.

Organisation for Economic Co-operation and Development. Transfer Pricing and Multinational Enterprises: Three Taxation Issues. Paris: OECD Publications, 1984.

Organisation for Economic Co-operation and Development. Trends in International Taxation. Paris: OECD Publications, 1985.

Osborn, J.E. "Renegotiation of the United States-British Virgin Islands Tax Convention: Prelude to the End of Treaty Shopping?" Virginia Journal of International Law Vol. 22, 1982, pp. 381-412.

Osgood, R.K. "Interpreting Tax Treaties in Canada, the United States, and the United Kingdom." Cornell International Law Journal Vol. 17, 1984, pp. 255-297.

Ott, K.T. "Economic Recovery Tax Act of 1981, Section 223: The Suspension of IRC Regulations Regarding the Allocation of R&D Expenses to Foreign and Domestic Source Income." Law and Policy in International Business Vol. 14, 1982, pp. 885-904.

Painter, Therese Eve and Dianne Zomper. "A Bibliography of Current Issues in International Business Transactions: Investment Regulation, Antitrust, Acquisitions and Mergers, Transfer of Technology, Joint Ventures, Taxation, Dispute Resolution, Transnational Tort Claims, and Export Controls." Texas International Law Journal Vol. 21, 1985, pp. 165-197.

Palmieri-Egger, N.W. "Worldwide Tax Allocation Norm v. Worldwide Combination Method of Taxation." [Summaries in English, French, and German] Intertax 1983, pp. 390-402.

Pardue, B.W. "International Taxation: Hedging." Vanderbilt Journal of Transnational Law Vol. 13, 1980, pp. 825-834.

Petkin, Lisa B. "Foreign Investment in Real Property Tax Act of 1980." Dickinson International Law Annual Vol. 1, 1982, pp. 11-34.

"Proposed Congressional Limitations on State Taxation of Multinational Corporations." Georgia Journal of International and Comparative Law Vol. 11, 1981, pp. 343-363.

Quinn, M.L. "Temporary Regulations Implementing FIRPTA's Withholding Tests Are Major Clarifications." Journal of Taxation Vol. 63, August 1985, pp. 98-105.

Raupach, A. "Die Verdeckte Nutzungseinlage in Kapitalgesellschaften, ein unbewaltigtes Problem bei der Besteuerung nationaler und internationaler Konzerne?" Wallis Collection pp. 309-326.

"Resolution Against Unitary Taxation." [Summaries in English, French, and German] Intertax 1980, pp. 204-208.

Rhoades, R.V. "Tax Aspects of Financing the Pacific Basin Enterprise." UCLA Pacific Basin Law Journal Vol. 2, 1983, pp. 137-179.

Rosenbloom, H.D. "Tax Treaty Abuse: Policies and Issues." Law and Policy in International Business Vol. 15, 1983, pp. 763-831.

Rosenbloom, H.D. and S.I. Langbein. "United States Tax Treaty Policy: An Overview." Columbia Journal of Transnational Law Vol. 19, 1981, pp. 359-406.

Rothschild, Jr., and R.E. Anthony. "World-Wide Combined Reporting: Recent Legislative Developments." Bulletin for International Fiscal Documentation Vol. 37, Fall 1983, pp. 59-64.

Ruchelman, S.C. and K.K. Imamura. "Intercompany Transfer Pricing Including Tax Treaty Relief." New York University Institute on Federal Taxation Vol. 42, 1984, pp. 35.1-35.43.

Sangal, P.S. "Taxation of Multinational Corporations." Journal of the Indian Law Institute Vol. 21, 1979, pp. 512-526.

Scarborough, K. "The Foreign Investor in the United States: Disclosure, Taxation and Visa Laws." International Lawyer Vol. 19, 1985, pp. 85-115.

Scholsen, J.-U. "EC: The Proposal for a Council Directive on the Elimination of Double Taxation (Arbitration Procedure)." [Summaries in English, French, and German] Intertax 1982, pp. 424-435.

Simmons, D.L. "Worldwide Unitary Taxation: Retain and Rationalize or Block at Water's Edge?" Stanford Journal of International Law Vol. 21, 1985, pp. 157-194.

Singer, S.R. and M.J.A. Karlin. "Multinationals and New Customs Law Will Have Broad Impact on Intercompany Pricing." Journal of Taxation Vol. 58, 1983, pp. 226-231.

Spitz, Barry, International Tax Planning, 2d ed. London: Butterworth, 1983.

"Stapled Stock and I.R.C. Section 269b: Ill-Conceived Change in the Rules of International Tax Jurisdiction." Cornell Law Review Vol. 71, 1986, pp. 1066-1094.

"State Taxation of Multinationals and the Unitary Business Concept: A Contemporary View." Brooklyn Journal of International Law Vol. 10, Winter 1984, pp. 115-156.

"State Unitary Tax: The 'Risk' of Container Corporation of America v. Franchise Tax Board [103 S.Ct. 2933]. Hastings International and Comparative Law Review Vol. 9 Fall 1985, pp. 59-76.

"State Unitary Taxes Imposed on Foreign Based Multinational Groups: A Post Container Analysis." Wayne Law Review Vol. 31, 1984-1985, pp. 219-246.

Streng, W.P. "United States: Taxation of International Business Transactions 1983." [Summaries in English, French, and German] Intertax 1984, pp. 137-148.

Strobl, J. "German Tax Audits of Foreign Subsidiaries in Germany: Practice and Experience." European Taxation Vol. 20, 1980, pp. 273-292.

Strobl, J. "Kritische Anmerkungen zum Bericht des OECD - Steuerausschusses ueber Verrechnungspreise im Konzern." Recht der internationalen Wirtschaft Vol. 26, 1980, pp. 407-410.

"The Supreme Court Upholds Worldwide Unitary Taxation by the States of Multinational Corporation Income: Container Corporation of America v. Franchise Tax Board [103 S.Ct. 2933]." Boston College Law Review Vol. 25, May 1984, pp. 645-683.

"Tax - A Deterrent for U.S. Firms." International Herald Tribune 3 October 1978, p. 9.

"Tax Aspects of Foreign Investment: A Symposium." Hasting's International and Comparative Law Review Vol. 5, 1982, pp. 473-674.

"Tax Avoidance - Tax Evasion: National Report." [Summaries in English, French, and German] International Fiscal Association, Cahiers de Droit Fiscal International No. 68A, 1983. Canada: pp. 295-315; France: pp. 373-399; Japan: pp. 477-489; United Kingdom: pp. 581-599; United States: pp. 333-355; West Germany: pp. 193-210. General: p. 15.

"Tax Reform Act of 1984 - International Related - Party Factoring - A Major Tax Loophole for Multinational Corporations is Closed." Georgia Journal of International and Comparative Law Vol. 1985, 1985, pp. 125-133.

"Tax Reform Act of 1984 - Netherlands Antilles - Effect of the Repeal of the Withholding Tax on Portfolio Interest Payments to Foreign Investors." Georgia Journal of International and Comparative Law Vol. 15, 1985, pp. 111-123.

"Taxation - Congress Amends Internal Revenue Code to Comport with the Foreign Corrupt Practices Act, Tax Equity and Fiscal Responsibility Act of 1982. Public Law No. 97-248, 96 Stat. 324 [codified as amended in scattered sections of 26 U.S.C." Texas International Law Journal Vol. 18, 1983, pp. 407-412.

"Taxation of French Direct Investment Abroad." [Summaries in English, French, and German] Intertax [I] August 1980, pp. 301-308; [II] September 1980, pp. 350-355; [III] October 1980, pp. 395-400; [IV] November-December 1980, pp. 430-438.

"Taxation - Renegotiation of the United States-Netherlands Antilles Tax Treaty. Convention with Respect to Taxes on Income and Certain Other Taxes. April 29, 1948, United States-Netherlands, 62 Stat. 1757, T.I.A.S. No. 1855." Texas International Law Journal Vol. 18, 1983, pp. 400-407.

"Taxation - State Taxation of Multinational Corporations: Container Corporation of America v. Franchise Tax Board, 103 S.Ct. 2933." Creighton Law Review Vol. 17, 1983-1984, pp. 857-884.

"Taxation - State Taxation on Multinational Corporations - ASARCO, Inc. v. Idaho State Tax Commission, 102 S.Ct. 1303 (1982); F.W. Woolworth Co. v. Taxation and Revenue Dept., 102 S.Ct. 3128 (1982)." Harvard International Law Journal Vol. 23, 1983, pp. 480-487.

"Taxation: Summons to Secure Business Records of a Foreign Subsidiary." Harvard International Law Journal Vol. 22, 1981, pp. 704-710.

Teschner, P.A. "Foreign Discovery of Head Office Tax Records: By Invitation Only." Taxes Vol. 64, 1986, pp. 326-334.

Thompson, Samuel C. Federal Income Taxation of Domestic and Foreign Business Transactions: Text, Cases and Problems. Indianapolis, Indiana: Bobbs-Merrill Co., 1980.

Tindall, Robert E. Multinational Enterprises: Legal and Management Structures and Interrelationship with Ownership, Control, Antitrust, Labor, Taxation and Disclosure. Dobbs Ferry, New York: Oceana, 1975.

Turpin, K. "Taxation: Treasury Regulation Interpreting Definition of Control as Contained in Internal Revenue Code 957." Texas International Law Journal Vol. 14, 1979, pp. 495-512.

"United Kingdom: International Tax Avoidance." [Summaries in English, French, and German] Intertax 1982, pp. 83-89.

"United Kingdom: Taxation of International Business." [Summaries in English, French, and German] Intertax 1983, pp. 186-200.

"United Kingdom: The Transfer Pricing of Multinational Enterprises." [Summaries in English, French, and German] Intertax 1981, pp. 301-306.

"United Kingdom versus Unitary Taxation." Bulletin for International Fiscal Documentation Vol. 38, 1984, pp. 157-161, also pp. 51-59, 153-156.

United States Department of Treasury, Internal Revenue Service. "Regulations Concerning the Taxation of Foreign Investment in U.S. Real Property." 1983. (Reprinted in International Legal Materials Vol.22, 1983, pp. 883ff.)

"United States Attitudes Towards Multinational Corporations." (Various articles: Vagts: control & protection; Tillinghast: tax; Ehrenhaft: anti-dumping; Surrey: Foreign Corrupt Practices Act; Loss: Extraterritoriality in FSC) Harvard International Law Journal Vol. 20, 1979, pp. 233-330.

"United States: IRS Could Better Protect US Tax Interest in Determining the Income of Multinational Corporations." [Summaries in English, French, and German] Intertax 1982, pp. 5-11.

"United States: Loan Between Foreign Subsidiaries May Constitute Constructive Dividend to U.S. Parent." [Summaries in English, French, and German] Intertax 1982, pp. 259-263.

van Waardenburg, D.A., et al. "Taxation of Profits Derived Through Subsidies in Low Tax Areas." European Taxation Vol. 23, 1983, pp. 179-188.

Verlage, H.C. "Transfer Pricing by Multinational Enterprises: Issues and Developments." [Summaries in English, French, and German] Intertax 1982, pp. 285-293.

Vogel, K. "Double Tax Treaties and Their Interpretation." International Tax and Business Lawyer Vol. 4, 1986, pp. 1-85.

Ward, David A. Taxation of Income of Foreign Affiliates Toronto: Carswell, 1983.

White, A.S. "Taxation: Foreign Corporations." Texas International Law Journal Vol. 18, 1983, pp. 388-400.

Whittaker, D.R. "An Examination of the OECD and UN Model Tax Treaties: History, Provisions and Application to U.S. Foreign Policy." North Carolina Journal of International Law and Commercial Regulation Vol. 8, 1982, pp. 39-60.

Willens, R. "The Corporate Provisions of the Tax Reform Act of 1986." Tax Advisor Vol. 17, 1986, pp. 624-661.

Wootton, R.R. "Section 382 After the Tax Reform Act of 1986." Taxes Vol. 64, 1986, pp. 874-889.

Yang, W. and D.W. Nelson "Post Reconstruction Section 367: New Rules and Changes." Tax Advisor Vol. 17, 1986, pp. 102-111.

Yelpaala, K. "The Efficacy of Tax Incentives within the Framework of the Neoclassical Theory of Foreign Direct Investment: A Legislative Policy Analysis." _Texas International Law Journal_ Vol. 19, 1984, pp. 365-414.

Yelpaala, K. "In Search of Effective Policies for Foreign Direct Investment: Alternatives to Tax Incentive Policies." _New England Journal of International Law and Business_ Vol. 7, 1985, pp. 208-266.

21. TRANSBORDER DATA FLOWS

"Advice to the U.S. Corporation Operating Abroad: The Costs of Transporting Information." ASILS International Law Journal Vol. 9, Winter 1985, pp. 61-86.

"Commercial Speech, Transborder Data Flows and the Right to Communicate under International Law." International Lawyer Vol. 17, 1983, pp. 87-95.

Coombe, G.W., Jr. and S.L. Kirk. "Privacy, Data Protection, and Transborder Data Flow: A Corporate Response to International Expectations." Business Lawyer Vol. 39, November 1983, pp. 33-66.

"The Development of Canadian Law on Transborder Data Flows." Georgia Journal of International and Comparative Law Vol. 13, 1983, pp. 825-855.

Donaghue, H.P. "Transborder Flows: Its Implications in Canada-U.S. Relations." Canada-United States Law Journal Vol. 11, 1986, pp. 289-294.

Eger, J.M. "Emerging Restrictions on Transnational Data Flows: Privacy Protection or Non-Tariff Trade Barriers?" Law and Policy in International Business Vol. 10, 1978, pp. 1055-1103.

Grossman, S. "Transborder Data Flow: Separating the Privacy Interests of Individuals and Corporations." Northwestern Journal of International Law and Business Vol. 4, Spring 1982, pp. 1-36.

Hardy, I.T., Jr. "Transborder Data Flow: An Overview and Critique of Recent Concerns." Rutgers Computer and Technology Law Journal Vol. 9, 1983, pp. 247-264.

Hyde, A. "Rights for Canadian Members of International Unions Under the (U.S.) Labor - Management Reporting and Disclosure Act." Washington Law Review Vol. 61, 1986, pp. 1007-1039.

bLandwehr, Martha L., ed. Private Investors Abroad - Problems and Solutions in International Business in 1982. Parts I, II, III, IV: "Privacy, Telecommunications and Transborder Data Flows - U.S. Multinational Response to European Expectations." (Articles: G.W. Coombe, Jr., R.E.L. Walker, H.P. Donaghue, and L.A. Hummer) New York: Matthew Bender, 1982.

Robinson, P. "Legal Issues Raised by Transborder Data Flow." Canada-United States Law Journal Vol. 11, 1986, pp. 295-316.

United Nations Centre on Transnational Corporations. Transborder Data Flows: Access to the International On-Line Database Market. UN Sales No. E.83.II.A.1.

United Nations Centre on Transnational Corporations. Transborder Data Flows and Brazil. UN Sales No. E.83.II.A.3.

United Nations Centre on Transnational Corporations. Transnational Corporations and Transborder Data Flows: A Technical Paper Sales No. E.82.II.A.4.

22. TRANSFER OF TECHNOLOGY

Brown, R.D. "Tax Aspects of Technology Transfers Between the United States and Canada: A Canadian Viewpoint." Canada-United States Law Journal Vol. 11, 1986, pp. 227-246.

Cabanellas, G. and L. Bertone. "Host Country Taxation of Transfer of Technology Transactions." Georgia Journal of International and Comparative Law Vol. 1981, 1981, pp. 495-516.

Clauser, H.R. "Foreign Investment and the Technology Drain." Research Management Vol. 19, September 1976, pp. 2-3.

Fikentscher, Wolfgang (for the Max Planck Institute for Foreign and International Patent, Copyright, and Competition Law). The Draft International Code of Conduct on the Transfer of Technology. Weinheim: Chemie, 1980.

Fisher, W. Halder. Technology Transfer as a Motivation for United States Direct Investments by European Firms. Battelle Memorial Institute, Columbus Laboratories, 1977.

"Foreign Investment: Foreign Economic Contract Law - the Foreign Economic Contract Law of the People's Republic of China, reprinted in 24 ILM 799 (1985) (unofficial transcript); and The Regulation of the People's Republic of China Governing Contracts for the Imports of Technology, reprinted in 24 ILM 801 (1985) (unofficial transcript)." Harvard International Law Journal Vol. 27, 1986, pp. 275-283.

"Foreign Investment in Industries Which Do Not Need Foreign Technology Has Been Stopped." Financial Times 15 March 1985, p. 4. Reported in Bulletin of Legal Developments, No. 6, 10 April 1985, p. 59.

Frank, H. "International Code of Conduct on Transfer of Technology: Some Basic Observations from a Transnational Enterprise's Viewpoint and Some Related Conclusions." German Yearbook of International Law Vol. 24, 1981, pp. 367-376.

Goodrich, G.G. "U.S. Tax Aspects of Technology Transfers Between the United States and Canada." Canada-United States Law Journal Vol. 11, 1986, pp. 213-226.

Hawkins, Robert G. and A.J. Prasad. Technology Transfer and Economic Development, Vol. 2 of H. Peter Gray, ed., Research in International Business and Finance. Greenwich, Connecticut: JAI Press, 1981.

Joelson, Mark R. "International Technology Transfers and U.S. Anti-Trust Laws." Journal of International Law and Economics Vol. 8, 1973, p. 85-112.

LeGall, J.-P. "Fiscalite des transferts internationaux de technologie: nouvelles technologies, nouveaux modes de transfert." [In French and English] Revue de Droit des Affaires Internationales/ International Business Law Journal 1985, pp. 617-634.

McFadden, D.L. "A Selected Bibliography on Hazardous Activity, Technology and the Law: Bhopal and Beyond." International Lawyer Vol. 19, 1985, pp. 1459-1475.

McFetridge, D.G. "Government Intervention in International Technology Transfer: More or Less?" Canada-United States Law Journal Vol. 11, 1986, pp. 331-344.

Modiano, G. "Contrats de Transfert de Technologie." Droit et Pratique du Commerce International Vol. 9, 1983, pp. 553-591.

"Multinational Corporations and the Lesser Developed Countries - Foreign Investment, Transfer of Technology, and the Paris Convention: Caveat Investor." University of Dayton Law Review Vol. 5, 1980, pp. 105-154.

Oh, Moonsong David. The Role of International Corporations in the Transfer of Technology of Developing Countries. Ann Arbor, Michigan: University Microfilms, 1970.

Ozawa, Terutomo. "Technology Imports and Direct Foreign Investment in Japan." Journal of World Trade Law Vol. 7, 1973, pp. 666-679.

Painter, Therese Eve and Dianne Zomper. "A Bibliography of Current Issues in International Business Transactions: Investment Regulation, Antitrust, Acquisitions and Mergers, Transfer of Technology, Joint Ventures, Taxation, Dispute Resolution, Transnational Tort Claims, and Export Controls." Texas International Law Journal Vol. 21, 1985, pp. 165-197.

Payne, Kenneth E. and Richard L. Stroup. "U.S. Antitrust Aspects of the International Transfer of Technology." North Carolina Journal of International Law and Commercial Regulation Vol. 5, 1980, pp. 91-120.

Perlmutter, Howard V. "Perplexing Routes to M.N.E. Legitimacy: Codes of Conduct for Technology Transfer." Stanford Journal of International Studies Vol. 11, pp. 169-199.

Roffe, P. "Transfer of Technology: UNCTAD's Draft International Code of Conduct." International Lawyer Vol. 19, 1985, pp. 689-707.

Roffe, P. "UNCTAD Transfer of Technology Code: Fifth Session of the UN Conference." Journal of World Trade Law Vol. 18, 1984, pp. 176-182.

Rudway, R.J. and F.T. Hoet-Linares. "Venezuela Revisited: Foreign Investment, Technology and Related Issues." Vanderbilt Journal of Transnational Law Vol. 15, 1982, pp. 1-45.

Smith, S. "Should There Be More Canadian Government Intervention in Technology Transfer Arrangements Between Canadian and Foreign Firms?" Canada-United States Law Journal Vol. 11, 1986, pp. 321-329.

Stewart, Frances. International Technology Transfer: Issues and Policy Options. World Bank Staff Working Paper No. 344, 1979.

Sweezy, E., J. Baranson and J. Hopper. *Field Survey to Assess Feasibility of Collection of Data for Analysis of Foreign Direct Investment and Technology Transfer*. Washington, D.C.: Institute of Public Administration, 14 October 1980.

Technology Transfer and International Trade. Boston: Boston Publishing Company, 1986.

Timberg, S. "Impact on the Transnational Corporation of the International Code of Conduct on the Transfer of Technology." *International Review of Industrial Property and Copyright Law* Vol. 12, 1981, pp. 133-152.

"Transfer of Technology in the International Marketplace: A Symposium." *British Columbia International and Comparative Law Review* Vol. 7, 1984, pp. 235-352.

United Nations Centre on Transnational Corporations. *The Acquisition of Technology from Multinational Corporations by Developing Countries*. UN Sales No. E.74.II.A.7.

United Nations Centre on Transnational Corporations. *Measures Strengthening the Negotiating Capacity of Governments in Their Relations with Transnational Corporations: Technology Transfer Through Transnational Corporations*. UN Sales No. E.79.II.A.6.

Wilner, Gabriel M. "Applicable Law and Dispute Settlement in the Transfer of Technology Code." *Journal of World Trade Law* Vol. 17, 1983, pp. 389-396.

Wilson, P.J. "The Legal Structures Governing Technology Transfers and Joint Ventures with the People's Republic of China." *International Tax and Business Lawyer* Vol. 3, 1985, pp. 1-51.

Zaphiriou, G.A. "International Code of Conduct on Transfers of Technology." *International and Comparative Law Quarterly* Vol. 26, 1977, pp. 210-218.

23. UNITED STATES

Abrams, Lee N., et al. "Antitrust and U.S. Trade Law." (Various articles) Proceedings of the Twenty-Ninth Annual Spring Meeting of the Section of Antitrust Law of the American Bar Association, Washington, D.C., 1981. Antitrust Law Journal Vol. 50, 1981, pp. 751-799.

Abrutyn, M. and N. Boidman. "The New Canada-United States Tax Convention." International Lawyer Vol. 20, 1986, pp. 125-152.

"The Act of State Doctrine: A Shield for Bribery and Corruption. Clayco Petroleum Corp. v. Occidental Petroleum Corp., 712 F.2d 404." University of Miami Inter-American Law Review Vol. 16, 1984, pp. 167-176.

"Act of State Doctrine - Anti-Trust Law." Denver Journal of International Law and Politics Vol. 3, 1973, pp. 133-140.

Adams, G.B. "European and American Antitrust Regulation of Pricing by Monopolists." Vanderbilt Journal of Transnational Law Vol. 18, 1985, pp. 1-70.

Adisert, R.J. "Federal Courts and Extraterritorial Antitrust Law: Enlightened Self-Interest or Yankee Imperialism?" Journal of Law and Commerce Vol. 5, 1985, pp. 415-432.

"Advice to the U.S. Corporation Operating Abroad: The Costs of Transporting Information." ASILS International Law Journal Vol. 9, Winter 1985, pp. 61-86.

"Advising Foreign Investors: A Symposium." Chicago Bar Record Vol. 61, 1980, pp. 255-258.

Allen, D.G.M. "Regulating Foreign Investments in the United States." Solicitors' Journal Vol. 125, 1981 pp. 838-840.

"Amenability of Foreign Corporations to United States Employment Discrimination Laws." Vanderbilt Journal of Transnational Law Vol. 14, 1981, pp. 197-221.

"Amending the Foreign Corrupt Practices Act of 1977: A Step Toward Clarification and Consolidation." Journal of Criminal Law and Criminology Vol. 73, 1982, pp. 1740-1773.

American Bar Association. Committee to Study Foreign Investment in the U.S. A Guide to Foreign Investment Under U.S. Law, by the Section of Corporation, Banking, and Business Law of the American Bar Association, principally drafted by project coordinator Allan R. Roth. New York: Law & Business, 1979.

American Law Institute. Restatement of the Law: Conflict of Laws. St. Paul, Minnesota: American Law Institute Publishers, 1934.

American Law Institute. Restatement of the Law (Second): Conflict of Laws. St. Paul, Minnesota: American Law Institute Publishers, 1971.

American Law Institute. Restatement of the Law (Second): Foreign Relations Law of the United States. St. Paul, Minnesota: American Law Institute Publishers, 1965.

American Society of International Law. "International Protection of Acquired Rights: Selections from the Harvard Draft Convention on International Responsibility of States for Injuries to Aliens." (Panel Discussion) Proceedings of the Fifty-Fourth Annual Meeting, 28-30 April, 1960, Washington, D.C., 1960, pp. 102-120.

American Subsidiaries of German Firms. New York: German-American Chamber of Commerce, 1971.

"America's Reliance on Foreign Funds to Fight the Deficit: Repeal of the 30% Withholding Tax." Brooklyn Journal of International Law Vol. 12, 1986, pp. 127-159.

Andrews, Gregory E. "An Evaluation of the Need for Further Statutory Controls on Foreign Direct Investment in the United States." Vanderbilt Journal of Transnational Law Vol. 8, 1974, pp. 147-188.

Angel, Juvenal L. Directory of Foreign Firms Operating in the United States. New York: World Trade Academy Press, 1986.

"The Antibribery Provisions of the Foreign Corrupt Practices Act of 1977: Are They Really As Valuable As We Think They Are?" Delaware Journal of Corporate Law Vol. 10, 1985, pp. 71-95.

"Antitrust - Foreign Import Cartels are Liable under the Sherman Act Although Domestic Export Competitors are Shielded within Webb-Pomerance Exemption; Daishowa International v. No. Coast Export Co. 1982-Z Tr.Cas. No. 64,774." Vanderbilt Journal of Transnational Law Vol. 16, 1983, pp. 645-665.

Antitrust Implications of Trade Law: Japan, the European Communities, and the United States: A Panel." American Society of International Law Proceedings Vol. 76, 1982, pp. 120-130.

"Antitrust - Noerr-Pennington [Eastern R.R. Presidents Conf. v. Noerr Motor Freight, Inc., 81 S.Ct. 523] Extends Immunity from Sherman Act to Foreign Litigation and Foreign Acts that Result in Alleged Antitrust Violations. Coastal States Marketing, Inc. v. Hunt, 694 F.2d 1358." Vanderbilt Journal of Transnational Law Vol. 16, 1983, pp. 623-644.

Applebaum, Harvey M. "Are U.S. International Trade and Commerce Conduct Laws in Harmony with Traditional Antitrust Law and Policy?" Antitrust Law Journal Vol. 49, 1980, pp. 1207-1216.

Arab Investments in the United States: General Outlook Plus Special Report on Kuwait. Atlanta, Georgia: Conway Research, Inc., 1974.

"Arbitration and Securities Regulation - Conflict between the Federal Arbitration Act and the Securities Exchange Act in an International Transaction." Missouri Law Review Vol. 40, 1975, pp. 527-535.

"Arbitration Clauses in International Contracts and the Extraterritorial Reach of the Securities Exchange Act of 1934 in Light of Scherk v. Alberto-Culver Co. (94 S.Ct. 2449)." Syracuse Law Review Vol. 26, 1975, pp. 995-1015.

Arpan, Jeffrey S. and David A. Ricks. Directory of Foreign Manufacturers in the United States. Atlanta, Georgia: College of Business Administration, Georgia State University, 1985.

Arpan, Jeffrey S. and David A. Ricks. "Foreign Direct Investments in the U.S. and Some Attendant Research Problems." Journal of International Business Studies Spring 1974, pp. 1-7.

Arpan, Jeffrey S. and David A. Ricks. "The Impact on the U.S.A. of Investments Made by Foreign Firms." Paper prepared for Allied Social Science Meetings, New York, December 1973.

Arthur, T.C. "Farewell to the Sea of Doubt: Jettisoning the Constitutional Sherman Act." California Law Review Vol. 74, 1986, pp. 263-376.

Atchinson, B.K. "Foreign Corrupt Practices Act: A Practical Look." New York State Bar Journal Vol. 53, 1981, pp. 342-347.

Atwood, James R. and Kingman Brewster. Anti-Trust and American Business Abroad, 2d edition. New York: McGraw Hill, 1981.

Atwood, James R. "International Ventures and the U.S. Anti-Trust Laws." Akron Law Review Vol. 10, 1976-1977, pp. 609-621.

Augustyn, F.M. "An Antitrust Analysis of Joint Research and Development Agreements in the European Economic Community and the United States." Georgia Journal of International and Comparative Law Vol. 16, 1986, pp. 45-71.

"Auslandsinvestitionen in Amerika gestiegen." Frankfurter Allgemeine Zeitung 29 August 1980, p. 12.

Aviel, David. "Volkswagen's Investment in the U.S.: A Pacesetter for Foreign Investment?" Fletcher Forum Vol. 4 1980, pp. 165-179.

Baade, H.W. "Multinationale Gesellschaft im americanen Kollisionsrecht." [Summary in English] Rabels Zeitschrift fuer auslaendisches und internationales Privatrecht Vol. 37, 1973, pp. 5-35.

Bagby, J.W. "Enforcement of Accounting Standards in the Foreign Corrupt Practices Act." American Business Law Journal Vol. 21, 1983, pp. 213-235.

Baker, Donald I. "Antitrust Conflicts Between Friends: Canada and the United States in the mid-1970s." Cornell International Law Journal Vol. 11, 1978, pp. 165-194.

Baklanoff, Eric N. and William R. Bennett. "Foreign-Based Investments in Alabama: An Interim Report." Paper prepared for a meeting of the Academy of International Business, Atlanta, Georgia, 31 October 1979.

Baklanoff, Eric N. and William R. Bennett. "Foreign-Based Investments in Alabama: An Interim Report." Alabama Business August 1978, pp. 2-5.

Balbach, A. "Foreign Investment in the United States - A Danger to Our Welfare and Sovereignty?" Federal Reserve Bank St. Louis Review October 1973.

Bank of America. Direct Investment in the United States from Abroad: Survey for the International Investor. New York: Bank of America, 1978.

Barivich, Richard. "Congress Looks at the Multinational Corporation." Columbia Journal of World Business Vol. 5, November/December 1970, pp. 75-79.

Barnes, Louie Burton, III. "State Regulation of Foreign Investment." (Note) Cornell International Law Journal Vol. 9, 1975, pp. 82-100.

Batista, P.A. "Confronting Foreign 'Blocking' Legislation: A Guide to Securing Disclosure for Non-Resident Parties to American Litigation." International Lawyer Vol. 17, 1983, pp. 61-85.

Bauer, D. Foreign Direct Investment in the U.S.: A Profile by State and Industry. Conference Board Record, February 1974.

Becker, J.D. "Antitrust and International Arbitration - the New American Synthesis." International Business Lawyer Vol. 13, 1985, pp. 445-447.

Behrman, Jack N. "The Multinational Enterprise and United States Foreign Economic Policy." Indiana Law Journal Vol. 52, 1977, pp. 601-626.

Behrman, Jack N. U.S. International Business and Governments. New York: McGraw-Hill, 1971.

Berberian, D. and Menck, T. "Comparison of U.S. and German Intercompany Pricing Regulations." [Summaries in English, French and German] Intertax 1981, pp. 410-420.

Berger, R.G. "Applying Uniform Margin Requirements to Foreign Entities Attempting to Acquire U.S. Corporations." Virginia Journal of International Law Vol. 24, 1984, pp. 543-574.

Berle, Adolf A. Power without Property: A New Development in American Political Economy. London: Sidgwick & Jackson, 1960.

Bierman, J.N. "The 1983 Export Administration Act Legislation: The Extraterritoriality Issue." Law and Policy in International Business Vol. 15, 1983, pp. 1181-1185.

Bishop, R.D. and S. Burnette. "United States Practice Concerning the Recognition of Foreign Judgments." International Lawyer Vol. 16, 1982, pp. 425-442.

Blechman, Michael D. "Antitrust Jurisdiction, Discovery and Enforcement in the International Sphere: An Appraisal of American Developments and Foreign Reactions." Antitrust Law Journal Vol. 49, 1980, pp. 1197-1206.

Blechman, Michael D. "Neue Entwicklungen in der amerikanischen Wettbewerbspolitik." Wirtschaft und Wettbewerb Vol. 32, March 1982, pp. 173-188.

Boddewyn, J. "Western European Public Policies toward American Investors." Project working paper, New York University Graduate School of Business Administration, October 1972.

Boehme, R. "Current Issues in U.S.-German Financial and Economic Relations." [Summaries in English, French, and German] Intertax 1982, pp. 129-135.

Bondurant, Ward S. "Extraterritorial Jurisdiction - Antitrust - The Impact of the British Protection of Trading Interests Act on the United States Antitrust Suit Brought by Laker Airways against British Airways and British Caledonian." (Recent Developments) Georgia Journal of International and Comparative Law Vol. 14, 1984, pp. 181-200.

Born, G.B. "Recent British Responses to the Extraterritorial Application of United States Law: The Midland Bank [Midland Bank v. Laker Airways, Slip Op. (C.A. July 30, 1985)] Decision and Retaliating Legislation Involving Unitary Taxation." Virginia Journal of International Law Vol. 26, 1985, pp. 91-108.

Boston Consulting Group. The Prospect for Japanese Direct Investment in the United States 1974-80. January 1974.

Boyer, A. "Form as Substance: A Comparison of Antitrust Regulation by Consent Decrees in the U.S.A., Reports of the Monopolies and Mergers Commission in the U.K., and Grants of Clearance by the European Commission" International and Comparative Law Quarterly Vol. 32, 1983, pp. 904-930.

Brennan, B.A. "Amending the Foreign Corrupt Practices Act of 1977: 'Clarifying' or 'Gutting' a Law?" Journal of Legislation Vol. 11, 1984, pp. 56-89.

"Bribes, Kickbacks, and Political Contributions in Foreign Countries - the Nature and Scope of the Security and Exchange Commission's Power to Regulate and Control American Corporate Behavior." (Comment) Wisconsin Law Review Vol. 1976, 1976, pp. 1231-1268.

Bricker, William L. Jr. and James M. Boyd, Jr. "Foreign Acquisition of a U.S. Business: The Tax Considerations." Case Western Reserve Journal of International Law Vol. 11, 1979, pp. 487-534.

Bridge, J.W. "The Law and Politics of United States Foreign Policy Export Controls." Legal Studies Vol. 4, 1984, pp. 2-29.

Brock, W.E. "Progress Report on Efforts to Amend the Foreign Corrupt Practices Act." Detroit College of Law Review Vol. 1983, 1983, pp. 1083-1093.

Brown, R.D. "Tax Aspects of Technology Transfers Between the United States and Canada: A Canadian Viewpoint." Canada-United States Law Journal Vol. 11, 1986, pp. 227-246.

Bruyneel, A. "Restrictions on Foreign Investment: Developments in U.S. Law." Journal of Comparative Corporate Law and Securities Regulation Vol. 3, 1981, pp. 330-338.

Bryan, Greyson. "Overseas Investment: Liability of U.S. Government under Expropriation Insurance Contract - ITT Corporation, S.A. v. Overseas Private Investment Corp., 13 ILM 1307 (American Arbitration Association, 1974)." Harvard International Law Journal Vol. 16, 1975, pp. 721-739.

Buckley, P.J. "Entry Strategy of Recent European Direct Investors in the United States of America." Journal of Comparative Corporate Law and Securities Regulations Vol. 3, July 1981, pp. 169-191.

Butler, E.B. "The Extraterritorial Reach of the U.S. Export Administration Act: Reflections on the Yamal Pipeline Controversy." Journal of Business Law Vol. 1983, 1983, pp. 275-283.

Canada. Eleventh Report of the Standing Committee on External Affairs and National Defence Respecting Canada-U.S. Relations. 28th Parliament, Second Session. Ottawa, 1970.

"The Canada-United States Memorandum of Understanding Regarding Application of National Antitrust Law: New Guidelines for Resolution of Multinational Antitrust Enforcement Disputes." New England Journal of International Law and Business Vol. 6, 1984/1985, pp. 1065-1095.

"Canada-United States Transnational Business Activities: Current Tax and Other Developments." (Various articles) Canada-United States Law Journal Vol. 4, 1981, pp. 90-173.

Carnulutti, A. and F. Delon. "États face aux éffets extraterritoriaux du droit de la concurrence des États-Unis d'Amérique: l'exemple de la France." Revue Française de Droit Aérien Vol. 36, 1982, pp. 15-41.

Carroll, Mitchell B. "Taxation of U.S.-Based Transnational Corporations." Mercer Law Review Vol. 27, 1976, pp. 441-468.

Carroll, Terence M. "Securities and Exchange Commission," in the chapter "Administrative Survey: October 1975 to September 1976: IV Investment Regulation," in Law and Policy in International Business Vol. 9, 1977, pp. 231-236.

Casey, Thomas A. "Japanese Investments in Alaska." Alaska Seas and Coasts Vol. 4, 1976, pp. 5-7.

Chilton, F.R., Jr. "United States Tax Developments during 1983 That Can Affect International Transactions." Hastings International and Comparative Law Review Vol. 1984, 1984, pp. 333-375.

Choate, Alan G. "U.S. Taxation of Foreign Direct Investment." Dickinson International Law Annual Vol. 1, 1982, pp. 35-58.

Chung, William K. and Gregory G. Fouch. "Foreign Direct Investment in the United States, 1977." Survey of Current Business (U.S. Department of Commerce) Vol. 58, August 1978, pp. 39-52.

Chung, William K. and Gregory G. Fouch. "Foreign Direct Investment in the United States in 1979." Survey of Current Business (U.S. Department of Commerce) Vol. 60, August 1980, pp. 38-51.

Clagett, Brice M. "Protection of Foreign Investment under the Revised Restatement." Virginia Journal of International Law Vol. 25, 1984, pp. 73-98.

"Closing the Open Door to FDI." Cornell International Law Journal Vol. 15, 1982, pp. 121-147.

Cohen, B.C. and G. Schachter. "Recent Trends in European Investment in the U.S." Bankers Magazine Vol. 153, Spring 1970, pp. 82-86.

Cohen, B.E. "In Personam Jurisdiction in Federal Courts Over Foreign Corporations: The Need for a Federal Long-Arm Statute." Denver Journal of International Law and Policy Vol. 14, 1985, pp. 59-73.

Cole, P.E. "New Challenges to the U.S. Multinational Corporation in the European Economic Community: Data Protection Laws." New York University Journal of International Law and Politics Vol. 17, 1985, pp. 893-947.

Columbia University, Conservation of Human Resources. Economic Impact of the Japanese Business Community in the United States. New York: The Japan Society, October 1979.

"Commercial Dispute Settlement in China-United States Trade: Conciliation in Perspective." Fordham International Law Journal Vol. 6, 1982-1983, pp. 172-201.

"Comparison of the F.C.P.A. and the Draft International Agreement on Illegal Payments." Vanderbilt Journal of Transnational Law Vol. 13, 1980, pp. 795-823.

"Compelling Production of Documents in Violation of Foreign Law: An Examination and Re-evaluation of the American Position." Fordham Law Review Vol. 50, 1982, pp. 877-908.

Conway, J.D. "The Proposed Tax Straddle Reform Act of 1983 - Unjust Treatment for Many United States-Owned Foreign Corporations." Taxes Vol. 62, 1984, pp. 256-270.

Conway Research, Inc. Arab Investments in the United States: General Outlook Plus Special Report on Kuwait. Atlanta, Georgia, 1974.

Corcoran, J.I.W. "The Trading with the Enemy Act: The Impact of the Amended Foreign Assets Control Regulations On Canadian Corporations Owned by Americans." McGill Law Journal Vol. 16, 1970, pp. 460-487.

Craig, William Laurence. "Application of the Trading with the Enemy Act to Foreign Corporations Owned by Americans: Reflections on Fruehauf v. Massardy." Harvard Law Review Vol. 83, 1970, pp. 579-601.

Culver, John C. "Foreign Investment in the United States." Foreign Policy, No. 16, Fall 1974, pp. 157-164.

Dachs, R.A. "Enforcement of Foreign Tax Judgments in the United States." George Washington Journal of International Law and Economics Vol. 14, 1980, pp. 281-299.

Dalebroux, Jeffrey M. "Foreign Investment - Mandamus Action to Enforce the Hickenlooper Amendment." Law and Policy in International Business Vol. 7, 1975, pp. 968-973.

Damm, W. "The Economic Aspects of European Direct Investment in the U.S," in S.E. Rolfe and W. Damm, eds., The Multinational Corporation in the World Economy. New York: Praeger, 1970.

Davidow, Joel. "U.S. Antitrust and Doing Business Abroad: Recent Trends and Developments." North Carolina Journal of International Law and Commercial Regulation Vol. 5, 1980, pp. 23-36.

Davis, R.W. "Antitrust, the Trade Deficit, and U.S. International Competitiveness: A Time for Rethinking." New York University Journal of International Law and Politics Vol. 18, 1986, pp. 1235-1279.

Deagan, James R. Japanese Investment in Alaska. Juneau: State of Alaska Division of Economic Enterprise, August 1974.

Degnan, T.E. and K.A. Coyle. "Final Regulations for FIRPTA Code Section 897." Oil and Gas Tax Quarterly Vol. 35, September 1986, pp. 50-72.

Dehner, W.J. Jr. "Multinational Enterprise and Racial Non-Discrimination: United States Enforcement of an International Human Right." Harvard International Law Journal Vol. 15, 1974, pp. 71-125.

Dickey, W.L. "Aspects of the Legal, Political and Policy Issues That Will Confront the U.S.-Japan Trading Community During the Remainder of the 1980's." Case Western Reserve Journal of International Law Vol. 15, 1983, pp. 445-468.

Dinkins, C.E. "Merger Guidelines: A Return to Reason." South Texas Law Journal Vol. 27, 1986, pp 507-518.

Dinur, D.D. and C.H. Coffin. "FIRPTA: An Update on Substance and Procedure." New York University Institute on Federal Taxation Vol. 42, 1984, pp. 30.1-30.44.

Directory of Japanese Companies in the U.S.A., 1979-1980. New York: Economic Salon, Ltd., 1980.

Dolzer, Rudolph. "Notstandsrecht in den Vereinigten Staaten von Amerika und seine Reform ("Stellungnahmen")." Zeitschrift fuer auslaendisches oeffentliches Recht und Voelkerrecht Vol. 40, 1980, pp. 101-121.

Donaghue, H.P. "Transborder Flows: Its Implications in Canada-U.S. Relations." Canada-United States Law Journal Vol. 11, 1986, pp. 289-294.

Done, Kevin. "Beecham Expanding in North America." Financial Times: "Finance and Company News" 9 March 1978.

"Draft Restatement Revised." American Society of International Law Proceedings Vol. 76, 1982, pp. 184-205.

Dreher, M. and C. Stewart. "Merger Guidelines des U.S. Department of Justice." Recht der internationalen Wirtschaft Vol. 29, 1983, pp. 906-915.

"Dresser Industries: The Failure of Foreign Policy Trade Controls Under the Export Administration Act." Maryland Journal of International Law and Trade Vol. 8, 1984, pp. 122-143.

Dunfee, T.W. and A.S. Friedman. "The Extraterritorial Application of United States Antitrust Laws: A Proposal for an Interim Solution." Ohio State Law Journal Vol. 45, 1984, pp. 883-932.

Dunn, R.R. "Taxation: Foreign Corrupt Practices Act." Texas International Law Journal Vol. 18, 1983, pp. 407-412.

Dunning, John H. American Investment in British Manufacturing Industry. London: Allen & Unwin, 1958.

Dunning, John H. "British Investment in the United States, 1860-1913," in J.H. Dunning, Studies in International Investment. London: Allen & Unwin, 1970.

Eaton, T. "Illinois Replaces 'Profit' for 'Presence' in Determining Long-Arm Jurisdiction over Foreign Corporations." Illinois Bar Journal Vol. 69, 1981, pp. 676-682.

Edwards, A.C. and A.D. Issa. "Foreign Direct Investment in Michigan." Paper prepared for a meeting of the Academy of International Business, Atlanta, Georgia, 31 October 1979.

Ehrenhaft, Peter D. Review of James A. Rahl, "Common Market and American Antitrust - Overlap and Conflict." Law and Policy in International Business, Vol. 3, 1971, pp. 649-658.

Ekblom, H.E. "European Direct Investment in the U.S." Harvard Business Review Vol. 51, July/August 1973, pp. 16-27.

Ellicott, J. "Trends in Export Control Regulation." Business Lawyer Vol. 38, 1983, pp. 533-553.

Ellis, Clarke N. "United States Multinational Corporations: The Impact of Foreign Direct Investment on United States Foreign Relations." San Diego Law Review Vol. 11, 1973, pp. 1-26.

Ellis, J.J.A. "Legal Aspects of European Direct Investment in the U.S.A," in S.E. Rolfe and Walter Damm, eds., The Multinational Corporation in the World Economy. New York: Praeger, 1970.

Elmer, B.C. and D.A. Johnson. "Legal Obstacles and Foreign Acquisitions of United States Corporations." Business Lawyer Vol. 30, 1975, pp. 681-698.

Evans, Alona E. "Expropriation - Cuba - Extraterritorial Effect - Act of State - Trademark Infringement - Bretton Woods Agreement - Hickenlooper Amendment." American Journal of International Law Vol. 68, 1974, pp. 325-330.

Evans, Alona E. "Self-Executing Treaties in the United States of America." British Yearbook of International Law Vol. 30, 1953, pp. 178-205.

"An Examination of Compensation Terms in the U.S.-Egypt Bilateral Investment Treaty." Case Western Reserve Journal of International Law Vol. 16, 1984, pp. 287-302.

"Exchange of Information under the OECD and U.S. Model Tax Treaties." Loyola of Los Angeles International and Comparative Law Journal Vol. 5, 1982, pp. 129-142.

"The Expanding Extraterritorial Jurisdiction of the Sherman Antitrust Act: Intent and Effects in the Balance?" Loyola of Los Angeles International and Comparative Law Journal Vol. 6, 1983, pp. 463-482.

"Expropriated Property, Frozen Assets, and Sovereign Immunity: Legal Obstacles to United States-China Trade Regulations." Columbia Journal of Transnational Law Vol. 15, 1976, pp. 254-276.

"Extraterritorial Application of the Sherman Act to Foreign Corporations." Delaware Journal of Corporate Law Vol. 11, 1986, pp. 513-534.

"Extraterritorial Application of U.S. Export Laws: Dresser Industries." Wisconsin International Law Journal Vol. 1983, 1983, pp. 138-159.

"The Extraterritorial Enforcement of U.S. Antitrust Laws and Retaliatory Legislation in the United Kingdom and Australia. Denver Journal of International Law and Policy Vol. 13, 1984, pp. 377-386.

"Extraterritoriality: Current Policy of the United States." Syracuse Journal of International Law and Commerce Vol. 12, 1986, pp. 493-519.

Faith, Nicholas. The Infiltrators: The European Business Invasion of America. New York: E.P. Dutton & Co., 1972.

Fanning, E.P. "U.S. Investment in Ireland." Journal of Transnational Law Vol. 17, 1984, pp. 563-630.

Fascell, D.B., and V.M. Schlundt. "United States International Communications and Information Policy: A Crisis in the Making?" Northwestern Journal of International Law and Business Vol. 5, 1983, pp. 486-509.

"FCPA: Curse or Cure?" American Business Law Journal Vol. 19, 1981, pp. 73-86.

Fedders, J.M., F.B. Wade, and M.D. Mann. "Waiver by Conduct? - A Possible Response to the Internationalization of the Securities Markets." Journal of Comparative Business and Capital Market Law Vol. 6, March 1984, pp. 1-54.

Feldman, M.B. "The Restructuring of National Security Controls Under the 1985 Amendments to the Export Administration Act: Multilateral Diplomacy and the Extraterritorial Application of United States Law." Stanford Journal of International Law Vol. 21, 1985, pp. 235-279.

Fisher, Bart S. "The Multinationals and the Crisis in United States Trade and Investment Policy." Boston University Law Review Vol. 53, 1973, pp. 308-366.

Fisher, Bart S. "The Multinationals at Bay: The Foreign Taxation Provisions of the Tax Reduction Act of 1975." Journal of International Law and Economics Vol. 10, April 1975, pp. 61-88.

Fisher, B.M. "Canada's Foreign Investment Review Act as a Model for Foreign Investment Regulation in the United States." Canada-United States Law Journal Vol. 7, 1984, pp. 61-91.

Fisher, W. Halder. Technology Transfer as a Motivation for United States Direct Investments by European Firms. Battelle Memorial Institute, Columbus Laboratories, 1977.

Fletcher, William M. Cyclopedia of the Law of Private Corporations. Chicago: Callaghan & Co., 1931-1933.

Flowers, Edward B. "Oligopolistic Reaction in European and Canadian Direct Investment in the United States." Journal of International Business Studies Vol. 7, Fall/Winter 1976, pp. 43-56.

Flowers, Edward B. "The Wane of Oligopolistic Reaction as an Explanation for Direct Foreign Investment in the U.S." Paper prepared for the annual meeting of the Academy of International Business, June 1979.

"Foreign Corrupt Practices Act: Domestic and International Implications: A Symposium." App. I: "FCP Act of 1977"; App. II: "Senate Bill 708"; App. III: "ITT Code of Corporate Conduct." Syracuse Journal of International Law and Commerce Vol. 9, 1982, pp. 235-378.

Foreign Direct Investment in the Southeast: West Germany, the United Kingdom and Japan. Atlanta, Georgia: Southern Center for International Studies, August 1979.

"Foreign Investment: Investment Disclosure Requirements - Amended Regulations to Implement the International Investment Survey Act of 1976, 46 Fed. Reg. 23,225 (1981) (to be codified in 15 C.F.R. Part 806)." Harvard International Law Journal Vol. 22, 1981, pp. 694-697.

Foreign Investment in Pennsylvania. Harrisburg, Pennsylvania: University of Pennsylvania, Wharton School, 1973.

"Foreign Investment in the United States: A Symposium." "United States Taxation of Foreign Nationals." C.R. Irish, M.G. Reinecke; Other articles: "Foreign Acquisitions of U.S. Banking Institutions: The Current Climate." T.J. Sheehan; "Foreign Direct Investment in the United States; a Legal Analysis." R.W. Shepro. Wisconsin International Law Journal Vol. 4, 1985, pp. 1-63.

"Foreign Investment in the U.S." (4 articles including a bibliography, 1976-1980) Stanford Journal of International Law Vol. 17, Winter 1981.

"Foreign Investment in U.S. Real Property - the Withholding Requirements." Suffolk Transnational Law Journal Vol. 9, 1985, pp. 27-55.

The Foreign Investor in the American Marketplace. New York: Hill & Knowlton, 1979.

"Foreign Statutory Response to Extraterritorial Application of United States Antitrust Law." Dickinson International Law Annual Vol. 1, 1982, pp. 125-155.

"Foreign Subsidiaries Are Not Immune to Employment Discrimination Laws." Washington University Law Quarterly Vol. 60, 1982, pp. 663-674.

Forry, John I. and M.J.A. Karlin. "Current Planning for Foreign Investors in U.S. Real Estate and Other Direct Investments". New York University Institute on Federal Taxation Vol. 38, 1986, pp. 21.1-21.55.

Forry, John I. A Practical Guide to Foreign Investment in the U.S., 2d edition. Washington, D.C.: Tax Management International, 1982.

"Forum Non Conveniens and the Extraterritorial Application of United States Antitrust Law." Yale Law Journal Vol. 94, 1985, pp. 1693-1714.

Fouch, Gregory G. and L.A. Lupo. "Foreign Direct Investment in the United States in 1978." Survey of Current Business (U.S. Department of Commerce) Vol. 59, August 1979, Part I, pp. 38-51.

Franko, Lawrence G. European Business Strategies in the United States. Geneva: Business International, 1971.

Franko, Lawrence G. The European Multinationals: A Renewed Challenge to American and British Big Business. London: Harper & Row, 1976.

Franko, Lawrence G. "Multinationals: The End of U.S. Dominance." Harvard Business Review Vol. 56, November-December 1978, pp. 93-101.

Fugate, Wilbur L. "Antitrust Aspects of the Revised Restatement of Foreign Relations Law." Virginia Journal of International Law Vol. 25, 1984, pp. 49-71.

Fugate, Wilbur L. "Antitrust Aspects of U.S.-Japanese Trade." Case Western Reserve Journal of International Law Vol. 15, 1983, pp. 505-525.

Fugate, Wilbur L. "Export Trade Exceptions to the Antitrust Laws: The Old Webb-Pomerane Act and the New Export Trading Company Act." Vanderbilt Journal of Transnational Law Vol. 15, 1982, pp. 673-707.

Furr, D.M. "The FIRPTA Withholding Rules: A Review of Internal Code Section 1445(a) and the Temporary Regulations." North Carolina International Law and Commercial Regulation Vol. 11, 1986, pp. 67-80.

Gann, P.B. "The U.S. Bilateral Investment Treaty Program." Stanford Journal of International Law Vol. 21, 1986, pp. 373-459.

Garfinkel, E.I. "Disclosure of Confidential Documents under the Trade Agreements Act of 1979: A Corporate Nightmare?" Law and Policy in International Business Vol. 13, 1981, pp. 465-493.

Garvey, G.E. "Foreign Trade Antitrust Improvements Act of 1981." Law and Policy in International Business Vol. 14, 1982, pp. 1-46.

German American Chamber of Commerce. American Subsidiaries of German Firms. New York: German American Chamber of Commerce, 1971.

"German Firms in the American Southeast: Problems and Prospects." Atlanta, Georgia: Georgia World Congress Institute, 1980.

"German-U.S. Tax Treaty: German Memorandum on the Questions of Dividend Taxation." [Summaries in English, French, and German] Intertax 1980, pp. 246-262.

Gerowin, Mina. "U.S. Regulation of Foreign Direct Investment: Current Developments and the Congressional Response." Virginia Journal of International Law Vol. 15, 1975, pp. 611-647.

"The G.M.-Toyota Joint Venture and Its Implications under the National Labor Relations Act." Detroit College Law Review Vol. 1984, 1984, pp. 647-685.

Goodrich, G.G. "U.S. Tax Aspects of Technology Transfers Between the United States and Canada." Canada-United States Law Journal Vol. 11, 1986, pp. 213-226.

Gordon, Edward. "Extraterritorial Application of United States Economic Law: Britain Draws the Line." International Lawyer Vol. 14, 1980, pp. 151-166.

Gotlieb, A.E. "Canadian-U.S. Relations: Legislation, Regulation and the Management of Conflict." Canadian Business Law Journal Vol. 9, 1984, pp. 485-496.

Gotlieb, A.E. "The Legal Aspects of International Investment: The Canadian-U.S. Experience." American Society of International Law Proceedings Vol. 76, 1982, pp. 47-55.

Grabar, N.H. "Antitrust: Effect of Foreign Disclosure Limitation on Discovery in United States Courts." Harvard International Law Journal Vol. 22, 1981, pp. 177-186.

Graham, E.M. "A Defensive Theory of Foreign Direct Investment and European Direct Investment in the United States." Massachusetts Institute of Technology: Sloan School of Management, 1976.

Graham, E.M. "Oligopolistic Imitation and European Direct Investment in the United States." Ph.D. dissertation, Massachusetts Institute of Technology, 1974.

Granwell, A.W. "Current United States International Tax Developments." Canada-United States Law Journal Vol. 8, 1984, pp. 43-60.

Granwell, A.W. "Treaty Shopping: Recent United States Developments." [In French and English] Revue de Droit des Affaires Internationales/International Business Law Journal Vol. 13, 1985, pp. 103-120.

Green, C.J. "New Protectionism." Northwestern Journal of International Law and Business Vol. 3, Spring 1981, pp. 1-20.

Greiff, T.E., C.R. Stevens and J. Leow. "Applicability of U.S. Employment Discrimination Laws to Foreign Corporations in the United States - the Circuit Court Decisions in Spress v. C. Itoh and Company (American), Inc., [643 F.2d. 353] and Avagliano v. Sumitomo Shogi American Inc. [638 F.2d. 552]." UCLA Pacific Basin Law Journal Vol. 1, 1982, pp. 153-161.

Grendell, Timothy J. "The Antitrust Legislation of the United States, the European Community, Germany and Japan." International and Comparative Law Quarterly Vol. 29, 1980, pp. 64-86.

Griffin, Joseph P. "Antitrust Constraints on Acquisitions by Aliens in the United States." International Lawyer Vol. 13, 1979, pp. 427-448.

Griffin, Joseph P. "The Power of Host Countries over the Multinational: Lifting the Veil in the European Economic Community and the United States." Law and Policy in International Business Vol. 6, 1974, pp. 375-435.

Gudgeon, K.S. "United States Bilateral Investment Treaties: Comments on Their Origin, Purposes, and General Treatment Standards." International Tax and Business Lawyer Vol. 4, 1986, pp. 105-135.

Gurley, Franklin L. "Zur Diskussion um den Entwurf fuer ein neues Kartellgesetz: Das amerikanische Wettbewerbsrecht." Neue Zuercher Zeitung, 7 September 1979, p. 14.

Hacker, Louis M. Foreign Investments in America's Growth. Washington, D.C.: U.S. Information Service, November 1, 1967.

"Hague Evidence Convention: A Practical Guide to the Convention, United States Case Law, Convention-Sponsored Review Commissions (1978 and 1985), and Responses of Other Signatory Nations; with digest of cases and bibliography." Georgia Journal of International and Comparative Law Vol. 16, 1986, pp. 73-107.

Halverson, J.T. "U.S. Industrial Competitiveness and Section 7 of the Clayton Act: Are they Compatible?" Introductory remarks. Other articles: "Some Form of Secton 7 Relief Must Be Granted to United States Industries." R.B. Peabody; "Necessary Flexibility Is Already Present Under the 1982 and 1984 Merger Guidelines." J.P. McGrath; "Antitrust and Problems of Adjustment in Distressed Industries." R. Pitofsky; "The Administration's Legislative Proposal and Its Ramifications." M. Baldridge; Panel discussion. Antitrust Law Journal Vol. 55, 1986, pp. 3-49.

Hammesfahr, R.W. and R.L. Blatt. "Extraterritorial Application of American Antitrust Laws: An Overview." Chicago Bar Record Vol. 65, 1983, pp. 106-112.

Hasebe, T. "Japan's Overseas Investment and Monetary Policy." Paper prepared for the Third Meeting of Japan-Hawaii Economic Council, Honolulu, Hawaii, 1974.

Hawk, Barry E., et al. "Antitrust and International Trade - Special Rules." (Various articles) Proceedings of the Twenty-Eighth Annual Spring Meeting of the Section of Antitrust Law of the American Bar Association. Antitrust Law Journal Vol. 49, 1980, pp. 1185-1223.

Hawk, Barry E., ed. International Antitrust: Annual Proceedings of the Fordham Corporate Law Institute (1978). New York: Law and Business, 1979.

Hawk, Barry E. International Anti-Trust Manual: U.S., Common Market, and International Antitrust: A Comparative Guide. New York: Law and Business, 1979.

Hawk, Barry E. "International Antitrust Policy and the 1982 Acts: The Continuing Need for Reassessment." Fordham Law Review Vol. 51, 1982, pp. 201-254.

Heck, A. "U.S. Misinterpretation of the Hague Evidence Convention." Columbia Journal of Transnational Law Vol. 24, 1986, pp. 231-278.

Heller, H. Robert and Emily E. Japanese Investment in the United States - with a Case Study of the Hawaiian Experience. New York: Praeger, 1974.

Hellman, Rainer. The Challenge to U.S. Dominance of the International Corporation. New York: Dunellen, 1970.

Hermann, Don H.J. "Criminal Prosecutions of U.S. Multinational Corporations." Loyola University of Chicago Law Review Vol. 8, 1976-1977, pp. 465-498, 619-641.

Hibey, R.A. "Practical Necessity for Amendment of the Foreign Corrupt Practices Act: S708 - the Current Legislative Initiative." Hofstra Law Review Vol. 10, 1982, pp. 1121-1136.

Hilinski, C.C. "U.S. Tax Aspects of European Direct Investment in the U.S." Commerce in Belgium September 1975.

Hodges, J.W. "The Trading with the Enemy Act of 1917 - Foreign-Based Subsidiaries of American Multinational Corporations: A Time to Abstain from Restraining." (Comment) San Diego Law Review Vol. 11, 1973, pp. 206-226.

Hoelzer, Heinrich. "Neuere Initiativen zum U.S. Antitrust - Ein Ueberblick -." Wirtschaft und Wettbewerb Vol. 30, 1980, pp. 728-740.

Honerman, L. "Japan's Direct Investment in California and the New Protectionism." Journal of World Trade Law Vol. 18, 1984, pp. 309-319.

Honigsberg, C.C. "Uniform Foreign Money-Judgments Recognition Act: A Survey of the Case Law." Vanderbilt Journal of Transnational Law Vol. 14, 1981, pp. 171-196.

Houck, J.B. "The New American Law Institute Restatement of the Foreign Relations Law of the United States - Problems for Practitioners." Private Investors Abroad Vol. 1983, 1983, pp. 37-61.

Howenstine, Ned. G. "Gross Product of U.S. Affiliates of Foreign Companies." Survey of Current Business (U.S. Department of Commerce) Vol. 59, January 1979, pp. 28-36.

Howenstine, Ned G. "Selected Data on the Operations of U.S. Affiliates of Foreign Companies, 1977." Survey of Current Business (U.S. Department of Commerce) Vol. 60, July 1980, pp. 32-44.

Hughes, Kent M. Trade, Taxes, and Transnationals: International Economic Decision Making in Congress. New York: Praeger, 1979.

Hui, C. and R.G. Hawkins. Foreign Direct Investment and the U.S. Balance of Payments. The American Statistical Association, 1972.

bHyde, A. "Rights for Canadian Members of International Unions Under the (U.S.) Labor - Management Reporting and Disclosure Act." Washington Law Review Vol. 61, 1986, pp. 1007-1039.

Imbert, Bernard. "French Investments in the American Southeast." Atlanta: Georgia World Congress Institute, August 1979.

"In Support of Azania: Divestiture of Public Pension Funds As One Answer to U.S. Private Investment in South Africa." Black Law Journal Vol. 9, 1985, pp. 167-188.

Inouye, Daniel K. "Political Implications of Foreign Investment in the United States." Mercer Law Review Vol. 27, 1976, pp. 597-614.

"Institutional Investor Disclosure Act: An Analysis of the Consumer Benefits." Yale Law Journal Vol. 83, 1974, pp. 1271-1290.

"International Implications of the 1982 Merger Guidelines." Georgia Journal of International and Comparative Law Vol. 13, 1983, pp. 797-824.

"International Joint Ventures in the United States: The GM-Toyota Deal." Columbia Journal of Transnational Law Vol. 22, 1984, pp. 505-540.

International Monetary Fund. "German Direct Investments in the United States." International Financial News Survey 15 May 1970.

"International Transactions: Jurisdictional Developments; Applicability of American Employment Discrimination Legislation to Domestically Based Foreign Companies; and Governmental Restrictions on International Economic Transactions." 1985 Annual Survey of American Law Vol. 1985, 1986, pp. 409-438.

"Intra-Enterprise Conspiracy Under Section 1 of the Sherman Act: A Suggested Standard." Michigan Law Review Vol. 75, 1976-1977, pp. 717-744.

"The Investment Company Act of 1940." Yale Law Journal Vol. 50, 1941, pp. 440-457.

Jackson, Bruce H. "Application of U.S. Antitrust Law to International Investment: Joint Ventures, Mergers and Aquisitions." North Carolina Journal of International Law and Commercial Regulation Vol. 5, 1980, pp. 141-164.

Japan Ministry of Foreign Affairs. Hawaii's Reaction to Japanese Investments in the Islands. Hawaii International Services Agency, September 1973.

Japanese Investment in Alaska. Alaska Department of Economic Development: August 1974.

Japanese Investments in Hawaii. Honolulu, Hawaii: Economic Salon, Ltd., October 1973.

Jedel, Michael Jay and Duane Kujawa. "Management and Employment Practices of Foreign Direct Investors in the United States." Georgia State University, March 1976.

Jennings, R.Y. "Extraterritorial Jurisdiction and the United States Anti-Trust Laws." British Yearbook of International Law Vol. 33, 1957, pp. 146-175.

Joelson, Mark R. "Challenges to United States Foreign Trade and Investment: Antitrust Law Perspectives." International Lawyer Vol. 14, 1980, pp. 103-114.

Joelson, Mark R. "International Technology Transfers and U.S. Anti-Trust Laws." Journal of International Law and Economics Vol. 8, 1973, pp. 85-112.

Joelson, Mark R. and Joseph P. Griffin. "Legal Status of Nation-State Cartels under United States Anti-Trust and Public International Law." International Lawyer Vol. 9, 1975, pp. 617-645.

Joelson, Mark R. and Joseph P. Griffin. "Multinational Joint Ventures and the U.S. Anti-Trust Laws." Virginia Journal of International Law Vol. 15, 1975, pp. 487-538.

Joelson, Mark R. "Proposed International Codes of Conduct as Related to Restrictive Business Practices." Law and Policy in International Business Vol. 8, 1976, pp. 837-874.

Johnson, Alan R. "The Initial FIRPTA Regulations." Tax Lawyer Vol. 36, 1983, pp. 713-749.

Johnson, Gregg Allen. "Comment: The Foreign Direct Investment Regulations, 1973: Balance of Payments Remedy or Regulation of Multinational Corporations?" San Diego Law Review Vol. 11, 1973, pp. 267-285.

Johnson, J.C. and K.C. Schneider. "Fifty Years (1936-1986) of the Robinson-Patman Act Mystique." Transportation Practitioners Journal Vol. 53, 1986, pp. 400-412.

Johnson, Richard T. and W.C. Ouchi. "Made in America Under Japanese Management." Harvard Business Review Vol. 52, 1974, pp. 61-69.

Johnson, Richard T. "Success and Failure of Japanese Subsidiaries in America." Columbia Journal of World Business Vol. 12, Spring 1977, pp. 30-37.

Joliet, René. Monopolization and Abuse of Dominant Position: Study of the American and European Approaches to the Control of Economic Power. (Lièges Faculté de droit: Collection scientifique de la faculté de droit de l'Université de Lièges 31) The Hague: Nijhoff, 1970.

Joliet, René. The Rule of Reason in Anti-Trust Law: American, German and Common Market Laws in Comparative Perspective. The Hague: Nijhoff, 1967.

Jones, Robert T. "Extraterritoriality in U.S. Antitrust: An International 'Hot Potato'." International Lawyer Vol. 11, 1977, pp. 415-435.

Jones, Robert T. "Practical Legal Aspects of Doing Business in the U.S." New Law Journal Vol. 124, 16-23 May 1974, pp. 465-467, 478-480.

"Jurisdiction over a Foreign Corporation on the Basis of its Subsidiary's Activities in New York: Bulova Watch Co. v. K. Hattori & Co. [508 F.Supp. 1322]." Brooklyn Journal of International Law Vol. 9, 1983, pp. 91-113.

"Jurisdiction over Foreign Corporations - In re Marc Rich and Co. A.G., Marc Rich and Co., A.G. v. United States, 707 F.2d 663." Harvard International Law Journal Vol. 25, 1984, pp. 250-257.

Kaplan, P.T. "The Unitary Tax Debate, The United States Supreme Court, and Some Plain English." British Tax Review Vol. 1983, 1983, pp. 203-220.

Kaplan, P.T. "U.S. Tax Act 1982: Provisions of Special Interest to Firms Doing Business Internationally." [Summaries in English, French, and German] Intertax 1982, pp. 463-475.

Karzon, A.U. "International Tax Evasion: Spawned in the United States and Nurtured by Secrecy Havens." Vanderbilt Journal of Transnational Law Vol. 16, 1983, pp. 757-832.

Katz, Julius L. "Foreign Direct Investment in the U.S. - Advantages and Barriers." Case Western Reserve Journal of International Law Vol. 11, 1979, pp. 473-486.

Katz, S.S. for the Commission on International Trade and Investment Policy. Foreign Direct Investment in the United States Vol. 1. Washington, D.C.: U.S. Government Printing Office, 1971.

Kessler, S.A. "Adjusting to FIRPTA." Taxes Vol. 61, 1983, pp. 960-971.

Kindred, H.M. and W. Biggs. "Trade and Investment Issues: Pattern of Canadian-American Economic Problems." Canada-United States Law Journal Vol. 1, 1978, pp. 114-131.

King, H.T., Jr. "Foreign Restrictions on U.S. Investment." San Diego Law Review Vol. 11, 1973, pp. 452-467.

Kleinberg, J.P. "The Extraterritorial Application of the United States." Hastings International and Comparative Law Review Vol. 8, 1985, pp. 187-195.

Knox, G.R., S.E. Alley, and D.B. Person. "The U.S. Tax Regime Affecting Mexican Nationals Who Desire to Conduct Business or Invest Within the United States." Houston Journal of International Law Vol. 8, 1985, pp. 87-118.

Kolluri, Bharat R. and Richard C. Torrisi. "Foreign Direct Investment in the United States: Some Empirical Results." Department of Economics, University of Hartford, Connecticut, September 1980.

Kooiman, K. "Article 16: The U.S. Attitude to Treaty Shopping." Bulletin for International Fiscal Documentation Vol. 37, 1983, pp. 195-200.

Kotkin, Joel. "Japan is Building Economic Empire in American West." International Herald Tribune 3 August 1978, p. 1.

Kramer, Lee C. Japanese Investment in Alaska. Juneau: State of Alaska Department of Economic Development, April 1971.

Krause, Lawrence B. "Evolution of Direct Foreign Investment: The United States and Japan," in J.B. Cohen, ed., Pacific Partnerships: United States-Japan Trade. Lexington, Massachusetts: Heath & Co., 1972.

Krause, Harry D. "The Multi-Corporate International Business under Section 1 of the Sherman Act - Intra-Enterprise Conspiracy Revisited." Business Lawyer Vol. 17, 1962, pp. 912-938.

Kubin, Konrad. "German Direct Investments in the U.S. and American Investments in the Federal Republic of Germany." Indiana University: Institute of German Studies, 1978.

Lahoud, N.J. "'Non-discriminatory' United States Generalized System of Preferences: De Facto Discrimination Against the Least Developed Developing Countries." Harvard International Law Journal Vol. 23, 1982, pp. 1-47.

bLandwehr, Martha L., ed. Private Investors Abroad - Problems and Solutions in International Business in 1982. Parts I, II, III, IV: "Privacy, Telecommunications and Transborder Data Flows - U.S. Multinational Response to European Expectations." (Articles: G.W. Coombe, Jr., R.E.L. Walker, H.P. Donaghue, and L.A. Hummer) New York: Matthew Bender, 1982.

Langbein, V. "U.S. Unitary Taxation Methode hier: Container Corp. of America v. (California) Franchise Tax Board." Recht der internationalen Wirtschaft Vol. 29, 1983, pp. 673-676.

Langley, M. "International Investment Survey Act: The High Cost of Knowledge." Law and Policy in International Business Vol. 14, 1982, pp. 481-504.

Lansing, P. and E.C. Rose. "The Japanese Industrial Policy Complex: An Appropriate Legal Model for the United States?" Brooklyn Journal of International Law Vol. 11, 1985, pp. 237-281.

Larose, L.A. "Conflicts, Contacts, and Cooperation: Extraterritorial Application of the United States Securities Laws." Securities Regulation Law Journal Vol. 12, Summer 1984, pp. 99-137.

Lawrie, R.F.C. "Corporate Freezeouts: A Comparison of Controls in the United States and England." New York University Journal of International Law and Politics Vol. 14, 1982, pp. 595-641.

Lebedoff, G. and C. Raievski. "A French Perspective on the United States Ban on the Soviet Gas Pipeline Equipment." Texas International Law Journal Vol. 18, 1983, pp. 483-507.

Leftwich, Robert. "Foreign Direct Investment in the United States in 1973." Survey of Current Business (U.S. Department of Commerce) Vol. 54, August 1974, pp. 7-9.

Leftwich, Robert. "Foreign Direct Investments in the United States, 1962-1971." Survey of Current Business (U.S. Department of Commerce) Vol. 53, February 1973, pp. 29-40.

"Legislation - The Overseas Private Investment Corporation Amendment of 1974 - OPIC's Functions are to be Gradually Phased Out and its Programs are to be Transferred to the Private Insurance Industry. 22 U.S.C.A. Sec. 2191-2200a, as amended (- U.S.C.A. Sec. -)." (Note) Texas International Law Journal Vol. 10, 1975, pp. 402-410.

Leigh, M. "Restating the Restatement: The Foreign Relations Law of the United States," in Private Investors Abroad. New York: Matthew Bender, 1985.

Leleux, Paul. "Corporation Law in the U.S. and in the EEC." Common Market Law Review Vol. 133, 1967-1968, pp. 133-176.

Lenrow, Jay Laurence. "Foreign Direct Investment in the United States: Possible Restrictions at Home and a New Climate for American Investment Abroad." American University Law Review Vol. 26, 1976, pp. 109-153.

Lillich, R.B. "The Gravel Amendment to the Trade Reform Act of 1974: Congress Checkmates a Presidential Lump Sum Agreement." American Journal of International Law Vol. 69, 1975, pp. 837-847.

Lillich, R.B. "Requiem for Hickenlooper." [Amendment to the Foreign Assistance Act of the United States.] American Journal of International Law Vol. 69, 1975, pp. 97-100.

Lindsay, Robert. "Japanese Beachhead in California." New York Times 21 August 1977, Section 3, p. 1.

Little, Jane Sneddon. "Locational Decisions of Foreign Direct Investors in the United States." New England Economic Review Vol. 23, July/August 1978, pp. 43-63.

Little, L.E. "Out of Woods [Woods v. Interstate Realty Co., 304 U.S. 64] and Into the Rules: The Relationship Between State Foreign Corporaton Door-Closing Statutes and Federal Rule of Civil Procedure 17(b). Virginia Law Review Vol. 72, 1986, pp. 767-809.

Litvak, I. and C.J. Maule. "Canadian Small Business Investment in the U.S. - Corporate Forms and Characteristics." Business Quarterly Winter 1978, pp. 69-77.

Long, D.R. "More Foreign Firms Putting Money in U.S. Plants." Industry Week October 1973, pp. 30-35.

Lupo, Leonard A. and Gregory G. Fouch. "Foreign Direct Investment in the United States in 1975." Survey of Current Business (U.S. Department of Commerce) Vol. 56, August 1976, pp. 34-63.

Maiers, J.D. "New Tax Withholding Rules for Foreign-Owned U.S. Real Estate." Georgia Journal of International and Comparative Law Vol. 15, 1985, pp. 29-37.

Maitland-Walker, J., ed. International Anti-Trust Law. Oxford: ESC Publishing, 1984. (2 Vols.) Vol. 1: A review of national laws; Vol. 2: Recent developments in EEC and U.S. Anti-Trust Laws.

Maktouf, L, and M. Milliet-Einbinder. "Grandeur et décadence de la taxation unitaire aux États-Unis." [In French and English] Revue de Droit des Affaires Internationales/ International Business Law Journal Vol. 13, 1985, pp. 573-601.

Mandell, Stuart L. and Carl Dan Killian. An Analysis of Foreign Investment in Selected Areas of the United States: A Research Project on Behalf of the New England Regional Commission. Boston: International Center of New England, November 1974.

Mantel, Ida May. "Foreign Direct Investment in the United States, 1976." Survey of Current Business (U.S. Department of Commerce) Vol. 57, October 1977, pp. 26-44.

Mantel, Ida May. "Foreign Direct Investment in the United States in 1974." Survey of Current Business (U.S. Department of Commerce) Vol. 55, October 1975, pp. 36-42.

Marans, J.E., et al., eds. Foreign Investment in the United States - 1980: Legal Issues and Techniques. Washington, D.C.: The District of Columbia Bar, 1980.

"Marc Rich [Marc Rich and Co., A.G. v. U.S., 707 F.2d 663]: An Expansion of U.S. Criminal Jurisdiction Over Foreign Defendants." New England Journal of International Law and Business Vol. 6, 1984, pp. 615-645.

Marcuss, S.J. and E.L. Richard. "Extraterritorial Jurisdiction in United States Trade Law: The Need for a Consistent Theory." Columbia Journal of Transnational Law Vol. 20, 1981, pp. 411-479.

McClaren, Richard. "International Investment and the U.S. Antitrust Laws." Address delivered in London, 1 December 1969.

McClure, C.E. "Federal Law and State Corporate Income Taxes." Vanderbilt Journal of Transnational Law Vol. 18, 1985, pp. 275-310.

McDermid, John F. "Merger Directions in the United States and EEC: an Ominous Picture for United States Multinationals." George Mason University Law Review Vol. 3, 1980, pp. 1-62.

McNamara, D.E. "Foreign Direct Investment in the United States: Disclosure Regulations." Georgia Journal of International and Comparative Law Vol. 12, 1982, pp. 193-207.

Meal, D.H. "Governmental Compulsion as a Defense under United States and European Community Antitrust Law." Columbia Journal of Transnational Law Vol. 20, 1981, pp. 51-131.

"Merger Policy and Enforcement." J. Sims, introductory remarks. Other articles: "Merger Policy and Enforcement at the Antitrust Division: The Lawyer's View." R.B. Andewelt; "Merger Policy and Enforcement at the Federal Trade Commission: The Lawyer's View." J.E. McCarty; "Merger Policy and Enforcement at the Antitrust Division: The Economist's View." F.R. Warren-Boulton; "Merger Policy and Enforcement at the Federal Trade Commisssion: The Economist's View." D.T. Scheffman; Panel discussion. Antitrust Law Journal. Vol. 54, 1985, pp. 93-128.

Mestmaecker, E.-J. and R. Richter, eds. "Competition Policy: German and American Experiences - A Symposium." Zeitschrift fuer die gesamte Staatswissenschaft No. 3, 1980, pp. 385-592.

Miller, Arthur S. "Toward the 'Techno-Corporate' State? - An Essay in American Constitutionalism." Villanova Law Review Vol. 14, 1968, pp. 1-73.

Millstein, Ira M., et al. "Extraterritorial Application of U.S. Antitrust Law (Economic Imperialism or Protecting Competition Against Foreign Invasion?)." (Debate) Proceedings of the Twenty-Ninth Annual Spring Meeting of the Section of Antitrust Law of the American Bar Association Washington, D.C., 1981. Antitrust Law Journal Vol. 50, 1981, pp. 617-644.

"Modifying the Foreign Corrupt Practices Act: The Search for a Practical Standard." Northwestern Journal of International Law and Business Vol. 4, 1982, pp. 203-233.

Moeschel, W. "Konglomerate Zusammenschlusse im Antitrustrecht der Vereinigten Staaten von Amerika." Rabels Zeitschrift fuer auslaendisches und internationales Privatrecht Vol. 44, 1980, pp. 203-256.

Morgan Guaranty Trust Company. "Foreign Investment: The Two-Way Street." Morgan Guaranty Survey, October 1970, pp. 3-7.

Morgan Guaranty Trust Company. "Foreign Investors - Bullish on America". New York, September 1978, pp. 2-4.

Morgan, H.V., Jr. "Advising the Foreign Investor in the Southeastern U.S.: Perspectives on Foreign Investment in the Southeastern U.S. An Introduction." Other articles: "The U.S. Policy Toward Foreign Direct Investment." H.E. Bale, Jr.; "Determinants of Foreign Plant Start-ups in the U.S.: Lessons for Policymakers in the Southeast." M.I. Luger and S. Shetty; "An Evaluation of Current Trends in Foreign Direct Investment in the Southeastern U.S." C.L. Suzman and J.A. Heslin; "Federal Law and State Corporation Income Taxes." C.E. McLure, Jr.; "Attribution of a Multinational Corporation's Net Income: The Position of Unitary States Regarding Combined Reporting." W.D. Dexter; "The Foreign Investor: Current Approaches Towards U.S. Immigration Law." A.T. Fragomen, Jr. and G.M. Robosson; "Foreign Investment in the U.S.: A Survey of Current Legal Literature." I.I. Kavass. Vanderbilt Journal of Transnational Law Vol. 18, 1985, pp. 191-480.

Mueller-Dott, J.P. "California Franchise Tax und Unitary Tax Concept." Recht der internationalen Wirtschaft Vol. 26, Fall 1980, pp. 109-116.

Murphy, D.T. "Moderating Antitrust Subject Matter Jurisdiction: the Foreign Trade Antitrust Improvements Act and the Restatement of Foreign Relations Law (Revised)." University of Cincinnati Law Review Vol. 54, 1986, pp. 779-827.

National Industrial Conference Board. Foreign Direct Investment in the United States: Policy, Problems and Obstacles. New York: National Industrial Conference Board, 1974.

Neale, A.D. The Antitrust Laws of the United States of America: A Study of Competition Enforced by Law, 2d ed. Cambridge: Cambridge University Press, 1970.

Negandhi, Anant R. and Martin Welge. Global Rationalization Strategies of American, German and Japanese Multinational Companies. Greenwich, Connecticut: JAI Press, 1984.

"The New Wave: Foreign Capital Investment in the United States - A Survey." The Economist 25 October 1980, pp 1-26 following p. 72.

Newmark, M.N. and D.M. Lang. "Subchapter S Revision Act of 1982." *Tax Lawyer* Vol. 37, 1983, pp. 93-132.

Niehuss, John M. "Foreign Investment in the United States: A Review of Government Policy." *Virginia Journal of International Law* Vol. 15, 1975, pp. 65-102.

Nielsen, Asger M. "The Economic Impact of Foreign-Based Multinational Firms Operating in the United States." Ph.D. dissertation, University of Michigan, 1975.

Nothstein, G.Z. "Multinational Corporations and the Extraterritorial Application of the Labor Management Relations Act." *Cornell International Law Journal* Vol. 10, 1976, pp. 1-58.

O'Reilly, James T. *Federal Information Disclosure: Procedures, Forms, and the Law.* (Two looseleaf volumes) Colorado Springs, Colorado: Shepard's/McGraw-Hill, 1977.

Olmer, L.H. "Barriers to U.S. Foreign Investment." in *1983 Private Investors Abroad*. New York: Matthew Bender, 1983, pp. 63-72.

Olson, T.H. "Tax Considerations in Structuring Foreign Investment in the United States." *Brigham Young University Law Review* Vol. 1983, 1983, pp. 713-754.

Ongman, John Will. "Be No Longer a Chaos: Constructing a Normative Theory of the Sherman Act's Extraterritorial Jurisdictional Scope." *Northwestern University Law Review* Vol. 6, 1977, pp. 733-766.

Osborn, J.E. "Renegotiation of the United States-British Virgin Islands Tax Convention: Prelude to the End of Treaty Shopping?" *Virginia Journal of International Law* Vol. 22, 1982, pp. 381-412.

Osgood, R.K. "Interpreting Tax Treaties in Canada, the United States, and the United Kingdom." *Cornell International Law Journal* Vol. 17, 1984, pp. 255-297.

Ott, K.T. "Economic Recovery Tax Act of 1981, Section 223: The Suspension of IRC Regulations Regarding the Allocation of R&D Expenses to Foreign and Domestic Source Income." Law and Policy in International Business Vol. 14, 1982, pp. 885-904.

Ozawa, Terutomo. "Japan's New Industrial Offensive in the United States." Michigan State University Business Topics Autumn 1972.

Park, J.G. "Extraterritorial Impact of United States Antitrust Laws and Commercial Bribery Considerations." Dickinson International Law Annual Vol. 1, 1982, pp. 105-124.

Parker, Paul S. "Foreign Relations Law." (Recent Decisions) Vanderbilt Journal of Transnational Law Vol. 8, 1974, pp. 223-230.

Parsky, G.L. "OPEC Investment in the U.S." Middle East Economic Survey Vol. 18, 21 March 1975, Supplement.

Paterson, R.K. "The GATT and Restrictions on Foreign Investment: the U.S. Challenge to Canada's Foreign Investment Law." UCLA Pacific Basin Law Journal Vol. 1, 1985, pp. 224-246.

Pattison, J.E. "The United States-Egypt Bilateral Investment Treaty: A Prototype for Future Negotiation." Cornell International Law Journal Vol. 16, 1983, pp. 305-339.

Paugh, Jon. "The Application of U.S. Economic Regulations to International Commerce: A Comparison of the Sherman Act and U.S. International Trade Regulation Laws." Law and Policy in International Business Vol. 13, 1981, pp. 961-995.

Peay, T. Michael. "The Foreign Sovereign Immunities Act of 1975: Reflections on Old Problems in a New Bill." The Black Law Journal Vol. 5, pp. 270-279.

Peppas, Spero C. "A Comparative Study of Promotional Activities to Attract Foreign Investment: An Application of Marketing Theory to the Efforts of the Southeastern States." Ph.D. dissertation, Georgia State University, Atlanta, 1979.

Pengilley, W. "New England Commerce Legislation: The Likely Impact on Commercial Conduct in the Light of Australian Experience." 1986 New Zealand Law Journal 1986, pp. 111-118.

Perlmutter, Howard V. and Franklin R. Root. Foreign Investment in Pennsylvania. Harrisburg, Pennsylvania: Pennsylvania Department of Commerce, 1973.

Peterson, C.H. "Law Applicable to Multinational Corporations from the Perspective of the United States," in Hazard, J. ed., Law in the United States of America in Social and Technological Revolution. Brussels: Emile Bruylant, 1974, pp. 173-194.

Petkin, Lisa B. "Foreign Investment in Real Property Tax Act of 1980." Dickinson International Law Annual Vol. 1, 1982, pp. 11-34.

"Phillips Petroleum Company v. Shutts [105 S.Ct. 2965]: Multistate Plaintiff Class Actions: A Definite Forum, But Is It Proper?" The John Marshall Law Review Vol. 19, 1986, pp. 483-499.

Pizer, Samuel and Zalie Warner. Foreign Business Investments in the United States. U.S. Department of Commerce, Office of Business Economics, 1962.

Pizer, Samuel and Frederick Cutler. "Private Foreign Investment Near $37 Billion." (Special Article) Survey of Current Business (Department of Commerce) Vol. 38, September 1958, pp. 15-23.

Porrata-Doria, Jr., R.A. "Amending the Foreign Corrupt Practices Act of 1977: Repeating the Mistakes of the Past?" Rutgers Law Review Vol. 38, 1985, pp. 29-67.

"Potential Havens from American Jurisdiction and Discovery Laws in International Antitrust Enforcement." Univerisity of Florida Law Review Vol. 33, 1981, pp. 240-271.

Probe Directory of Foreign Direct Investment in the United States. Stamford, Connecticut: Probe International, Inc., 1986.

"A Proposal for Uniform Regulation of Foreign Investment in American Real Estate." Cornell International Law Journal Vol. 18, 1985, pp. 147-178.

"Proposed Congressional Limitations on State Taxation of Multinational Corporations." Georgia Journal of International and Comparative Law Vol. 11, 1981, pp. 343-363.

Quinn, M.L. "Temporary Regulations Implementing FIRPTA's Withholding Tests Are Major Clarifications." Journal of Taxation Vol. 63, August 1985, pp. 98-105.

Rahl, James A. Common Market and American Antitrust - Overlap and Conflict. New York: McGraw-Hill, 1970.

Ramos, F. "First Application by the Spanish Supreme Court of the New York Convention of June 10, 1958 to the Exequatur of Foreign Arbitral Awards." [Summary in French] Droit et Pratique du Commerce International Vol. 10, 1984, pp. 95-116.

Ramsey, S.D. "The United States-Australia Antitrust Cooperation Agreement: A Step in the Right Direction." Virginia Journal of International Law Vol. 24, 1983, pp. 127-169.

Ray, Dennis M. "The Causes of Expropriation of American Property Abroad." Stanford Journal of International Studies Vol. 11, 1976, pp. 122-152.

Ray, Dennis M. "Corporations and American Foreign Relations," in D.H. Blake, "The Multinational Corporation." The Annals of the American Academy of Political and Social Science Vol. 403, September 1972, pp. 80-92.

"Recent Legal Developments in U.S.-China Economic Relations." Business Lawyer Vol. 36, 1981, pp. 1699-1732.

Reicin, C.V. "Act of State Doctrine: Applicability of United States Antitrust Laws." Harvard International Law Journal Vol. 23, 1982, pp. 117-123.

Reinsch, W. "Export Trading Company Act of 1981." Law and Policy in International Business Vol. 14, 1982, pp. 47-127.

Ritomsky, B.A. and R.M. Jervis. "Doing Business in America: The Unfinished Work of Sumitomo Shoji America, Inc. v. Avagliano [102 S.Ct. 2374] Harvard International Law Journal Vol. 27, 1986, pp. 193-225.

Robinson, D.R. "Conflicts of Jurisdiction and the Draft Restatement." Law and Policy in International Business Vol. 15, 1983, pp. 1147-1155.

"The Robinson-Patman Act Revisited in Its 50th Year." Introduction by R.D. Paul; Other articles: "The Robinson-Patman Act: the Great Issues and Personalities." P.H. LaRue; "The Robinson-Patman Act: A Critical Appraisal." H.L. Shniderman; Panel discussion. Antitrust Law Journal Vol. 55, 1986, pp. 133-170.

Rocour, Jean-Luc. "Management of European Subsidiaries in the United States." Management International Review Vol. 1, 1966, pp. 13-28.

Roemer, J.E. "Japanese Direct Foreign Investment in Manufactures: Some Comparisons with the U.S. Pattern." Quarterly Review of Economics and Business Vol. 16, Summer 1976, pp. 91-111.

Rosenbloom, H.D. and S.I. Langbein. "United States Tax Treaty Policy: An Overview." Columbia Journal of Transnational Law Vol. 19, 1981, pp. 359-406.

Rosenthal, Douglas E. "Relationship of U.S. Antitrust Laws to Formulation of Foreign Economic Policy, Particularly Export and Overseas Investment Policy." Antitrust Law Journal Vol. 49, 1980, pp. 1189-1196.

Rowe, Frederick M. "Antitrust Aspects of European Acquisitions or Joint Ventures in the United States." Paper presented at a conference on "The U.S. Antitrust Laws/Die U.S. Antitrust Gesetze: the legal implications for those entering or operating in the U.S. market." Practising Law Institute (New York)/German-American Lawyers Association (Bonn), Cologne, June 1979.

Sametz, Arnold W. "The Foreign Multinational Company in the U.S." Working Paper No. 9, Solomon Brothers Center, New York University, October 1973.

Sametz, Arnold W. and J. Backman. "Why Foreign Multinationals Invest in the United States." Challenge March-April 1974, pp. 43-47.

Sampson, Anthony. The Sovereign State - The Secret History of ITT. London: Hodder & Stoughton, 1973.

Sawyier, Michael T. "Encouraging Foreign Investment in the United States by Limiting the President's Emergency Authority under the Trading with the Enemy Act." Mercer Law Review Vol. 27, 1976, pp. 681-716.

Sayler, R.H. and A. Heck. "Neue Rechtlinien zur Fusionskontrolle in den USA und ihre praktischen Auswirkungen." Recht der internationalen Wirtschaft Vol. 29, 1983, pp. 77-81.

Scarborough, K. "The Foreign Investor in the United States: Disclosure, Taxation and Visa Laws." International Lawyer Vol. 19, 1985, pp. 85-115.

Schmidt, H.R. "The Extraterritorial Application of the United States Antitrust Laws." Journal of Law and Commerce Vol. 5, 1985, pp. 321-345.

Schmidt, I. "Different Approaches and Problems in Dealing with Control of Market Power: A Comparison of German, European, and U.S. Policy Towards Market-Dominating Enterprises." Antitrust Bulletin Vol. 28, 1983, pp. 417-460.

Schweitzer, Thomas A. "The United Nations as a Source of Domestic Law: Can Security Council Resolutions Be Enforced in American Courts?" Yale Studies in World Public Order Vol. 4, 1978, pp. 162-273.

Servan-Schreiber, Jean-Jacques. The American Challenge. London: Hamish Hamilton, 1968.

Shemanski, Donald R. "Obtaining Evidence in the Federal Republic of Germany: The Impact of the Hague Convention on German-American Judicial Cooperation." International Lawyer Vol. 17, 1983, pp. 465-487.

Shenefeld, J.H. "Thoughts on Extraterritorial Application of the United States Antitrust Laws." Fordham Law Review Vol. 52, 1983, pp. 350-373.

"Shortening the Long Arm of American Antitrust Jurisdiction: Extraterritoriality and the Foreign Blocking Statutes." Loyola Law Review Vol. 28, 1982, pp. 213-280.

"Should Investment Capital Stay Home? A Canadian-U.S. Dialogue," Proceedings of the 68th Annual Meeting (1974). Washington, D.C.: American Society of International Law, 1975.

"The Siberian Pipeline Dispute and the Export Administration Act: What's Left of Extraterritorial Limits and the Act of State Doctrine." Houston Journal of International Law Vol. 6, Autumn 1983, pp. 63-91.

Silcox, C.R. "Unfair Methods of Competition: The Courts Revive Proof of Injury to Competition in Antitrust Cases under Section 5 of the Act." Antitrust Bulletin Vol. 29, 1984, pp. 423-474.

Silverstein, D. "Antitrust Guide for International Operations - Another Point of View." International Lawyer Vol. 13, 1979, pp. 693-701.

Simson, G.J. "Return of American Banana: A Contemporary Perspective on American Anti-Trust Abroad." Journal of International Law and Economics Vol. 9, 1974, pp. 233-265.

Singer, Stuart R. Regulation of Foreign Investments in the United States. New York: Practicing Law Institute, 1976.

Snyder, J.L. "International Competition: Toward a Normative Theory of United States Antitrust Law and Policy." Boston University International Law Journal Vol. 3, 1984, pp. 257-324.

Sornarajah, M. "Extraterritorial Enforcement of U.S. Antitrust Laws: Conflict and Compromise." International and Comparative Law Quarterly Vol. 31, 1982, pp. 127-149.

Southern Center for International Studies. Foreign Direct Investment in the Southeast: West Germany, the United Kingdom and Japan. Atlanta, Georgia, August 1979.

"Soviet Reaction to the U.S. Pipeline Embargo." Maryland Journal of International Law and Trade Vol. 8, 1984, pp. 144-155.

Stanford, J.S. "The Application of the Sherman Act to Conduct Outside the United States: A View from Abroad." Cornell International Law Journal Vol. 11, 1978, pp. 195-214.

"Stapled Stock and I.R.C. Section 269b: Ill-Conceived Change in the Rules of International Tax Jurisdiction." Cornell Law Review Vol. 71, 1986, pp. 1066-1094.

Starrels, A.J. "A Proposal for Uniform Regulation of Foreign Investment in American Real Estate." Cornell International Law Journal Vol. 18, 1985, pp. 147-178.

"State Securities Regulation: Merit Review of Foreign Equity Offerings." Virginia Journal of International Law Vol. 25, 1985, pp. 939-965.

"State Unitary Tax: The 'Risk' of Container Corporation of America v. Franchise Tax Board [103 S.Ct. 2933]. Hastings International and Comparative Law Review Vol. 9, Fall 1985, pp. 59-76.

Stein, Eric and Thomas L. Nicholson, eds. Enterprise (American) in the European Common Market: A Legal Profile. (2 Vols.) Ann Arbor: University of Michigan Law School, 1960.

Stephens, Richard A. "Re-evaluation of Disclosure Requirements for Foreign Issuers: Securities Exchange Act of 1934." George Washington Law Review Vol. 45, 1977, pp. 135-178.

Stewart, Milton Dudley, Jr. "Foreign Direct Investments in the United States." Ph.D. dissertation, University of Texas, Austin, 1972.

Streng, W.P. "United States: Taxation of International Business Transactions 1983." [Summaries in English, French, and German] Intertax 1984, pp. 137-148.

Stuermer, U. "Neuere Entwicklung der extraterritorialen Anwendung amerikanischen Securities Regulations." Recht der internationalen Wirtschaft Vol. 29, 1983, pp. 641-646.

"A Summary of the Forthcoming Restatement of the Foreign Relations Law of the United States (Revised)." Columbia Journal of Transnational Law Vol. 24, 1986, pp. 677-685.

Sun, Emily. "An Empirical Study of Direct Foreign Investment in the U.S." Paper prepared for an annual meeting of the Academy of International Business, August 1978.

Takitani, Kenji. "A Prototype for Japanese Investment in the United States?" Columbia Journal of World Business Vol. 8, Winter 1973, pp. 31-33.

"Tax - A Deterrent for U.S. Firms." International Herald Tribune 3 October 1978, p. 9.

"Tax Reform Act of 1984 - International Related - Party Factoring - A Major Tax Loophole for Multinational Corporations is Closed." Georgia Journal of International and Comparative Law Vol. 1985, 1985, pp. 125-133.

"Tax Reform Act of 1984 - Netherlands Antilles - Effect of the Repeal of the Withholding Tax on Portfolio Interest Payments to Foreign Investors." Georgia Journal of International and Comparative Law Vol. 15, 1985, pp. 111-123.

"Taxation - Congress Amends Internal Revenue Code to Comport with the Foreign Corrupt Practices Act, Tax Equity and Fiscal Responsibility Act of 1982. Public Law No. 97-248, 96 Stat. 324 [codified as amended in scattered sections of 26 N.S.C.]" Texas International Law Journal Vol. 18, 1983, pp. 407-412.

"Taxation - Renegotiation of the United States-Netherlands Antilles Tax Treaty. Convention with Respect to Taxes on Income and Certain Other Taxes. April 29, 1948, United States-Netherlands, 62 Stat. 1757, T.I.A.S. No. 1855." Texas International Law Journal Vol. 18, 1983, pp. 400-407.

"Taxation - State Taxation of Multinational Corporations: Container Corporation of America v. Franchise Tax Board, 103 S.Ct. 2933." Creighton Law Review Vol. 17, 1983-1984, pp. 857-884.

"Taxation - State Taxation on Multinational Corporations - ASARCO, Inc. v. Idaho State Tax Commission, 102 S.Ct. 1303 (1982); F.W. Woolworth Co. v. Taxation and Revenue Dept., 102 S.Ct. 3128 (1982)." Harvard International Law Journal Vol. 23, 1983, pp. 480-487.

Thiesing, Jochen. "Antitrust and International Law as Viewed from the United States and the European Common Market." Record of the Association of the Bar of the City of New York Vol. 25, 1970. pp. 206-224.

Thompson, R.B. "United States Jurisdiction over Foreign Subsidiaries: Corporate and International Law Aspects." Law and Policy in International Business Vol. 15, 1983, pp. 319-400.

Thompson, Samuel C. Federal Income Taxation of Domestic and Foreign Business Transactions: Text, Cases and Problems. Indianapolis: Bobbs-Merrill, 1980.

"Title VII of the Civil Rights Act of 1964 and the Multinational Enterprise." Georgia Law Journal Vol. 73, 1985, pp. 1465-1498.

Tittman, H.H. "Extraterritorial Application of U.S. Export Control Laws on Foreign Subsidiaries of U.S. Corporations: An American Lawyer's View from Europe." International Lawyer Vol. 16, 1982, pp. 730-737.

Toms, B.C., III. "French Response to the Extraterritorial Application of U.S. Antitrust Laws." International Lawyer Vol. 15, 1981, pp. 585-614.

"Transnational Discovery: The Balancing Act of American Trial Courts and the Northern District of Illinois' New Approach to the Hague Convention." Washington and Lee Law Review Vol. 42, 1985, pp. 1285-1310.

Tsurumi, Yoshi. "The Best of Times and the Worst of Times: Japanese Management in America." Columbia Journal of World Business Vol. 13, Summer 1978, pp. 56-61.

Tsurumi, Yoshi. The Japanese Are Coming: A Multinational Spread of Japanese Firms. Cambridge, Massachusetts: Ballinger, 1976.

Tsurumi, Yoshi. "The Strategic Framework for Japanese Investments in the United States." Columbia Journal of World Business Vol. 8, Winter 1973, pp. 19-25.

Turpin, K. "Taxation: Treasury Regulation Interpreting Definition of Control as Contained in Internal Revenue Code 957." Texas International Law Journal Vol. 14, 1979, pp. 495-512.

"United States and Japanese Government Procurement: The Impact on Trade Relations." Washington University Law Quarterly Vol. 62, Spring 1984, pp. 127-164.

"United States Antitrust Law and Industrial Policy: International Joint Ventures and Global Competition After GM-Toyota [103 F.T.C. 374]." Fordham International Law Journal Vol. 9, 1985/1986, pp. 257-294.

"United States Attitudes Towards Multinational Corporations." (Various articles: Vagts: control & protection; Tillinghast: tax; Ehrenhaft: anti-dumping; Surrey: Foreign Corrupt Practices Act; Loss: Extraterritoriality in FSC) Harvard International Law Journal Vol. 20, 1979, pp. 233-330.

"United States Bilateral Investment Treaties: Egypt and Panama." Georgia Journal of International and Comparative Law Vol. 13, 1983, pp. 491-514.

United States Chamber of Commerce. "Foreign Investment in the U.S. - Task Force Report." Mexican-American Review Vol. 42, February 1974, pp. 19-27.

United States Chamber of Commerce. Foreign Investment in the United States. Washington, D.C.: U.S. Government Printing Office, 1974.

United States Congress. Hearings before the Senate Committee on Foreign Relations on Executives E, G, and H. 84th Cong. 2d sess. 3-5, 1976.

United States Congress, Joint Economic Committee, Subcommittee on Foreign Economic Policy. The Multinational Corporation and Internal Investment, Part 4. Washington, D.C.: Government Printing Office, July 1970.

pUnited States Congress, Senate Committee on Banking, Housing and Urban Affairs. Report to the Securities and Exchange Commission on Questionable and Illegal Corporate Payments and Practices. 94th Cong. 2d sess. 3-5, 1976.

United States Congress, Senate Committee on Finance, Subcommittee on International Trade. Multinational Corporations: A Compendium of Papers Submitted to the Subcommittee. Washington, D.C.: Committee Printing, 1973.

United States Congress, Senate Committee on Finance, Subcommittee on International Trade. World Trade and Investment Issues, Part I. Washington, D.C.: Government Printing Office, May 1971.

United States Department of Commerce. Foreign Investment in the United States. 1976.

United States Department of Commerce. "U.S. International Economic Policy in an Interdependent World. July 1971.

United States Department of Commerce, Bureau of the Census. Selected Characteristics of Foreign-Owned Firms: 1975-1976. November 1978.

United States Department of Commerce, Bureau of Foreign and Domestic Commerce. Foreign Investments in the United States. Washington, D.C.: U.S. Government Printing Office, 1937.

United States Department of Commerce, Bureau of International Commerce. "Foreign Direct Investment in the United States." Conference Paper No. 6, 15 April 1969.

United States Department of Commerce, Bureau of International Commerce. Foreign Direct Investors in the United States. October 1973.

United States Department of Commerce, Bureau of International Commerce. Invest in the U.S.A.: An Invitation from the President of the United States. 1969.

United States Department of Commerce, Bureau of International Economic Policy and Research. Economic Models and Methodologies to Determine the Impact of Foreign Direct Investment in the U.S. November 1977.

United States Department of Commerce, International Investment Division. "Benchmark Survey of Foreign Direct Investment in the United States, 1974." Survey of Current Business Vol. 56, May 1976, pp. 35-51.

United States Department of Commerce, International Trade Administration. "International Direct Investment: Global Trends and the U.S. Role." August, 1984.

United States Department of Commerce, International Trade Administration. _Invest in the USA: A Guide for the Foreign Investor_. March 1981.

United States Department of Commerce, International Trade Administration. _Investment Climate in Foreign Countries_. (Vol.1: OECD and Other European Countries [includes Canada and Japan]; Vol. 2: Africa; Vol. 3: Asia [excluding Japan]; Vol. 4: Western Hemisphere [excluding Canada]) August, 1985.

United States Department of Commerce, International Investment Division. "U.S. Business Enterprises Acquired or Established by Foreign Direct Investors in 1979." _Survey of Current Business_ Vol 61, January 1981, pp. 28-39.

United States Department of Commerce, Office of Business Economics. "Foreign Assets in the United States." _Survey of Current Business_ Vol. 39, August 1959, pp. 28-29.

United States Department of Commerce, Office of Business Economics. "Foreign Business Investments in the United States." _Survey of Current Business_ 1962, Supplement.

United States Department of Commerce, Office of Business Economics. _Foreign Business Investments in the United States_. Washington, D.C.: U.S. Government Printing Office, 1962.

United States Department of Commerce, Office of Business Economics. "Foreign Investments - Summary and Analysis of Recent Census: Current Trends and Economic Effects." _Survey of Current Business_ Vol. 40, August 1960, pp. 15-24.

United States Department of Commerce, Office of Business Economics. "Foreign Investments in the United States." _Survey of Current Business_ Vol. 38, September 1958, p. 22-23. (Fourth part of Special Article by Samuel Pizer and Frederick Cutler. "Private Foreign Investment Near $37 Billion," pp. 15-23)

United States Department of Commerce, Office of Business Economics. "Record Growth of Foreign Investments." Survey of Current Business Vol. 37, August 1957, pp. 22-30.

United States Department of Commerce, Office of Foreign Investment in the United States. Canadian Direct Investment in the United States. July 1980.

United States Department of Commerce, Office of Foreign Investment in the United States. Foreign Direct Investment in the United States: 1976 Transactions - A1 Forms; 1974-76 Acquisitions, Mergers and Equity Increases. December 1977.

United States Department of Commerce, Office of Foreign Investment in the United States. Foreign Direct Investment in the United States - 1979 Transactions. September 1980.

United States Department of Commerce, Office of Foreign Investment in the United States. Foreign Investment in the United States: Hawaii. March 1980.

United States Department of Commerce, Office of Foreign Investment in the United States. List of Foreign Direct Investments in the United States - Pending and Completed. 1977-1979.

United States Department of Commerce, Office of Foreign Investment in the United States. OPEC Direct Investments, 1974-1979. December 1980.

United States Department of Commerce, Office of International Policy. Foreign Direct Investment in the United States. August 1980.

United States Department of Commerce. U.S. Direct Investment Abroad. Washington, D.C.: U.S. Department of Commerce, 1982.

United States Department of Housing and Urban Development. The Impact of Foreign Direct Investment on U.S. Cities and Regions. June 1979.

United States Department of Justice, Antitrust Division. Antitrust Guide for International Operations. Washington, D.C.: Department of Justice, 1977.

United States Department of Labor, Office of Foreign Economic Research. _Production Strategies and Practices of Foreign Multinationals in the United States_. December 1980.

United States Department of the Treasury. _Foreign Assets Control Regulations_. Washington, D.C.: Government Printing Office, 8 July 1963.

United States Department of the Treasury, Internal Revenue Service. "Regulations Concerning the Taxation of Foreign Investment in U.S. Real Property." 1983. (Reprinted in _International Legal Materials_ Vol. 22, 1983, pp. 883 ff.)

United States Department of the Treasury, Office of the Secretary. _Census of Foreign-Owned Assets in the United States_. Washington, D.C.: U.S. Government Printing Office, 1945.

United States Federal Trade Commission, Bureau of Competition, Premerger Notification Office. _Premerger Notification Compliance Guide: An explanation of the application and operation of the premerger notification rules implementing the Hart-Scott-Rodino Anti-Trust Improvements Act of 1976_. 18 September 1978.

United States General Accounting Office. _Are OPEC Financial Holdings a Danger to U.S. Banks or the Economy?_ 11 June 1979.

United States General Accounting Office. _Changes Needed to Improve Government's Knowledge of OPEC Financial Influence in the U.S._ 19 December 1979.

United States General Accounting Office. _Controlling Foreign Investment in National Interest Sectors of the U.S. Economy_. 7 October 1977.

United States General Accounting Office. _Emerging Concerns Over Foreign Investment in the United States_. 24 March 1975.

United States General Accounting Office. _Impact of Foreign Investments: Case Studies in North and South Carolina_. 26 April 1976.

United States General Accounting Office. Should Canada's Screening Practices Be Used by the United States? 6 September 1979.

"United States: IRS Could Better Protect US Tax Interest in Determining the Income of Multinational Corporations." [Summaries in English, French, and German] Intertax 1982, pp. 5-11.

"United States: Loan Between Foreign Subsidiaries May Constitute Constructive Dividend to U.S. Parent." [Summaries in English, French, and German] Intertax 1982, pp. 259-263.

United States National Commission for the Review of Antitrust Laws and Procedures. Report to the President and the Attorney General. Washington, D.C., 22 January 1979.

United States President Emergency Management Office, Coordinator of Inter-American Affairs Office. Foreign Investments in the United States: History and Nature of Investments. Washington, D.C.: U.S. Government Printing Office, June 1944.

United States Temporary National Economic Committee. Direct Foreign Investments in American Industry, 1937. Monograph No. 6, Part 2. Washington, D.C.: U.S. Government Printing Office, 1941.

"United States v. First National City Bank of Chicago [699 F.2D 34]: Limiting American Extraterritorial Authority to Order the Production of Documents in Violation of Foreign Law." DePaul Law Review Vol. 33, Fall 1983, pp. 183-206.

"U.S. Challenges BASF's Purchase." International Herald Tribune 19 April 1979, p. 7.

U.S. International Economic Policy in an Interdependent World. Williams Commission Report. Washington, D.C.: Government Printing Office, July 1971.

"U.S. Regulation of Foreign Direct Investment: Current Developments and the Congressional Response." Virginia Journal of International Law Vol. 15, 1975, pp. 611-647.

Vagts, Detlev F. "United States and Its Multinationals: Protection and Control." Harvard International Law Journal Vol. 20, 1979, pp. 235-251.

Vagts, Detlev F. "The United States of America and the Multinational Enterprise," in H.R. Hahlo, ed., Nationalism and the Multinational Enterprise: Legal, Economic and Managerial Aspects. Dobbs Ferry, New York: Oceana, 1973.

van Roy, Y. "Commerce Amendment Act 1983 - Necessary Procedural Change for Mergers and Takeovers." Victoria University Wellington Law Review Vol. 14, May 1984, pp. 203-219.

Veltius, M.A. "Neueste Entwicklungen der extraterritorialen Anwendung des U.S. Antitrust-Rechts." Recht der internationalen Wirtschaft Vol. 28, 1982, pp. 157-161.

Vernon, Raymond. America's Foreign Trade Policy and the GATT. Princeton, New Jersey: Princeton University Press, 1954.

Vernon, Raymond. Sovereignty at Bay: The Multinational Spread of U.S. Enterprises. London: Longman, 1971.

Vila, A.M. "Legal Aspects of Foreign Direct Investment in the United States." International Lawyer Vol. 16, 1982, pp. 1-49.

Waldmann, Raymond J. "A Guide to Foreign Investment in the U.S." District Lawyer October/November 1979.

"Wall Street's Rush to Beat the New Merger Rules." The Economist 17 March 1979, pp. 113-114.

Waller, S.W. "Redefining the Foreign Compulsion Defense in U.S. Antitrust Law: The Japanese Auto Restraints and Beyond." Law and Policy in International Business Vol. 14, 1982, pp. 747-817.

Ward, James J. The European Approach to U.S. Markets: Product and Promotion Adaptation by European Multinational Corporations. New York: Praeger, 1973.

Ward, James J. "Product and Promotion Adaptation by European Firms in the U.S." Journal of International Business Studies Vol. 4 Spring 1973, pp. 79-85.

Webley, Simon. Foreign Direct Investment in the United States: Opportunities and Impediments. London: British-North American Committee, 1974.

Weems, P.R. "Reporting Requirements for U.S. Corporations: The International Investment and Trade in Survey Act." International Lawyer Vol. 19, 1985, pp. 1293-1302.

Wehle, Louis B. "Government-Controlled Business Corporations in America and Europe." Address delivered 8 May 1935 in Washington, D.C. Washington, D.C.: American Bar Association, 1935.

Weisner, C. "Determinants of Foreign Investment Patterns in the United States." Paper presented at an annual meeting of the Southwestern Social Science Association, March/April 1977.

Wengler, Wilhelm. Die Mitbestimmung und das Voelkerrecht: Ein Gutachten ueber die Vereinbarkeit der Mitbestimmungsgesetzgebung in der Bundesrepublik mit dem deutsch-amerikanischen Handelsvertrag. Baden-Baden: Nomos Verlaggesellschaft, 1975.

Whichard, Obie G. "Employment and Employee Compensation of U.S. Affiliates of Foreign Companies, 1974." Survey of Current Business (U.S. Department of Commerce) Vol. 58, December 1978, pp. 23-30.

Whittaker, D.R. "An Examination of the OECD and UN Model Tax Treaties: History, Provisions and Application to U.S. Foreign Policy." North Carolina Journal of International Law and Commercial Regulation Vol. 8, 1982, pp. 39-60.

Wilkins, Mira. Foreign Enterprise in Florida - The Impact of Non-U.S. Direct Investment. Miami: University Presses of Florida, 1979.

Willens, R. "The Corporate Provisions of the Tax Reform Act of 1986." Tax Advisor Vol. 17, 1986, pp. 624-661.

Wilner, Gabriel M. and Terri K. Smith. "Is Georgia on Their Minds? - Some Legal Aspects of Investment and Trade by Foreign Business Enterprises." Mercer Law Review Vol. 27, 1976, pp. 629-656.

Wilson, Robert Renbert. The International Law Standard in Treaties of the United States. Cambridge, Massachusetts: Harvard University Press, 1953.

Wilson, Robert Renbert. United States Commercial Treaties and International Law. New Orleans, Louisiana: Hauser Press, 1960.

Witherspoon, R.A. "Multinational Corporations - Governmental Regulation of Business Ethics under the Foreign Corrupt Practices Act of 1977: An Analysis." Dickinson Law Review Vol. 87, 1983, pp. 531-593.

Wittman, Joseph I. "International Mergers under Section 7 of the Clayton Act and Article 86 of the Common Market Treaty of Rome: A Comparative Perspective." Washburn Law Journal Vol. 18, 1979, pp. 512-534.

Yang, W. and D.W. Nelson "Post Reconstruction Section 367: New Rules and Changes." Tax Advisor Vol. 17, 1986, pp. 102-111.

Young, J.H. "Acquisition of United States Businesses by Foreign Investors." Business Law Vol. 30, November 1974, pp. 111-128.

Young, S. "Foreign Direct Investment into Louisiana." Paper presented at the Academy of International Business, Atlanta, Georgia, 31 October 1979.

Zaphiriou, G.A. "The U.N. Economic Charter and U.S. Investment and Policy." Mercer Law Review Vol. 27, 1976, pp. 749-780.

Zaucha, J.J. "The Soviet Pipeline Sanctions: The Extra-territorial Application of U.S. Export Controls." _Law and Policy in International Business_ Vol. 15, 1983, pp. 1169-1179.

Zeitler, Arthur W. "Foreign Investment in the United States - Reporting Requirements." _Houston Journal of International Law_ Vol. 3, 1981, pp. 221-240.

Zupnick, Elliot. "Foreign Investment in the U.S: Costs and Benefits." _Headline Series_ No. 249, New York: Foreign Policy Association, 1980.

Zwarensteyn, Hendrik. _Some Aspects of the Extraterritorial Reach of the American Antitrust Laws_. Deventer: Kluwer, 1970.